Ian A. Fraser.

March, 1991.

ENGLISH PLACE-NAME SOCIETY VOLUME LXII/LXIII

FOR 1984-5 & 1985-6

General Editor
KENNETH CAMERON

THE PLACE-NAMES OF SHROPSHIRE

PART ONE

ENGLISH PLACE-NAME SOCIETY VOLUME LXII/LXIII

FOR 1984-5 & 1985-6

THE PLACE-NAMES OF SHROPSHIRE

By

MARGARET GELLING in collaboration with H.D.G. FOXALL

PART ONE

THE MAJOR NAMES OF SHROPSHIRE

ENGLISH PLACE-NAME SOCIETY
1990

Published by the English Place-Name Society

ISBN: 0 904889 14 9

Printed in Great Britain
by Woolnough Bookbinding, Irthlingborough.

The Camera-ready Copy of this volume
has been produced by Mrs Esmé Pattison
on equipment provided
by
Messrs Allied Breweries plc
and by
Messrs Advent Desktop Publishing Limited

CONTENTS

Maps

INTRODUCTION

This is the first time that the initial volume of an EPNS survey has consisted of an alphabetical arrangement of the major settlement-names for the whole county. The rest of the Shropshire survey will be presented on the usual regional basis, with brief summaries of the discussions of those names which have been treated in Part I. The first of these regional volumes will deal with the hundreds of Ford and Condover.

The reasons for presenting all names of parishes and Domesday manors in a single volume are twofold. First, I am anxious to make available a book which covers the whole county, so that the Shropshire people who have helped me for so long may see a satisfactory result of their labours. Second, an initial sorting-out of major names is expecially useful in this county because of the unparalleled quantity of name-repetition, particularly in regard to compounds with **tūn**. If the Astons, Nortons, Suttons, Westons, and the Actons, Bourtons, Brocktons, Eatons, Hattons, Hoptons, Moretons, Prestons, Uptons, Woottons, were not assembled and studied as complete groups it is unlikely that the correct assignment of early forms among them would be achieved. Assemblage of these groups is necessary, also, for an appreciation of the significance of such names. Something will be said below about the possible historical reasons for this salient characteristic of Shropshire toponymy, but before beginning a discussion of the material it is appropriate to record some facts concerning the genesis of the county survey and its history to date.

The Shropshire survey is a result of the activities of the Extra-Mural Department of Birmingham University (now the School of Continuing Studies). In 1959 the warden of the residential centre at Attingham Hall, Sir George Trevelyan, organised a weekend school on Shropshire place-names at which I lectured. This led to a request for a session of lectures, and I conducted these in the following year. The group which attended these lectures refused to disband at the end of them, and I was pressurised by local enthusiasm into the instigation of a research group for the collection of material for a full EPNS survey. This group functioned from 1961 to 1988. Three members - George Foxall, John Pagett and Peter Selwyn Smith - were with it for the whole period. Others who were with us for a long time include Mr D.B. Corbyn (decd.), Miss J. Haseler (decd.), Mr E. Jenks, Mrs Jones, Miss E. Lambert, Miss R. Lees, Mrs S. Nelson, Mr L.T. Rouse (decd.), Mr R. Selwyn

Smith, Miss M. Strain, Mrs D.G. Turner and Mr and Mrs P.T. Watkins. A number of others worked on the project for a few years. It was in every way a rewarding experience, and I owe a deep debt of gratitude to everyone concerned. In its initial stages the project owed much to the enthusiasm of the late John Pilgrim, who was Birmingham University's tutor-organiser for Shropshire.

The initial venue was Attingham Hall, after which we were for a short time at a centre in College Hill, Shrewsbury, finally transferring to the Local Studies Department of Shrewsbury Library. This last was an ideal venue, since a major part of our work consisted of extracting material from the vast collection of local deeds which are housed in the library. We also had access there to all relevant books, and we received much help from the librarian, Mr A. Carr, and his staff.

In 1988 our group failed to meet the new, more rigorous rules regarding numbers enrolling for Birmingham University external courses. At this point it seemed best to stop collecting material so that I could devote the remainder of my rapidly diminishing store of years to working up the material which I have. The sources for Shropshire place-name spellings are not, in practical terms, finite. The deeds in the public library number some 30,000. In the 1920s and 1930s E.W. Bowcock, the pioneer of Shropshire place-name studies, examined the first 4,000. Our group had reached number 10,000 when it was disbanded. In addition to the remaining 20,000 of these deeds there is unpublished material in the County Record Office which has not been studied. Some of the unstudied local material is, however, accessible at second-hand through the kindness of the historians working for the Victoria History of Shropshire. I am most grateful to Mr G. Baugh and his staff for much help, the fruits of which will be more apparent in the regional volumes than in the present one.

In addition to working through some 6,000 documents in Shrewsbury library, the research group extracted spellings from a vast quantity of printed material, including all the Public Record Office publications which are usually drawn upon for EPNS volumes. It was possible with their help to work through the voluminous series of Shropshire Parish Register publications, a task I should not have felt able to tackle on my own. In the present volume the benefits are particularly apparent of having comparatively late spellings, like those from parish registers, to add to the medieval ones. The later spellings document the development from Middle English forms to modern ones, and they provide unique information about local pronunciations in the Early Modern period. I should like to stress the importance of the very full documentation from all periods which is provided for most of the names presented here. The general meaning of most of the major names of Shropshire has been known since the 1930s, but the manner in which full documentation can enable refinement of earlier etymologies is illustrated by the articles on Atcham, Bayston, Bearstone, Boraston, Colehurst, Coreley, Crudgington, Glazeley, Kinnersley, Lydham, Marchamley, Milson, Myddle, Onibury, Romsley, Sheinton, Shrewsbury, Siefton, Stirchley, Stottesdon, Tong, and many other names.

Other benefits were derived from the research group in addition to the assembling of spellings. I was able to absorb information about the history and landscape of Shropshire from members who knew a great deal more than I could hope to learn by my own efforts. Chief among my informants was the late H.D.G. Foxall, whose death in March 1989 was a grievous loss to historical scholarship in Shropshire. His knowledge was encyclopedic, and his industry, generosity, modesty and humour were admired and enjoyed by all who worked with him. He knew that his name was to appear on the title-pages of this survey. E.W. Bowcock's collection of spellings, which was much larger than would be suspected from his book *Shropshire Place-Names* (1923), was bequeathed to the EPNS, and I took possession of it in 1961 and have incorporated much of it into my own collection.

Spellings collected by the research group and spellings from E.W. Bowcock's material are two components of the collection. A third major component derives from sources in the Public Record Office, London, which were extracted by successive research assistants of the EPNS, mostly by Dr A. Rumble, Dr Catherine Cubitt and Dr M. Bateson. The two major monastic cartularies, from Shrewsbury and Haughmond, have been made available in exemplary editions by Dr Una Rees.

The names included in Part I comprise those of all parishes and all identifiable Domesday manors. The terms 'Ancient Parish' and 'Civil Parish', applied to the first group, denote parishes which were functioning before 1833 and those which came into existence after that date. To label them in this manner gives a convenient indication of older and more recent administrative units, and only this is intended. The inclusion of all names recorded in Domesday Book brings into the volume a large number of places some of which are of minimal administrative status today; but since the Domesday geography of Shropshire is exceptionally difficult to unravel, this preliminary statement of identifications is a useful part of the framework for the whole survey. Unidentified DB manors are: *Aitone, Avochelie, Bolebec, Bosle, Buchehale, Burtone, Caurtune, Cheneltone, Chinbaldescote, Costeford, Estone, Halstune/Haustune, Hibrihteselle, Lai, Muletune, Newetone, Petelie, Slacheberie, Sudtelch, Tibeton, Tunestan, Udeford, Wlferesforde.* These are not included, but they will be discussed in the regional volumes under the headings of the hundreds in which they are believed to lie. The heroic work of Frank and Caroline Thorn in their 1986 edition of the Shropshire Domesday is gratefully acknowledged.

There are many Shropshire settlement-names for which there is excellent documentation beginning in the twelfth or thirteenth centuries which are not included in this volume on the arbitrary grounds that they are not parish-names and do not appear in DB. No criteria for inclusion could be wholly satisfactory, however, and the names which are included provide a representative sample from all parts of the county.

A full discussion of the historical and philological information which can be derived from Shropshire place-names will not be undertaken until all the material has been processed, but a preliminary notice of some salient features may be useful at this stage.

A feature which may occasion some surprise is the paucity of pre-English names. These are much less frequent in Shropshire than they are in Worcestershire, and the contrast with Herefordshire is striking. Herefordshire has a considerable number of names which may be considered to date at least from Roman times, and also many Welsh names of early medieval type which indicate continuous Welsh speech, such as Treville, Kilpeck, Hentland, in the Archenfield district south of Hereford. In Shropshire, major names of late Welsh type, such as Llanfair, Bettws-y-crwyn, Llanymynech, Llanyblodwel, only occur on the west boundary. There are numerous Welsh minor names in the western parishes, but these are probably mainly indicative of the return of Welsh speech in the post-Conquest period. Much information concerning the use of Welsh in the medieval and early modern periods will be furnished in due course by the minor names and field-names of the whole western half of the county, but this late Welsh influence is not found in major names as it is in Herefordshire.

The surviving pre-English names of Shropshire are:

1. RIVERS. Clun, Cound, *Giht* (in Ightfield), *Leden* in (Ledwyche), *Nene* (in Neenton), Roden, Tern and the first part of Perry. Others on the west boundary - Camlad, Ceiriog, Morda, Morlas, Tanat - belong to Wales rather than to Shropshire.
2. HILLS. Mynd, Wrekin, probably the first part of Wenlock. There are some possible instances of **crüg**.
3. SETTLEMENTS. Hints, Hodnet, Prees and the first part of Catherton.

A number of landscape features which might have been expected to retain their British names have failed to do so. Some fairly long rivers, such as Corve and Meese, have English names, and now that a full range of spellings is available this seems likely to be the case with Onny. Some of the names of major hill-massifs, particularly Clee, are more easily explicable as Germanic than as Celtic. The most impressive of the British survivals are the settlement-names Hodnet and Prees in the north-east of the county. These parishes adjoin each other, and Ightfield (which is partly British) is nearby. In most of the county, however, the incidence of surviving pre-English names is very low, and there is no likelihood that it will be significantly increased by further research. There must have been a drastic re-naming of settlements and landscape features after the area became part of the kingdom of Mercia.

The prevalence of English speech revealed by the place-names cannot, in this county, be ascribed to the presence in the early years of Mercian rule of a large number of English people. The pagan Anglo-Saxon archaeology of the midlands barely extends as far west as Staffordshire, and there is no trace of it in Shropshire, despite decades of scrupulous search by modern archaeologists. Some of the names discussed under Beslow may refer to vanished Anglo-Saxon tumuli, but this type of burial (even if it could be proved to exist in the county) would only denote the presence of a ruling caste.

The combination of total absence of pagan Anglo-Saxon archaeology with overwhelming predominance of Anglo-Saxon place-names presents a challenge to the historian. I have argued elsewhere that the coming of a small ruling class does not cause a change in the stock of place-names, and I intend to maintain this assertion, but to interpret the situation in Shropshire as an exception to the general rule. Here it is possible to adduce another salient feature of Shropshire toponymy, the extraordinary degree of repetition of some recurrent **tūn** compounds. Shropshire has ten Astons, eight Westons, seven Nortons and eight Suttons, and there are five Uptons, four Middletons and ten Newtons. Acton occurs eight times, Eaton six and Eyton five. There are four instances of Hatton, Mor(e)ton and Wootton. There are five Prestons. It is possible that such names were originally convenient labels used by Mercian administrators when referring to the component parts of large estates. Some, like Eaton and Hatton, could refer to the specialised contributions made by a place to a larger economic unit. The significance of each of these recurrent names is discussed in this volume under the appropriate headings. These names could have originated in the speech of Mercian administrators, who could have been in the habit of saying that a settlement was the *ēa-tūn* of a particular composite estate, or the *prēosta tūn* of a minster church. Such appellatives might gradually have come to be perceived as place-names, and ousted earlier British names of these places.

Pre-Conquest documentation for Shropshire is scarce, and this scarcity leaves room for speculation about the time-scale of the change from Welsh to English place-names. The document known as the Testament of St Mildburg cannot be called in evidence without qualification. It almost certainly incorporates the substance of a number of genuine seventh-century land-grants, but the place-names (as is pointed out *infra* under Chelmarsh and Clee) show unmistakable evidence of post-Norman-Conquest influence. They are predominantly English, but it is far from certain that the estates given to Wenlock were known by these names c.685, when the house was founded. There could have been several revisions of the original documents before the version used by St Mildburg's biographer was arrived at, and English names which had become current at any date between c.685 and the immediate post-Conquest period could have been substituted for obsolete British ones. Apart from the documents connected with Wenlock Priory, Shropshire has three pre-Conquest charters, dated 901, 963 and 975, two wills, dated c.975 and 1002-4, and a writ of Edward the Confessor. It is clear from these that in the eastern half of the county the place-names were English in the tenth century.

Shropshire contains the major part of Offa's Dyke within its boundary, and it seems possible that it was administered with particular thoroughness by the rulers of Mercia, and some of the phenomenal loss of British place-names may be due to this. The county has its fair share of names which mean 'x's estate', sometimes constructed with the genitive of the personal name, sometimes with the connective particle **-ing-**. These names can date from as early as the eighth century, but they were certainly still being formed in the tenth and eleventh centuries, when examples in Berkshire and Wiltshire can be shown to refer to documented land-owners. With only three Anglo-Saxon charters extant for Shropshire it is not surprising that we have no record of the *Alhmund* of Alcaston, the *Card* of Cardeston, or any other eponymous estate owners in the shire. Some of these names are formed with habitative generics other than **tūn**, such as **byrig** and **worðign**. Such place-names will in most instances have replaced earlier names for ancient settlements, and in this area the items replaced could well have been British.

In addition to the recurring **tūn** compounds and the names which mean 'x's estate', Shropshire has its fair share of unique and obscure toponyms. It is evident that in spite of the relatively late date at which the English names were coined the people responsible for them had a wide topographical vocabulary which contained archaic items not evidenced in literary sources. Discussions in this volume of exceptionally difficult names, such as Clee, Ercall and Haughmond, are intended to present the problems rather than to offer definitive solutions. Further discussion can be incorporated into the relevant regional volumes. In addition to these major *cruces* there are several obscure elements, such as **cwatt*, **pimbe* and **pulre*, which have not been noted outside Shropshire.

The less obscure items of topographical vocabulary used in Shropshire toponymy are many and varied, and can be related very precisely to landscape-forms. The precise meanings of some terms, such as **bæce**, **hlið**, **hop**, **ofer** and **wæsse** are particularly well-illustrated in this county; and less regionalised terms, such as **dūn**, **ēg** and **hōh**, had lost none of their precision when they were applied to features in the Shropshire landscape. In view of the negative archaeological evidence we cannot assume that the area was densely populated with English speakers in the centuries when

Anglo-Saxons lived in *grubenhäuser* and practised pagan burial, so it seems necessary to assume that the exactitude with which Old English landscape terms were used was still undiminished in the ninth century.

It is reasonable to envisage a growing English population in the eighth and ninth centuries. This would not be colonisation, since there is no reason to suppose a drastic alteration of earlier settlement patterns. It would rather be a process of gradual infiltration into lands which were the central province of the western part of Offa's Mercian kingdom. When the provision of local churches became common, probably from the tenth century onwards, the area conformed to the English practice of only very rarely jettisoning an earlier name for a new one which referred to the church. This replacement happened on a massive scale in Wales and in a significantly large number of instances in the Archenfield district of Herefordshire. Shropshire has a few Llan- names on the west boundary, but only Baschurch and Whitchurch have names with **cirice** as generic. The unexplained use of **cirice** in Chirbury is discussed under that name. There are occasional references to minster churches, as in Emstrey and Minsterley, but most of these also failed to displace ancient names like Morville, Shifnal and Stottesdon. The physical nature of Shropshire church-sites, with the very high incidence of raised curvilinear churchyards, owes something to Celtic traditions, but with a few exceptions the parish-names remained unaltered, as was the general fashion in English-speaking areas.

As regards my view of the process by which the lands included in the later shire became part of Mercia, there is a detailed account in my book *The West Midlands in the Early Middle Ages*, which will appear shortly after the present volume, and a briefer statement in a paper contributed to *The Origins of Anglo-Saxon Kingdoms*, ed. Steven Bassett (Leicester University Press 1989). I accept the thesis advanced by I. Forster in 1932, which was developed by H.P.R. Finberg, and more recently by Dr J. Rowland, which holds that the Welsh poetic tradition enshrined in the Cynddylan verses has no historical basis. I do not believe that there was a seventh-century war of conquest in which Penda of Mercia gained possession of eastern Powys. I believe that eastern Powys voluntarily became part of Penda's kingdom, as did many other originally independent units stretching from Shropshire to the east coast.

In geographical terms there is no barrier which would hinder the advance of Mercian influence from the east. Sir Frank Stenton (*Anglo-Saxon England* p.40) spoke of the Staffordshire forests of Morfe and Kinver as if they constituted a barrier between central Mercia and British kingdoms to the west. But the Roman road called Watling Street, the western stretch of which runs from Tamworth to Wroxeter, must have remained in use, since it became the modern A5. The River Severn has sufficient crossing places. North Shropshire, together with most of Cheshire, constitutes a great plain which continues into central Staffordshire. There is no serious barrier to westward movement until the Welsh mountains are reached, and this high ground determined the general nature of the English/Welsh border. There was no dense colonisation of the area in the pagan period, but the physical relationship to central Mercia, and the importance which Mercian kings must have attached to the governance of these lands, would render the area particularly liable to English infiltration in the ninth and tenth centuries. This is the likely explanation of the victory of the English language and the replacement of British place-names.

Shropshire was not subject to Norse settlement in the late ninth and early tenth centuries. There was a certain amount of this in Cheshire, mainly in The Wirral, and a very small amount in north-east Staffordshire and eastern Warwickshire. There are no Norse names in Shropshire, however, and the county is also free of the later Norse influence revealed in such Herefordshire names as Rowlestone, Swanstone, Arkstone, Durstone and Thruxton. The eponymous Hrolf, Swein, Arnketill, Thored and Thorkell of these late *-tūn* names were most probably thegns of King Canute, given estates in Herefordshire in the early eleventh century. No personal names of Norse origin have been noted in Shropshire.

A considerable number of Norman personal names and surnames became attached to English place-names in Shropshire, but there are few French place-names. Frankwell, a suburb across the Welsh Bridge from Shrewsbury, derives its name from *Francheville*, 'free town', a name which occurs also in the Isle of Wight, where it alternates with Newtown as the designation for a planted borough of the Bishopric of Winchester. The Isle-of-Wight borough was founded in 1256 (M. Biddle, *Medieval Archaeology* III, pp.202ff). The Shrewsbury name is recorded in HAC in the early thirteenth century. There are Norman names for castles, such as *Luvre* (discussed under Oswestry) and *Chastel Isobel* (Shrawardine Castle). Caus and Cantlop are more easily explained as French than as English, though the origin of both is far from certain.

Use of Norman French in new names is a very slight element in Shropshire toponymy, but indirect influence from the new administrative language has generally been considered to be much greater. The articles in this volume refer frequently to "Norman French pronunciation" as a factor in the development of name-forms; see, for instance, the discussions of Shrewsbury and Wroxeter. Ascription to Norman pronunciation of developments such as are found in these names is a time-honoured practice, common throughout EPNS publications. It is, however, about to meet a formidable challenge. I am privileged to have a pre-publication copy of a paper by Cecily Clark entitled "Towards a reassessment of 'Anglo-Norman influence' on English place-names". In this she exposes a number of improbabilities in the thesis advanced by R.D. Zachrisson eighty years ago, which was repeated in the introductory volume of the EPNS series. She shows it to be unlikely that either French scribes or French-speaking people in England were responsible for the distortions seen in the development of many English place-names after the Conquest. She suggests that, rather than invoking French difficulty with English sounds, place-name scholars should look for explanations based on native tendencies which may have operated more freely in place-names than in other elements of speech. The first volume of the Shropshire survey was already written when I encountered this paper, and it has seemed best to let the conventional references to 'Anglo-Norman influence' stand. The matter can be reconsidered when each of the names under which this shibboleth is invoked comes up for discussion in the regional volumes. Meanwhile it is some slight consolation to note that in my article on Wroxeter I had noted one of the points which features in Miss Clark's discussion, namely that French speakers should not wholly be blamed for the drastic reduction of **ceaster**.

As a conclusion to this Introduction it remains for me to thank the administrative team which manages the Society's activities. The Honorary Director, Professor Kenneth Cameron, has been the guiding spirit since 1967. He is ably supported by the Assistant Editor, Mr John Field. The Honorary Treasurer, Dr Geoffrey Lee, bears the constant anxiety which results from minimal funding. We have been able to sustain our publication programme by resorting to desk-top publishing, and this has been possible because of the outstanding skill of Mrs Esmé Pattison, The Society's Secretary. The EPNS survey proceeds because of the dedication of these officers, and because of the generosity of Nottingham University in providing us with accommodation in the Department of English. A major factor in this last arrangement is the goodwill of Professor Christine Fell. I very much hope that all of these will feel that my volume is worthy of their efforts.

The Survey is a major project of the British Academy, and we are, as always, grateful for their regular and continued support.

July 1990 Margaret Gelling
Birmingham

ABBREVIATIONS and BIBLIOGRAPHY

Abbreviations printed in roman type refer to printed sources and those in italic to manuscript sources.

a.	*ante.*
Abbr	*Placitorum Abbreviatio* (RC), 1811.
acc.	accusative.
AD	*Catalogue of Ancient Deeds* (PRO), 1890 and in progress.
AddCh	Additional charters in B.
adj.	adjective.
APW	*Calendar of Ancient Petitions relating to Wales*, ed. W. Rees, Cardiff 1975.
ASC	*The Anglo-Saxon Chronicle.*
Ass	Assize Rolls (PRO).
ASWills	*Anglo-Saxon Wills*, ed. D. Whitelock, 1930.
Ave.	Avenue.
Baugh	*Robert Baugh's Map of Shropshire 1808*, Shropshire Archaeological Society 1983.
BBCS	*The Bulletin of the Board of Celtic Studies..*
Bd	Bedfordshire.
Berks	Berkshire.
Bk	Buckinghamshire
BL	Documents in British Library.
Blome	Richard Blome, *A General Mapp of Shropshire with its Hundreds* (c.1675).
BM	*Index to the Charters and Rolls in the Department of Manuscripts, British Museum*, ed. H.J. Ellis and F.B. Bickley, 2 vols, 1900-12.
Bowcock	E.W. Bowcock, *Shropshire Place-Names*, Shrewsbury 1923.
Burton	*Charters of Burton Abbey*, ed. P.H. Sawyer, *Anglo-Saxon Charters* II, British Academy 1979.
c.	*circa.*
Ca	Cambridgeshire.
Cant	*The Register of Thomas de Cantilupe*, Canterbury and York Society II, 1907.
CartAntiq	*The Cartae Antiquae Rolls* 1-10, PRS NS 17, 1939; 11-20, PRS NS 33, 1960.
cent.	century.
Ch	Cheshire.

Ch	*Calendar of Charter Rolls* (PRO), 1903-27.
Ch 1, Ch 2	regnal dates, t. Charles I or II.
ChanR	*Calendar of various Chancery Rolls*, A.D.1277-1326 (PRO), 1912..
Charles	B.G. Charles, 'The Welsh, their Language and Place-Names in Archenfield and Oswestry', in *Angles and Britons: O'Donnell Lectures*, University of Wales Press 1963, pp. 85-110.
ChR	*Rotuli Chartarum*, ed. T.D. Hardy (RC), 1837.
Cl	*Calendar of Close Rolls* (PRO), in progress.
ClR	*Rotuli Litterarum Clausarum*, ed. T.D. Harcy (RC).
Co	Cornwall.
Coin(s)	spellings taken from coin-legends.
Corn.R.O.	Buller MSS in Cornwall Record Office, Truro.
Craven	Surveys of the Craven Estates in Shrewsbury Public Library (Class M.S.Accession 2480-3).
Ct	Court.
Cu	Cumberland.
Cur	*Curia Regis Rolls* (PRO), in progress.
CurR	*Rotuli Curia Regis* (RC), 1835.
D	Devon.
dat.	dative.
Db	Derbyshire.
DB	Domesday Book.
Denb	Denbighshire.
DEPN	E. Ekwall, *The Concise Oxford Dictionary of English Place-Names*, 4th ed., 1960.
Do	Dorset.
Du	County Durham.
Duignan	W.H. Duignan, *Notes on Staffordshire Place-Names*, London 1902.
e.	early.
E.	east.
ECWM	H.P.R. Finberg, *The Early Charters of the West Midlands*, Leicester 1972.
Ed 1, Ed 2 etc.	regnal date, t. Edward I, t. Edward II, etc.
el.	place-name element.
Eliz	regnal date, t. Elizabeth I.
EPN	A.H. Smith, *English Place-Name Elements*, Parts 1 and 2 (EPNS 25, 26), Cambridge 1956.

EPNS	publications of the English Place-Name Society.
ERN	E. Ekwall, *English River-Names*, Oxford 1928.
ERY	East Riding of Yorkshire.
Ess	Essex.
et freq	*et frequenter*: and frequently (thereafter).
et seq	*et sequenter*: and subsequently.
Eyton	SRO 665/37-8, an uncatalogued collection of 16th, 17th and e.18th cent. indentures from the Condover estate which came to SRO from the Eyton family.
Eyton	R.W. Eyton, *Antiquities of Shropshire*, London 1854-60.
FA	*Feudal Aids* (PRO), 1899-1920.
Fees	*The Book of Fees* (PRO), 1920-31.
Feilitzen	O. von Feilitzen, *The Pre-Conquest Personal Names of Domesday Book*, Uppsala 1937.
fem.	feminine.
ff.	and the pages following.
FF	*Feet of Fines* (PRSoc 17, 20, 23, 24), 1894, 1896, 1898, 1900. Some FF forms have been taken from SAS vols; these are referenced (e.g.) SAS 2/X(FF).
FFW	*Fouke Fitz Warin, Roman du XIV° Siecle* ed. Louis Brandon, Paris 1930.
Fine	*Calendar of Fine Rolls* (PRO), in progress.
Fli	Flintshire.
Fm	Farm.
f.n., f.ns.	field-name(s).
FN	H.D.G. Foxall, *Shropshire Field-Names*, Shrewsbury 1980.
For	*Select Pleas of the Forest*, ed. J.G. Turner, Selden Soc. 13, 1901.
ForProc	Forest Proceedings in PRO.
Fr	French.
freq	frequently.
G	German.
Gazetteer	H.D.G. Foxall, *A Gazetteer of Streets, Roads and Place Names in Shropshire*, 2nd ed., Shrewsbury 1967.
gen.	genitive.
GeolSurv	T.H. Whitehead and R.W. Pocock, *Dudley and Bridgnorth*. Memoirs of the Geological Survey of England and Wales, HMSO 1947.
Gir	*Giraldi Cambrensis Opera* (RS), 1861-91.
Gl	Gloucestershire.

G.R.	national grid reference.
Ha	Hampshire.
HAC	*The Cartulary of Haughmond Abbey*, ed. Una Rees, Cardiff 1985.
Harl 433	*British Library Harleian Manuscript 433*, ed. Rosemary Horrox and P.W. Hammond, 4 vols., Richard III Soc. 1979-83.
He	Herefordshire.
Ho	House.
Hobbs	J.L. Hobbs, *Shrewsbury Street-Names*, Shrewsbury 1954.
Howard	C. Howard, *The Roads of England and Wales*, 1883.
Hrt	Hertfordshire.
HTR	*The Shropshire Hearth-Tax Roll of 1672*, ed. W. Watkins-Pitchford, Shrewsbury 1949.
Hu	Huntingdonshire.
Hunt	*Henrici Huntendunensis Historia Anglorum* (RS), 1879.
Hy 1, Hy 2 etc.	regnal date, t. Henry I, t. Henry II etc.
ib, *ib*	*ibidem* (referring respectively to published and unpublished sources).
InqMisc	*Calendar of Inquisitions Miscellaneous* (PRO), in progress.
Ipm	*Calendar of Inquisitions Post Mortem* (PRO), in progress.
Jas 1, Jas 2	regnal date, t. James I, t. James II.
JEPN	Journal of the English Place-Name Society.
John	regnal date, t. John.
K	Kent.
Kelly	*Kelly's Directory of Shropshire.*
Kynnersley Brown	Letter from W.J. Kynnersley Brown, The Hall, Leighton, date 31st Jan. 1933, filed in E.W. Bowcock's material.
l.	late.
L	Lincolnshire.
La	Lancashire.
LCA	*Index to Llyfr Coch Asaph, Archaeological Cambrensis* 3rd series, Vol. 14, 1868.
Lei	Leicestershire.
Leland	*Leland's Itinerary in England and Wales*, ed. L. Toulmin Smith, 5 vols., London 1964.
LHEB	K. Jackson, *Language and History in Early Britain,*

	Edinburgh 1953.
Lib	*Calendar of Liberate Rolls* (PRO), in progress.
Lil	Lilleshall Cartulary, BL AddMS 50121.
Lilco	Records of the Lilleshall Company.
m.	mid.
Margary	I.D. Margary, *Roman Roads in Britain*, 2 vols., London 1955-7.
masc.	masculine.
ME	Middle English.
MemR	*The Memoranda Roll of the King's Remembrancer for* 1230-31 (PRS NS 11), 1933; - *for the Michaelmas Term of the First Year of the Reign of King John* (PRS NS 21), 1943.
MGS	C.H. Drinkwater, *The Merchants' Gild of Shrewsbury.* a series of articles in SAS. Most of these are bound in a volume in the Local Studies Library, Shrewsbury, (D 36.1 Acc No 1695).
MHG	Middle High German.
Mills	A.D. Mills, *Dorset Place-Names: Their Origins and Meanings,* Wimborne 1986.
MinAcc	Ministers' Accounts (PRO).
MM	*Mappa Mundi* in *The Historical Works of Gervase of Canterbury,* ed. W. Stubbs, Vol. II (RS), 1880.
ModE	Modern English.
Mont	Montgomeryshire.
Morden	*The County Maps from William Camden's Britannia 1695* by Robert Morden. A Facsimile (1972).
MorganTs	R. Morgan, *Welsh Place-Names in Shropshire* (typescript) 1988.
MS, MSS	Manuscript(s).
Mx	Middlesex.
N.	north.
Nb	Northumberland.
NCPNW	B.G. Charles, *Non-Celtic Place-Names in Wales,* London 1938.
n.d.	undated.
NED	*A New English Dictionary,* ed. J.A.H. Murray and others, Oxford 1888-1933.
Nf	Norfolk.
NLW	MSS in the National Library of Wales.

nom.	nominative.
Norwich	*The Valuation of Norwich*, ed. W.E. Lunt, Oxford 1926.
NRY	North Riding of Yorkshire.
NS	New Series in a run of publications.
Nt	Nottinghamshire.
Nth	Northamptonshire.
O	Oxfordshire.
obl.	oblique case.
OE	Old English.
Ogilby	J. Ogilby, *Itinerarium Angliae*, London 1675.
OHG	Old High German.
OLG	Old Low German.
ON	Old Norse.
OrdVit	*The Ecclesiastical History of Ordericus Vitalis*, ed. M. Chibnall, 6 vols., Oxford 1968-80.
OS	Ordnance Survey.
p.	page.
p.	*post*.
(p)	place-name used in a person's surname.
P	Pipe Rolls (PRS), in progress.
part.	participle.
Pat	*Calendar of Patent Rolls* (PRO), in progress.
pers.n.	personal name.
P.H.	Public House.
Pk	Park.
pl.	plural.
Plymley	J. Plymley, *General Survey of the Agriculture of Shropshire*, London 1803.
p.n., p.ns.	place-name(s).
PN	EPNS survey of the county indicated by the abbreviation which follows.
PRAlveley etc.	MS transcripts of parish registers in Shrewsbury Borough Library.
PR	*Shropshire Parish Registers*, Shropshire Parish Register Society. (H) Hereford Diocese; (L) Lichfield Diocese; (StA) St Asaph Diocese.
PrGerm	Primitive Germanic.
PRO	Public Record Office, London.
PRS	Pipe Roll Society.
PrW	Primitive Welsh.

PW — *The Parliamentary Writs and Writs of Military Summons* --- (RC), 1827-30.
QW — *Placita de Quo Warranto* (RC), 1818.
R. — River.
R 1, R 2 etc. — regnal date, t. Richard I, t. Richard II etc.
Rad — Radnorshire.
RB — Romano-British.
RBE — *The Red Book of the Exchequer*, ed. H. Hall (RS), 3 vols., 1896.
RC — Record Commission.
Rd — Road.
Redin — M. Redin, *Studies on Uncompounded Personal Names in Old English*, Uppsala 1919.
RentSurv — Rentals and Surveys in PRO.
RH — *Rotuli Hundredorum* (RC), 1812-18.
RS — Rolls Series.
Ru — Rutland.
S — P.H. Sawyer, *Anglo-Saxon Charters, an annotated list and bibliography*, Royal Historical Society, 1968.
S. — South.
s.a. — *sub anno.*
Sa — Shropshire.
SAC — *The Cartulary of Shrewsbury Abbey*, ed. Una Rees, 2 vols., National Library of Wales, 1975.
Saints — *Die Heiligen Englands*, ed. F. Liebermann, Hanover 1889.
SAS — *Transactions of the Shropshire Archaeological Society.* The series is numbered in arabic figures, the volume in roman, e.g. 1/IX, 4/III. If no series no. is given the ref. is to the current series, and the volume no. is in arabic.
Saxton — Saxton's *Map of Shropshire*, 1577.
SBL — A collection of Shropshire documents in The Local Studies Department of Shropshire Libraries, Shrewsbury.
Searle — W.G. Searle, *Onomasticon Anglo-Saxonicum*, Cambridge 1897.
Sf — Suffolk.
ShelveMap — Map of 1650 displayed in Shelve church.
sing. — singular.
Slack — *The Lordship of Oswestry 1393-1607*, ed. W.J. Slack,

Shrewsbury 1951.

s.n. — *sub nomine.*

So — Somerset.

SNQ — *Shropshire Notes and Queries* Vols. I and II, Shrewsbury 1886 (items collected from *The Shrewsbury Chronicle* 1884-86).

Sr — Surrey.

SR — *The Shropshire Lay Subsidy Roll of 1 Edward III, 1327*, ed. W.G.D. Fletcher, reprinted from SAS, Oswestry 1907.
The Lay Subsidy Roll of 1334, ed. R.E. Glasscock, British Academy 1975.

SRO — Documents in Shropshire Record Office.

St — Staffordshire.

Strange — *Le Strange Records*, ed. Hamon le Strange, London 1916.

StRO — Documents in Staffordshire Record Office.

s.v. — *sub voce.*

Swin — *Registrum Ricardi de Swinfield, Episcopi Herefordensis*, ed. W.W. Capes, Canterbury and York Society VI, 1909.

Sx — Sussex.

t. — *tempore.*

TA — Tithe Award.

TAMap — Map accompanying *TA*.

Templars — *Records of the Templars in England in the Twelfth Century*, ed. B.A. Lees, British Academy 1935.

Tengstrand — E. Tengstrand, *A Contribution to the Study of Genitival Composition in Old English Place-Names*, Uppsala 1940.

TN — *Taxatio Ecclesiastica Angliae et Walliae, auctoritate Papae Nicholai IV, c.1291*, ed. S. Ayscough and J. Caley, London 1802.

Tong — G. Griffiths, *A History of Tong, Shropshire*, Newport 1894.

Townson — R. Townson 'A Sketch of the Mineralogy of Shropshire' in *Tracts and Observations in Natural History and Physiology*, London 1799.

TRE — *tempore Regis Edwardi*, the DB term for 'on the day that King Edward the Confessor was alive and dead'.

VCH — *The Victoria History of the County of Shropshire*, in progress.

VCH — Victoria County History notes, held at Shropshire Record

	Office. Sometimes followed by note of ultimate source, e.g. *VCH(Longleat)*, *VCH(Hereford)*.
VE	*Valor Ecclesiasticus*, ed. J. Hunter (RC), 1810-34.
W	Wiltshire.
W.	West.
WATU	M. Richards, *Welsh Administrative and Territorial Units*, Cardiff 1973.
Wd	Wood.
We	Westmorland.
WMidl	west-midland.
Wo	Worcestershire.
Wom	Wombridge Cartulary, *BL EgMs 3712*.
WRY	West Riding of Yorkshire.
WSax	West-Saxon.
Wt	Isle of Wight.
Y	Yorkshire.
*	a postulated form.

Words printed in bold type, e.g. **āc**, **tūn**, are recognised place-name elements. Most of these are discussed in EPNS XXV-XXVI; some are to be found in the Elements sections of later volumes.

If a source-abbreviation is printed in italics, e.g. *Wom*, this indicates that the source is unpublished.

Long and short vowels are indicated thus: ā, ă

PHONETIC SYMBOLS

p	*p*ay	j	*y*ou	ɔ	p*o*t
b	*b*ay	x	lo*ch* (Scots)	ɔ:	s*aw*
t	*t*ea	h	*h*is	ɔi	*oi*l
d	*d*ay	m	*m*an	e	r*e*d
k	*k*ey	n	*n*o	ei	fl*ay*
g	*g*o	ŋ	si*ng*	ɛ	jam*ais* (Fr.)
ʍ	*wh*en	r	*r*un	ɛ:	th*ere*
w	*w*in	l	*l*and	i	p*i*t
f	*f*oe	tʃ	*ch*ur*ch*	i:	b*ea*d
v	*v*ote	dʒ	*j*u*dg*e	ou	l*ow*
s	*s*ay	ɑ:	f*a*ther	u	g*oo*d
z	*z*one	ɑu	c*ow*	u:	b*oo*t
ʃ	*sh*one	a	m*a*nn (German)	ʌ	m*u*ch
ʒ	a*z*ure	ai	fl*y*	ə	ev*er*
þ	*th*in	æ	c*a*b	ə:	b*ir*d
ð	*th*en			?	wa*t*er (Cockney, glottal stop)

Phonetic symbols are enclosed in square brackets: [ ].

The symbols used in the expression of Brit and PrWelsh forms are those used in LHEB.

ABDON SO 575866 Ancient Parish

Abetune 1086 DB, *Abeton'* c.1200 *ForProc*(p), *Abeton* Hy 2 (1346) Ch, 1316 FA, 1332 Ch, *Abetun'* 1255-6 *Ass*
Abbetona 1155 SAC, *Abbeton* 1255 RH *et freq* to 1504 Ipm
Abint' c.1200 *ForProc, Abinton'* 1261-2 *ib* (p)
Habeton' 1255-6 *Ass*
Alberton' 1271-2 *Ass, Albeton, Alberton* 1315 Ipm
Abbedon 1301 Ipm
Abdon 1503,4 Ipm, 1535 VE *et seq*
Abton 1577 Saxton, *Apton* 1695 Morden

'Ab(b)a's estate'; the second element is **tūn**, with late substitution of **dūn** 'hill'. The two spellings with *-in-* from *ForProc* do not constitute sufficient evidence for an alternative form with *-ingtūn.*

Abcott in Clungunford contains the same personal name.

ACTON

Shropshire contains eight examples of the place-name Acton, from OE *āc-tūn*, 'oak settlement or estate'. Acton Burnell and Pigott are here counted as a single instance, and this, together with Acton Reynald, Acton Round and Acton Scott, comprises the examples which are of sufficiently high administrative status to be included in the present work. Full lists of spellings for these are given below. The four minor names are:

1. Acton in Lydbury parish, well-recorded from 1255 onwards.
2. Stoneacton in Rushbury (*Staniacton'* 1242 Fees, *Stoniacton* 1255 RH)
3. Boreatton in Baschurch (*Acton'* 1291-2 *Ass* (p), *Acton* 1545 (1773) *SBL 17285, Boreatton* 1577 Saxton, 1609 *SBL 17410, Boracton* 1672 HTR)
4. Shotatton in Ruyton-XI-Towns (*Acton' iuxta Knokyn* 1291-2 *Ass, Schettatton* c.1300 *SBL 3587, Setacton'* 14th *SBL 3588, Acton* 1553 Pat)

The affix to Stoneacton is OE *stānig* 'stony'. The affix to Boreatton could be OE *bār* 'boar' or a word **bor* 'hill' believed to occur in Boreham (Ess, Hrt, Sx and W). This second possibility would suit the topography and would balance well with the probable nature of the affix to Shotatton, the *Acton* from which Boreatton is being distinguished. Shot- is probably the topographical term *scēat* 'something projecting'. On the other hand **bor* is an archaic place-name element, so unlikely to be found in Shropshire, and other etymologies are possible for the affix in Shotatton. The problems posed by the terms used to distinguish some of the Shropshire Actons may be left aside for the present; it is more relevant here to consider the significance of the compound *āc-tūn*.

The limited distribution of this place-name in the country as a whole has not hitherto been appreciated. With the single exception of Acton near London, examples are in the west midlands and the north. (The Denbighshire instance can be loosely counted as in the west midlands). The corpus has been plotted by Mr J. Pagett on Fig. 1. It should be noted that in the north *āc-tūn* sometimes becomes Aughton or Aighton, showing the same development of *-ct-* as is found in Broughton from *brōc-tūn*.

In assembling a corpus of any type of place-name there will be difficult decisions about items for which the early spellings are not conclusive. My corpus includes Acton Turville, Gl, for which E. Ekwall and A.H. Smith preferred the etymology 'Ac(c)a's *tūn*'. Three of the four spellings on which they base this (*Achetune* DB, *Aketon'* 1236 Fees, 1287 *Ass*) can be explained, as can comparable spellings for some of the Shropshire Actons, as manifesting the inorganic *e* which developed between consonants in Norman-French pronunciation of Germanic names; and the fourth irregular Acton Turville spelling, *Achentona* 1169 P, may fairly be dismissed as erratic, like the solitary *Akerton'* for Acton Burnell. These are heavily outnumbered by *Acton'* spellings. For two likely instances in Staffordshire, Acton near Whitmore and Acton Hill near Eccleshall, there are as yet no early spellings available. When some difficulties of this kind have been acknowledged, however, the body of material plotted on Fig. 1 is sufficiently reliable to form a basis for discussion, and the curiously limited distribution must be noted in any attempt to explain the name. Since Shropshire has eight examples and no other county has more than four the subject is particularly relevant to a study of Shropshire place-names.

The standard explanations of Acton/Aughton are that the name means 'farm built of oak', 'farm by an oak-tree' or 'farm among oak-trees'. It is, however, difficult to explain the limited distribution if any of these is accepted, since they must have been equally appropriate in many areas where the name does not occur. Compounds of **tūn** with some other tree-names, e.g. Ashton/Eshton, and Alderton/ Allerton/ Ollerton/ Orleton, are fairly frequent but more widely distributed. The only such compound which shows similar preferential distribution to Acton/Aughton is Thornton, which has a predominantly east-midland and north-country distribution, sixteen of its occurrences in major names being in Yorkshire. It is necessary to conclude that something in the significance attached to the compound *āc-tūn* made it specially applicable to settlements in the west midlands, and that *þorn-tūn* denoted a type of settlement especially common in Yorkshire.

A tentative explanation of Acton based on the characteristics of the eight Shropshire examples is that places so called had special functions in the processing or distribution of oak timber. The places can easily be seen as component parts of large multiple estates. The four minor names are situated in large parishes which contain a number of settlements, and Acton Reynald (here counted a 'major' name because it is in DB) is similarly placed in the large parish of Shawbury. As regards the three which have become parishes - Acton Burnell, Acton Round and Acton Scott - the areas of the parishes are modest, quite different from those of Rushbury, Shawbury, Lydbury North or Baschurch. The hidage given in DB for the five names mentioned there is 3 for Acton Pigott, Acton Reynald and Acton Scott, 3½ for Acton Burnell, and 4 for Acton Round. (Acton Pigott is a DB estate later in the parish of Acton Burnell). The splitting up of large composite estates might result in the creation of just such units as these.

To account for the geographical distribution, it would have to be assumed either that the handling of oak timber became a specialised function for subordinate settlements at the period when

English place-names were replacing Welsh ones in the west midlands and in Yorkshire, or that the pre-English economy of those areas had been characterised by such specialisation, and that this was recognised in the new English names.

This suggestion is the most tentative of hypotheses. The aim of the discussion is to present the eight Shropshire Actons in their distributional setting.

ACTON BURNELL SJ 534019 Ancient Parish

Actune 1086 DB, *Akton' Burnell* 1198 FF, *Acton'* 1242 Fees, *Acton' Burnel* 1255 RH *et passim* with variant spellings *Acton* and *Burnell; Actonbornell* 1458 Fine *Acton Bornell* 1461 Cl, *Ackton Bornel* 1716 PR(H) 16, *Acton Burnhill* 1742 PR(H) 1

Akerton' 1229 Cur

This place and Acton Piggott may reasonably be seen as a single instance of the place-name Acton, though by the time of the Domesday Survey two considerable estates, of 3½ hides and 3 hides respectively, had become established in the hypothetical area once known as 'oak farm or estate'. DB does not mention woodland under Acton Burnell, but for Acton Piggott wood for 20 swine is noted. VCH VIII, p.3, says that woodland has been an enduring feature of the parish landscape, most of it lying on Acton Burnell Hill.

The Burnell family are mentioned in connection with the manor from the late 12th century (VCH VIII, p.7). Parliament met here in 1283.

ACTON PIGOTT SJ 542027 DB Manor

Æctune 1086 DB

Acton' Picot 1242 Fees, *Acton Pygod* 1270 Pat, *Acton' Pichot* 1272 Cl, *Acton Picot* 1279 Cl, *- Pycod* 1280 Pat, *- Pigot* 1291 Ipm *et freq* with variant spellings *- Pygot, - Pig(g)ott; - Pycot* 1295 Cl, 1316 Pat

Aketon Bygot 1271-2 *Ass*

See the discussion of Acton Burnell. The affix in this instance is from the name of William Fitz Picot, who was living in 1203 (VCH VIII, p.9). The *Æ*- of the DB spelling suggests that there was an alternative form from **ǣc**, dative of **āc**.

ACTON REYNALD SJ 535232 DB Manor

Achetone 1086 DB, *Aketon* 1203-4 *Ass* (p)
Actona c.1185-90 HAC, *Acton'* 1242-3 Fees (p), - *Reyner'* 1255-6 *Ass et freq* with variant spelling *Acton Reyner* to 1615 (copy) *SBL 15755, Actone* 1274 RH (p), *Acton Reigner* 1416 AD, - *Reignold* 1654 PR(L) 20, - *Rinoll* 1675 Ogilby, - *Reynold* 1697 PR(L) 7, - *Reynalds* 1699 PR(L) 1

The manor was held by a family surnamed *de Acton*, three of whom had the Christian name *Reyner.* Eyton (X, p.61) says that the first Reyner de Acton was a frequent witness of deeds from 11951220.

An *Acton' monachorum* is mentioned in 1255-6 *Ass* together with places (Hadnall, Harlascott and Albrightlee) in the vicinity of Acton Reynald, and in 1291-2 *Ass* there is a reference to *Acton Reyner et Frates.* Haughmond Abbey had some property here (Eyton X, p.65), and *monachorum* and *Frates (?recte Fratres)* might refer to this.

DB notes woodland for 30 swine at this Acton.

ACTON ROUND SO 634956 Ancient Parish

Achetune 1086 DB, *Aketon'* 1251 Cl
Acton' c.1200 *ForProc et freq* with variant spellings *Acton(e)* to 1272 Cl, *Acton la Runde* 1283 Ipm, *Acton Rotunda* 1283 (1348) Pat, *Acton Round* 1284-5 FA, *Actone Rotunda* 1291-2 *Ass, Acton' la R(o)unde* 1292-5 *Ass, Rounde Acton* 1300 Ipm, *Acton Rounde* 1302 Ipm *et freq* to 1535 *SBL 7180, Acton la Rounde* 1302 Ipm, 1307 Pat, 1315 *SBL 8649*, 1320 Cl, *Acton' le Roun'* 1308 Cl, *Rondeacton* 1397 Pat, *Acton Rownd* 1500 Ipm, *Round*

Acton 1566 *SBL 8384*, 1675 Ogilby, 1787 PR(H) 17, *Acton Round* 1716 PR(H) 3 *et seq*

This Acton lies in a belt of land where estates mentioned in DB are not stated to have woodland; a number of oak trees are, however, mentioned in a perambulation of Spoonhill Wood, on the boundary of Acton Round and Much Wenlock, in 1255-6 *Ass.*

The affix to this name has been a source of speculation. It is Latinised as *Rotunda*, so must have been considered by government officials to be the adjective *round*, which is a ME loan from OFr *rond.* This word is rare in place-names (leaving aside those of modern origin). EPN notes only the present name and two instances of Roundhay in YW and Nth.

The most convincing suggestion offered for *la Runde* etc. in the Sa name is probably that put forward by E.W. Bowcock in a letter to a Shropshire newspaper dated 25th July 1924, found among his papers. This suggests that the affix is a playful variant of the name *Arundel.* The manor belonged to the Earls of Arundel, and the Sussex place-name might have been interpreted by French speakers as containing *rond.* It is spelt *Arondel(l)* in 1273-91 and 1303, *Aroundell* in 1330 (PN Sx 136-7).

Other explanations have not been substantiated. There is nothing especially circular in the topography, and there is no evidence for the former existence of a round church, traditions about which probably arose from the name. This last suggestion is discussed by Eyton (IV, p.121 n.2) with considerable scepticism.

ACTON SCOTT SO 454893 Ancient Parish

Actune 1086 DB, *Acton* 1255 RH, *Acton' Longefeud'* 1255-6 *Ass*, *Acton' in longefeld'* 1261-2 *ForProc*, *Acton' longfeld* 1271-2 *Ass*, *Acton in Longefeld* 1284-5 FA, *Scottes Acton*, *Skottesacton* 1289 InqMisc, *Actone Schottes* l.13th *ForProc*, *Acton' Scottes* 1291-2 *Ass*, *Acton Scot* 1301 SAC, 1675 Ogilby, *Scotus Acton* 1316 FA, *Actonscott* 1502 Ipm, *Acton of the Hill* 1702 PR(L) 16, *Acton Scote* 1718 PR(H) 16

Oak trees are referred to again in the name Oakwood in this parish, which is *Hokwode* 1271-2 *ForProc, Ocwode* 1291-2 *Ass.*

The affix *Longefeud', in Longefeld* is a district-name which has survived as the name of two settlements, Cheney Longville and Longville in the Dale, lying S.W. and N.E. of Acton Scott. The 'long open land' was a strip of ground at the foot of the chain of hills which separates these settlements from the valley of Church Stretton. The surviving affix is a family name; Reginald *Scot'* was in possession of the manor in 1255 RH. The affix *of the Hill* survived into modern times; Foxall's Gazetteer gives 'Acton Scott (or Acton on the Hill)'.

ADDERLEY SJ 661395 Ancient Parish

Eldredelei 1086 DB, *Aldel', Arderdel'* 1255-6 *Ass, Aldrideleye* 1283 Ch, *Aldredelegh'* 1291-2 *Ass, Aldredele* 1320 Fine

Ethdredesh' c.1182 SAC

Addirdel 1255 RH, *Adderdeleye* 1314, 30, 41 Cl, 1334 SR, *Adderdelegh* 1319 Pat, *Adderdeleygh* 1323 Pat, *Adderdele* 1330 Pat, 1339 Cl, *Adderdeley* 1360 Pat, *Addurdeley* 1369 Pat

Addradel' 1255-6 *Ass, Addridelegh'* 1271-2 *Ass, Addredeleye* 1286 Pat, c.1291 TN, *Addreddelegh'* 1291-2 *Ass, Addredele* 1309,39 Cl, *Addredelegh* 1318 Pat, *Addridele* 1324,7 Fine

Adredelegh, Adredelegth 1271-2 *Ass, Adredeleye* 1284-5 FA, 1328 Ipm

Adurdeleye 1306-7 *Ass, Aderdelye* 1315 Ch, *Aderdeleye* 1316 FA *et freq* to 1343 Cl, *Aderdele* 1329 Ipm, 1331 Cl

Adderleye 1309 Cl *et freq* to 1390 Pat, *Adderle* 1350 Pat, *Addirlegh* 1361,4 Pat, *Adderlee* 1363 Ipm, *Adderley* 1386 Cl, 1535 VE *et freq, Addyrley* 1430 Cl

Addridleye, Addrydleye 1318 Cl, *Addridleye* 1318 Fine, Pat

Final element *lēah*, perhaps in the late sense 'meadow'. The first element is a feminine personal name, which might be *Ealdthrȳth* or *Ælfthrȳth* or *Æthelthrȳth.* Alderley, Cheshire, is a similar, perhaps identical name, but the development is different. The spellings for Alderley show that that name consistently retained the *-l-* of the first syllable (with occasional vocalisation to *-u-*),

PLACE-NAMES DERIVED FROM *āc-tūn* OR *eik-tūn*

Yorkshire	Aketon	SE	352 521
	Ackton		412 220
	Aughton		701 387
	Aughton	SK	455 866
Lancashire	Aighton	SD	670 397
	Aughton		391 054
	Aughton		550 677
Cumberland	Aikton	NY	274 530
Cheshire	Acton	SJ	631 536
	Acton Hall		593 753
	Acton Grange		597 850
	Agden Hall		715 855
Denbighshire	Acton	SJ	340 520
Shropshire	Shotatton	SJ	366 228
	Boreatton		413 229
	Acton Reynald		535 232
	Acton Burnell and Pigott		534 019, 542 027
	Acton	SO	314 849
	Acton Scott		454 894
	Stone Acton		507 937
	Acton Round		634 956
Staffordshire	Acton Trussell	SJ	937 174
Worcestershire	Acton	SO	845 674
Herefordshire	Acton Beauchamp	SO	679 503
Gloucestershire	Iron Acton	ST	680 834
	Acton Turville		808 809
Greater London	Acton	TQ	201 802

N.B. Acton Fm in Charing, Kent, is a doubtful specimen, more likely to be 'Aca's tūn', as *Aketon'* and the like is more common than *Acton'* in the available early spellings (J.K. Wallenberg, *The Place-Names of Kent*, p. 388).

Acton Essex is OE *Acantune, Acyntune.*

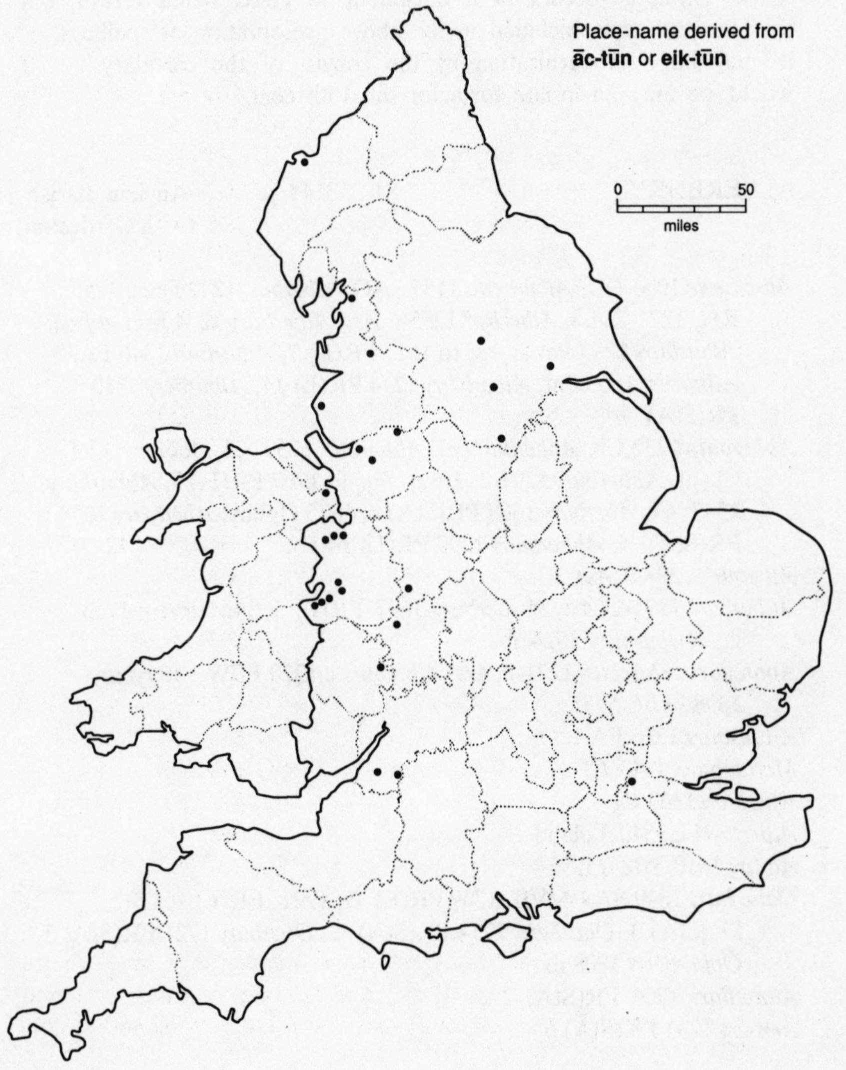

Place-name derived from
āc-tūn or eik-tūn
0
50
miles

whereas in the Shropshire name *-l-* was quickly assimilated to give *Add-* instead of *Ald-*.

Addurley occurs in a document in HAC dated c.1213, but this has not been included in the above presentation of spellings, as it may be a modernisation by the copyist of the cartulary. It would be an appropriate form for the 15th cent.

ALBERBURY SJ 358144 Ancient Parish (with Cardeston)

Alberberie 1086 DB, *Alberberia* 1155 SAC, *Alberbur'* 1242 Fees, 1255 RH, 1271-2 *Ass*, *Alberbyr'* 1255-6 *Ass*, *Alberbury* 1274 Ipm *et freq;* *Alburbury* 1293 Pat *et freq* to 1617 PR(L) 7, *Alburburi* 1346 FA, *Alburbiry* 1363 Pat, *Alberberry* 1744 PR(L) 14, *Alburbery* 1810 PR(StA) 3

Abberbure 1232 Ch, *Abberbur'* (p), *Abburbur'* 1259 Cl, *Abberbir* 1268 Cl (p), *Abberbury* 1291-2 *Ass et freq* to 1767 PR(H) 7, *Abburbury* 1347 Cl, *Aberbury* 1607 PR(StA) 4, 1675 Ogilby, *Aberberry* 1658 PR(StA) 4, *Abberberry* 1799 PR(L) 20

Albebur' 1271-2 Ass

Auberburi 1271-2 *Ass*, *Awberbury* 1697 PR(L) 1, *Awburbery* 1703 ib, *Awburbury* 1724 ib

Abbrebur', *Aldrebur'* 1271-2 *Ass*, *Albreburs* c.1320 FFW, *Albrybury* 1398 *SBL 5435*

Albresbury 1316 FA

Malberbury 1343 Cl

Atterbury 1363 Cl

Albertbyri c.1540 Leland

Albury 1610 *SBL 15757*

Obberbury 1649 SAS 4/VII, 1709 PR(L) 12, 1721 PR(L) 1, 1797 PR(StA) 3, *Obarberry* 1714 PR(StA) 2, *Oberbury* 1721 PR(StA) 3, *Obberberry* 1808 ib

Allderbury 1703 PR(StA) 2

Aerbery 1733 PR(StA) 6

'Manor-house of Aluburg', second element **byrig.** The personal name is feminine. The absence of *-k-*, which might have been expected from the *-h-* of the commoner name *Ealhburg,* favours Ekwall's alternative suggestion of *Aluburg.*

This is a very well-recorded place-name, and the influence of written forms may have contributed to the survival of the long form Alberbury, rather than the once-recorded shortened form *Albury.*

It is clear from the parish-register spellings that a form with vocalised *-l-* was current locally. This developed from *Awburbury* to *Obberbury,* which the Introduction to PR(H) 7, published 1902, cites as the local pronunciation. The present-day pronunciation mostly corresponds to the modern spelling, though the *Awburbury* form is sometimes heard.

There was also, from 1232 to 1799, a form in which the *-l-* was assimilated to *-b-* to give *Abber-*.

The place has a Welsh name, Llanfihangel, from the church-dedication to St Michael. This is *Llanui(h)angel* 1265 *NLW Peniarth MS 231* (ex. inf. R. Morgan). *MorganTs* p.2 shows that the affix *Llychantyn,* found with Llanfihangel in 16th-cent. sources, is the Welsh version of Loton, an adjacent settlement *(q.v.).*

ALBRIGHT HUSSEY SJ 502175 DB Manor

Abretone, Etbretone 1086 DB, *Abrighton'* 1292-5 *Ass*
Adbricton', At- 1242 Fees, *Atbryghton'* c.1275 SAC, *Netheradbrighton'* 1291-2 *Ass, Addbrithton' Hese* 1301 SAC, *Adbrygton Husee* 1309 Pat, *Adbrighton Huse* 1316, 46 FA, 1406 Pat, - *Husee* 1353 Pat, 1410 Ch, 1428,31 FA, *Adbryhton Heseye* 1394 Cl, *Adbryghton Huse* 1409 Pat, *Adbrighton Hussey* 1794 PR(L) 1
Albrighton' Husey 1291-2 *Ass, Albrighton Hussey* 1535 VE, 1586 *SBL 6022*
Adbriton Huse 1332 Ch
Hussey 1535 VE, 1590 *SBL 5795,* 1688 *SBL 3469A*
Abright Hussey 1586 *SBL 6022, Abrightt* - 1647 *SBL 6032A, Abrid Husee* 1675 PR(L) 7, *Adbrid* - 1681 ib, *Adbright Hussey* 1688 *SBL 3469,* 1699 PR(L) 1, 1722 *SBL 3451, Albright Hussey* 1690-1 *SBL 5230*

Albright Hussey is in the modern parish of Albrighton near Shrewsbury *(infra)*, and the name Albrighton was anciently used for both settlements. The two manors described in DB which are identified with Albright Hussey were held by Rainald the Sheriff, most of whose manors appear later in the possession of the Fitz-Alans. In 1242, Fees notes Walter Hose(y) as the holder of half a fee in *Adbricton'* or *Atbricton'* in the barony of the Fitz-Alans. When the surname Hussey had been affixed, the whole name was shortened by dropping *-ton-*. In the 16th cent. the affix was occasionally used by itself as the place-name.

ALBRIGHTLEE SJ 524162 DB Manor

Etbretelie 1086 DB, *Edbrittleg* 1217 (1285) Ch, *Adbruteleg'* 1271-2 *Ass, Edbrit'leg'* 1395 *SBL 16293, Edbritlleg* 1443 (copy) *SBL 15752*

Edbricteleg' 1221-2 *Ass*(p), *Eadbrichteleg'* 1255-6 *Ass, Edbrictel'* 1261-2 *ForProc, Adbrictelegh', Adbrychtelegh'* 1271-2 *Ass, Adbrithelegh'* 1301 SAC, *Atbrighteleye* 1320 *SBL 5410, Adbryghtley* 1369 *SBL 5859, Adbryhtleg'* 1394 Cl, *Adbrightley* 1555 Pat, *Adbrightlee, Adbrightly* 1599 *SBL 5951, Adbrightlee* 1651 *SBL 6045*, 1653 *SBL 5920*, 1669 *SBL 15748*

Radbricteleg' 1261-2 *ForProc*

Abbrythleye 1291-2 *Ass, Abbryghtle* 1570 *SBL 5769, Abrightlye* 1584 *SBL 5976, Abright Lee* 1672 HTR

Albrightlee 1695 Morden, *Allbright Lee* 1736,8,61 PR(L) 20, *Allbrightlee* 1757 ib

Probably 'woodland clearing adjacent to Albrighton'. The spellings do not preclude 'Ēadbeorht's clearing', which would be an independent place-name referring to the same Anglo-Saxon landowner from whom Albrighton near Shrewsbury is named. The absence of genitival *-s-* would be more difficult to explain in Albrightlee than it is in Albrighton, however, and the persistent *-e-* of forms like *Edbricteleg'* could result from the dropping of **tūn** from an original **Ēadbeorht(es)tūnlēah.*

There was a *leuuede* of wood at the time of DB, and the reference in 1394 Cl is to a wood of *Adbryhtleg'* ; but since the place was a small manor in 1086 the translation 'clearing' is perhaps more apt than 'wood' for **lēah** in this instance.

Albrightlee is in the parish of Uffington.

ALBRIGHTON (near Shrewsbury) SJ 496181 Civil Parish

Etbritone 1086 DB, *Edbryton'* 1256 SAC
Eadburtona 1121 SAC, *Edburtona* 1138, 1155 SAC
Adbrictun 1167-82 SAC, *Adbrichton'* 1241 Cl, 1272 SAC, *Adbrichton Monacorum Salop'* 1255 RH, *Adbricton'* 1261-2 *ForProc*, 1271-2 *Ass*, *Adbrighton'* l.13th *SBL 5840*, 1344 *SBL 3622*, 1392 Pat, *Adbryghton'* 1393 *SBL 4534*, 1413 *SBL 3720*, *Adbrighton* 1535 VE, 1682 PR(L) 1 *et freq* to 1728 *SBL 3453*, *Adbrington* 1702 PR(L) 1
Edbricton' 1208-9 *ForProc*, *Edbrictone* 1204-14 SAC(p), *Eadbrichtone* 1235 SAC
Albriton' 1241 Cl(p), *Albrythton'* 1271-2 *Ass*, *Albrighton' monachor'* 1291-2 *Ass*, *Albrington* 1691 PR(L) 12, *Albrighton* 1715, 87 PR(L) 12, 1783 PR(L) 14
Abricton' Monacorum 1261-2 *ForProc*, *Abbrykton* 1318 *SBL 5427*, *Abrighton* 1585 PR(L) 12 *et freq* to 1688 *SBL 3469A*, *Abrington* 1607 PR(H) 1, 1694, 1704 PR(L) 12, 1735 *SBL 3434*, *Abbrighton* 1667 PR(L) 1
Adbriston' 1271-2 *ForProc*, 1271-2 *Ass* (p)
Monkes Adbrithon' 1301 SAC
Abriton 1650 PR(L) 15, *Abretton* 1656 ib
Old Brighton 1650 *SBL 3447*
Adbrighton alias Albrighton alias Albrington 1688 *SBL 3469A*, *Abrighton also Adbrighton* 1700 *SBL 3500*

The etymology is clearly 'Ēadbeorht's estate', but the original structure of the name requires some consideration. At first sight this would appear to be an instance of the use of an uninflected personal name as qualifier, a practice which is characteristic of northern England. This would, however, be unusual in Shropshire, where personal names are usually in the genitive when used in place-names. There may have been a tendency for compounds of **tūn** with personal names ending in *-beorht* to lose the genitival *-s-* at a very early date. Apparently uninflected personal names in *-beorht* occur in Aylburton Gl (for which see Albrighton near Shifnal); Ebrington Gl (a doublet of Albrighton near Shrewsbury); Emberton Bk and Amerton St *(Ēanbeorht)*; Kemberton Sa *(infra)*; Tibberton Gl, Sa, and Tyberton He *(Tīdbeorht)*; Wilbrighton St *(Wilbeorht)*. The genitival *-s-* is, however, preserved in Ebberston YN, which is another 'Ēadbeorht's **tūn**'.

ALBRIGHTON (near Shifnal) SJ 809044 Ancient Parish

Albricstone 1086 DB
Aibbricton 1221-2 *Ass*
Albrichton 1232 Ch, *Albricton'* 1232 Cl, 1251-2 Fees, *-ton* 1253 Ipm, 1284-5 FA, 1285 Pat, *Albrighton* 1271-2 *Ass et freq* with variant spelling *-bryght-; Albrigton* 1291 *Ass*
Aubricton' 1242 Fees
Albriton 1255 RH, 1276 Cl, 1301,5 Ipm, *-tone* 1325 Pat
Aylbrihton 1285 Ipm, *Ailbriȝton* 1301 Cl, Ipm, *Aylbrighton* 1303 ChanR, InqMisc
Abryton 1597 PR(H) 3
Albrington 1690, 1725,36,38 *PRShifnal*
Allbridgton 1787 PR(H) 16

Probably 'Æthelbeorht's estate', *v.* **tūn**. If the personal name be correctly identified, this place-name is a doublet of Aylburton Gl, but in the Gl name the *Ail-, Ayl-* spellings predominate over those with Al-, whereas they are in a small minority for the Sa name.

A genitival *-s-* may have been lost from this name and from Aylburton Gl for the reason suggested under Albrighton near Shrewsbury. DB *Albricstone* probably has *-cst-* as a Norman-French spelling for OE *-ht-*.

ALCASTON SO 459870 DB Manor

Ælmundestune 1086 DB
Agemundeston' 1194,5 P
Alhameston 1255 RH, *Alchamston'* 1255-6 *Ass, Alkhameston'* 1261-2 *ForProc, Alhamestan* c.1270 InqMisc, *Alghamston', Alhamston'* 1271-2 *Ass, Alhamstun* 1274 Ipm, *Alcaneston* 1284-5 FA, *Alghameston* 1301 SAC, 1492 Ipm, *Alkamston* 1302 Ipm, *Alghhamston* 1307 Pat, *Alghamston* 1347 Cl, Pat, 1399 Pat, *Alghampton* 1347 Pat, *Alghampston* 1353,4 Pat, *Alcamston* 1504 Ipm
Halkamston', Halkameston' 1255-6 *Ass, Holghamton'* 1271-2 *Ass, Halthamstan, Halchamstan* 1274 Ipm, *Halchameston* 1276 Ipm
Aleyghamstone l.13th *ForProc*
Aulkaston 1577 Saxton, *Allcaston* 1786 PR(H) 17
Orson 1732 PR(H) 8

'Alhmund's estate', *v.* **tūn**. The development to *Alhameston* is perhaps due to the insertion of a vowel between *Alh-* and *mund* by Norman-French speakers, a practice reflected in DB *Alchemond* for a Yorkshire landowner whose name was OE *Alhmund*, and paralleled in many other DB spellings for names which had medial consonant-groups. The inserted vowel is usually *-e-*, but occasionally *-a-*. A hypothetical late-11th cent. form **Alchamundeston* could have become *Alhameston, Alghamston* by the dropping of the middle element.

The substitution of the hard *-c-* of the modern name for the OE sound represented by *-h-* appears from the spellings to have been a relatively late development. The *-gh-* of many spellings probably represents the sound spelt *-h-* in OE.

Alcaston is in Acton Scott parish.

ALDON SO 436795 DB Manor

Alledone 1086 DB, *Auldoun* 1391, 1425 Cl, *Auldon* 1395,6, 1416 AD, 1577 Saxton, *Alden* 1500 Ipm, *Aldon* 1503,4 Ipm
Euledon' 1221-2 *Ass*, 1242 Fees, *-don* 1255-6. 1271-2 *Ass, -done*

1271-2 *Ass* (p), *-den* 1284-5 FA, *Ewledon* 1346 FA, *Euldon'* 1334 SR, *Euldon* 1428 FA
Gueledon 1271-2 *Ass*
Eweldon' 1291-2 *Ass*, 1318 Ipm, 1348 Cl (p)
Eauldon 1356 Ipm

'Hill with a spring', OE **æwell-dūn.* Research by Mrs Ann Cole in southern counties suggests that the rare 'spring' terms *æwell* and *æwelm* (literally 'river-source') were reserved for particularly copious springs.

Aldon lies just below the tip of a hill projecting into the area between the R. Onny and a tributary which flows past Stokesay Court. The hamlet overlooks a deeply-cut valley in which one of the headstreams of this tributary rises.

The 6in. map shows Upper and lower Aldon Fm on either side of the hamlet. These are *Over Euledon', Nither Eweledon'* 1291-2 *Ass, Overe Eweledon, Nether* - 1318 Ch.

ALKINGTON SJ 531392 DB Manor

Alchetune 1086 DB
Alkinton' 1255-6 *Ass*, *-ton* 1577 Saxton
Alghynton 1320 Pat, 1399 AD
Alyngton 1483-5 *Harl 433*
Alkington 1695 Morden *et seq*
Uckington 1703 PR(L) 7

Probably OE **Ealhingtūn*, 'settlement connected with Ealha'. The suggested personal name is not on record, but *Ealh-* is a common theme in compound personal names.

Alkington is a township of Whitchurch parish.

ALVELEY SO 759845 Ancient Parish

Alvidelege 1086 DB, *Aluedelea* 1189,90 P, *-lega* 1191,2,3,4 P,

Aluideleya 1230 P, *Alvedelegh* 1316 FA, *Alvidele(y)* 1337 Pat, *Alvedelei* 1346 FA, *-leye* 1346 Pat, *-ley* 1349 Ipm, 1390 Pat, *-le* 1349,72 Pat, 1369,70 Ipm, *Alvidele* 1361 Pat, *Alvydeleye* 1361 Ipm, 1366 Pat, 1387 Fine

Aluielea 1160,1 P, *Ailuiel'* 1162 P, *Alveleia* 1199 Cur (p), *Alvetheley alias Alveley* 1401 Pat, *Alveleye* 1406 Fine, *-ley* 1484 Cl, 1492 Ipm, 1774 PR(L) 7, *Allveley, Alvely* 1553 Pat, *Allvalley* 1618 *PRAlveley, Alvely* 1654 *ib, Alvelly* 1801 PR(H) 7

Alveðelea 1177 P, *Aluitheleg'* 1195 P *et passim* with variant spellings *Aluitheléé, Aluithel', Aluitheleh, Alvytheleg(e), Alvitheley(e), Aluytheleghe, Alvythele(ye)* to 1381 Fine, *Alvutheleg'* 1212 AD, *Alvithleye, Alvyth-* 1271-2 *Ass, Alvethele* 1330 Fine, 1339 Pat, *-leye* 1333-4 *ForProc* (p), 1347,72,82 Pat, *Alvethley* 1399 Pat

Avitheleg' 1199 Cur

Auvillers 1266 Pat

Alvitleg' 1274 RH, *Alvetele* 1328 Pat

Hauedeleye (ter) 1284-5 FA

Aveley 1577 Saxton, 1675 Ogilby, 1736 PR(H) 3

Alverley 1734-5 *PRLudford*

'Ælfgȳð's clearing'; the personal name is feminine, and the compound is similar to Adderley, *supra.*

In spite of the occasional appearance of shortened forms from 1160 to 1199, it is clear that the longer form did not succumb till the early 15th century; and it may have been the memory of the second element of the personal name which prevented the smooth reduction of the place-name to a disyllable after that date. The parish register spelling of 1734-5, *Alverley,* presumably reflects the local persistence of a trisyllabic form.

There was another *Ælfgȳðelēah* in Essex, which became modern Aveley. The spellings set out in PN Ess 120-1 are similar in many respects to those for the Sa name. The earliest *Avel(e)y* spellings are 16th-cent., and it is interesting that the Sa name also had a form *Aveley,* recorded in 1577, 1675 and 1736. The single *Auvillers* from 1266 is paralleled by a number of similar 13th-cent. spellings for the Ess name; and P.H. Reaney, the author of the Ess survey, suggested that these were due to association with

French names ending in *-vill(i)ers.*

The BBC pronouncing dictionary gives a disyllabic pronunciation for the Sa name, with short *A-* and loss of the first *-l-*; but local informants give [a:vli], with long *A-*. The Ess name is pronounced as spelt.

AMASTON (now in Heath Fm) SJ 378112 DB Manor

Enbaldestune 1086 DB
Amboldeston' 1251 Fees, *Ambaldeston* 1255, 74 RH,
Ambaldeston' 1271-2 *Ass, Hambaldeston'* 1255-6 *Ass*
Ambaston 1346 FA (p), 1381 Cl, 1416 AD, 1421 Cl, 1633 PR(H) 6
Amaston 1571 *SBL 6664,* 1651 PR(H) 6, 1707 *SBL 6042,*
Ameston 1672 HTR, 1778 PR(H) 7
Amason 1644 PR(H) 6, *Amasson* 1775 PR(H) 7

'Ēanbald's estate'. Another OE *Ēanbaldestūn* has become Ambaston in Db.

Amaston is not marked on modern maps, though it is still in use locally. It was a 2-hide manor in DB, and there is a motte and bailey earthwork at Heath Fm; but its ancient union with the manor of Rowton probably militated to some extent against its survival as a separate entity. It was, however, still a township of Alberbury with Cardington in the 19th cent., and VCH VIII p.192 suggests that a recognisable hamlet survived until the 1690s.

Besides showing Amaston as a township and as the name of buildings corresponding to Heath Fm, the 1st edition 1" map shows a building named *Emmerson* a short distance to the E., perhaps corresponding to modern Wood End Fm. *Emmerson* may be an alternative development of the name Amaston. Both names occur on the 1881 OS 6", and Amaston is marked on Bacon's *New Survey Map of Staffordshire and Shropshire,* of about 1901.

ASHFORD BOWDLER SO 519705 Ancient Parish

Esseford 1155 BM, 1242 Fees
Esford 1203, 1230 Eyton
Eschford 1221 Eyton
Asford Budlers 1255 RH, 1271-2 *Ass, Asford Bulers* 1255-6 *Ass, Asford Boudlers* 1271-2 *Ass, Asford Boulers* 1287 Ipm
Asseford Bulers 1255-6 *Ass*
Aysford Bullers 1271-2 *Ass*
Assheford Boulers 1287 Cl, *Assheford Boudlers, Asscheford Boudlers* 1308 Ipm, *Ascheford Boulers* 1346 FA, *Asscheford Boudelers* 1428 FA
Asshford Bowdelers 1498 Ipm, *Ashford Bowdler* 1675 Ogilby

'Ash-tree ford'; the name occurs also in Devon and Derbyshire. Henry de *Bodlers* is the holder 1242 Fees. Eyton (V, pp.228-9) has an earlier reference to Roger de *Bouler* in 1203.

The river-crossing may have been on the site of the bridge which takes the road from Caynham to Richard's Castle across the Teme, but the position of the church immediately beside the river perhaps indicates a site downstream from the bridge. Ashford is one of a series of -ford names running from Ludford to Rochford in Worcestershire, but it is the only one to have given name to settlements on both sides of the R. Teme. See Ashford Carbonel *infra.*

ASHFORD CARBONEL SO 525701 Ancient Parish

Esseford 1086 DB, 1221-2 *Ass*, 1242 Fees
Hesford 1174-85 Eyton
Aysford Carbonel 1255 RH, 1271-2 *Ass*, 1308 Ipm, *Ayseford Carbonel* 1309 Cl
Asford Carbunel 1255-6 *Ass, Asford Carbonell* 1284-5 FA, *Asford Carbonel* 1287 Ipm
Assheford Carbonel 1287 Cl, 1348 Ipm, *Ascheford Carbonel* 1346, 1428 FA
Eshford Carbonel 1291-2 *Ass*

Hasseford' 1291-2 *Ass*
Ashford Carbonel 1303 InqMisc *et seq, Ashford Cardinal* 1733 PR(H) 16
Ahsford Carbonel 1356 AD, *Ahsford Carbonell* 1361 AD, *Achford* 1366 Ipm
Nether Assheford 1389 AD

See Ashford Bowdler *supra.* John *Carbonel* is mentioned in connection with this estate in 1221-2 *Ass.* Eyton (V, 81-2) has earlier references to the family, including a 17th-cent. transcript of a charter of 1174-85 granting Ashford and Overton to William *Carbunel.*

This manor was *Nether Ashford* by contrast to the manor called Ashford Jones (*Ahsford Jones* 1337 AD, *Ascheford Jones* 1346 FA, *Assheford Jones* 1349 Pat, 1431 FA), which Eyton (V, 79) equates firmly with *Upper Ashford (Ouerashford'* 1291-2 *Ass, Over Assheford* 1389 AD). The 19th-cent. 1" map marks Ashford Jones where the modern 1" has Ashford Ho, N.E. of Ashford Carbonel. Jones is probably from *John* de Esseford who is mentioned as the tenant of this manor from 1240-56.

It is possible that the ocasional spellings *Ahsford, Achford* represent a metathesised form such as is found in Axford in Ramsbury W and Axford in Nutley Ha.

ASTLEY SJ 530188 Civil Parish

Hesleie 1086 DB
Estleg' 1208-9 *ForProc*, 1248 Cl, 1255 RH, *Estleg' iuxta Haghemon* ?14th *SBL 5834*
Astleyg' 1261-2 *ForProc et freq* with variant spellings *Astleg(h)', Astleye, Astle; Astleye sub Haweman* 1271-2 *ForProc, Astleye by Berewyk* 1303 Ipm, *Hastley* 1394 *SBL 5434*
Asteleg(t)h 1271-2 *Ass* (p), *Asteley* 1291-2 *Ass*, l.13th *SBL 5840,* 1499 Ipm, 1552 Pat, *Asteleye by Haghemon* 1318 Pat, *Asteleye iuxta Hadenhale* 1358 *SBL 5850*
Asley 1701 PR(L) 1

'East clearing', probably named from its position in relation to Albrighton. The manor was rated as 3 hides in DB, and the settlement is probably an ancient one, the choice of **lēah** as the generic being a reference to the woodland setting. Place-names suggest that there was a narrow belt of ancient woodland running from near Lee Brockhurst to the R. Severn.

Various affixes - 'under Haughmond', 'near Hadnall', 'near Berwick' - were used in the 13th and 14th centuries, but the name must have been felt to be sufficiently distant from other Astleys not to require such distinction, since none of these stuck.

ASTLEY ABBOTS SO 709962 Ancient Parish

Estleia, Alia Esteleia c.1090 SAC, *Estleg'* c.1198 SAC *et freq* with variant spelling *Estlegh'* to 1275 Ipm

Astleg' c.1225 SAC *et freq* with variant spellings *Astlegh, Astley(e), Astlee; Astleg' subter Shyrlet* 1261-2 *ForProc, Astleg' iuxta Bruges* c.1270 SAC, *Astleye iuxta Brugges* 1291-2 *Ass, Astleye Abbatis* l.13th *ForProc, Astleg' Abbatis* 1291-2 *Ass, Astleye Abbots* 1304 Pat, *Abbots Astley* 1329 AD, *Astley Abbots* 1407 Cl, *Astley Abbots alias Astley Bridge* 1544 *SBL 4564, Abbot's Astley* 1730 PR(H) 16, *Astly Haberts* 1764 PR(H) 3

Esteleya c.1270 SAC

Astelegh iuxta Bruge 1316 FA, *Asteleye* 1327,8 Pat, 1387 Fine, *Asteley Abbatis* 1395 Pat, *Asteley Abbots* 1403 Cl, 1404 Pat, *Abbotesasteley* 1427 Cl, *Asteley Brugge* Hy8 *RentSur*

Asly Abbots 1664 PR(H) 1, *Asley Abbotts* 1704 ib, *Asley Abuts* 1750 ib, *Assley* 1731 PR(H) 3

'East clearing', named in relation to Morville, which was the centre of a great estate including Astley at the time of the DB survey. The affix *Abbots* (which ousted the other affixes, 'under Shirlet' and 'near Bridgnorth') refers to the ownership of the manor by the Abbey of Shrewsbury. There is an unexplained reference in 1696 (copy) *SBL 8894B* to *Astley Regis alias Astley Abbots.*

The estate designated *alia Esteleia* in c.1090 (which seems to have no modern equivalent) is referrred to as *(subtus) Parvam*

Estleham and *Parva Estleg'* c.1225 SAC. Eyton (I, p.49) gives Astley Home as another name for this. A William Kynnesley of *Asteleyhome* is mentioned in 1429 and 1430 Fine, but this does not seem certain to be Little Astley in Astley Abbots.

The third Astley in Shropshire is a hamlet in Alveley parish. Asterley in Pontesbury has *ēasterra* 'more eastern' as first element.

ASTON

Aston means 'east settlement or estate', and it can be classed with names in which a *tūn* is characterised as 'north', 'south', 'west' or 'middle'. In the country as a whole, *ēast tūn* (which can become Aston, Easton or Eston) is probably the commonest of these names. It is certainly the commonest in Shropshsire where, in addition to the six places which have sufficient past or present administrative status to be included in this study, there are four Astons of lesser importance. These are Aston E. of Claverley, Aston N.E. of Shifnal, Aston Pigot and Rogers N.E. of Worthen, and Aston on Clun N.E. of Clunbury. The 'major' names are set out below.

ASTON (near Oswestry) SJ 325271 DB Manor

Estone 1086 DB, *Estune* c.1217 HAC
Astona 1201 HAC, *Aston* 1272 Ipm *et freq, Aston' iux' Westfelton'* 1292-5 *Ass, Aston Abbots* 1404 Cl, - *Abbottes* 1553 Pat
Elston 1272 Cl
Easton 1630 PR(StA) 4
Estyn c.1640, c.1700 *MorganTs, Eastyn* 17th *ib*

In this instance 'east' refers to the position of the settlement in the great estate which became centred on the castle of Oswestry. It may originally have been named in relation to Maesbury. In 1553 Pat *Aston Abbottes* is said to be 'late of Haughmond Abbey'.

ASTON in Wellington parish SJ 613097

Eastun 975 (12th) S 802
Estona c.1144 SAC *et freq* with variant spelling *Eston'* to 1249 SAC, *Hestuna sub Wrekena* c.1187 SAC
Aston' 1231-40 SAC *et freq* with variant spellings *Aston(e); Aston' iuxta Wrokene* 1261-2 *ForProc* (p), *Aston' sub Wrekene* 1271-2 *ib*, *Astoun under the Wrekene* 1397 Cl, *Aston subtus Wreken* 1535 VE

The village is a mile E. of Uppington. The area to which it is central forms a well-defined corner of Wellington parish, but is not a parish in its own right or a Domesday manor. It has been included in this study of ancient and modern administrative centres because it was a pre-Conquest estate of 3 hides, the subject of a royal charter dated A.D. 975. In the boundary survey of this the S.E. boundary is given as 'along the Wrekin'.

ASTON in Wem parish SJ 531287 DB Manor

Estune 1086 DB
Aston' 1271-2 *Ass et freq* with variant spelling *Aston; Aston' iuxta Wemme* 1292-5 *Ass*

The settlement is E. of Wem. The name was apparently not felt to require an affix (the use of *iuxta Wemme* in an Assize Roll is probably a clerical convention).

ASTON BOTTERELL SO 632841 Ancient Parish

Estone 1086 DB, *Eston'* 1186-90 SAC *et freq* to 1272 Cl, *Eston' Boterell* 1255 RH, *Eston Boterel* 1263 Ch, *Eston Boterell* 1272 Ipm
Aston' 1242 Fees, *Astone Boterell* 1255 RH, *Haston* 1284-5 FA, *Boterel Aston* 1336 Pat (p), *Aston Boterel* 1346 FA, *Botrell Aston* 1438,9 Fine, *Boterell Aston* 1455 Fine, *Bottrells Aston* 1591 PR(L) 14, c.1612 *SBL 15691*, 1740-1 *PRLudford, Aston Bottrell*

1761 PR(H) 1, *Aston Bottrel* 1779 PR(H) 3
Asseton Boterel 1316 FA

Aston Botterell is not east of any place on which it seems likely to have been dependent, and no improvement can be offered on Eyton's comment (I, p.222) that it 'took its name probably from lying to the *East* of the Great Clee Hill'. Eyton gives references to William *Boterell* from the beginning of the 13th cent.

•

ASTON EYRE SO 653941 Civil Parish

Estone 1086 DB, *Eston'* 1242 Fees
Whetene Aston 1255 RH, *Wetenaston'* 1261-2 *ForProc, Wetene Aston'* 1271-2 *ib, Wetoneston* 1271-2 *Ass, Wethenaston'* 1272 Cl, *Wetenestone* 1272 Ipm, *Whetenaston'* 1291-2, 1292-5 *Ass*, 1373-4 *ForProc, Wheteneaston* 1313 Ipm, *Wheaten Aston* 1695 Morden
Aston 1284 Pat
Aston Aer 1284-5 FA *et seq, Aston Eyres* 1293 Ipm, *Aston Ayer* e.14th *SBL 5923*, 1346 FA, 1357 Cl, *Aston Eir* 1402,3 Cl, *Aston Ayre alias Wheateon Aston* e.17th SAS 4/III

The significance of the name is unresolved in this instance. Cf. Eyton I, 199, 'Aston or Easton, wherever it occurs, implies a *town* situated to the *East* of something else. If this Aston and the hamlet of Weston, about four miles distance, were each so called with reference to some common centre, we can fix such a centre nowhere but at Monk Hopton. Howbeit no early mention of the latter will warrant a presumption of such by-gone importance as might have reflected a name on its neighbouring localities'.

The affix Wheaten ('characterised by wheat-growing') has been attached to another Aston in St, and in that instance the modern form is Wheaton Aston. The affix which stuck in the Sa name is from the family surnamed *Fitz Aer*, who are frequently mentioned as owners. Eyton suggested that they were the descendants of the DB tenant *Alcher*, and that *Aer* was a derivative of his name. This is repeated in DEPN; but without clear evidence for the connection it should not be assumed that OE *Ealhhere* (which lies behind the DB form *Alcher*) would develop into ME *Aer*.

ASTON MUNSLOW SO 513866 DB Manor

Estune 1086 DB, *Estona* 1167 P, *Eston'* 1189 P, 1242 Fees
Aston 1255 RH *et freq* with variant spelling *Aston'; Aston in Corvedale* 1303, 1410 Pat, *Aston by Munselowe* 1343 InqMisc, *Aston in Monslowe in Corfedale* 1402 Cl, *Aston in Corfedale* 1463 Cl, *Monslows Aston* 1565 PR(H) 15, *Aston Coruistram* 1695 Morden

The DB manor is rated at 8½ hides, which is high for this county, and it should probably be considered to include Munslow, which is not named in DB. The name Aston may perhaps be seen as referring, not to the actual village, but to the whole land-unit which survives as the parish of Munslow; and 'east' may refer to the position of this unit in relation to that of Eaton under Haywood. It is possible that several of the parishes in the area were once dependent settlements in a larger unit.

The affix 'in Corvedale' probably gave rise to the corrupt form in Morden. For Munslow, see the parish-name *infra*.

CHETWYND ASTON SJ 755175 Civil Parish

Estona 1155 SAC, *Eston'* 1251 Cl
Great Aston (*sic* printed) 1199 (1265) Ch, *Aston' iuxta Novum Burgum* c.1240 SAC, *Aston Magna* 1255 RH, 1281 *SBL 4127*, 1596 *SBL 3463*, 1606 *SBL 4680*, *- Major* 1274 RH, *Magna -* 1320 *SBL 4664*, *Aston by Newport* 1332 Ch, *Muchelaston* 1391 Pat, Cl, *Mikelaston* 1401 Cl, *Mickle, Much, or Great Aston* 1490 Ipm, *Aston'* 1501 *SBL 16170*, *Greate Aston* 1597 *SBL 4675*, *Greate Aston alias Chetwynde Aston* 1619 *SBL 4744*, *Aston Magna alias Chetwinde Aston* 1630 *SBL 5693*, *Chetwinds Aston* 1689 *SBL 5207*

Church and Chetwynd Aston are named in relation to Edgmond, which was the ecclesiastical parish. The two Astons were probably a single unit at one time, though they were separate by 963, as explained under Church Aston. The affix which stuck is the surname of a family called 'of Chetwynd'; John *de Chetewind'* is mentioned in connection with *Eston'* in 1251 Cl. Eyton calls the place 'Great Aston, now Chetwynd-Aston, or Field-Aston.'

CHURCH ASTON SJ 743179 Civil Parish

Eastun 963 (12th) S 723
Aston 1252 Ch, 1317 Ipm, *Parua Aston'* 1294-9 *Ass*, 1310 *SBL 16200*, 1422 *SBL 16181, Parua Astone* c.1271 *SBL 16196, Chirche Aston* c.1300 *SBL 16197, Churche Aston'* 1323 *SBL 16199, Aston Parva* 1596 *SBL 3463*, 1629 *SBL 4127, Church Aston SBL 4127, Church Aston als Aston Parva* 1707 *SBL 5326*

See Chetwynd Aston, to which this place is adjacent. The late Mr D.B. Corbyn has shown, in an unpublished study of the boundary survey, that the charter of A.D. 963 refers to Church Aston. Previous commentators have taken this survey to include Chetwynd Aston, but there is no doubt that the boundary runs between the two land-units. Eyton (who has little information about this place) considers the affix 'church' to be a reference to the chapel, though this was not an independent church as both Astons were in the parish of Edgmond.

ATCHAM SJ 541092 Ancient Parish

Atingeham 1086 DB, 1241 Cl (p), *Ætingeham* 1194 P (p), *Hattingeham* 1291-2 *Ass, Atyngeham* 1315 Pat
Etingeham 1149-59 SAC, 1195,7,8,9 P (p), *Ettingeham* 1195, 6,7 P (p)
Etringham 1193 P (p)
Etingehale 1194,6 P (p)
Etingham 1194,8,9, 1200 P (p), *Ettingham* 1197,8 1201 P

(p), 1217 (1285) Ch, 1395 *SBL 16293*, 1443 (copy) *SBL 15752*

Etchingeham 1195 P (p), *Ethingeham* 1196 P (p), 1203-4 *Ass* (p), *Ethtingham* 1200 P (p), *Eching'* 1221 SAC

Attingham 1203-4 *Ass* (p), c.1291 TN, 1292 Cl, 1785 *et freq* PR(L) 14, *Atingham* 1255-6 *Ass*, 1284 Cl, 1293 Pat, 1324 Ipm, *Attyngham* 1328 Cl (p), 1346 Pat, 1535 VE, *Atyngham* 1338 Pat, 1395 *SBL 4482* (p)

Ekin(g)ham 1234 Cl (p)

Attinham 1255 RH, *Etinham* 1255-6 *Ass*, *Atineham* 1316 FA

Attinsham 1271-2 *Ass, Athinch'ham* 1305-6 *Ass* (p), *Atyncham* 1334 SR, 1350 SAS 1/XI

Aticham 1418-19 SAS 52

Acham 1535 VE, c.1540 Leland, 1663 *et seq* PR(L) 8,14, *Attyngham alias Acham, the grange of Attyngham* 1548 Pat, *Atcham* 1669 *SBL 15748*, 1712 *et seq* PR(L) 14, *Achum* 1675 Ogilby

'Land in a river-bend belonging to the followers of Ēata' is a likely etymology, but everything about this name is open to controversy. The simplest point at issue is the nature of the final element. The spellings only suggest **hām** 'village', but in midland names with only post-Conquest spellings it is legitimate to suspect that the word involved is **hamm** if the situation of the place is particularly suited to that term. One of the best-evidenced uses of **hamm** is for land in the bend of a river, a sense which is found in Shropshire, and persists in field-names (see FN, pp.19,20).

For the middle element the choice lies between **-inga-**, genitive of **-ingas** 'people of', and the connective particle **-ing-**, used as a variant of the genitive inflection to connect a person's name with a word for the type of property of which the person was owner or tenant. Frequent *-inge-* spellings, such as are manifested for this name, are conventionally held to prove derivation from **-inga-**; but it has recently been suggested (*Nomina* 1982, p.35) that *inge-* spellings may result when *-ing* is followed by a final element beginning with *h-, w-* or a vowel.

The third matter for controversy is whether the first element of Atcham is the name of an early Anglo-Saxon landowner or whether it is the name of the saint to whom the church is dedicated. The dedication to St Eata (successively Abbot of Melrose and Bishop of Lindisfarne and Hexham in the second half of the 7th century) is known to be an ancient one because it is mentioned by the historian Orderic Vitalis, writing c.1127. Orderic was born and christened at Atcham, and he says that the 'second birth' of his baptism took place *apud Etingesham in æcclesia sancti confessoris Eattæ quæ sita est super Sabrinam fluuium.* There is nothing in this to suggest that Orderic connected the place-name with the dedication, but the possibility was noted by later historians. Eyton (VIII, p.245) says 'It is perhaps possible that an Abbot and Bishop of the seventh century, being bound by no law of celibacy, may have left descendants, and that those descendants, removing into Mercia, may have colonized Atcham and dedicated its Church to their canonized progenitor.' In terms of modern historical thinking a more likely explanation would be that the dedication arose from the place-name. This is believed to have happened elsewhere, examples being the dedication of Boston church to St Botolph and that of Warburton (Cheshire) to St Werburgh.

Finally, the formal development of the name requires discussion. Eyton calls it 'Atcham, formerly Attingham', and the short form, first evidenced in the mid-16th century, would probably have ousted the longer one completely if the latter had not been revived (perhaps as a conscious archaism) for the great house, which is an 18th-century foundation.

Atcham is one of a small group of names once ending in *-ingham* which exhibit not only assibilation (development of *-ingham* to *-incham*) but also metathesis of that assibilation, so that it is transferred to the first syllable of the name. This is best evidenced in names which had *-ting(e)h-* in their early form. Another example is Watchingwell in the Isle of Wight, earlier *Watingewelle.* The development may be found in Whicham Cumberland, earlier *Whittingham,* but in that name the modern form could be considered to be a shortening of an assibilated form such as *Whittincham.* This explanation would have sufficed for Atcham were it not for the few early spellings like *Etchingeham* 1195, *Eching'* 1221, which show that the *-t(t)-* of the first syllable had been affected long before the name was shortened to a disyllable.

The phenomenon may be more common than has been recognised; only abundant documentation could make it apparent, and this is not available for all the possible examples. Some degree of assibilation may be reflected in Orderic's spelling *Ettingesham.*

The frequent spellings with (p) are mostly from the surnames of two men called Elias de Attingham. The first of these was, from 1184 to 1199, a royal official in charge of a house at Feckenham Wo, and his salary is regularly entered in the Pipe Rolls. A second *Helyas de Ettingham* flourished c.1226-1250.

BADGER SO 768996 Ancient Parish

Beghesoure 1086 DB, *Beggesoure* 1255 RH (p)
Baggesour' 1203-4 *Ass* (p), *Baggesoure* 1255 RH (p) *et freq* to 1502 Ipm, *Baggeshouere* 1287 Ipm, *Baggesouere* 1291-2 *Ass,* 1308 Ipm, *Baggesovere* 1404 Cl
Begesaur' 1203-4 *Ass* (p), *Begesour'* 1255-6 *Ass*
Baiesovre 1210-12 RBE (p)
Bagesoure 1212 P (p), *Bagesour'* 1228 Cur (p), *Bagesovere* 1255 RH (p), 1443 (copy) *SBL 15752, Bagesover* 1258 Ipm (p), 1285 Pat
Beggesor' 1229 Cl
Baggesore 1258 Ipm (p) *et freq* with variant spellings *Baggesor* to 1505 Ipm, *Baggeshore* 1327 Pat (p)
Bagesore 1258 Ipm (p), 1331 (1348) Pat, 1338-9 *ForProc* (p), *Bagisore* 1353 Pat (p)
Baddeshovere c.1291 TN
Badger 1549 Pat, *Badgor* 1577 Saxton, *Bagsore als Badger* 1694 PR(H) 16

'Bæcg's ridge-tip'. The first element is probably a strong form of the personal name *Bæcga,* evidenced in a number of place-names. The second element is **ofer**, the precise meaning of which is discussed under Condover *infra.* The present settlement at Badger is beside, not on, the ridge. The site is confined, and the nature of the topography is difficult to evaluate from the access roads.

BARLOW SO 383840 DB Manor

Berlie 1086 DB, *Berleg* 1254 Pat, *Berleye* 1291-2 *Ass, Berley* 1302 Ipm, 1455 Cl, 1675 Ogilby, *Borley* 1577 Saxton
Barlow 1753 PR(H) 17

'Barley clearing', OE **bere-lēah.* The late development to -low may be due to the proximity of Brunslow.

BARROW SJ 658001 Ancient Parish

Barwa c.1200 *ForProc* (p), *Barewe* 1221-2 *Ass* (p), 1255 RH, 1262 (1329) Ch, l.13th *ForProc, Barwe* 1261-2 *ib, Bareuue* 1283 (1348) Pat, *Barew* 1331 (1348) Pat, *Barowe* 1413 Pat, *Barrowe* 1535 VE, *Barrow* 1577 Saxton

'Grove', OE **bearu**. The manner in which **bearu** is used in place-names suggests that it refers to a wood of limited extent. There are other instances besides the Sa name in which the place is on the outskirts of a heavily wooded area.

BASCHURCH SJ 220425 Ancient Parish

Bascherche 1086 DB, *Baschirche* Hy1 (1267) Ch, 1221-2 *Ass* (p), 1255 RH, 1346 Pat, *Baschirge* c.1220 (1292) Ch (p), *Baschyrche* 1271-2 *Ass, Baschurche* 1316 FA *et freq, Baschurch* 1393 Pat *et freq, Bas Church* 1672,5,9 PR(L) 4
Basecherch(e) 1086 DB, *Basechirche* 1222 Cur (p), *Basechurch* 1602 PR(H) 1, 1675 *SBL 8546*
Bassecherche 1204 P (p), 1221-2 *Ass* (p), 1256 (1346) Ch, *Bassechirch* 1256 (1332) Ch, c.1291 TN, *Bassechirch'* 1261-2 *ForProc* (p), *Bassechurch* 1508 AD, 1628 PR(L) 19
Bastchyrch' 1327 SAS 3/V, *Bastchurch* 1654-5 PR(StA) 4, 1718 PR(L) 12
Bass Church 1671 PR(L) 4, 1719 PR(H) 6, 1762 *PR Little Wenlock*, 1769 PR(L) 14, *Basschurch* 1737 *et seq* PR(L) 4,

1744 PR(StA) 2, 1811 PR(StA) 3

'Bas(s)a's church'. The personal name is not on independent record but can be conjectured from an Old High German parallel, and from a number of place-names.

OE **cirice**, modern *church*, is rather rare in settlement-names as compared with Welsh, Cornish and Gaelic equivalents. Herefordshire has nine examples, but some of these are translations of Welsh Llan- names. Kent has five, but it is significant that four are in the south-east corner of the county, where much of the settlement is related to the drainage of Romney Marsh in the middle/late Anglo-Saxon period. Devon has four, and most other counties have two or three, though some, such as Berkshire and Sussex, have none. Shropshire has three: Chirbury, Baschurch and Whitchurch. Baschurch is one of ten English place-names in which **cirice** is certainly combined with the genitive of an Old English personal name; there are another five possible examples.

Since *cirice* is not frequent in settlement-names, most villages must have acquired their churches without this development leading to a name change. It may be that when settlement-names do refer to churches this indicates that their church was acquired at an early stage, so that it was felt to be remarkable by the people of surrounding settlements. Another possibility is that the provision of a church for an estate would stimulate a process of nucleation, and a nucleated village which grew up in the vicinity of a church might acquire such a name. When the meaning is 'x's church' it is reasonable to suppose that the person referred to is the founder.

The name Baschurch is taken back, perhaps to the mid-9th century, by the appearance of a Welsh translation, *Eglwysseu Bassa*, in the cycle of poems known as *Canu Heledd*. The use of the plural, *eglwysau*, may indicate that the poet took the name to refer to a Celtic *clas*, which would contain a number of small churches. The traditions incorporated in the poetry may have reference to the great earthwork, The Berth, which is in the parish of Baschurch; but it is likely that when the poem acquired its final form, perhaps in the 9th century, the English name Baschurch had superseded the earlier name of the fort and the surrounding area. Berth is from OE **burh** 'fort'.

BATTLEFIELD SJ 512173 Ancient Parish

Hayteleyfeld 1406, 9 Pat
Bateleyfield 1410 Ch
Batelfeld 1419 *SBL 5437*, 1535 VE, *Bataylfelde, Batailfeld* 1446 Cl, *Batelfelde* 1471 *SBL 5438*, 1535 VE, *Battelffilde* 1539 AD, *Battlefeild* c.1540 Leland, *Battelfild* 1546 AD, *Battelfelde* 1549 Pat, *Battell Filde* 1562 *SBL 13455*, *Battlefield* 1587 PR(L) 12

It seems probable that the battle of Shrewsbury (A.D. 1403) was fought in an area called *Hayteley*; but there is no early record in which the name appears independently of the battle and the collegiate church which was founded on the site, so the existence of an ancient name *Hayteley* cannot be proved. It would be a compound of OE *hǣðiht* 'heathy' and **lēah**, and can be paralleled in surviving names in Ch and St, which have the modern form Heatley. The addition *-feld* is probably to be understood as '(battle)field'. *Hayteleyfeld* was probably transformed into Battlefield by popular etymology.

A collegiate church was founded on the site of the battle by Roger Ive, a member of a burgess family of Shrewsbury, who was Rector of Albright Hussey, the ecclesiastical parish in which it lay. By 1548, the date at which the college was dissolved, this church had replaced Albright Hussey chapel as the parish church, and the parish was styled Battlefield.

BAVENEY SO 689795 DB Manor

Barbingi 1086 DB
Babbeleye 1255-6 *Ass*
Babbeneye 1291-2 *Ass* (p), 1305 Ipm, Cl, 1330 Ch
Babeney 1399 Cl
Babney 1652 PR(H) 17
Baveny 1709 PR(H) 17, *Baveney* 1714 ib, *Baveney Wood* 1777 ib, *Bavniey-Wood* 1806 ib
Bavin Wood 1822 PR(H) 17

'Babba's island', *v.* **ēg.** The two earliest forms are garbled. Baverstock W and Bavington Nb, which also contain the personal name *Babba*, show the same development to *-v-* in the modern form.

The place was assessed at half a hide in DB, but in spite of this low valuation it is stated to comprise two earlier manors, and these may fairly be equated with Upper and Lower Baveney. Lower Baveney is still on OS maps. Upper Baveney is shown on the 19th-cent. 1" map and on the 1902 6" as the name of the farm which the 1967 1" calls Overwood Common, (Overwood Common appears on the 6" as an area immediately W. of Upper Baveney). Baveney Wood and Brook take their names from these two ancient settlements.

Neither of the farms has a site which is a typical **ēg**, but Upper Baveney, on a promontory made by the 500' contour with small streams on two sides and Baveney Brook on a third, has a type of position for which **ēg** is occasionally used elsewhere.

BAYSTON SJ 492082 DB Manor

Begestan 1086 DB, *Beyeston'* 1255-6 *Ass*
Bethstan 1208-9 *ForProc* (p)
Beestan' 1208-9 *ForProc* (p), *Beestane* 1251 InqMisc, *Beeston* 1670 PR(H) 18
Beyston 1255 RH, 1261-2 *ForProc*, 1434 Fine, 1486 Ipm, 1580 *SBL 6586*, 1585, 1664 PR(L) 6, *Beystan* 1271-2 *ForProc et freq* to 1386 *SBL 6271* (p), *Baystan* 1284-5 FA, *Beistan* 1306-7 *Ass, Beiston'* 1344-5 *ForProc* (p), *Baystone* 1613 PR(L) 6
Berstan 1271-2 *ForProc*
Bestan 1291-2 *Ass, Beston* 1577 Saxton, 1586, 1595 *SBL 7065, 9501*, 1600 PR(L) 6
Byston 1585 PR(L) 6, 1586 *SBL 6883*, 1598 *SBL 7022, Biston* 1616 PR(L) 6, *Bieston* 1621 ib, *Bystone* 1674 ib, 1695 Morden, 1727 PR(H) 18

BAYSTON HILL is *Beystaneshull* 1301 SAC, *Beystonhull'* 1364-6 *ForProc, Beiston Hill* 1667 PR(H) 18, *Byston Hill* 1677 PR(L) 6,

Baiston Hill 1781 ib, *Baston Hill, Beaston Hill* 1802 PR(H) 18

Probably 'Bēage's stone', from OE **stān** and the feminine personal name which ocurs also in Bibury Gl. DEPN says 'Bǣga's stone', *Bǣga* being a weak masculine name which occurs in a number of place-names, the best-documented example probably being Bayworth Berks. The full range of spellings now available for Bayston shows more resemblance to that for Bibury than to the forms for Bayworth. There are many more *-e-* than *-a-* spellings, and the alternative development to *Byston, Bieston, Beaston* suggests a closer affinity with Bibury. But the eventual survival of the Bayston form might be considered to favour *Bǣga.* DEPN sugests that the same personal name is to be found in Betton Abbots, which adjoins, but a full collection of spellings demonstrates that Betton is a wholly different name.

stān is sometimes used of rock outcrops, and there is such a feature at The Burgs, a short distance to the north. The approach lane to Lower Bayston appears to have been cut through rock in places.

VCH VIII, p.35, says "The former hamlet of Bayston, now known as Lower Bayston to distinguish it from the squatter settlement of Bayston Hill, stood on the site of Bayston Farm'. The G.R. reference given above is for Lower Bayston.

BEARSTONE SJ 724397 DB Manor

Bardestune 1086 DB, *Bardeston* 1284-5 FA
Beggardeston' 1255-6 *Ass (ter), Begardeston'* 1271-2 *Ass*
Bearston' 1271-2 *Ass, Bearstone* 1281 Ipm, 1607 PR(L) 18, *Bearston* 1303 Pat, 1577 Saxton, 1694 *et freq* PR(L) 18, *Beerston* 1655 SAS 1/XLVII, *Berston* 1662 ib
Byardeston' 1291-2 *Ass*
Byarston' 1291-2 *Ass*
Beardstone Halle e.17th SAS 4/III

Possibly 'Bæghard's estate', *v.* **tūn**. The personal name is not on record, but both elements are evidenced, and it is a reasonable conjecture.

The spellings present some difficulty. It spite of the form in 1255-6 *Ass*, there cannot have been *-cg-* or *-gg-* in the original name, as a consonant from this would have survived. *Byardeston'* 1291-2 *Ass* is the development most easily paralleled from a hypothetical **Bæghardestūn*, and it is easy to accept the contemporary shortened form *Byarston'*. Similar developments are found elsewhere in place-names containing the personal name *Wighard*. *Bearston(e)* is probably an alternative ME spelling for the pronunciation represented by *Byarston'*; this possibly prevailed because of association with the word *bear*. There must have been an alternative shortened form *Bardestūn* at the end of the OE period, to account for the DB spelling, and it is interesting that a form with *-d- (Beardston)* survived till the early 17th century.

BECKBURY SJ 765015 Ancient Parish

Becheberie 1086 DB, *Beccheberia* 1155 SAC, *Beckebir'* 1229 Cl *et freq* with variant spellings *Beckebur', -bury, -buri, Bekkebury* to 1376 Pat
Bekebir' 1203-4 *Ass* (p), *Bekebur'* 1242, 51 Fees (p), *Bekebir'* 1251 ib (p), *Bekebury* 1255 RH, 1325 Pat (p)
Be(c)kesbir' 1230 P
Bukkebur', Bakkebur' 1242 Fees (p)
Beckbur' 1255 RH, *Beckburi* 1284-5 FA, *Bekbury* 1379 Pat, 1502 Ipm, *Becbury* 1505 Ipm, *Beckbury* 1535 VE, 1577 Saxton

'Becca's manor house', second element **byrig**, dat. of **burh**.

BEDSTONE SO 368757 Ancient Parish

Betietetune 1086 DB
Bedeston' 1176 P (p), 1255 RH, 1271-2 *Ass (ter)*, 1291-2 *Ass*, *Bedestone* 1272 Ipm, *Bedeston* 1283 Ipm, *Bediston* 1297 ChanR
Bedestan(e) 1271-2 *Ass*
Budeston' 1271-2 *Ass*

Bodeston' 1272 Cl
Bedston 1577 Saxton *et freq, Bedstone* 1705 PR(H) 13
Bedson 1579 PR(H) 18
Beaston 1695 Morden

Probably 'Bedgēat's estate', *v.* **tūn**. This is Ekwall's solution in DEPN, and nothing better can be offered. The personal name is not on record, but both elements are evidenced. This etymology assumes that the genitival *-s-* has been omitted in the DB spelling, and that the two *-stan(e)* spellings from 1271-2 *Ass* can be disregarded. The dropping of the middle element, so that **Bedgēatestūn* became ME *Bedestone*, is a normal procedure.

If the DB spelling be accepted as in any degree reliable the final element must be **tūn** not **stān**; but it is curious that this is the only name in a wide area in which *-tūn* has become modern *-tone* rather than *-ton.*

BELSWARDYNE HALL SJ 603033 DB Manor

Belleurdine 1086 DB, *Bellewrðe* 1205 P (p)
Bedleswurth' c.1200 *ForProc et freq* with variant spellings *-worthe, -wurthin, -worthin, -worthyn, -wordin, -wardyn* to 1301 SAC, *Beddeleswordyn* l.13th *ForProc, Bedeleswortyhn'* 1291-2 *Ass, Bedeleswarthyn* 1317, 21 Pat, *Bedeleswardyn* 1317 Cl, *Bedelesworthyn* 1347 Pat
Belleswrðe (p), *Belleswrth'* 1204 P, *Beleswurth'* 1236 Cl, *Beleswrthin* 1242 Fees, *Belleswardyn* 1421 Cl
Beclesworþin 1255 RH
Beldeswrth' 1255-6 *Ass*
Bedlewrthin, Bedlewarthin, Bedleswardin, Bedeswarthyn, Bledeleworth' 1271-2 *Ass*
Bedresworth' 1291-2 *Ass*
Belserdyne 1577 Saxton, *Beleardyne* 1690 PR(L) 2, *Belzardine* 1718 ib, *Belserdine* 1695 Morden
Belsadine 1662 PR(L) 20, *- Hall* 1675 Ogilby, *Belzadine* 1692, 4 PR(L) 14
Belswardine 1690 PR(L) 20, 1700 *et freq* PR(L) 14

Beswardine 1690 PR(L) 14

'Bēdel's enclosed settlement', *v.* **worðign**. The personal name would be a derivative of *Bēda*. OE *bydel*, influenced or replaced by OFr *bedel*, 'beadle', is theoretically possible, but unlikely; Belswardine was only assessed at half a hide in DB, but it is too considerable a property to be owned by the sort of official who might be designated 'beadle'. The spelling *Belzadine* represents the local pronunciation.

BENTHALL SJ 658026 Ancient Parish

Benetala 1120 (copy) Eyton IV, p.134 (p), *Benethala* 1167 P, *Benethal(e)* 1221-2 *Ass* (p) *et freq* with variant spelling *Benethal'* to 1421 Cl
Benithal' 1204,5 Cur (p)
Benedhal 1255 RH (p), *Bendhale* 1271-2 *Ass* (p)
Bynthehal' 1271-2 *Ass* (p), *Bentehale* 1291-2 *Ass* (p)
Benthale 1271-2, l.13th *ForProc*, 1348 Pat, 1363 Cl, 1364 Ipm, 1416 AD, 1421 Cl, *Benthall* 1698 PR(L) 14 *et seq, Benthull* 1740 PR(L) 18, *Benthal* 1755 ib
Bental 1577 Saxton, 1734 PR(L) 18, *Bentoll* 1664 PR(H) 1, *Bentall* 1670 PR(L) 14

'Bent-grass nook', *v.* **beonet, halh**. The spelling on Saxton's map is the earliest to represent the modern pronunciation. The trisyllabic form is the commonest till 1421.

The G.R. given above relates to the church and hamlet called Benthall on the 19th-cent. 1" map, which lies to the west of the settlement now bearing the name. Here, as at Posenhall a short distance south, very careful local study would be required before suggestions could be made about the nature of the **halh**.

BENTHALL (in Alberbury parish) SJ 394139 DB Manor

Benehale 1086 DB

Benthale 1291-2 *Ass*, 1308 Ipm, *Benthall* 1601 *SBL 12706*, 1673 PR(H) 6, *Bentall* 1610 PR(H) 6, *Bentoll* 1679 ib

Another 'bent-grass nook'. This is an area of shallow gullies and indeterminately-shaped hollows.

BERRINGTON SJ 529070 Ancient Parish

Beritune 1086 DB, *Beritona* 1121 SAC, *Beriton* 1382 Pat, 1577 Saxton, *Beryton* 1535 VE
Biritona c.1090 SAC *et freq* with variant spellings *Byriton', Biryton', Biriton', Byryton'* to 1449 Fine
Beringtun' 1226 Cur, *Beryngton* 1535 VE, *Berrington* 1596 PR(L) 6 *et seq, Berington* 1728 PR(L) 19, 1730 *SBL 4246*, 1790 PR(L) 1, 1812 PR(L) 6
Birinton' 1255-6 *Ass, Byrynton* c.1291 TN, *Byrrynton* 1535 VE
Bireton 1271-2 *Ass*
Buritone 1274 RH (p), *Buritona* c.1280 HAC
Berynton 1361 Pat, *Berinton* 1675 Ogilby
Birrington 1565 PR(H) 12, 1588 PR(L) 1, *Byrrington* 1594 PR(L) 6
Burrington 1642 PR(L) 15
Barrington 1771 *SBL 5747*

'Settlement associated with a fort', from **byrig**, dat. of **burh**, and **tūn**.

In the country as a whole, the compound of **burh** in the nom. with **tūn** is found in over forty examples of Burton, eleven of Bourton, and nine of Broughton. It is also found (with an unusual modern spelling) in Boreton in Condover, on the opposite side of Cound Brook from Berrington. The compound *byrhtūn*, with the gen. of **burh**, is found in five examples of Burton, two of Buerton, and in Bierton, Bk. The third form, *byrigtūn*, gives rise to four instances of Berrington and two of Burrington; this form is the most westerly, occurring in Gl, He, Wo, Sa and So.

It has hitherto been assumed that these names could arise from three separate situations, which were:

(a) the proximity of a *tūn* to an ancient fort,

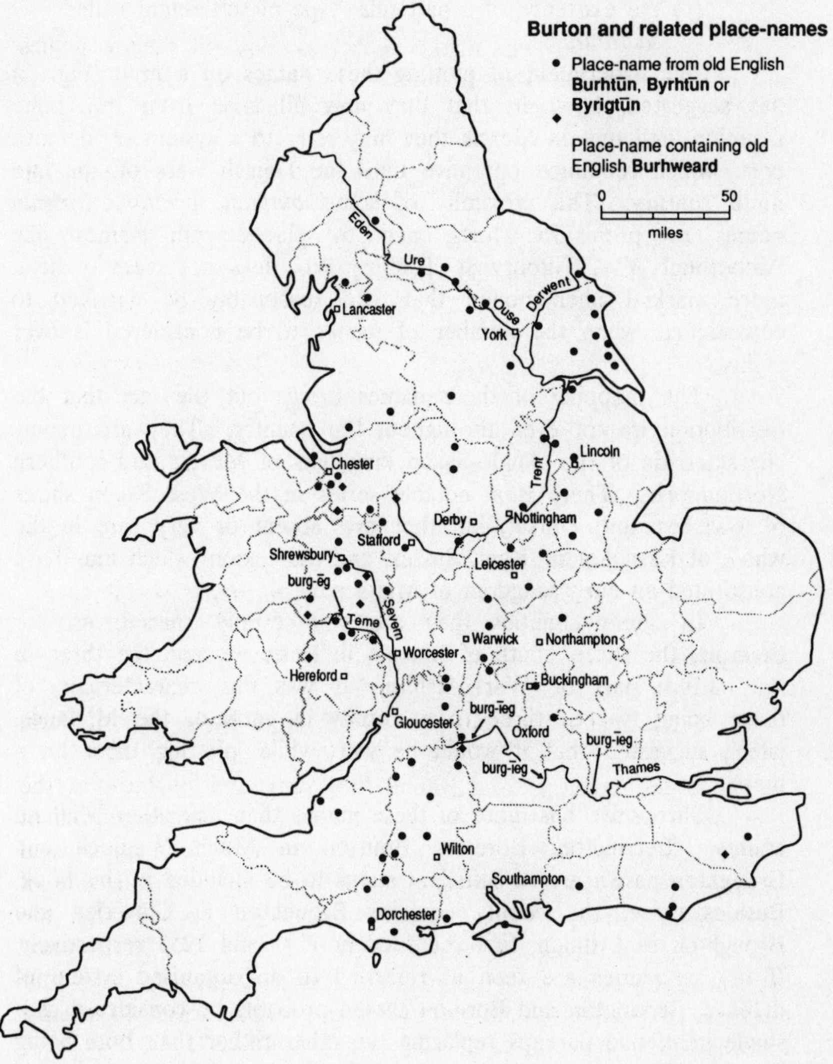
Burton and related place-names
Place-name from old English Burhtūn, Byrhtūn or Byrigtūn
Place-name containing old English Burhweard
0
50
miles
Eden
Ure
Ouse
Derwent
Lancaster
York
Lincoln
Trent
Chester
Derby
Nottingham
Stafford
Shrewsbury
burg-ēg
Leicester
Severn
Teme
Warwick
Northampton
Worcester
Hereford
Buckingham
burg-īeg
Gloucester
Oxford
burg-īeg
burg-īeg
Thames
Wilton
Southampton
Dorchester

(b) the proximity of a *tūn* to a more important settlement with a name ending in *-burh* or *-byrig*,

(c) the existence of a particular type of settlement called *burhtūn*.

The experiment of plotting these names on a map (Fig. 2) has suggested, however, that they may all arise from the same situation, and that in Mercia they may refer to a system of defence posts which remained operative until the Danish wars of the late ninth century. The proximity of some *burhtūn, byrhtūn, byrigtūn* names to prehistoric forts, and to places with names like Aldborough YW, Tutbury St, Tenbury Wo, does not seem to be a more marked phenomenon than can reasonably be ascribed to coincidence when the number of names to be considered is over eighty.

The mapping of these names brings out the fact that the distribution is not even throughout the country. They are mainly characteristic of the Anglo-Saxon kingdoms of Mercia and southern Northumbria. There is a notable series in the West Saxon shires of Wiltshire and Dorset, but they are absent or very rare in the whole of East Anglia, Kent, Sussex, and the region which may have constituted an early kingdom of Middlesex.

In some counties they are very evenly spaced, as, for example, the three south of Lincoln in Kesteven, and the three in the eastern part of Warwickshire. It was this characteristic, of there being two or three to a county in parts of the Midlands, which suggested that it would be worthwhile plotting them on a map.

Shropshire has more of these names than any other Midland county. Berrington, Boreton, Bourton in Much Wenlock and Broughton parish are of sufficient status to be included in this book. Besides these, the county contains Broughton in Claverley and Broughton in Lydham, first recorded in 1191 and 1255 respectively. If the six names are seen as referring to an organised system of defence, Berrington and Boreton should probably be considered as a single item, one perhaps replacing the other rather than both being in operation at the same time. The distribution of the *byrigtūn* type suggests that it is the latest of the three forms of the compound; a *burhtūn* at Boreton could have been replaced by a *byrigtūn* at

Berrington. The majority of places with these names in Mercia developed into DB manors and/or parishes (though only Burton on Trent became a town), and the relatively high administrative status of four of the six Shropshire places accords with the general pattern.

In addition to the six *burhtūn, byrigtūn* names, Shropshire has Trebirt (Upper and Lower) in Llanfair Waterdine parish, about a mile W. of Offa's Dyke. Early spellings are *Treburt* 1284 Cl, 1381 *SRO 552/1/20, Trefburt'* 1345 *SRO 552/1/11*, and this is an obvious Welsh rendering of Burton.

Names containing OE *burhward* 'fort guardian' show a distributional relationship to the *burhtūn, byrhtūn, byrigtūn* names, and a marked clustering in the Welsh Marches. Shropshire has Broseley and Burwarton *(infra)*, and the interesting name Treverward in Clun (*Treboreward* 1284 Cl), which is a Welsh rendering of Burwarton. Also relevant is the compound *burh-ēg* 'fort-island', which has become Burway near Ludlow. This should be considered in conjunction with three names along the R. Thames (Laleham Burway, Sr, Borough Marsh near Sonning, Berks, Burroway near Bampton, O), which are shown on Fig. 2.

Whatever may be thought about the hypothesis advanced here concerning the significance of these names, it should be noted that there is no obvious explanation for Berrington and Boreton in terms of proximity to prehistoric forts or to more important places with names ending in *-byrig.*

BERWICK GROVE SJ 540105 DB Manor

Berewic 1086 DB, *Berewik'* 1242 Fees *et freq* with variant spellings *Berewyk(e)* to 1428 FA; *Berrewyk* 1326 Ipm

Berwyk' 1261-2 *ForProc* (p), *Berwyk* 1324 Fine, *Berwik* 1346 FA, *Berwyke* 1548 Pat, *Berwicke* 1713, 17 PR(L) 14, *Berwick* 1713 ib *et seq, Berwick Grove* 1807 ib

Birewike 1272 Ipm

Berewyk Mauvesyn 1397 InqMisc, *Barwicke Mavison* 1585 *SBL 3424, Berwick Maviston* 1783 PR(L) 14

At the end of the OE period **berewīc** meant 'outlying grange, dependent farm'. It is used in an OE document of c. 963 to describe outlying estates belonging to Peterborough Abbey, and it is the usual term in DB for the dependent settlements in a large estate. It has given rise to at least sixteen major settlement-names, but is less common in the country as a whole than the probably synonymous *beretūn*, which is the source of about forty examples of Barton. To some extent the distribution of **berewīc** complements that of *beretūn*; it is found in W, Hrt, Sx, Ess and Sa, where *beretūn* is not evidenced. It is possible that it superseded *beretūn* as the common appellative for a particular type of settlement. The first element of both terms is OE *bere* 'barley'; the grange farms may at one time have been thought of as places where grain was stored.

This Berwick was sometimes distinguished from the other Shropshire example by the affixing of the surname *Mavison*, borne by a family evidenced from the mid-13th cent. This is a Norman nickname meaning 'bad neighbour'.

The house called Berwick Grove is here treated as the surviving representative of the settlement which is called Berwick Maviston on the 1st ed. of the OS 1" map. This was centred on the road-fork S. of Berwick Wharf, at G.R. 533107. To the N.E. of this, the 1st ed. map marks Berwick New Fm, and this building is shown on the modern 1", though it is not named.

BERWICK HOUSE, UPPER BERWICK SJ 473148, 472160
DB Manor

Berewic 1086 DB, *Berewic'* 1223 Cur *et freq* with variant spellings *Berewyk(e), Berewyc', Berewik(e)* to 1316 FA

Berwic' 1223 Cur *et freq* with variant spellings *Berwyk', Berwyk, Berwik* to 1342 *SBL 6298; Berrick* 1632 PR(H) 3, *Berwick* 1682 PR(L) 12 *et seq, Barwick* 1685 PR(L) 4, 1695 Morden, *Barwicke* 1696 PR(L) 4, *Berwick otherwise Barwick* 1780 *SBL 3398*

Salopia Berewyk 1291-2 *Ass, Berwyk' iuxta Roshale* 1294-5 *Ass*

Berewyk Leyburne 1291-2 *Ass, Little Berwyk* 1383 Pat, *Berwyke Parva* 1608 *SBL 3455, Berwyke Parva alias Berwyke Leyborne*

1619 *SBL 3425, Little Barwick alias Barwick Leyborne* 1719 *SBL 3385,* 1728 *SBL 3388, Berwick Leyburne* 1796 PR(L) 12
Ouere Berewyk' 1294-9 *Ass*
Barwick Major 1549 Pat, *Barwick Magna* 1577 Saxton, *Berwyke Magna* 1608 *SBL 3455, Great Berwicke* 1682 *SBL 6319, Great Barwick* 1717 *SBL 3392*

See Berwick Grove for the meaning of the name.

The application of the various affixes is not clear. In DB, Berwick is a single estate of 1½ hides, and the account of Great Berwick in Eyton (X) gives the impression that the whole manor described in DB later belonged to the family surnamed *de Leyburn.* In some 17th- and 18th-century references quoted above, however, Berwick Leyburn is equated with Little Berwick. If there were two centres to the settlement in the medieval period it would be reasonable to suppose that the more northerly, called Upper Berwick on modern OS maps, was the *Ouere Berewyk'* of 1294-9 *Ass.* There is considerable fluctuation in the manner of referring to the two centres in post-1800 sources:
1) Baugh's map (1808) shows 'Berwick' (with a big house and a church) and 'Upper Berwick' (with a big house and some lesser buildings);
2) The OS 1" of the 1860s has 'Great and Little Berwick and Newton' in capitals as a township name, and 'Berwick Hall' (with an adjacent 'Chapel'), and 'Great Berwick' and 'Great Berwick Farm' where the modern map has Upper Berwick;
3) The TA map of 1847 (for the township of Great and Little Berwick and Newton) shows 'Berwick House' and 'Berwick Chapel' and marks 'Upper Berwick House' where the 19th-cent. OS map has Great Berwick;
4) Kelly's Directory for 1934 has an entry for 'BERWICK, consisting of Great and Little Berwick and the hamlets of Alkmond Park, Newton and Rose Hill, in the parish of St. Mary, Shrewsbury'. The two first Private Residents listed in this entry have 'Upper Berwick' and 'Berwick house' as their addresses;
5) Eyton, while not making allowance for two estates, speaks on p.223 of his account of 'Great Berwick and its member, Little Berwick'.

The two affixes in the Assize Rolls for 1291-2 and 1294-5, where we have *Salopia Berewyk* and *Berwyk' iuxta Roshale*, may be alternative suggestions for distinguishing the whole unit from Berwick in Atcham parish.

BESFORD SJ 551250 DB Manor

Betford 1086 DB
Beyford 1244 Ch
Besford 1249 *SBL 5409 et freq* with variant spelling *Besford'; Besfort'* 1569 *SBL 5769*
Besseford 1254 Ipm *et freq* with variant spelling *Besseford'* to 1394 Cl
Bessford 1271-2 *Ass*, 1657 PR(StA) 4, 1807 PR(StA) 3, 1833 OS
Basseford' 1271-2 *Ass* (p), *Basford* 1346 FA, *Bassford* 1804, 36 PR(L) 19

'Betti's ford'. The development to Besford is paralleled in Besford Wo, for which there is an OE spelling *Bettesford*. The personal name *Betti* is also the first element of Beslow, which is not too far away to be associated with the same man.

The ford would be where the road from Moreton Corbet crosses a small tributary of the R. Roden. Besford is in Moreton Corbet parish.

BESLOW SJ 580087 DB Manor

Beteslawe 1086 DB
Bezlawa 1177 P (p)
Besselauwe 1255 RH (p) *et freq* with variant spellings *Besselawe, Besselo(u)we* to 1450 *SBL 3057*
Beslaw 1577 Saxton, *Beslow* 1725 PR(L) 2

'Betti's mound', probably named from the same man as Besford *supra*. The spelling *Bezlawa* exhibits Anglo-Norman *-z-* for OE *-t(e)s-*. This is well-evidenced in the forms for the Wo Besford.

Beslow is one of seven Shropshire names in which OE **hlāw** is certainly or probably combined with the genitive of a masculine personal name. The other six are Longslow, Munslow, Onslow, Purslow, Walkerslow and Whittingslow. Wolferlow He is another such compound.

hlāw is the usual midland term for a tumulus. Barrow-burial is characteristic of the late 6th and early 7th centuries, and although no tumuli have yet been identified at these sites, it is tempting to think of the men whose names ocur in these place-names as the last generation of pagan Angles in Shropshire. Some of the names, expecially Whittingslow, could refer to natural hill-spurs rather than to artificial mounds, but a natural abrupt hill does not exist at Beslow. It seems necessary to postulate a tumulus at Beslow in order to explain the name.

BETTON (ABBOTS and STRANGE) SJ 515079, 507093

DB Manor

Betune 1086 DB, *Bettone Abbatis* 1271-2 *Ass, Betton Extranea* 1284-5 FA, *Betton'* l.13th *ForProc, Betton Lestraunge* 1322 Pat, *Betton* 1328 Pat *et seq, Straungebetton* 1373 Fine, *Betton Strange* 1569 *SBL 6621 et seq, Abbots Betton* 1583 *SBL 6738A et seq, Great, Little Betton* 1701 *SBL 4244, Betton Strange otherwise Little Betton, Abbots Betton otherwise Great Betton* 1758 *SBL 4248*

Beitona 1127,38, c.1155 SAC, *Beydon'* 1220 Cur, *Beiton'* 1223 Cur, *Beyton'* 1255 Cur

Parva Becton' 1167-82, 1256 SAC, *Bechton'* c.1248 SAC, *Bekton' Abbatis* 1271-2 *Ass, Becton'* 1291-2 *Ass*

Beketon' 1291-2 *Ass, Beccheton* 1301 SAC

Beetton 1717 PR(L) 15, *Beeton* 1718-19 ib

The OE form seems likely to have been **Bēctūn*, which is probably 'beech-tree farm or estate', from **bēce** and **tūn**. 'Settlement in a stream-valley', from **bæce**, seems less likely, as there are no *Bac-* spellings, and the area does not contain one of the well-marked valleys to which this term is applied in Shropshire.

The phonological development is similar in some respects to that of Petton, *infra*, from **pēac** and **tūn**. Another parallel is provided by two examples of the name Bratton, in Devon and Somerset, which appear as *Bratona*, *Bratone* in DB, but have later spellings with *Brac-*. The *-ei-* and later *-ee-* spellings for Betton may be partly due to influence from Bayston, which adjoins; but see the discussion of Betton-in-Hales.

As regards the affixes, Betton Abbots was acquired by Shrewsbury Abbey soon after 1086. In the latter part of the 12th cent. it was called *Parva* for distinction from Betton-in-Hales, which also belonged to the Abbey. Betton Strange was held as a separate manor in the mid-12th cent. by Hamon *le Strange*. In the 17th cent. (when the need for distinction from Betton-in-Hales was no longer felt), Betton Abbots and Strange were called Great and Little. On Ogilby's map of 1675 *Betton* is shown for the former and *Little Betton* for the latter.

BETTON IN HALES SJ 692370 DB Manor

Baitune 1086 DB, *Beitona* 1087-94, 1127, c.1135, 1138, 1155, 1175-c.1190 SAC

Bectona 1121 SAC, *Bectun' sub Lima* 1167-82 SAC, *Becton* 1236-50 SAC, *Bectone sub Lima* c.1242 SAC, *Becton' subtus Limam* 1256 SAC, *Bekton' subtus Lyme* 1271-2 *Ass*, *Becton' subtus Lyme* 1292-5 *Ass*

Batona c.1190-c.1219 SAC

Betton 1255-6 *Ass*, 1352 Pat, 1411 SAC, 1437 AD, *Betton subtus Limam* 1256 (1332) Ch, *Bettone sub Lima* 1276 SAC, *Betton'* 1294 SAC, *Betton in Hales* 1318 Cl, *Betton' sub Lyme* 1334 SR, *Betton under Lynde* 1492 Ipm, *Betton' alias dict' Betton' subtus Lyne* 1540 *SBL 6083*, *Betton under Line* 1672 HTR

Apparently another 'beech-tree settlement' from **bēce** and **tūn**, the same name as Betton Abbots. The DB spelling *Baitune* and the 12th-cent. *Beitona* forms from SAC present a serious problem, however; there seems to be no parallel to this development from an OE **Bēctūn*.

The objection to **bæce** 'stream-valley' as first element of Betton-in-Hales is the absence of a significant number of *-a-* spellings.

The affix 'under Lyme' refers to the upland district called Lyme, which stretched along the east boundary of Cheshire to the south-east border of Lancashire. The surviving affix, *in Hales*, is discussed under Market Drayton.

BETTWS-Y-CRWYN SO 205814 Ancient Parish

Betteus 1256,76 Cant, *Bethous'* 1305-6 *Ass*, *Bethous* 1331 (1348) Pat, *Bettus* 1577 Saxton, 1675 Ogilby, 1717 PR(H) 13, *Bettws* 1723 ib, *Bethouse* 1724 ib

'Prayer house', referring to a medieval chapel. The first reference is to *capelle de Betteus.* Welsh *bettws*, an adaptation of ME *bedhus*, occurs in other place-names in Wales. It is interesting that a form with English *-house* was current for the Sa name in 1724.

Baugh's map (1808) shows Bettws without an affix. The earliest printed appearance of *y Crwyn* appears to be on the 19th cent. OS map, where it has its modern spelling. *MorganTs* has an earlier occurrence, *Bettws y Crewin* 1811, from Powys Archives at Llandrindod. *TA* spells the affix *y Cruen.* DEPN suggests that it is Welsh *crowyn* 'pigsty'.

BICTON SJ 447150 Civil Parish

Bichetone 1086 DB, *Biketon'* 1255 RH (p), 1292-5 *Ass*, *-ton* 1286 Pat, 1346 FA (p), *Byketon* 1404 Fine (p), *Bykton* 1535 VE, *Bickton* 1577 Saxton, *Bicton* 1670 PR(L) 7

Bikedoun c.1200-12 HAC (p), *Bikedon, Bukedon* 1203-4 *Ass* (p), *Bikedene* 1212 P (p), *Bukedon* 1255 RH, *Bikedon'* ib (p) *et freq* with variant spellings *Bykedon(e), Bikedon(e)* to 1362 *SBL 3792* (p), *Bekedon* 1316 FA

Bickedon 1248 HAC (p)

Bikedon and variants form the largest category of spellings between c.1200 and 1362, and **dūn** 'hill' may fairly be considered to be the true final element, despite the DB form.

Bicton is situated at the 'waist' of a long, rather narrow hill, on the 250' contour, which makes fairly sharp projections to the N. and S. of the village. The shape is clearly shown by the hachuring on the 19th-cent. OS map. The first element is probably the OE word ***bic** or ***bica** which place-name specialists have proposed for a number of place-names, notably Purbeck in Dorset. The meaning would be 'bill' or 'beak'. The gen.pl. of a strong noun ***bic** would be appropriate here, giving an etymology 'hill of the beaks', which could refer to the N. and S. ends of the hill.

There is another Bicton at SO 289827, near Clun, but the sparse early spellings available for this (*Biggeton* 1271-2 *Ass* (p), *Biketon* 1284 Cl, *Bikedon* 1302 Ipm, *Bykidon* 1397 InqMisc) are insufficient for a decision as to whether **tūn** or **dūn** is the final element.

BILLINGSLEY SO 704853 Ancient Parish

Billingesle 1087-94 SAC, *Billingesleya* 1138-48, 1147-8 SAC, *Billingesleg'* c.1194-1238 SAC, *Billingesle* 1261 Ipm *et freq* with variant spellings *Byllyngesley(e), Billingesley(e), Billyngeslegh, Billyngesley(e), Byllynggesley(e)* to 1577 Saxton; *Bylingesleye* 1319 Ipm, *Belyngesley* 1453 Cl, *Byllyngsley* 1535 VE, *Byllingsleye* 1580 PR(H) 18, *Billingsley* 1678-9 PR(H) 3, *Bellingsly* 1713 ib

Byllingelegh', Billingele 1255 RH *et freq* with variant spellings *Billingeleye, Billyngeleye* to 1291-2 *Ass, Billynggeleye* c.1291 TN

Billinglesle 1271-2 *Ass*

Billingleya 1271-2 *Ass, Billingleye* 1291-2 *Ass, Bilyngleye* 1394 Pat

Billinsley 1751 PR(H) 16, *Billinsly* 1766 PR(H) 3

Possibly 'woodland clearing of the hill called *Billing*', *v.* **lēah**. There is good evidence in place-names for the use of *Billing* as a hill-name. It has been variously explained as a derivative of OE *bill* 'sword' or *bile* 'beak'; the former seems preferable. *Billing* might have been the name of the low ridge with a pointed tip which runs N.W. from the village of Billingsley.

If this etymology be accepted, the spellings with *-s-* can be seen as representing a formation in which **lēah** has been added to the gen. of the hill-name. Those without *-s-* could be from an alternative compound in which the hill-name was in the dat. The *-s-* spellings are earlier and more numerous. It is possible that *Billing* is a personal name, but a topographical term is perhaps more likely to occur with and without the genitival *-es.*

DEPN gives *Bylgeslege*, from ASC (C) s.a. 1055, under this name, but the event referred to is more likely to have taken place at Billingsley in Holme Lacy He, as implied in Stenton, *Anglo-Saxon England*, p.573.

BISHOP'S CASTLE SO 324886 Ancient Parish

Castrum Episcopi 1255 RH, 1255-6 *Ass*, 1271-2 *ForProc*, 1316 FA, *Chastel Eveske* 1318-19 APW, *Chastel Episcopi* 1394 Ch

Bisshopescastel 1282 ChanR *et freq* with variant spellings *Bisshopescastell*, *Bishoppes Castel* to 1540 Leland, *Bisshopcastel* 1322 Pat, *Bysshopuscastel* 1369 Pat, *Bysshop Castell* 1502 Ipm, *Bishop's Castle* 1577 Saxton

Bishops Towne, Byshops Towne, Bishoppes Towne c.1540 Leland

The castle was erected c.1127 in the Bishop of Hereford's great estate of Lydbury North, and the town is believed to have been planted in the late 12th century. MSS in Welsh refer to the town as *Trefesgob* from the late 15th cent. *(MorganTs)*; this corresponds to Leland's *Bishops Towne.*

BISHTON (in Boningale parish) SJ 804018 DB Manor

Bispetone 1086 DB

Bispeston' c.1200 *ForProc*, *Bispiston'* 1255-6 *Ass* (p), *Bispeston* 1284-5 FA

Buspeston 1221-2 *Ass* (p)

Bisopeston' 1255-6 *Ass* (p), *Bisshopeston'* 1306-7 *Ass* (p),

Bishipeston' 1346 FA (p)
Bisshton 1397 Cl, *Byssheton* 1429 Fine, *Byshton* 1599 PR(L) 3, *Little Bishton* 1729 ib

'Bishop's estate'. There are several other places called Bishton, a number called Bishopstone, and one Bushton (W) from this source. Presumably the manor belonged in pre-Conquest times to the Bishop of Lichfield, but there is no record of ecclesiastical ownership in DB, so it must have been alienated before 1066.

Foxall's Gazetteer lists Little and Big Bishton as well as Bishton Hall. The 19th-cent. OS map shows a single settlement called Bishton, and the modern 1" shows Bishton Manor there.

BITTERLEY SO 563774 Ancient Parish

Buterlie 1086 DB *et freq* with variant spellings *-le(e), -leg', -legh, -ley(e)* to 1349 Ipm, *Butterlega* 1172-7 HAC *et freq* with variant spellings *-le(e), -leye, -leghe* to 1655 *SBL 8557*, *Buturley* 1326 AD
Butreley 1266 Cl (p), *Burteleye* 1356 Pat
Byterleye 1306-7 *Ass* (p), *Biterleye* 1330 Fine, *Bitterley* 1346 FA, 1399 Cl, 1577 Saxton, *Bitterleye* 1346 Cl (p), 1348 *SBL 5235*, 1356 Ipm, *Bytterleye* 1392 Pat, *Bitturley* 1399 Cl (p), 1431 FA, *Biterley* 1694 *PRCulmington*
Boterleye 1306-7 *Ass* (p), *Boterley* 1322 Pat

'Butter pasture', identical with Butterleigh D, Butterley Ch, Db, He. In this compound **lēah** is used in its late OE sense of 'pasture, meadow', the earlier senses of 'wood' and 'clearing' being possibly obsolescent when the name was coined. In spite of the late English name, Bitterley is likely to be an ancient settlement, and its British name may have persisted into the 10th century, though there is no trace of it in surviving records.

The establishment of the modern form was relatively late. In *SBL 8557*, dated 1655, the place is called 'Bitterly or Butterley or Bitterlay'. The same document speaks of 'Over Bitterly or Over Bitterlay'. Another reference to *Over Bitterley* occurs 1596 *SBL 8550*.

BOLAS MAGNA SJ 647213 Ancient Parish

Belewas 1198 Fees
Boulewas 1199 (1265) Ch *et freq* to 1443 *SBL 15752*, *Bowlewas* 1255 RH, 1405 *SBL 3716*, 1447 *SBL 4432*, *Boulwas* 1316, 1437 Cl, 1334 SR, 1338,59 Cl (p), 1398, 1402,7 Pat
Bewlw' 1249 Ipm, *Beulewas* 1255 RH (p), 1271-2 *Ass*
Bulewas 1255-6 *Ass* (p)
Bolewas 1271-2 *ForProc* (p), 1284-5 FA
Bo(u)ldwas 1284-5 FA, *Bouldwas* 1316 FA
Bowelwas 1291-2 *Ass*
Baulwas 1316 Ipm
Boughelas 1359 *SBL 4495*
Bolas 1520 AD, 1577 Saxton *et seq*, *Bollas* 1535 VE, *Bolus* 1750 PR(L) 1
Bollwas 1616 *SBL 5120*
Bowlas 1711 PR(L) 11, 1721,2 PR(L) 13

The second element is OE **wæsse**, a term discussed in detail in Gelling, *Place-Names in the Landscape*, pp.59-60, where it is shown that it denotes riverside land which floods and drains with dramatic swiftness. The sites are by meanders. The R. Tern has been straightened near Great Bolas, but the parish boundary shows the earlier course.

The first element might be the gen.pl. of an OE **bogel* 'little bend'. The site presents a contrast to that of Buildwas, the other major name in the county which contains **wæsse**, in that the river-bends are squiggles, whereas those at Buildwas are great curves. There is no other evidence for an OE diminutive of **bog** 'bend', but analogous formations are well-represented in place-names.

The modern pronunciation has ō.

Little Bolas (in Hodnet parish) is *Parva Boulewas* 1342 Pat (p), *Little Bolas* 1705 PR(L) 11, *Bolas Parva* 1717 ib. The first use of an affix noted for Great Bolas is *Bowlas Magna* 1655 *SBL 5573*. It is *Greate Bolas* 1672 HTR, *Big Bolas* 1755 PR(L) 10. Modern maps show *Bolas Magna* for the parish-name, *Great Bolas* for the settlement.

BONINGALE SJ 810027 Ancient Parish

Bolingehal' c.1200 *ForProc, Bollinggehale, Bolyngehale* 1291-2 *Ass*
Boligbale 1203-4 *Ass* (p), *Bolighale* c.1300 *SBL 5406*
Bolingchal 1221-2 *Ass* (p)
Bolinghale (p), *Bollinghall* 1255-6 *Ass, Bolinghal'* 1261-2 *ForProc* (p) *et freq* with variant spellings *Bolinghall, Bolinghale, Bolynghale* to 1446 Fine, *Bollynghale, Bolinghull'* 1291-2 *Ass, Bollynghall'* 1539-40 *RentSur*
Boninghal 1276 Cl (p), *Bonynghall* 1535 VE, *Bonyngale* 1577 Saxton, *Boningall(e)* 1600 PR(L) 3, *Bonninghall* 1610 *SBL 15757, Boningall* 1671 PR(H) 3, *Bonningale* 1472 HTR, *Bonningal* 1720 PR(H) 16, *Bonning Hall* 1765 *SBL 9642*

'Nook associated with Bola', *v.* **halh**. There are not enough forms with *-e-* to support an etymology 'nook of Bola's people'. The original form is more likely to have contained a connective **-ing-** than to have had **-inga-**, gen. of **-ingas**.

halh is common in the place-names of the area between Shifnal and Wolverhampton, and in this region it probably refers to shallow, rather shapeless hollows which provided sheltered settlement-sites.

Bolinghale became *Boninghale* by dissimilation of the first *-l-*. The modern pronunciation has ŏ

BORASTON SO 614700 Civil Parish

Bureston 1188 P, 1203-4 *Ass* (p), *Bureston(e)* 1255 RH (p), *Bureston'* 1255-6, 1271-2 (p) *Ass*
Buraston' 1255-6 *Ass* (p), 1274 RH, *Buraston* 1633 PR(H) 16, *Burraston* 1671 ib, 1803 Plymley
Burston' 1255-6 *Ass*
Burweston' 1271-2 *Ass* (p)
Boraston' 1271-2, 1291-2 *Ass, Boraston* c.1291 TN, 1311 Pat, 1690 PR(H) 16, *Borastone* 1366 Ipm (p), *Borraston* 1804 PR(H) 16
Baraston' 1291-2 *Ass*
Boreyston 1255 Pat

The *-as-* of the modern form is well-represented in 13th-cent. spellings, and as this is not likely to have developed from a gen.sing. inflection Ekwall's etymology (DEPN) '**tūn** of the *gebur* or peasant' is not satisfactory.

It is possible that this place and Aston Court in Knighton-on-Teme (in Wo but adjoining) were once a single unit called *Ēast tūn*, and that Boraston was later distinguished by having **burh** 'fort' prefixed. Both places belonged to the bishopric of Worcester. Aston in Knighton-on-Teme is difficult to explain as an 'east settlement', but if the unit included Boraston it could be thought of as immediately E. of Burford (which has **burh** as first element).

BORETON SJ 513077 DB Manor

Burtune 1086 DB *et freq* with variant spellings *Burton(a), Burton'* to 1726 PR(L) 6, *Burton' iuxta Betton'* 1291-2 *Ass*
Borton 1255-6 *Ass* (p), 1808 Baugh, *Borton' Abbatis* 1291-2 *Ass*
Bourton' 1301 SAC, *Boorton* 1634 PR(H) 11, *Bourton* 1706 PR(L) 6, 1833 OS
Boerton' 1425 *SBL 6693*
Boreton 1785 PR(L) 6

'Fort settlement', see the discussion under Berrington; this is a unique instance of development to the modern form Boreton. *Abbatis* because it belonged to Shrewsbury Abbey.

BOSCOBEL SJ 837083 Extra-Parochial

The extra-parochial district shown on OS maps as Boscobel is called White Ladies in PR(L) 3. The latter name refers to the Augustinian canonesses of the Priory of St Leonard, Brewood, which was established in the 12th cent. The area round the priory was extra-parochial and extra-manorial.

Boscobel ('fair wood' in Italian) was the name given to the half-timbered mansion built near the site of the priory c.1606. An account of this is given in PR(L) 3, in the Introduction to the register of White Ladies. The name is recorded as *Baskabell* 1707, *Boscobel* 1784. Charles II took refuge at White Ladies in 1661 after his defeat at Worcester.

BOULDON SO 545851 DB Manor

Bolledone 1086 DB, *Boledon'* c.1230 SAC (p), *Bolledon* 1255, 1271-2 *Ass*, 1295 Ipm, 1346 FA, *Boledon* 1271-2 (p), 1291-2 *Ass, Bolledon'* 1334 SR
Bul(l)ardone 1166 RBE (p), *Bularddun', Bullarddun, Bulardon* 1203-4 *Ass* (p), *Bulardun* (p), *Bullardun* 1205 Abbr, *Bollardedon'* 1242 Fees, *Bullerdon* 1271-2 *Ass* (p)
Bulledon' 1255-6, 1271-2, 1291-2, 1294-9 *Ass*, 1284-5 FA, *Buldon', Bulledon'* 1259 Cl (p), *Buledon'* 1255-6, 1291-2 *Ass, Buledun', Buledon'* 1261-2 *ForProc* (p), *Bulledon* 1274 RH (p)
Bolyndon', Bolydon' 1291-2 *Ass*
Bouledon 1291-2 *Ass*
Boldon 1431 FA, *Bouldon* 1495 Ipm, 1743 PR(H) 15, *Boulden* 1631 ib, 1840 *SBL 6120, Bowldon* 1729 PR(H) 15
Bowden 1732 PR(L) 4
Boulton 1845 *SBL 6121*

The second element is **dūn**, which does not suit the present position of the village, in the valley of the Clee Brook. It is necessary to assume a change of site.

The first part of the name is obscure. There is an unusual degree of variation in the spellings, sometimes in the same entry, as *Bouledon* and *Bolydon'* in 1291-2 *Ass.* To account for the *Bullardun* type, DEPN suggests that there were two forms, one containing **-ware** 'dwellers'. It is possible, however, that the *Bulardone, Bollardedon', Bullerdon* spellings derive from the original form, and that *Bolledone, Bulledon'* etc. result from an early shortening. If so, 'Bulla's hill', suggested by Ekwall, could not be the etymology. The element **dūn** is only rarely qualified by a reference to a group of people. The commonest qualifiers in **dūn** names are descriptive terms, personal names and plant-names. An unrecorded plant-name is perhaps involved.

The modern pronunciation is [bouldən].

BOURTON SO 597963 DB Manor

Burtune 1086 DB *et freq* with variant spellings *Burton'*, *Burton* to 1833 OS
Bureton' 1226-8 Fees (p)
Burnton' 1251 Cl
Burgton 1255-6 *Ass*, *Burghton* 1316 FA
Bourton 1291 Ch, c.1291 TN, 1535 VE *et seq; -ton'* 1305-6 *Ass*
Borton 1405 Pat, 1746 PR(H) 1 *et freq* to 1784 PR(L) 6
Boreton 1732 PR(H) 3

'Fort settlement', OE **burhtūn**: see the discussion under Berrington. This Bourton (in Much Wenlock parish) is not near an ancient hill-fort or a settlement with a name containing **burh**.

BRATTON SJ 637142 DB Manor

Brochetone 1086 DB, *Brocton' iuxta Welinton'* 1294-9 *Ass*
Brothton' 1255-6 *Ass*
Bronton' 1255-6 *Ass*
Broghton' 1292-5 *Ass*
Bratton 1602 *et seq* PR(L) 8, *Braton* 1649, 1728,64,66 ib, *Bratten* 1699 *et freq* to 1721 ib

'Brook settlement'. The compound of **brōc** with **tūn** usually develops to Broughton or, in Shropshire, Brockton. Bratton in Wrockwardine parish is one of two instances of this atypical development, the other being Bratton Seymour in Somerset.

Bratton is by a tributary of the R. Tern.

BRIDGNORTH SO 720930 Ancient Parishes

(apud) Brugiam Hy 1 (1267), 1155 (1468) Ch, *Bruges* 1121 CartAntiq *et freq* to 1459 Cl, *Brug'* 1155 CartAntiq (p) *et freq* to 1307 Ch, *(apud) Brugiaez* 1155 (1327) Ch, *Brugis* 1170 *et seq* to 1194 P, *Brugg'* 1261 Cl *et freq* to 1276 Cl, *Brugge* 1291-2 *Ass* (p), 1312 Cl, 1315 Ipm, 1328 AD, 1339 InqMisc, 1349 Ipm, *Brugges* 1273,5 Cl, 1293, 1325 Pat, 1311,18,41 Fine, *Bruge* 1308 Cl, *Brugg* 1341 Cl, 1350 Ipm, *Brug* 1380 Fine, 1443 (copy) *SBL 15752*, *Bruges alias Bruggenorth* 1446 Ch, *Bruges als. Bridg(e)north* 1675 Ogilby

Brig' 1161 P, *Briges* 1175 P, 1235-6 Fees, 1255-6 *Ass*, 1259 Cl, 1264 Pat, *Brigg* 1275 Cl, 1383 Fine, *Brigges* 1297 Cl, *Brigge* 1485 Cl

Bregenorth c.1200 Strange, *Bregge* 1342 Cl

Burges 1230 P

Brugg' Norht 1282 Cl *et passim* with variant spellings *Brugge North', Brugge North(e), Bruggenorth(e)* to 1498 Cl, *Brugenorth* 1316 Pat *et freq* with variant spelling *Brugenorthe* to 1550 Pat, *Brugysnorth* 1321,31 Pat, *Brugnorth* 1332 Pat, *Bruggesnorth* 1334,54 Pat, *Broggesnorth* 1352 Pat, *Bruggenorth or Brugges* 1484 Cl, *Brudgenorthe* 1548 Pat, *Brudgnorthe* 1559,60 PR(H) 3

Briggenorth 1322 Cl *et freq* with variant spellings *Briggenorthe, Bryggenorth* to 1506 AD, *Briggeinorth* 1341 Cl (p), *Brygenorth* 1530 AD, *Bridgenorth, Bridge North* c.1540 Leland, *Brydgenorth* 1549 Pat, 1560 AD, *Brigenorth* 1553 Pat, *Bridgnorthe* 1566 AD, *Bridgnorth* 1661 PR(L) 4, *Bridgenorth* 1770 PR(H) 18, 1833 OS, 1834 *SBL 5552*

'Bridge', OE **brycg**. The final *-s* of many of the spellings is not an indication that the name was plural. The Anglo-Norman nom. ending *-s* was sometimes added to English names in the post-Conquest period, particularly to short names, like Barnes Sr, Staines Mx. The spellings with *-u-* predominate, and without the influence of standard English *bridge* the name might have developed to *Brudge, like Rudge from OR **hrycg**.

Only the post-Conquest spellings are given above. A place in this area is referred to in pre-Conquest sources, and in post-Conquest chronicles drawing on such sources, in connection with the Danish wars of the late 9th and early 10th centuries. A good account of these references is given by J.F.A. Mason, 'The Norman Castle at Quatford', SAS 57 (1961-4), pp.37ff. The forms derived from them are:

æt Cwatbrucge c.924 (s.a. 895) ASC A
æt Brycge, æt Brygcge 11th cent. (s.a. 896) ASC D
æt Bricge 912 Mercian Register
Cantbricge c.1000 (s.a. 910) Æthelweard
Quattbrycge, Cwatbrycge, Brycge c.1130 'Florence of Worcester'

The event chronicled under the years 895-6 is the wintering of a Danish army and their construction of a fort. The event of 910 described by Æthelweard is the crossing of the R. Severn by a band of Danes who were subsequently defeated at Tettenhall St. (The greater part of the bridge-name, *-antbricge*, can be read in the charred remains of the Æthelweard MS, so the form is not due to a misreading by the copyist from whom most of the text is known; but A. Campbell in his edition of 1962 emends to *Cuatbricge* and translates 'Bridgnorth'). The series of annals known as the Mercian Register records that in 912 the lady Æthelflæd built one of her fortresses at *Bricge.* The chronicle known as Florence of Worcester, in addition to a reference to the wintering of the Danes at *Quattbrycge, Cwatbrycge* in 895-6, says that the *burh* built by Æthelflæd was on the western bank of the Severn in the place called *Brycge*; and when speaking of the rebellion of Robert de Bellême against Henry I this chronicle says that Robert refortified the fort which Æthelflæd had built at *Brycge.*

The primary source for the last event is the chronicler Ordericus Vitalis, who wrote between 1123 and 1141. He records the transfer in 1101-2 of Robert de Bellême's headquarters from Quatford to Bridgnorth. The passage runs 'Oppidum de Quatfort transtulit, et Brugiam, munitissimum castellum, super Sabrinam fluvium condidit'. The new headquarters is referred to as *Brugiam* and *Brugiæ* in Orderic's subsequent account of its siege and capture by the king.

It seems probable that there was a bridge at Bridgnorth in the 9th century, and that the structure remained in continuous use thereafter. There is no reason to postulate a bridge at Quatford. The bridge at Bridgnorth and the ford at Quatford were both named from a feature called *Cwat(t)* in OE, and this name survives uncompounded in the settlement-name Quatt. OE *Cwat(t)* probably has to be considered as a district-name covering an area extending at least from Quatt to Bridgnorth, a distance of 4 miles. An alternative hypothesis would be that it was originally the name of the settlement at Quatt, and that this was the centre of a large estate to which the areas of Bridgnorth and Quatford were subordinate; but the recorded history of Quatt gives no hint of such a status. The term *Cwat(t)* appears to have no parallel among other place-names, and no suggestion is available about its meaning. Ekwall (s.n. Quatford) favours OE *cwēd* 'dirt', but is clearly aware that this is not really satisfactory. There is a word *quat*, first recorded in 1579, which means 'pimple'. This could be derived from an OE **cwat(t)*, but the meaning is not suitable for our hypothetical district-name.

The settlement at Bridgnorth (which may fairly be assumed to have been there before the arrival of Robert de Bellême) had probably lost the first part of its name and become known simply as 'Bridge' in local speech by the end of the OE period. The records suggest that the affix 'north' was added to this simplex name in the latter part of the 11th cent. There has been a general assumption that 'north' distinguished a bridge built by Robert de Bellême from one at Quatford. This assumption was challenged by J.F.A. Mason in the articles cited above. He pointed out that in 12th-cent. and later deeds referring to Quatford there is mention only of the ferry and the ford, never of a bridge, and he considered it probable that if there was a bridge at Quatford it was destroyed soon after Robert de Bellême moved to Bridgnorth. As stated above, there is no reason to suppose that Quatford ever had a bridge; but even if it had, and this had survived into the 13th cent., it does not seem likely that the more northerly bridge would have been distinguished in this way. It would have been more natural to have called it *Northbridge or *Newbridge. The placeing of 'north' *after* the simplex name suggests a pseudo-manorial construction, distinguishing Bridgnorth from other places in England called 'Bridge' which had acquired, or were in the process of acquiring, suffixes referring to their manorial owners. Such names are Bridgerule D, Bridgwater So and Bridge Sollers He.

It was suggested by Arthur Oswald in *Country Life* May 1957 that -north was for distinction from Bridgwater. Frank Noble (*Offa's Dyke Re-viewed*, M.Phil. thesis, Open University 1977, p.245) suggests that it is for distinction from Bridge Sollers. The reference is perhaps less precise, however. There may have been a feeling among government officials that Bridgnorth should be characterised as the most northerly of several places called 'Bridge' with which they had to deal.

Leland (c.1540) records a belief that the suffix is the forest-name *Morfe*. This is obviously not possible, but it suggests that there was in his time some bafflement about the meaning of -north in Bridgnorth.

BROCKTON

Shropshire contains six names derived from OE *brōctūn* 'brook settlement'; five have the modern form Brockton, one *(supra)* has become Bratton. These forms are echoed in St, where there are two Broctons, and in So and YN, where the compound has become Bratton and Brotton. Elsewhere *brōctūn* has become Broughton in at least nineteen major settlement-names.

None of the Shropshire Brocktons has become a parish, but three of them qualify for inclusion in this study by virtue of being named in DB. The Brocktons which did not achieve this distinction are a village W. of Worthen, which is first recorded in 1271-2 *Ass*, and one W. of Lydbury North, which appears 1208-9 *ForProc.*

brōc is used in place-names for fairly substantial streams, and a settlement called *brōctūn* is likely to have had at least a good water-supply. The Shropshire places had low assessments in DB, however. The highest - 2 hides - is for Brockton in Shipton. Bratton is assessed at 1½ hides, Brockton in Longford parish at ½ hide, and Brockton in Sutton Maddock at only 1 virgate 8 acres. It was perhaps because of their modest status that the places were not felt to require distinguishing affixes.

BROCKTON (in Longford parish) SJ 728168 DB Manor

Brochetone 1086 DB
Brotton 1255-6 *Ass*
Brokton' 1271-2 *Ass, Broktone* c.1271 *SBL 16196, Brocton'* 1341 *SBL 4127* (p)

Named from its position by a substantial tributary of the Strine Brook.

BROCKTON (in Shipton parish) SO 579938 DB Manor

Broctune 1086 DB, *Brocton'* 1242 Fees, 1255 RH, *Brochton* 1255-6 *Ass, Brokton* 1271-2 *Ass*, 1401,53 Cl, *Brocton* 1284-5 FA *et freq, Brockton* 1548 Pat, 1636 *et seq* PR(H) 1
Brotton 1503 Ipm

This Brockton is by a rather small tributary of the R. Corve.

BROCKTON (in Sutton Maddock parish) SJ 721035 DB Manor

Broctone 1086 DB, *Brocton'* 1212 Fees *et freq* with variant spellings *Brocton, Broctun, Brokton; Brochton'* 1226-8 Fees, *Brocthon* 1272-3 Ipm, *Broctone by Sutton Madok* 1318 Ch, *Brockton* 1544 *SBL 4564*

Situated by Mad Brook.

BROMFIELD SO 482769 Ancient Parish

Bromfelde 1060-1 ECWM, *Bromfeld* 1203-4 *Ass et passim* with variant spellings *Bromfeud', Bromfeld', Bromfel, Bromfild, Bromfylde* to 1535 VE, *Bromfeild, Bromefeld* c.1540 Leland, *Bromefield* 1596 PR(H) 18, *Bromfield* 1634 AD

Brunfelde 1086 DB, *Brumefeld* Hy 2 (1235) Ch, *Brunfeld* 1194, 5 P, *Brumfeld* 1203-4 *Ass*, 1292 Pat, 1293 Cl, 1319 InqMisc (p), *Brumfeud, Breumfeud* 1255-6 *Ass, Brumfeud* 1271-2 *Ass, Brumfelde* 1317 Ch
Bramfeld' 1208-9 *ForProc*
Bremesfeld 1251 Fees
Brompfeld 1318 InqMisc (p)
Broumeld 1346 FA
Brimfield 1826 PR(H) 18

'Open land where broom grows'; identical with Bramfield Sf, Broomfield Ess, K, So, and Brimfield He about 6 miles S. of this place. The 'open land' is referred to again in Felton and Clayfelton, which lie in Bromfield parish. The name appears in French as *Champ Geneste* c.1320 FFW.

feld is most commonly used in ancient settlement-names to denote a contrast with adjacent woodland or with adjacent higher ground. The second sense may be the relevant one here, where the valley of the R. Corve is just about to broaden into the Plain of Hereford.

The earliest reference is to the minster church of St Mary at Bromfield. Most of the post-Conquest references are to the Benedictine Priory, founded in 1135. In the 13th and 14th centuries there were two estates. *Bromfeld Parva* occurs 1284-5 FA, and *Lutelbromfeld, Muchelbromfeld* are mentioned 1377 Cl.

BROMPTON (in Berrington parish) SJ 548079 DB Manor

Brantune 1086 DB, *Brantone* 1121, c.1130 SAC, *Bramtona* 1155 SAC
Bromptona c.1140 SAC, *Brompton'* 1255-6, 1291-2 *Ass, Brompton* 1256 (1322) Ch, 1583 PR(L) 14 *et freq*
Brampton by Atingham 1327 Pat, *Brampton* 1577 Saxton
Brumpton 1271-2 *Ass*
Bromton 1646,59, 1715 PR(L) 14

'Broom settlement'. This fairly common name has become Brompton in Mx and Y (several instances), but more frequently

Brampton, as in Little Brampton in Hopesay parish. The two Sa examples included here are both *Brampton* on Saxton's map. Other modern forms of the compound include Braunton D, Brympton So.

BROMPTON (and Rhiston) SO 250934 Civil Parish

Bromton 1228 Lib
Brompton' 1255-6 *Ass*, *Brompton* 1299, 1301 Ipm, 1318 Cl, InqMisc, 1346 FA, 1352 Pat, 1380 Fine, 1431 FA
Brampton 1404 Pat, 1577 Saxton

'Broom settlement', see the preceding article. The Book of Fees, in 1242, has *Brocton'* for this place; this is a clear error for *Bromton'*.

BROOM (in Ellesmere Rural parish) SJ 379317 DB Manor

Bruma 1086 DB
Bromam 1157-72, c.1179 HAC, *Brome* c.1177 HAC *et freq* to 1336 Pat

'Broom'. Two other Shropshire hamlets with this name are Broome *infra* and Broome in Hopesay parish, the latter being first recorded in 1255-6 *Ass*.

DEPN lists Brome (Sf), Broom (Bd, Du, Wo) and Broome (Nt, Sa, Wa).

BROOME (in Cardington parish) SO 525981 DB Manor

Brame 1086 DB
Brome 1255-6 *Ass*, 1261-2 *ForProc* (p), 13th InqMisc, 1327 Pat, 1689 PR(H) 16
Broom 1770 *PRCardington*

See Broom *supra*.

BROSELEY SJ 673020 Ancient Parish

Burewardeslega 1177 P (p), *Burewordesl'* 1195 P (p), *Burewordesleg'* 1197,8 P (p), *Burwardesle* 1203-4, 1271-2 *Ass*, 1316 FA, 1383 Pat, *Burawardesleia* 1205 P (p), *Burewardesleg'* 1212 P (p), 1242 Fees (p), 1255 RH, *Burwardeslegh* 1229 Pat (p), *-leg'* 1271-2 *ForProc*, *Burrewardeslee* 1291-2 *Ass* (p), *Burwardesleye* 1359 Pat, *-ley* 1407,61 Cl, *Burwardesley alias Broseley* 1701 *SBL 14802*

Burwarleg' 1177 P (p)

Burgardeslege 1194 P, *Burghwardelee* 1291-2 *Ass*, *Burghwardesley* 1363 Pat

Burwardelega Warini 1194 P, *Burewardele* 1228 Pat (p), *Burewardel'* 1229 Cl (p), *Burwardel'* 1230 Cur (p), *Burewardeleg'* 1231 Cur (p), 1261-2 *ForProc*, *Burwardelleg'* 1255 RH (p), *Burwardele* 1261 Ipm, *Burwardleg* 1262 Pat

Borewardleg' 1230 P (p), *Borewardel'* 1274 RH

Borewardesleg' 1242 Fees, *Borewardesle(gh')* 1271-2 *ForProc*, *Borewardesleye* 1291-2 *Ass* (p), 1360, 1402 Cl, 1418 Fine, *Borewardusleg'* 1274 RH, *Borwardeslegh'* 1291-2 *Ass* (p), *Borewardesley* 1310 Ipm, *Borwardesleie* 1319 Ipm, *Borewardisleye* 1331 (1348) Pat

Borewarsleye l.13th *ForProc*, 1327,8 Pat

Barwardesley alias Borsley 1548 Pat

Brosley 1535 VE, 1625 PR(H) 6, 1706 ib 9, *Broseley* 1577 Saxton, 1675 Ogilby, *Brooseley* 1619 PR(L) 20, *Broasley* 1699 PR(H) 3

'Woodland clearing of the fort-guardian', second element **lēah**.

OE **burhweard** occurs in a number of place-names, and these are plotted on Fig. 2. In this name and in Burwardsley Ch *burhweard* is combined with **lēah**, but more frequently it qualifies a habitative term such as **tūn** or **cot**. Burwarton *infra* is one of the compounds with **tūn**. If it be accepted that a defence-system from before the time of the Danish wars is represented by the *burhtūn, byrhtūn, byrigtūn* names, it could be argued that the *burhweard* names refer to ownership of estates by officials in charge of a number of fortified sites. *Burgweard* could, on the other hand, be an ordinary OE personal name belonging to a landowner with no special military status or function; but it is noteworthy that 7 out of a corpus of 10 names in which this term occurs are in Cheshire, Shropshire and Herefordshire.

The late appearance (1535, 1548) in the records of a shortened form *Brosley, Borsley* may be deceptive; spellings like *Burwardesley* may have continued to be used after a shorter form was current in local speech. Shorter forms are recorded earlier for Burwardsley Ch, which is *Borosley* 1499, *Bursley* 1524 (PN Ch 4, 93), and the longer form may have been restored to that name by antiquarian influence. In Broseley there has been metathesis as well as shortening. The long vowel may be a spelling-pronunciation due to the casual insertion of *-e-*, giving *Broseley* rather than *Brosley.*

The *Warin* whose name is once used as an affix is mentioned *freq* in the Pipe Rolls.

BROUGHTON SJ 497242 Ancient Parish

Burtune, Burtone 1086 DB, *Buretona* c.1228 *SBL 5285* (p)
Burcton', Burchtune 13th *SBL 5394,6,7* (p), *Burhton* (p), *Burchton* 1255 RH, *Burhtone* 1274 RH (p), *Burghton'* 1291-2 *Ass, Burgton'* 1292-5 *Ass, Burghton* 1346 FA (p), 1350 *SBL 3656* (p)
Boruton' 13th *SBL 5398* (p)
Bourton' 1291-2 *Ass*
Bourghton' 1334 SR
Broughton 1544 *SBL 4564*, 1577 Saxton *et seq, Browton* 1748 PR(L) 4

'Fort settlement'; see the discussion under Berrington. DB describes two estates, assessed at 2 and 5 hides, which suggests that the area known as *Burtune* must have been appreciably larger than the present small parish. There is no village; the G.R. given above is for Broughton Fm.

BUCKNELL SO 355739 Ancient Parish

Buchehalle 1086 DB, *Buckenhale, Bockenhale* 1333 Fine, *Bukenhale*

1334 ib

Bukehill' 1175 P (p), *Bukehull* 1271-2 *Ass*

Bukenhull' 1208-9 *ForProc* (p), *Buckenhulle, Bukenhull* 1255-6 *Ass* (p), *Bukenhull* 1270 Ch, 1271-2 *Ass* (p), 1305 Cl, *Bukenhulle* 1272 Ipm

Bockenhul 1242 Fees, *Bockenhul(l)* 1255 RH (p), *Bokenhulle* 1272 Cl, *Bokenhull'* 1291-2 *Ass, Bokenhull* 1305 Ipm *et freq* to 1431 FA

Bykynhull 1316 FA

*Bucknell*1535 VE, 1577 Saxton *et seq, Bucknyll* 1587 PR(H) 18, *Bucknill* 1602 *PRBucknell*, 1626 PR(H) 2, *Bucknel* 1787 ib

'Bucca's hill' or 'hill of the he-goat'. Buckton, 2 miles S.E. in He, has the same first element combined with **tūn**, and this might be considered evidence in favour of the personal name rather than the animal. Bucknell PN O 203 is another instance of the place-name.

This is an area where all the hills are pointed, so it is natural that **hyll** should be the generic, rather than **dūn**. The name presumably refers to Bucknell Hill, which overlooks the village.

BUILDWAS SJ 637048 Ancient Parish

Beldewes 1086 DB, *Beldewas* 1170 P, 1271-2 *Ass, Parua Beldewas* 1271-2 *Ass*

Billewus 1158 P, *Billewas* 1160,2 P, *Parva Billewas* 1189 CartAntiq, *Builwas* 1655 SAS 1/XLVII

Buldewes c.1160 SAC, *Buldewas* 1175-6 SAC *et freq* to c.1540 Leland, *Parva Buldewas* 1253 (1292) Ch (p), 1255 RH, 1255-6 *Ass*, 1261-2 (p), 1271-2 *ForProc*, 1334 SR, *Buldiwas* 1272 Ipm, *Buldywas Parva, -Maugna* l.13th *ForProc, Buldewas Parva* 1316 FA, *Buldewasse* 1332 Cl, *Buldwas* 1340 Cl, c.1540 Leland, *Buldewace* 1344 Cl

Bildewas 1189 CartAntiq *et freq* with variant spelling *Byldewas* to 1513 AD, *Bildwas* 1277 Pat, 1535 VE, 1604 PR(L) 3, 1720-1 PR(H) 17, 1745 PR(L) 14, *Lytyll Byldwas* 1535 VE

Biltewas 1203-4 *Ass*

Buildewas 1255-6 *Ass, Buildwas* 1301 Strange, 1680 PR(L) 14 *et seq*

Billedewas 1271-2 *Ass*

Burlewas 1328 Pat

Billevoise, Belvoys c.1540 Leland

Bildas Parva, - Magna 1577 Saxton, *Bildas* 1604 PR(L) 3, 1637 PR(L) 20, 1666 PR(H) 1, 1684 PR(L) 13, *Byldas* 1684 PR(L) 13, *Bildass* 1711, 1715 PR(H) 13

Budas 1695 Morden

Byldews 1590 PR(L) 20, *Byldeous* 1591 ib, *Bildoes* 1747 PR(H) 8, *Byldows* 1766 PR(L) 2

See the discussion of Bolas. Buildwas would serve as the 'type-site' to illustrate the meaning of OE **wæsse**. The village stands on raised ground at the edge of the flood-plain of the R. Severn, and there is a series of great meanders extending several miles upstream. The flooding and draining of the meadows by these meanders occurs with dramatic swiftness.

The first element must have had a form such as **bylde, *byldan*. DEPN suggests either 'building' or 'builder', but this was put forward before the nature of a **wæsse** had been established. The one activity which would not take place on a **wæsse** is building, so it is advisable to seek another OE root for the qualifying term (though the modern spelling is probably due to association with the word *build*).

The OE verb *bieldan, byldan* 'to encourage', and the noun *byldu* 'boldness, confidence' and adjective *gebyld* 'courageous', might be considered. These words, which are related to OE *beald*, modern *bold*, are discussed in NED under *bield*. An adjective with a more concrete sense, such as 'swelling, surging', would suit the action of the flood-water at Buildwas.

There are modern pronunciations with and without *-w-*, and the parish-register spellings suggest that both forms were current in the 16th-18th centuries. The occasional local development to *Bildoes* or *Byldows* is noteworthy. The commonest modern pronunciation is [bildəs].

BURFORD SO 583680 Ancient Parish

Bureford 1086 DB, 1209 P *et passim* with variant spelling *Bureford'* to 1386 Pat
Bireford' 1255-6 *Ass*
Burford 1284 InqMisc *et freq*, *-e* 1535 VE, c.1540 Leland, 1577 *SBL 5239*
Boreford c.1291 TN *et freq* to 1431 FA, *-vord* 1304 Ipm, *Boreford-upon-Temede* 1332 Cl
Bereford 1316 FA, 1337 Cl
Borford 1365 Ipm
Bourforde 1390 Cl

'Fort ford', first element **burh**. The other instance of this name is Burford Oxon, which was sometimes called *Burford upon the Wold*; it is possible that *-upon-Temede* for the Sa place in 1332 is for distinction from this.

Burford is one of a series of 'fort' names on the R. Teme. Berrington Wo is one mile W. See the discussion of Berrington *supra*, and Fig. 2.

BURWARTON SO 618850 Ancient Parish

Burertone 1086 DB
Burwardton' 1194,5 P
Bureworton' 1199, 1200 P, *Burewarton* 1221-2 *Ass*, 1255 RH, c.1270 InqMisc, 1271-2 *Ass*, *Burewareton* 1255-6 *Ass*
Burwarton' 1225 Cur, *Burwarton* 1290 Ipm *et seq*, *Burwardon* 1498 Ipm
Borewarton' 1242 Fees *et freq* with variant spelling *Borewarton* to 1431 FA
Barewarton 1274 RH
Borwarton 1305 Ipm, 1349 Pat, *Boruarton under the Clee* 1327 Pat
Burewarston' 1242 Fees, *Burwarston* 1271-2 *Ass* (p), *Borewardston* 1331 Ch
Brewarton' 1291-2 *Ass*
Burwolton' 1291-2 *Ass*

Bourwarton 1359 Fine
Borghwarton 1369 Ipm
Burwayton 1581 PR(H) 2
Burton 1615-16 *PRChetton*
Burwinton 1761 PR(H) 17

'Burgweard's estate' or 'estate belonging to a fort-guardian', see the discussion of Broseley and Fig. 2.

Treverward in Clun is *Treboreward* 1284 Cl, and this is a Welsh version of OE *burhwardtūn.* The two settlements called Treverward lie 1-1½ miles E. of Offa's Dyke.

BUTTERY SJ 688171 DB Manor

Buterel 1086 DB
Buthereia c.1175 SAC, *Butereia* 1200 Cur (p), *Buthereya* 1226-7 SAC, *Butterie* 1655 SAS 1/XLVII, *Buttery House* 1700 PR(L) 13, *Buttery* 1703 ib
Botreye 1291-2 *Ass, Botereya* 1249 SAC, *Botereye* 1301, l.14th SAC
Butry Houses 1695 Morden

'Butter island'; the name is an oblique reference to the quality of the pasture.

This is one of five names in the Weald Moors which have ēg as first or second element, see Eyton and Kinnersley. One of the other names is Adeney (first recorded in 1209 P), a larger modern settlement than Buttery, occupying a more extensive area of raised ground to the N.E. Buttery itself can hardly have been more than a single farm, since its site is so constricted, but it was the centre of a one-hide DB manor with land for 2 ploughs. Adeney may have been part of this estate. Both places are now in the parish of Edgmond.

CALVERHALL SJ 602372 DB Manor

Cavrahalle 1086 DB, *Kauerhal'* 1255-6 *Ass* (p)
Chalurehal' 1219 SAC, *Calfrehall* 1255 RH, *Kaluerhal'* (p), *Caluerhale* 1255-6 *Ass, Calurehale* (p), *Calferhal* 1271-2 *Ass,*

Calverhalle 1284-92 HAC, *Caluerhale* 1291-2 *Ass, Kaluerhale* 1306-7 *Ass* (p), *Calverhale* 1308 InqMisc, 1315,39,99 Cl, 1337,46 Pat, *-hall* 1490 Ipm, 1654 *SBL 5305 et seq*
Callerall 1427 Cl
Colverhall 1672 HTR
Coverhall 1699 PR(L) 18

'Calves' nook', second element **halh**. OE **calf** has *-r-* in the plural; it could be nom. or gen. in this name, but 'of the calves' seems more satisfactory.

This could be one of the names in which 'dry ground in a marsh' is the likeliest meaning of *halh*; see the discussion of Whixall.

Calverhall was a township of Prees in 1843, when the *TA* for that parish designated it *Corrar.* The form *Corra* is still current locally. It was formed into an ecclesiastical parish in 1858, from Moreton Say and Prees. Modern maps show it as lying in the civil parish of Ightfield.

CANTLOP SJ 523058 DB Manor

Cantelop 1086 DB, *Cantilop* 1221-2 *Ass* (p), *Cantolop* 1255 RH, *Cantilup* 1255-6 *Ass, Kantelhope* 1271-2 *Ass. Cantelop'* ib *et freq* with variant spellings *-op(e)* to 1694 *SBL 9955, Cantelhop'* 1271-2 *Ass, -hope* 1274 RH (p), 1294 Ipm, 1334 SR, 1394 *SBL 6687*, 1416 AD, *Cantelhop* 1294 InqMisc, 1316 FA, *Cantilhope* 1315 Ipm, *Cantilope 1430 Fine*
Cantlopp 1579 *et freq* PR(L) 14, *Cantlop* 1613 *et freq* ib, *Cantlope* 1648 ib, 1672 HTR, 1702 *SBL 13394, Cantlap* 1702 *SBL 13457*

Cantlop is situated on a level shelf of ground overlooking Cound Brook. The final element of the name appears to be **hop** 'remote enclosed place', but it is difficult to discern the precise reference here. There is no possibility of the 'enclosed valley' sense which is the usual one S. of the R. Severn, and 'enclosure in marsh' seems equally out of the question. The only established sense of *hop* which seems possible in Cantlop is 'enclosure in waste'.

The first element presents more formidable difficulties. There appears to be no parallel in OE names for *Cantel-*. If there was evidence for the existence earlier than the 14th cent. of the word *cantle* 'corner-piece, slice, projecting corner of land' this would be a possibility; but NED thinks that this word and *cant* 'edge, border, nook' are borrowings from Romanic. NED similarly thinks that Welsh *cant* 'edge of a circle' may be a borrowing from medieval Latin.

DEPN hints at a connection between the first element of Cantlop and the river-name Cound; but it is not clear how any derivative of this British river-name could have become OE **cantel*. If it is English, the name is an unsolved mystery.

There are numerous place-names in France derived from a phrase which means 'sing wolf', conjectured to be used of places where wolves could be heard howling. This appears as a surname in England with such forms as *de Cantelupo, de Cantelo.* If the place-name had been transferred from France to Shropshire, in the manner conjectured for Caus and Montgomery, this would suit the spellings for Cantlop, allowing for some association of the final element with OE **hop**.

Cantlop is in Berrington parish.

CARDESTON SJ 395123 Ancient Parish (with Alberbury)

Cartistune 1086 DB
Cardel 1255 RH
Cardeston' 1255-6 *Ass et freq* with variant spellings *Cardeston, Kardeston; Cardiston* c.1291 TN, 1649 PR(H) 6, 1794, 1821 PR(L) 14, *Cardaston* 1674-5 PR(H) 6, *Cardestan* 1675-6 ib
Cardeton 1271-2 *Ass*
Gardeston 1430 Fine
Karston 1535 VE, *Carston* 1599 *SBL 7033 et freq* to 1675 Ogilby, *Cardeston als Carston* 1646 *Eyton, Carston alias Cardeston* 1655 SAS 1/XLVII
Carson 1577 Saxton, 1631 *SBL 6889,* 1714 PR(H) 6, 1695 Morden, 1750 PR(L) 20, *Carsonne* 1658 PR(StA) 4
Cardston 1706 PR(H) 18
Cardidston 1749 PR(H) 12
Caerdeston 1800 PR(H) 12

'Card's estate', *v.* **tūn**. The personal name would be a strong form of *Carda*, believed to be evidenced in *cardan hlæw* ('Carda's tumulus') in a Berks boundary-survey of A.D. 949.

The modern pronunciation is that represented by the spelling *Carson*. The form *Caerdeston* suggests modern association of the first syllable with Welsh *caer* 'fort'.

CARDINGTON SO 507952 Ancient Parish

Cardintune 1086 DB, *Cardinton' Templariorum* 1170,89 P, *Kardintona* 1185 Templars, *Kardinton' militum Templi* 1190 P, *Kardinton* 1221 *Ass, -ton'* 1271-2 *ForProc, Cardinton* 1271-2 *Ass,* 1722 PR(H) 16, 1750 PR(H) 14, *Kardenton'* 1271-2 *Ass* (p), *Cardynton* 1308 Pat, *Cardenton* 1655 PR(L) 9
Carditona 1185 Templars *et freq* with variant spellings *-ton, -ton'* to 1577 Saxton, *Karditona* 1185 Templars, *Cardyton* 1327 Pat, 1334 SR
Kartington' 1200 P, *Cartinton'* 1201 P
Cridinton 1243 Pat
Kardington' 1271-2 *ForProc, Cardyngton* 1397 Pat, 1535 *SBL 7180,* VE, *Cardington* 1559-60 *CornR.O. et seq*

'Estate associated with Card(a)', an **-ingtūn** name. The personal name is discussed under Cardeston.

CATSLEY FM SO 725796 DB Manor

Cateschesleie 1086 DB, *Catekesle* 1255 RH
Cackesleg', K- 1242 Fees, *Kachesleg* 1274 RH, *Kackesleygh'* 1291-2 *Ass, Cackesleye* 1346, 1428 FA, *-lee* 1399 Cl
Cacheleg' 1261-2 *ForProc* (p), *Kakele(e)* 1291-2 *Ass*
Kattesley 1431 FA, *Catesley* 1578-9 *RentSur,* 1617-34 PR(H) 17, *Catsley* 1657 PR(H) 17, *Cattsley* 1754 ib, *Cattesley* 1804 ib

'Cattuc's clearing'. There is some evidence for a personal name *Catta*, and *Cattuc* would be a hypocoristic form of this.

The *Cacheleg', Kakele(e)* forms are formally indistinguishable from spellings for Caughley in Broseley, but the contexts connect them with Catsley, which is in Kinlet parish.

CAYNHAM SO 553733 Ancient Parish

Caiham 1086 DB, *Kayham* 1255-6 *Ass* (p), 1265 Ch, 1274 RH, 1291-2 *Ass* (p), 1297 ChanR, *Cayham* 1291-2 *Ass*, 1314 Ch
Cainham 1255 RH (p), 1686 PR(H) 18 *et seq*, *Kainham* 1255-6 *Ass*, *Caynham* c.1291 TN, 1748 PR(H) 14 *et seq*, *Kaynham* 1291-2 *Ass*, 1334 SR, 1394 Pat, *Cayneham* 1672 HTR, *Caineham* 1747 PR(H) 16
Keynham 1255-6 *Ass*
Keningheham 1271-2 *Ass*
Kynham 1316 FA
Keyenhom c.1320 FFW
Caynam 1399 Cl, 1535 VE, 1577 PR(H) 18, 1741 PR(H) 16, *Conam* 1577 Saxton, *Canum* 1707 *PRShifnal*

There are several possible interpretations of this name. The final element could be **hām** 'village' or **hamm** in the sense 'land between two streams'. Caynham is between two small tributaries of Ledwyche Brook, but the situation is not so strongly in favour of **hamm** as is the case with Atcham and several other Sa names ending in -ham.

The first element might be a personal name *Cǣga*, but early forms without the *-n-* of the genitive are more numerous than would be expected if this were the origin. A significant term or an earlier place-name is more likely than a personal name to give rise to two forms of a compound, one in which it is uninflected and the other in which it is in the genitive. There are a number of other place-names which require a first element *Cǣg(a)* or *Cǣge*. Four of these - Cainhoe and Keysoe Bd, Cashio Hrt and Kew Sr - are compounds with **hōh** 'hill-spur', and it has been suggested (M. Gelling, *Place-Names in the Landscape*, p.168) that the word **cǣg(e)**, modern *key*, might have been used as the name of the hills at these places. If the hill crowned by Caynham Camp was called 'The Key', Caynham could have been alternatively 'Key village (or promontory)' and 'village (or promontory) of Key'. In this second variant the hypothetical hill-name *Cǣge* would have its genitive form, *Cǣgan*.

The ramparts of the fort, which are very steep on the south side, give the hill a highly distinctive outline. An OE word **cæg* 'stone, boulder' has been conjectured as a place-name element, but this does not suit the topography in the present case, and the *-n-* forms require a weak noun or place-name.

Cay Brook is a back-formation from Caynham, perhaps (though not noted in records till 1729) going back to the 14th cent., when the form *Cayham* was still current. In FFW, *Keyenhom* is said to be named from *Chastel Key*, built by Key, the seneschal of King Arthur.

CHARLCOTTE SO 638861 DB Manor

Cerlecote 1086 DB, *Cherlecote* 1195 P *et freq* to 1302 Ipm
Cherlescote 1255-6 *Ass* (p), *Cherlescot'* 1261-2 *ForProc* (p)
Charlcote 1274 RH
Chalcot 1695 Morden, 1768 *PRAstonBotterell*, 1826 PR(H) 17

'Cottages of the free peasants', *v.* **ceorl, cot(e).** The same name has become Charlcote in W and Charlecote in Wa. The social class called *ceorlas* occurs more frequently in place-names in connection with settlements called **lēah** or **tūn**: see the discussions of Charlton and Chorley.

CHARLTON (lost place in Shawbury parish) DB Manor

Cerletone 1086 DB, *Cherlet'* c.1177 *SBL 5403*, *Cherleton* 1249 *SBL 5409 et freq* with variant spelling *-ton'* to 1395 *SBL 16293*, *Cherleton' iuxta Shawebury* 1334 *SBL 5413*, *- infra Morton Corbet* 1425 *SBL 5421*
Cheleton 1217 (1285) Ch
Chorlet' 13th *SBL 5405*

'Settlement of the free peasants', from *ceorla*, gen.pl. of **ceorl, and tūn**. Eyton (VIII, p.250) says that this lost *Charlton* lay between Shawbury and Moreton Corbet, and near a tributary of the R. Roden. *Charlton Grange* is shown as a township of Shawbury on the 19th-cent. OS map indexing Tithe Awards. There is another

Charlton in the parish of Wrockwardine, for which the earliest form noted is 1121 SAC.

This place-name, which becomes modern Charl(e)ton, Carl(e)ton or Chorlton, was discussed by H.P.R. Finberg in *Lucerna* (London 1964), pp.144-60. Finberg assembled 95 examples, and the map on which these are plotted (p.145) shows the two Shropshire places as the furthest-west examples in the Midlands. His conclusion was that a Charlton was a settlement on a great estate whose farmers could be called upon for extra labour services. He cites Charlton in Wrockwardine as an example for which this meaning is especially appropriate, because Wrockwardine was a royal manor before 1066. It is not so obviously appropriate in Shawbury.

CHELMARSH SO 721878 Ancient Parish

Celmeres 1086 DB, *Chelmersh* 1331 Cl, 1651 *PRAlveley, Chelemessh* 1372 Fine, *Chellemerssh* 1384,9 ib, *Chelmershe* 1535 VE, *-marshe* 1577 Saxton, *-marsh* 1618 *SBL 6332 et seq, -march* 1670 PR(H) 1, *-mish* 1743 PR(H) 16, *-mesh* 1769 PR(L) 2, *-mash* 1799 PR(H) 17

Cheilmere 1228 Cur *et freq* with variant spellings *Cheylmers(e), -mers(s)h, -mershe, Cheilmerch, -mers(s)h* to 1494 Cl, *Ceylmerys* 1252 Cl, *Chealmers* 1274 RH, *Cheylmarsh* c.1291 TN, *Cheilma(r)ssh* 1311 Ch, *Cheylemerch* 1317 Ipm, *-mersh* 1327 Fine, Pat, *Cheilmarsh* 1344 Cl, *Chail(e)mersche* 1399 Cl, *Cheelmarch* 1713 PR(H) 1

Chemers 1250 Fees, *Chaumers* 1266 Ch, *Cheymis* c.1270 InqMisc, *Chaum's* 1291-2 *Ass, Chemarsh* 1695 Morden

Chelmermersch 1316 FA

Cheilesmersh 1330 Ch

Shelmershe 1552 Pat

'Pole marsh', from OE **mersc**, and ***cegel**, a word which is not on independent record but would be the equivalent of OHG *kegil.* Kelmarsh Nth is probably identical with Chelmarsh, but with *K-* from ON influence, Cheylsmore Wa is 'marsh of the pole'. It is possible that wet ground at these places was marked out with posts. There is no marsh at Chelmarsh now, but the large hollow occupied by the reservoir might have been wet ground in Anglo-Saxon times.

A manor of *Nether Chelmersshe* is mentioned 1379 Pat.

The place is mentioned in the text known as *St Mildburg's Testament* (ECWM 197ff), but the spelling *Cheilmers*, is a ME one, so is not cited here as the earliest form.

CHELMICK SO 468914 DB Manor

Elmundewic 1086 DB
Chelmendewic', Chelesmundeswiche 1208-9 *ForProc, Chelmundewyk* c.1240 (1292) Ch (p), 1301 SAC, 1326 Ipm, *-wyk'* 1255-6 *Ass, Chelmondwik* 1329 Ipm (p), *Chelmondewyk* 1391 Fine (p)
Cheilmundewik 1255 RH
Chelmwyke, Chelmeswyke 1397 Cl (p), *Chelmeswyk* 1410 Pat (p)
Chelmyk 1577 Saxton, *Chelmick* 1672 HTR, *Chelmyck* 1725 *PRHope Bowdler.*

'Cēolmund's dairy farm', second element **wīc**. Chelmick is in Hope Bowdler parish.

CHENEY LONGVILLE SO 420849 DB Manor

Languefelle 1086 DB, *Langefeld* 1087-94, 1130,55 SAC, c.1200 *ForProc*, 1272 Cl, *Langafeld* 1121-6 SAC, *Langafelda* 1138 SAC, *Langefeud* 1242 Fees, 1255-6 *Ass*
Longefelda 1142-6 SAC *et freq* with variant spellings *-feud(e), -feld(e)*; *Longafeld* 1155 SAC, *Longesfeld'* 1255-6 *Ass, Longeford* 1271-2 *Ass, Longefelde Cheyne* 1421 Cl
Longfeld 1592 PR(H) 1, *Cheyny Longveld* 1641 SAS 3/IV, *Longvield* 1663 PR(H) 17, *Longveld, Longvild* 1670-1 ib
Chenes Longvill 1577 Saxton, *Longvile* 1662 PR(H) 17, *Longa Villa* 1667 ib, *Longville* 1674-5 ib, *Longvel* 1715 ib

'Long stretch of open land', *v.* **feld**. This was a district-name as well as a settlement-name; Acton Scott is 'Acton in Longfield' in 13th-cent. references, and Longville in the Dale, nine miles NE, may mark the other end of the strip of territory to which the name was applied. Longville in the Dale is first recorded in 1271-2 *Ass.* Felhampton, which has **feld** as first element, lies in this strip. **feld** always implies a contrast with land which is not so easy of access. The contrast is often with forest, but in this case it may be with the high ground of Wenlock Edge.

The development of *-feld* to *-ville* is found also in Morville *(infra)* and in Enville St. It is due to a combination of voicing of *-f-* to *-v-* and association with the French word *ville.*

The affix is from the surname of Roger *de Cheyny*, mentioned as the owner in 1315 Ipm. Cheney Longville is in Wistanstow parish.

CHERRINGTON SJ 666202 Civil Parish

Cerlintone, Cerlitone 1086 DB
Cherintona 1155 SAC *et freq* with variant spellings *-tun', -ton', -ynton'* to 1428 FA, *Cherenton'* 1200 Cur (p), *Cherrinton* 1227 Pat
Chirinton 1235-6 Fees (p)
Chorrinton 1318 Ch
Cheryngton 1376 Cl, 1535 VE, *Cherington* 1535 VE, 1589, 1681, 1765 PR(L) 20, *Cherrington* 1786 PR(L) 13
Charington 1535 VE
Cheryton 1577 Saxton

Perhaps 'settlement by a river-bend', *v.* **tūn**. The noun ***cerring**, which has been conjectured as the source of Charing in London, would be a suitable first element, as Cherrington is by a bend in the R. Meese. The name could, however, be an **-ingtūn** formation with the personal name *Ceorra* as first element.

CHESTHILL (lost, in Moreton Say and Stoke upon Tern parishes) DB Manor

Cestulle, Cesdille 1086 DB
Chell'hull' 1203 P (p)
Chesthull' 1203-4 *Ass* (p) *et freq* with variant spellings *Chesthul, Chesthull(e)* to 1535 VE, *Chestull* 1428 FA, *Chesthull al*

Chesthall 1696 *SBL 4992*
Chisthill 1206 P
Chestehull' 1214 P
Chesterhill, Chesterhull 1230 P (p)

The first element is probably OE **ceast** 'strife, contention', noted occasionally elsewhere as the likely qualifier in names on parish boundaries. (There are several words with this sense which are used in place-names, the most frequent being **þrēap**). The second element is **hyll**, used as the generic in a cluster of names in this area, the others being Tern Hill, *Burnhull* and *Redehull*, which are discussed below. **hyll** must have seemed the appropriate term for the higher points in the blocks of ground above the 250 ft. contour which adjoin the valleys of the R. Tern and Bailey Brook.

The area surrounds the meeting-point of the ancient parishes of Hodnet, Moreton Say and Stoke upon Tern. It included Tern Hill (SJ 636322, *Hulle* 1232, 1331 Ch, *Terynhyll* 1520 AD, granted to Combermere Abbey together with *Chesthulle* in 1232) and Stoke Grange (SJ 631311), which is called *Chatsall Grange otherwise Stoke Grange* 1813 *SRO 327/1*, this being the last occurrence noted of the name *Chesthill*. The bounds of *Chesthulle* and *Hulle* are given in 1331 Ch. The boundary-marks are *Stratford, Grymbaldesweye, le Bromhock, Burnhull*, Helshaw, Wollerton ford, R. Tern, Bailey Brook, *Redehull*, the Long Ford. The references to *Burnhull* and Helshaw are to their bounds, so *Burnhull* (for which there are references from 1155 SAC to 1696 *SBL 4992*) is probably another lost settlement. The name may be represented by *Bran(t) Hill* in the Stoke upon Tern *TA*; the two fields so named are on the parish boundary at GR 662223. There is no trace of *Chesthill* in Tithe Awards, and of the names in the 1331 bounds only *Burnhull*, Helshaw, Wollerton, *Bulebrok* (assumed to be Bailey Brook) and the Long Ford survive or appear in later references.

The land-unit of Chesthill, with its two settlement-foci at Stoke Grange and Tern Hill, must have been divided up between Moreton Say and Stoke upon Tern. In DB there were two small manors, each assessed at a little over one hide. These were later combined to form half a knight's fee (Eyton VIII, pp.200 ff.).

CHESWARDINE SJ 720298 Ancient Parish

Ciseworde 1086 DB
Chesewordin 1159-60 RBE *et freq* with variant spellings *-wurthin, -wardin, -werdyn, -worthyn, -wardyn, -warthyn, -wordyn* to 1428 FA, *Chesewurda* 1160 *et seq* to 1170 P, *Chesewrthe* 1166 RBE, 1203-4 *Ass, Chesewurða* 1177 P, *Cheseworthyn alias Cheselworthyn* 1322 Ipm
Chessewrda 1162 P, *Chessewurdin* 1189 *et freq* with variant spellings *-w(u)rðin, -wrdin, -worðin* to 1230 P, *Chessewurdi* 1200 P, *-wrdi* 1201 P, *-wrði* 1202,3 P
Chesworthin 1210-12 RBE, 1284-5, 1346 FA, *-wardin* 1255 RH, *-wordin* 1291-2 *Ass, -wardyn* 1322 Pat, 1373 Fine, 1376 Cl, 1408 Pat, 1443 Cl, *-warthyn* 1333 Cl, *-wardyne* 1577 Saxton, *Cheswardine* 1662 *et seq* PR(L) 18
Cheshardine 1586 PR(L) 20, *Cheserdyne* 1609 ib, *Chessardyne* 1639 ib, *Chessardine* 1643 ib, *Chezadine* 1671 PR(L) 9, *Chesserdin* 1682 ib, *Cheserdine* 1716 ib

'Cheese-producing settlement', final element **worthign**, perhaps alternating with **worth**. This appears to be the only instance of **cēse** being compounded with a settlement-term other than **wīc**.

DEPN comments that the numerous spellings with *-ss-* might tell against derivation from *cēse.* Early *-ss-* forms have only been noted in the Pipe Rolls, however, and in that source an erratic spelling is liable to be repeated in subsequent years.

Chezadine represents the local pronunciation.

CHETTON SO 663903 Ancient Parish

Catinton 1086 DB, *Chatinton'* 1167 P
Chetintone 1210-12 RBE (p) *et freq* with variant spellings *Chetinton, Chetynton* to 1334 SR
Chetelton 1217 (1285) Ch (p), 1256 Ipm, 1271-2 *Ass*
Thedinton' 1223 Cur, *Chediton* 1291 Pat
Chetyton' 1255 RH, 1290 Ipm, *Chetiton* 1255,74 RH, 1295 Ipm
Chetilinton 1256 Ipm (p)
Chetyngton 1270 Ch *et freq* with variant spelling *Chetington* to 1421 Cl

Chetindon' 1271 Cl, *Chetyngdon* 1364 Ipm
Cheton' 1271-2 *Ass* (p), *Cheton* 1316 FA, 1722 PR(L) 8, *Chetton* 1397 Pat, 1535 VE, 1577 Saxton *et seq*

Probably an **-ingtūn** name, 'settlement connected with Ceatta'. The *Chetel-*, *Chetil-* forms can be explained as evidencing Norman French confusion of *n* and *l*.

CHETWYND SJ 735214 Ancient Parish

Catewinde 1086 DB
Chetewint, Chetewind 1200 Cur (p), *Chetewinde* c.1200 *ForProc* (p) *et freq* with variant spellings *Chetewind, Chetewynd(e)* to 1440 Cl
Chetwind' 1203-4 *Ass* (p), *Chetwynde* c.1271 *SBL 16196*, 1281 Ipm, 1428,45 Cl, *Chetwinde* 1272 Ipm, *Chetwind* 1284-5 FA, 1687 PR(L) 8, 1706 PR(L) 4
Chettewinde 1233 Cl (p), *Chettewynd'* 1291-2 *Ass*
Chedewind' 1242 Fees, *Chedwynde* (p), *Chedewinde* 1255-6 *Ass, Chedewynd'* 1306-7 *Ass*
Cheotewynde 1332 Ipm (p)
Chetewyn 1345 Cl (p), 1428 FA, *Chetwin* 1577 Saxton *et freq* with variant spelling *Chetwyn* to 1744 PR(L) 20, *Chetwen* 1590 ib, *Chettwyn* 1606 PR(L) 19, *Chetwynne* 1726 PR(L) 2

'Ceatta's winding ascent'. second element OE **gewind**, which is recorded as a translation of Latin *circuitus ascensus.* There was presumably a winding path up the steepish oval hill which extends south from Chetwynd Park. The word does not apear to be used in this sense in any other place-name. The preservation of -d is noteworthy, since the spellings from Saxton onwards indicate a local form with *-win, -wyn.*

CHIPNALL SJ 727315 DB Manor

Ceppecanole 1086 DB
Schipcnol 1255 RH (p), *Chipknoll'* (p), *Chypknoll'* 1291-2 *Ass*
Chippeknol c.1240-60 HAC (p), *Chyppenoll'* 1291-2 *Ass, Chippenol*

1337 HAC
Chupeknoll' 1255-6 *Ass* (p)
Chipnall 1577 Saxton, 1672 HTR *et seq*
Chippall 1695 Morden

Probably 'Cippa's knoll'. The first element could be the gen.pl. of OE *cipp* 'log', but this does not seem specially appropriate with **cnoll**.

Chipnall is a township of Cheswardine parish.

CHIRBURY SO 261985 Ancient Parish

(æt) Cyricbyrig s.a. 915 (c.1000, c.1050) ASC B, C
Cireberie 1086 DB, *Chirebiri* 1227 Ch *et freq* with variant spellings *Chirebir', Chyrebyr', Chirebur', Chyrebury, Chirebury, Chirebyr', Chirebiry* to 1334 SR
Chiresbir', Cheresbir 1226-8 Fees
Cherebiri 1227,9 Ch, *-bir', -by'* 1233 Cl, *-bir'* 1253 Cl, *-bur'* 1255-6 *Ass*, *-bury* 1277, 1317 Cl, *-bery* 1296 Ipm
Chyrbury 1272 LCA, 1277 Cl, 1641 PR(H) 12, *Chirbiry* 1287 Pat, 1332 Ch, *Chyrbyry* 1299 Ipm, *Chirbury* 1321 Pat *et seq*
Shirbury 1281 ChanR, *Shirbry* 1729 PR(StA) 6
Churebyry 1287 Pat, *Churrebury* 1301 Ch, *Churbury* 1629 PR(H) 8
Cherbury 1295 Cl, 1629 PR(H) 8 *et seq* to 1811 PR(H) 12, *Cherbrie* 1623-4 PR(H) 2, *Cherbery* 1644 PR(H) 3
Chirchebury 1352 SAS 2/III

'Church fort or manor'. The use of OE **cirice** in this name is surprising. **mynster** was the OE term for a church which served a wide area and was staffed by a community of monks, nuns or priests. St Michael's at Chirbury was the mother church for a huge parish, and **mynster** would seem the more appropriate term, rather than **cirice**, which is generally used in place-names for a church serving a single estate.

Another historical problem concerns the nature of the **byrig**. The reference in ASC is to the building of a fort here by Æthelflæd, the ruler of Mercia, in her war against the Norsemen. On the whole it seems likely that this fort was built somewhere within the large estate already known as *Cyricbyrig*, but it is possible that the name was newly coined in 915. Archaeological investigations have so far failed to locate the Æthelflædan fort.

The Welsh name of Chirbury is Llanffynhonwen, 'white-spring church'; this is first noted c.1566 *(Morgan Ts).*

CHOULTON SO 378883 DB Manor

Cautune 1086 DB
Cheleston' 1251 Fees, *Scheleston', Chefton'* 1255-6 *Ass*
Chelewichton' 1255-6 *Ass*
Schelton 1272 Ipm
Sulton 1290 Ipm
Chelton' 1291-2 *Ass*
Culedon 1315 Pat
Choulton 1577 Saxton, 1641 SAS 3/IV
Chaulton 1695 Morden

This is almost certainly a much-corrupted OE *scelf-tūn*, 'settlement on a ledge', a well-evidenced name which usually becomes Shelton, Shilton or Skelton; cf. Shelton near Shrewsbury *infra.* 'Terrace on a hillside' is one of the senses in which **scelf** is used in place-names, and this suits the position of Choulton, on the lower slopes of the hill crowned by Billings Ring.

The pronunciation represented by Morden's spelling is still heard locally. Choulton is a township of Lydbury North parish.

CLAVERLEY SO 793934 Ancient Parish

Claverlege 1086 DB *et passim* with variant spellings *-lai, -lay, -lega, -le(a), -leia, -legh', ley(e), -ly; Claverley alias Clarely* 1610 *SBL 15757,* 1636 *SBL 6435*
Chaverlega 1190 P, *Chaverlye* 1297 Cl
Clavereleye 1323 Ipm
Clareley 1361 Ipm, 1363,95 Cl, 1410 Pat, 1430,2 Fine, 1544 *SBL 4564,* 1547 Pat, *Clarley* 1460 *SBL 4214, Clarely* 1667 PR(H) 1
Calverleye 1366 Pat
Clorley 1550 Pat, *Clorely* 1611 PR(L) 1
Clearly 1698 PR(L) 4

Cloverley 1837 *SBL 4301*

'Clover clearing', *v.* **clǣfre, lēah.** The copious recording of the name may have preserved the long form against the competition of short forms such as *Clareley, Clorley, Clearly.* There is a local pronunciation [cla:li], though *Clarley* only occurs once in the spellings.

The same name has become Cloverley in Ightfield parish.

CLEE ST MARGARET, CLEESTANTON, CLEOBURY MORTIMER, CLEOBURY NORTH, CLEETON (in Bitterley).

All the names in this group are considered together because they are all derived from the Clee Hills. Four of them qualify for inclusion in the book by reason of being parishes and/or DB manors. Cleeton, which is of a lesser administrative status, has been included because its spellings must be taken into account when discussing the name Clee.

Clee is the name of two large massifs, Brown Clee and Clee Hill - or of three massifs if Titterstone Clee is considered a separate entity from Clee Hill. These massifs are a major feature of the topography of S.E. Shropshire. The settlements named from them are widely scattered, with 9 miles separating Clee St Margaret from Cleobury Mortimer, and 6 miles between Cleestanton and Cleobury North.

Clee was in origin the collective name of the hills, but the settlements are referred to in records earlier than the hills, and it is the settlement-names which supply the material from which the hill-name must be explained. The spellings for the settlements are laid out at the end of this article. There was also a forest of Clee, which Henry II gave to Walter de Clifford as an appurtenance to the manor of Corfham; the area of this forest was Brown Clee Hill and its surroundings. The forms of the name used in references to the hills and the forest will be discussed after a consideration of the settlement-names.

It may be stated at the outset that Ekwall's suggestion, in the 4th ed. of DEPN, of an OE **clēo* related to the recorded word which has forms *clīewen, clēowen, clēowe* and means 'ball', is the most satisfactory solution available for this name. OE *clīewen* is the ancestor of the modern word *clew.* What is required for the place-name is a related word which does not have *-w.*

It is possible to regard most of the varied spellings of Clee as deriving from OE **clēo.* There are no pre-Conquest spellings. The supposed **Ufere Cleobyrig* ascribed in DEPN (following Bowcock) to Cleobury North is a mistake. The name in the charter (S 786, the foundation charter of Pershore Abbey) is *Hleobyrig,* modern Libbery, Wo. The form in the Testament of St Mildburg, which is discussed below, is ME, not OE.

Despite the rejection of Ekwall's supposed OE **Cleobyrig,* the salient point to emerge from the spellings of the settlement-names is the persistence of some with *-eo-* from 1235 to the present day. Some of the DB and ME forms can fairly be ascribed to association with the word *clay*; but if OE *clǣg* were really the basis of the name there would have been no reason for it to have been sometimes spelt with *-eo-.*

In the west midlands, an *eo* spelling of 1235 should represent a pronunciation ø, developed from an OE diphthong *eo.* The diphthong could be long or short. The ø sound came to be pronounced like the vowel in Clee, but the spelling *-eo-* persists into modern times in a number of place-names, such as Beoley and Weoley Wo, Beobridge Sa, which are considered to derive from OE words containing *ēo.* The *eu, ue, u* spellings, seen in forms for Clee St Margaret, Cleeton, Cleobury Mortimer, are acceptable occasional spellings for this sound. Spellings of the 13th and 14th centuries with *e(e)* probably represent the treatment of *ēo* in the northern, east-midland and south-midland dialects, where its ME reflex was unrounded during the 12th century, as opposed to remaining a rounded vowel in the west midlands until c.1400. A name which appeared frequently in government records would be likely to be influenced by sound-developments outside its own dialect. DB spellings with *e(e),* however, are too early to be explained in this way, and are probably due to Anglo-Norman sound-substitution for ø.

Clai-, Cley- spellings, and perhaps DB *Cleie,* can fairly be ascribed to association of this unusual name with OE *clǣg* 'clay'.

The remaining spelling-type which occurs frequently is *Clie, Clya, Clia,* for Clee St Margaret. This is not incompatible with an

OE **Clēo*. Grammarians have noted that ø from OE ēo could occasionally become y̆, then ĭ, in the west of England (see O. von Feilitzen, *The Pre-Conquest Personal Names of Domesday Book*, p.65 and n.1). Some place-name spellings require this development, and Redmarley Wo is one of the examples cited. This name, which contains OE *hrēod* 'reed', is spelt *Rid-* in 1086, 1296, 1323 and 1431. It is possible that OE **Clēo* developed a form *Cli*, which was Latinized to *Clia*, *Clya*, or, in *Clie*, had the inorganic Anglo-Norman *-e* which is very frequent in place-name spellings.

The only spelling among those set out below which cannot be derived from an OE **Clēo* is *Cleaton'* 1334 SR. This may not be the only early spelling with *-ea-*. Eyton (IV, p.374) cites *Cleaton* as the surname of a juror in 1292 *Ass.* Abstracts from the Assize Roll which have been made for the EPNS Shropshire collection, however, present this surname as *Cleton'*, and Eyton's form has not been traced. The *-ea* spelling occurs again in *Clea St Margaret(s)* 1421 and 1549, but this could be a Latinized form of *Cle*, or in the case of the 1549 example it could exhibit the modern *-ea-* spelling for ME *ē*. It is uncertain whether this small batch of spellings, one (possibly two) instances of *Cleaton'* and two late ones of *Clea*, should be given any weight. They cannot be explained as regular derivations of an OE *Clēo(tūn)*, so they must either be dismissed as erratic or taken as evidence for an alternative OE form of the name Clee.

It is time to consider the main alternative suggestion to Ekwall's *clēo* 'ball' which has been made for the etymology of Clee, since this alternative suggestion leans heavily on the *Cleaton* spelling. It was put forward in 1965 by Betty Hill. In an article in *Notes and Queries* July 1965 (pp.141-5), Dr Hill pointed out that there was in OE a poetic by-form, *clēo*, of the plural word *clēa* 'claws', and that this would suit the phonology of the Clee names. She suggested that another toponymic use of this word is evidenced in the surnames of John *atte Cleo* and Simon *de Cleo*, mentioned 1332 SR, in Clifton-upon-Teme and Kyre Magna, Wo. M. Löfvenberg (*Studies on Middle English Local Surnames,* Lund 1942, pp.37-8) also considered this surname to derive from a local toponymic formed from *clēo*, which he renders 'claw, cloven hoof'. It seems to me more likely, however, that the people surnamed *atte Cleo, de Cleo* came from Clee St Margaret, 12-15 miles from where they are recorded, in which case this is not an additional example of the place-name.

The strength of Dr Hill's argument is that while (as noted above) most of the spellings for Clee are consistent with derivation from an OE *Clēo*, she can ascribe the occasional *Clea-* forms to derivation from the commoner form, *clēa*, of the word she considers to be the base. The weakness of her case is that 'claws' is a less convincing etymology for this hill-name than a word meaning 'ball'. She cites a history of Cleobury Mortimer which says that the parish has 'two claws or horns' which meet on the summit of Titterstone Clee; but this is not relevant as the author is speaking of the area of the parish, not the form of the hill. The two massifs of Brown Clee and Clee Hill are sub-circular, rather than claw-shaped. They have peaks which are encircled by hill-fort ramparts. On the top of Brown Clee and on its western flank are the forts called Abdon Burf, Clee Burf and Nordy Bank, all of which have a rounded shape. The peak on the north end of Clee Hill, which is the site of Titterstone Camp has, by contrast, a very sharp outline, but this is more of a 'nose' than a 'claw'. The singular form, *clawu*, of the word proposed by Dr Hill, and its contraction *clēa* (which can be sing. or pl.), are occasionally used in place-names, but apparently more frequently of a tongue of land between rivers than of a hill. There is no evidence in place-names that the anatomical term *claw* would have been felt suitable for the naming of a great massif.

Betty Hill's article gives useful details of the occurrence in two ME poems of a word *cleo* used apparently in the general sense of 'hill, mountain'. Both texts are in the same manuscript, which was written in the west midlands between 1256 and 1300. One is the *Poema Morale*. Six of the seven extant texts of this have in line 351 the word *cliue* ('cliff'); but the west midland manuscript has *cleo* substituted for it. In the same manuscript is another poem which contains the line 'So the schef is of the cleo'. This enigmatic remark occurs in an 'ubi sunt' context. It can, as Dr Hill says, be associated with the statement in Proverbs xxvii, 25, about the hay being gathered out of the mountains. These two poetic occurrences suggest the currency in the west midlands of a ME word *cleo* meaning 'mountain'. Betty Hill thinks the reference is directly to the Shropshire name Clee, but the hypothetical OE **clēo* 'ball-shaped massif' could perhaps have survived in west-midland dialect in its own right, as well as giving rise to the

Shropshire name.

The forms taken by the name when used for the forest and the hills are characterized by frequent association with the English word *cliff* and the formally similar but unrelated Latin word *clivus* 'slope'. Corruption from these associations has not, however, occurred in the earliest reference to the forest, which is a statement in 1199 P about the royal grant to Walter de Clifford of 'manerio de Corfham, et de Haie, et de Ernestrie, et Desclus'. The form *Desclus* has French *des* prefixed to a ME plural of the form *Clu*, which is evidenced in the spellings for the settlement-names. Not all references to the forest use a plural name: Hubert, forester of *Clya*, attests a charter of c.1230 in SAC, and the forest is called *Clive* 1285 Cl, *Le Clee* 1362 Cl. But most 13th- and 14th-cent. references have *-s*, whether or not they are using the 'cliff' version of the name. Forms include *Clyes* 1200 SAS 2/X (FF), *Clyves* 1259 Cl, *Cleyes* 1260 Cl, *Cliues, Clyes* 1274 RH, *Clyes* 1279, 1314,18 Pat, *Cleies* 1347 Pat. The name is treated as a Latin plural in *Clyvarum* 1357 Pat, *Clivarum* 1396, 1407 Cl.

The earliest reference to the hills occurs in the document known as St Mildburg's Testament (ECWM pp. 197ff), which has been edited and discussed by Professor H.P.R. Finberg. This document recites a charter in the names of Merchelm and Mildfrith, said to be the saint's brothers, of land some of which is 'circa montem qui dicitur Clie'. Professor Finberg regards this as a copy of an authentic charter of A.D. 674-704, and the general form of the document is strongly in favour of that; but the place-name spellings, including *Clie*, have been 'modernised' either by the late-11th-cent. author of the saint's life or by the 13th-cent. copyist. (Another form from this charter is discussed under Chelmarsh).

Two other early references to the hills occur in 1230 Cur, where there is a reference to all the lands of Wenlock Priory which lie 'circa Clivas', and in 1292 QW. The last source has an account of John Giffard being questioned about his free chase in his manors of *Corpham* (*sic* print) and *Cleya.* The text then states 'Et Johannis ven' et dicit quod Cleya est quidam mons infra predictum manerium'. Later references to the hills include *the Cle Hilles* c.1540 Leland, *Lesclives alias Cley alias Cleys alias Browne Clee* c.1612 *SBL 15691, The Clee* 1650 *et freq* to 1693 PR(H) 9, *The Clee* 1664 ib, *Clea* 1743 ib, *Clayhill* 1766, 1770 *SBL 6110.*

There is a second discussion of Clee in *Notes and Queries*

for February 1974 (pp. 44-6). In this, Nicolas Jacobs suggests that the origin is a Welsh loan-word from Latin *clivus* 'slope, hill'. As noted above, the gen.pl. *Clyvarum, Clivarum* in 1357 Pat, 1396, 1407 Cl suggests that some government clerks associated Clee with Latin *clivus* (though the gen.pl. should have been *clivorum*). N. Jacob's suggestion is not related to this ME manifestation, however. He bases his argument on the occurrence of a Welsh word *hirgliw* in the Canu Llywarch Hen, noting that I. Williams, the editor, interprets this as 'long hill', with second element **cliw* 'hill'. Jacob says that this Welsh word, adopted from Latin *clivus*, could have become **clīo* in OE, **clēo* in some dialects. Ḥe suggests that the name Clee is an English version of a Welsh name **Cliw*, and that *cleo* in 'so the schef is of the cleo' shows that the word was borrowed in its own right into the English language.

This argument may be logically defensible, but it is not convincing. We know a good deal about the British and Old Welsh place-name-forming vocabulary for hills.. Surviving English names contain more pre-English words for hills than for any other landscape feature. The word **cliw* is not an established element, as are *barr, blain, breȝ, brig, brin, crūg, mönith* and *penn*. The Latin word *clivus* does not seem specific enough to be a useful addition to the Welsh place-name-forming terms for hills, and a British name for a major feature like the Clee Hills might be expected to be older than the Romano-British period, and so less likely to incorporate a Latin term.

It seems to me most satisfactory to consider that the base of Clee is an OE name **Clēo* which means 'ball-shaped massif'. The hills might be thought of as 'ball-shaped' by contrast with the long, narrow massifs - The Long Mynd, Wenlock Edge, the Aymestrey Limestone escarpment, the Stiperstones and The Long Mountain - which lie between them and the Severn Plain. The Caer Caradoc range consists of discrete hills, but these are dramatically pointed.

The name Clee is obviously open to discussion and liable to alternative explanations. It appears to be unique. The first element of Clulow in Cheshire has been compared (PN Ch I, 165-6), but the spellings for Clulow require a word **clēow*, whereas for Clee it is necessary to postulate a form without *-w*.

CLEE ST MARGARET SO 565845 Ancient Parish

Cleie 1086 DB, *Cleia* 1221-2 *Ass* (p)
Clie 1199 P, *Clia* c.1210 SAC, *Clye* 1259 Cl (p), *Clya Sancte Margarete* 1255-6 *Ass et freq* with variant spellings - *Margerete,* - *Margaret* to 1339 Pat, *Clye Sancte Margarete* 1284-5 FA, *Clia St Margaret* 1346 Cl
Cl'ies Sancte Marg' 1255 RH, *villa Sancte Margarete de Clyes* 1255-6 *Ass, Clyes* 1259 Cl, *Clyes St Margaret's* 1285 Cl
Cle St Margaret's 1280 Pat, *Clee Sancti Margarete* 1334 SR, *Clee* 1361 Ipm, *Clee St Margaret's* 1416 AD, *Sainct Margeretes Cle* c.1540 Leland, *St Merget Clee* 1577 Saxton
Margar' Cleu 1291-2 *Ass, Clue St Margaret* 1298 Pat
Clea St Margaret 1421 Cl, *Clea St Margarets* 1549 Pat

The affix is from the church dedication. This place and Cleestanton are both called 'Clee' in DB. It is possible that there was at one time a large land-unit called 'Clee', which was later split into the parishes of Clee St Margaret and Stoke St Milborough.

CLEESTANTON SO 573792 DB Manor

Clee 1086 DB
Stanton' 1250 Cl, *Staunto'* 1255 RH, *Staunton by Buterley* 1290 InqMisc, *Staunton* 1291 Ch
Cleo Staunton 1290 InqMisc, *Cleostantone* 1324 *SBL 5234, Cleostaunton* 1347-8, 1435 *SBL 5236, 5238, Cleestaunton* 1384 *SBL 5441, Clestaunton* 1351 *SBL 5237, Clee Staunton juxta Buterley* 1431 FA, *Cleestanton* 1602 PR(H) 1

Stanton (in Stoke St Milborough parish) was probably a subsidiary settlement in a large estate called 'Clee'. The name Stanton is discussed *infra* with other Shropshire instances.

CLEETON ST MARY (in the parish of Bitterley) SO 606795

Cleoton 1241 SAS 4/VI (FF), 1387 Pat, 1389,93 Cl, 1397,8 InqMisc, *La Cleoton* 1290 InqMisc (p)

Cletone 1255 RH *et freq* with variant spelling *Cleton* to 1410 Pat, *La Cleton'* 1291, 1306-7 *Ass* (p)
Cleeton' 1291-2 *Ass* (p), *Cleeton* 1427 Fine *et seq, Ye Clee Town* 1696 PR(H) 6
Cleaton' 1334 SR
Cluton 1316 PW
Cleyton 1535, 1577 *SBL 7180, 5239*

'Settlement by Clee Hill', *v.* **tūn.**

The addition of the church dedication is first noted in a directory of 1885. It was possibly made when Cleton became an ecclesiastical parish in 1879.

CLEOBURY MORTIMER SO 674757 Ancient Parish

Claiberie 1086 DB, *Claib'i* 1167 P, *Claiberi* 1201 SAS 2/X (FF), *Claibur'* 1242 Fees, *Claybir* 1266 Ch
Cleberie 1086 DB, *Clebury Mortimer* c.1270 InqMisc *et freq* with variant spelling - *Mortymer* to 1385 Fine, *Clebir'* 1235-6 Fees, *Cleburi Mortimer* 1287 Cl, *Clebury* 1300 Pat *et freq* to 1382 Cl, *Mortimers Clebyri* c.1540 Leland, *Cleburie Mortymer* 1552 Pat, *Cleberye* 1577 Saxton
Cleybur' 1242 Fees, *Cleybir* 1251 ib, *Cleybur' Mortem'* 1255 RH, *Cleibiry, Cleybiry, Cleybury* 1256 Pat, *vill' de Cleybur' Mortum' et Cleybur' Foreyn* 1291-2 *Ass, Cleybury Mortymer* 1291 *Ass, Cleybiry Mortimer* 1301 Pat, *Cleybury* 1303 Ipm
Cleobr' 1235-6 Fees, *Cleobury Mortymer* 1315 Pat, 1338 Cl, 1382 Fine, *Cloebury Mortimer* 1333 Ipm, *Cleobury* 1360 Cl *et seq, Cleobery Mortimer* 1382 Fine, *Cleobury Mortemer* 1387 Pat, *Cleobery* 1425 Cl, *Cleobury Mortimer* 1666 *SBL 6387, Mortimers Cleobury* 1690 *SBL 6335*, 1739-40 *PRLudford*, 1766 PR(H) 13
Clubury 1356 Cl
Clyberye Mortimer 1535 VE, *Clibbury Martimer* 1586 AD, *Clibury Mortimor* 1626 PR(H) 3

'Manor by Clee', *v.* **byrig.** Ralph de *Mortimer* is named as the holder in DB; the surname (which is sometimes Latinized to *de*

Mortuo Mare) is derived from Mortemer in Seine-Inferieure. In the 1291-2 *Ass* reference, the manorial affix is regarded as applying specifically to the town, and 'foreign', i.e. 'outside', is applied to the rest of the land-unit. (*Cleobury Farren* is listed in 1672 HTR).

Pronunciations include that represented by the spelling *Clibbury* (much the commonest local form), and one with the first element pronounced *Clee.* There is also a form with a diphthong which must be a spelling pronunciation.

CLEOBURY NORTH SO 623870 Ancient Parish

Cleberie 1086 DB, *Clebury North* 1283 Ipm, 1316 FA, 1334 SR, *Nortclebury* 1291 Ipm, *North Clebury* 1291-2 *Ass et freq* to 1714 PR(L) 14, *Northclebery* 1505 Ipm, *-burie* 1552 Pat
North Claibir' 1221-2 *Ass, Northclaibiry* 1222 SAS 3/VI (FF)
Northcleyburi 1255 RH, *Cleybiri North* 1258 Ipm, *Cleybir* 1267 Ch, *Northcleybur', Cleybyri North* 1271-2 *Ass, Cleybur' Nort* 1274 RH, *Cleyburi North* 1284-5 FA
Cleoburinorth' 1349 *SBL 6979, North Cleobury* 1696-7 *PRChetton,* 1741 *PRLudford, Cleobury North* 1753 PR(H) 1
Clybery North 1535 VE, *Clibbery North* 1702 PR(H) 18

Another 'manor by Clee'. For the use of *North* to balance the manorial affix of Cleobury Mortimer, cf. the discussion of Bridgnorth.

CLIVE SJ 515240 Civil Parish

Clive 1255 RH *et freq* with variant spellings *Clyve, Klive; Clyva* 1255-6 *Ass* (p), *La Clyve* 1255-6, 1271-2, 1305-6 (p) *Ass,* 1318 *SRO 2821/1, The Clive* 1585 *et seq* to 1808 PR(L) 12, *The Clyve* 1588 ib
La Cleve 1291-2 *Ass, Cleve* 1569 *SBL 5769,* 1577 Saxton, *Cleeve* 1589 PR(L) 12
Clyff 1499 Ipm, 1552 Pat, *Cliffe* 1695 Morden, *The Cliff* 1766 PR(L) 20

'Cliff', referring to the steepish slope on the south side of

Grinshill Hill. The name derives from *clife*, dat.sg. of **clif**. Some forms show the development to Cleeve, which is well-evidenced elsewhere in names from this source. The fairly frequent use of the definite article shows that the name continued to be meaningful, however, and this probably caused the current form of the word *cliff* to be used occasionally. The modern pronunciation is [kliv], by contrast with Clive in Cheshire, which is [klaiv] (PN Ch 2, 234-5).

DEPN quotes a spelling from 1176 P, but this belongs to King's Cliffe, Nth.

CLUN SO 300806 Ancient Parish

Clune 1086 DB *et freq* from 1160 P to c.1540 Leland, *Cluna* c.1160 SAC (p), 1255 RH, *Clun* c.1540 Leland, 1577 Saxton, 1742 PR(H) 18
Clone 1199-1200 RBE, 1255 RH, 1272 Cl *et freq* to 1658 *SBL 6561, Clon* 1535 VE
Cloune 1242 Fees, 1255 RH, 1272,95 Cl, 1302,5 Ipm, 1333,54 Pat, 1343 Cl, *Cloun alias Clune* 1272 Ipm, *Cloon, Cloun* 1322 Cl, *Cloun* 1455 Cl
Clawne 1267 Ipm
Clunne 1500 Ipm, 1641 SAS 3/IV, c.1540 Leland, 1586 PR(H) 2, 1625 PR(H) 18, *Clunn* 1670 PR(H) 8, 1672 HTR, 1675 Ogilby, 1685 *et seq* PR(H) 13, 1774 PR(H) 8
Klwne 1613 PR(StA) 4

Originally the name of the R. Clun, which gave name to two settlements (one later becoming Clungunford) and is the first element in Clunbury and Clunton. Spellings for these four names should be considered together.

Clun is derived from a British river-name **Colaunā*, of uncertain meaning. Other instances occur in Clowne Db, a lost *Clowne* and a place called Clumber near Worksop Nt, and (with an alternative development) in several examples of the river-name Colne. Jackson, LHEB p.309, gives the proximate source of Clun and Clowne as PrW **C'lūn*, OE **Clūn*. The long vowel of this form is represented by the ME spellings *Clun(e), Cloun(e)*. The vowel seems to have been shortened in all forms between 1455 and 1500.

Spellings with *Clon(e)* are more frequent than might have been expected with OE *Clūn* as the base. The DB spelling *Clone* for Clungunford can, however, be paralleled by DB *Done* for Down St Mary, D, which is from OE **dūn**. In 13th-cent. forms, *-o-* is an acceptable spelling for ŭ before a nasal, and the *Clone, Clon(e)-* spellings of 1200 onwards may indicate that the vowel had been shortened in one of the current pronunciations, though it remained long in others till at least 1455. This shortening is unequivocally shown in the *Clunn(e)* forms, which begin in 1500. There was no reason for the vowel to be shortened in the simplex name Clun, but shortening would be regular in the compounds Clunbury and Clunton, and in Clungunford when the affix had become part of the name; and these longer names probably influenced the development of Clun.

The Welsh form is Colunwy (*dref Golunwy, Colunwy* in the Brut y Tywysogyon, s.a. 1233, 1263, *Clun alias Colunwye* c.1540 Leland). Jackson, LHEB p.688, thinks this is from an alternative British form **Colaunóu̯iā̯*, the suffix of which became *-wy*.

CLUNBURY SO 371807 Ancient Parish

Cluneberie 1086 DB
Clumbire c.1155 (1348) Pat, 1221-2 *Ass, Plumbiri* 1272 Cl, *Clombury* 1293, 1347,53,4 Pat, 1347 Cl, 1416 Fine, 1593,6, 1604 PR(H) 18, *Clumbury* 1376 Pat, 1716 PR(H) 17, *Cleombury* 1638 PR(H) 18, *Clomburie* 1623-4 PR(H) 2, *Clumry* 1684 PR(H) 16, *Clumbery* 1685 PR(H) 13, *Clummery* 1690,7 ib
Clounebur' 1242 Fees
Clunburn', Clymbire 1271-2 *Ass*
Clunbir' 1272 Cl, *Clunburi* 1272 Ipm, *Clunbury* 1316 FA, 1327 Pat, 1346 FA, 1360 Ipm, 1535 VE, *et seq, Clunberry* 1699 PR(H) 13
Clonbiry 1281 Cl, *Clonbury* 1381 Pat, 1397 InqMisc, 1431 FA, *Clonburie* 1658 *SBL 6561, Clonnbury* 1672 HTR
Clonebury 1289 Cl, 1334 SR, 1347 Pat

'Fortified site on R. Clun', *v.* **byrig**. The reference is probably to a manor-house, rather than to a major fortification.

The development of *-n* to *-m* in the *Clumbire, Clombury, Clummery* forms is paralleled in Clumber Nt, which consists of the same river-name and British *bre* 'hill'. It is seen occasionally in other names with *-nb-*, as in *Fembi* c.1115 for Fenby L, *Humbi* 1086 for Hanby L (both from DEPN).

CLUNGUNFORD SO 395788 Ancient Parish

Clone 1086 DB, *Clongunford* 1272 Cl, c.1291 TN, 1553 Pat, 1668 *SBL 8241, Clongoneford'* 1306-7 *Ass, Clongenford* 1316 FA, *Clongeneford* 1334 SR, *Clongonford* 1346 FA, 1397 InqMisc, *Clonegonford* 1397 Pat, *Clongoneford* 1416 Fine, *Clonegoneford* 1431 FA, *Clongonforde alias Clongonwas* 1492 Ipm, *Clongonforde alias Clongonas* 1587 *SBL 6411*

Cloune Goneford 1242 Fees

Cluna' Gonnef' 1255 RH, *Clunegumford, Clune Gunford'* 1255-6 *Ass, Clungonvert* 1272 Ipm, *Clungunford* 1291-2 *Ass,* 1327 Pat, 1641 SAS 3/IV *et seq, Clunguneford* 1327 Pat, *Clungunford otherwise called Clungunwas* 1500 Ipm, *Clungonas* 1577 Saxton, 1695 Morden, *Clungunhlow* 1647 PR(H) 18, *Clungonnas* 1690 PR(H) 13, *Clungunnas* 1691 ib, 1748 *SBL 2872, Clungunno* 1702 PR(H) 13, *Clungunnos* 1703 ib, *Clungunnus* 1778 PR(H) 2

Clyngeford, Clunigunford, Clungeford 1271-2 *Ass*

Longonas 1669 PR(H) 8, *Langunford* 1761 *PRChetton*

Clangonas 1797 PR(H) 17

Originally 'Clun', a second estate named from the River. The affix is the name of the TRE owner named in DB, *Gunward.* This personal name was probably interpreted as a place-name in *-ford* in the 13th and 14th centuries. There is a local form [gʌnəs], which consists simply of the development of the affix seen in such spellings as *Clongonas, Clungunnus.*

CLUNTON SO 335813 DB Manor

Clutone 1086 DB

Cluntune c.1155 (1348) Pat, *Clunton* 1302 Ipm, 1327 Pat, 1577

Saxton *et seq*
Cloton' c.1225 SAC
Clonton 1255 RH, 1267 Ipm, 1304 Pat, 1621 PR(H) 2, 1641 SAS 3/IV, *Clonton'* 1291-2 *Ass*, 1334 SR
Clinton' 1255-6 *Ass*, *Clinton*, *Clynton* 1271-2 *Ass*, *Clynton'* 1291-2 *Ass*
Clumpton 1272 Ipm
Clountone 1331 (1348) Pat, *Clounton* 1672 HTR

'Settlement on the R. Clun', *v.* **tūn**. Clunton is in Clunbury parish.

COCKSHUTT SJ 435293 Civil Parish

La Cockesete 1270 AD
Kackeshute 1427 *SBL 4028*
Cokshote 1549 Pat, *Cockshutt(e)* 1557 SAS 4/X, *Cockshot* 1577 Saxton, *Cockshutt* 1588 *SBL 3648 et seq*, *Cocshut* 1644 PR(L) 12, *Cockshut* 1688 PR(L) 7, *Cockshute* 1772 *PRCockshutt*

A *cockshoot* is a woodland glade where nets were stretched to catch woodcock. The word is fairly common as a minor place-name (*v.* ***cocc-sciete**), but this Shropshire instance is probably the only one which has become a parish-name. An ecclesiastical parish was formed in 1872 from Ellesmere parish, and this became a civil parish in 1896. Saxton's map of 1577 marks 'Cockshot Chap.', and this chapel may have provided a focal point for a small settlement.

The identification of the c.1270 reference is not certain. AD (I, p.323) catalogues the deed with a marginal attribution to Shropshire. It is a grant of two messuages and land in *La Cockesete* by Stephen Dorelot to Hugh le Vavassur. There are other places with this name in Shropshire, but Cockshutt in Ellesmere is the most likely to have contained messuages c.1270.

COLEBATCH SO 319871 Civil Parish

Colebech' 1208-9 *ForProc et freq* with variant spellings *Kolebeche*,

Colebech(e) to 1271-2 *Ass, Colebach'* 1271-2 *Ass,* 1334 SR
Culbach', Colbach 1306-7 *Ass, Colbache* 1416 Fine, *Colbach* 1641 SAS 3/IV
Cowbach 1577 Saxton, 1675 Ogilby
Coldbach c.1830 OS

Perhaps 'Cola's stream-valley', but there are other possibilities for the first element. *col* 'charcoal' would yield good sense in this heavily-wooded area. Stream-names and spring-names with Col(e)- are frequently assumed to contain the OE adj. *cōl* 'cool', but this word is not unequivocally evidenced in place-names. Assuming it does occur in some names, it might be less appropriate with **bæce**, which denotes the valley as well as the stream, than with such elements as **brōc** and **well**.

Colebatch became a civil parish in 1934.

COLEHURST MANOR SJ 662314 DB Manor

Corselle 1086 DB
Colsisel 1242 Fees
Coleshasel 1255-6, 1291-2 *Ass, Culleshesel* 1255-6 *Ass, Colsesele, Koleshesele* 1291-2 *Ass* (p)
Cunshesel 1291-2 *Ass*
Colshasel 1291-2 *Ass* (p), *Culsasel* e.14th *SBL 4543, Colshesel* 1346 FA, *Colshesell* 1428 FA
Colsesene 1291-2 *Ass*
Colleshull 1431 FA
C(h)oulhurst 1517 *SRO 327, Col(e)hurst, Cowlehurst* c.1566 *ib, Colehurst als Coosich* 1671 *SBL 4242, Colehurst Mill* 1813 *SBL 4303*

'Col's hazel-clump'; the tree-name **hæsel** is probably used collectively, like **alor** in Longnor. A similar combination of **hæsel** with an OE pers.n. is found in Badsaddle Nth. The spellings *Corselle, Cunshesel, Colsesene* exhibit Norman French confusion of l-n-r. *Colleshull* and the *-hurst* forms show rationalising substitution of more familiar place-name generics. The local pronunciation is [cɔlʌs].

DB *Corselle* has been identified with Cross Hills on the

boundary between Hinstock and Chetwynd (Eyton VIII, p.24). It is probable, however, that the spellings set out above all refer to the same place as the DB entry, and Colehurst in Sutton on Tern parish seems to be the correct identification. This was suggested by R.C. Purton in SAS 48, on the basis of forms from 1346-1623. The case is greatly strengthened by the inclusion of 13th-cent. spellings, and the identification is clearly indicated by the context of three Assize Roll entries. In 1255-6 and in 1291-2 the place is associated with Wistanswick, Sutton upon Tern and Goldstone, and a second entry on the 1291-2 roll refers to the vills of *Golston' et Colsesene.*

COLEMERE SJ 433327 DB Manor

Colesmere 1086 DB
Colemere 1157-72, 1246-53 HAC, 1255 RH, 1271-2 *Ass*, 1319 Fine, *Colemor* 1255-6 *Ass*
Culmere 1279-80 *RentSur*, 1316 FA, 1320,30 Fine, 1349,82 1440 Cl, 1351 Pat, *Culmer* 1449 Cl
Colmor' 1306-7 *Ass, Colmere* 1319 InqMisc, Pat, 1334 SR, 1337 Pat, 1349 Ipm, 1397 InqMisc, *Colmare* 1331 Ch, 1335,6,7 Cl, 1377 Pat
Culemere 1318 Pat, 1321 Fine
Coulmere 1577 Saxton
Coomer 1655 PR(L) 9, *Coumer* 1704 ib
Crowmeer or Coulmeer 1695 Morden

'Cūla's lake', second element **mere**. The lake is *acqua de Colemere* 1271-2 *Ass.* The form *Coomer,* in a parish register of 1655, represents what is still the local pronunciation. The rather high proportion of *Col(e)-* spellings may represent an alternative form in which the *ū* of *Cūla* was shortened.

Colemere is a township of Ellesmere parish.

CONDOVER SJ 495058 Ancient Parish

Conedovre (ter), Conendovre 1086 DB, *Conedovera* c.1090, 1121,55 SAC, *Conedome* (v.r. *Conedoure*) 1167 P, *Conedovere* 1280

SAC *et freq* to 1366 Ipm
Cunedoura 1130 SAC *et freq* with variant spellings *-our(e), -over(e), -ovre* to 1267 Pat
Condoura 1177 P, *Condovere* 1291 Ipm *et freq* to 1421 Cl, *Condover* 1494 Ipm *et seq*
Cunesdour' 1235 Cl
Candever 1252 Pat
Cunnedever' 1252 Cl, *Cunn(e)dovre* 1265 Pat
Conedor' 1255-6 *Ass*, *Conedore* 1364 Ch
Goundovere 1258 InqMisc
Condore 1416 AD, 1437 Fine, *Conder* 1577 Saxton, *Condor* 1584 *SBL 6631*, *Condover alias Condor* 1586 *SBL 7035*
Cundover alias Condover 1580 *SBL 6586*, *Cundover* 1614 PR(StA) 2 *et freq* to 1799 PR(H) 7, *Cundofer* 1642 PR(H) 6
Cunder 1597 *SBL 6674*, *Cundover vulgo Cunder* 1675 Ogilby, *Cundor* 1694-5 PR(H) 3

'Flat-topped ridge overlooking the R. Cound'. See Cound for a discussion of the river-name, and Wentnor for the second element, **ofer**. The ridge at Condover is a low one, and the configuration is difficult to appreciate in the village, but it can be made out on OS maps, and is clearly shown by the hachuring on the 19th-cent. 1".

The shortened form spelt *Cunder/Cundor* survives in local speech, together with the longer forms represented by the spellings *Cundover/Condover.*

CORELEY SO 613739 Ancient Parish

Cornelie 1086 DB, *Corneleye* 1255-6 *Ass* (p), *Cornileye* 1274 RH, *Cornilee, Cornele* 1291-2 *Ass*
Cornleg' 1242 Fees, *Cornleye* 1255-6 *Ass*, 1305 Ipm, *Cornlegh* c.1270 InqMisc, *Cornleg* 1271-2 *Ass*, *Cornlay* 1399 Cl
Corley 1255 RH, 1346 FA *et freq* with variant spellings *Corle, Corleye* to 1710 PR(H) 9
Coreley 1577 Saxton *et seq*, *Corely* 1685, 1705 PR(H) 13, 1710,14 PR(H) 9
Corneye 1305 Cl
Goriey 1362 Cl

Curley 1770 *SBL 10308*

This name must be studied in conjunction with three names which occur in a late 10th-cent. boundary survey of Knighton-on-Teme, which is a Wo parish, S. of Coreley. The survey runs from *corna broc* to *corna wudu* to *corna lith*, then along the *lith* to the other *corna broc.* The first *corna broc* is the modern Corn Brook, which rises high on Clee Hill and flows past Coreley to the Teme. The boundary runs up its southern part, leaving it where the county boundary does, N. of Aston Bank. OE *corna wudu* is represented on the 19th-cent. 1" map by *Cornwood or Knighton Common*, which has become Knighton Common on modern maps. The 'other Corn Brook' is presumably Trapnell Brook, which forms the N.E. boundary of Knighton. The hollow hill-side called *corna lith* must be a relatively slight feature between Knighton Common and Trapnell Brook. Another Wo survey, of Pensax with Knighton, Lindridge and Stockton, has *hrycges* ('ridges') about where *corna lith* would be, and refers to Trapnell Brook as *cornbæce.* The documents are S 1185 and S 1595.

The name *corna lith* in the Knighton bounds has hitherto been considered the original form of the name Coreley. It would be possible for **hlið** 'concave hill-side' to be replaced by the much commoner generic **lēah**; but on other grounds it seems much more likely that Coreley is a separate name which has **lēah** as second element and the same first element as the *brōc, wudu, hlith* and *bæce* mentioned in the OE surveys. The village of Coreley is nearly 2 miles from the county boundary, along which *corna lith* must have extended; and in this countryside the *hlið* cannot have been a dominating feature such as might give name to an area.

Coreley is 'cranes' wood or clearing'. The first element (as in the other names listed above) is the gen.pl. of OE **corn**, a metathesised form of *cran, cron*, which is the modern English bird-name *crane.* This is a fairly common place-name element, and may have been used of the heron. Corley Wa has the same etymology.

CORFHAM SO 525850 DB Manor

Corfan 1086 DB

Corfham 1159-60 RBE *et passim, Corffham* 1280 Pat, 1407 Cl, *Korfeham* 1500 Ipm, *Corpham als Corfham* 1651 *SBL 6315*
Corfam 1162 , 1255 RH, 1391, 1419 Cl, 1492 Ipm
Cofham, Coffam 1255 RH

The second element is probably **hamm** 'land hemmed in by water', here used of the long tongue of land between the R. Corve and Pye Brook. This use of **hamm** is found in The Home in Wentnor (GR 376902), so it was certainly current in S. Shropshire.

The first element is the river-name Corve. Land "iuxta amnem qui Corf dicitur" is one of the endowments in the testament of St Mildburgh (ECWM p.203), and this is the earliest occurrence of the river-name. Later spellings include *Corve* 1250 Fees (p), 1255 RH. Corve Dale is *Corvedale* 1255-6 *Ass* (p) *et seq, Corfedale* 1402 Cl, *Cordale* 1675 Ogilby. Corve is OE **corf** 'valley, pass'. In the earliest record the name belongs to the river, but it may nevertheless have been used originally of the long valley between Wenlock Edge and the Clee Hill, and transferred from the valley to the river. The loss of the pre-English name for this major river is surprising.

Corfham Castle is in Diddlebury parish.

CORFTON SO 498848 DB Manor

Cortune 1086 DB
Croftona c.1090 SAC
Corfton 1221-2 *Ass* (p) *et passim* with variant spelling *Corfton'*
Coistun' 1252 Cl
Corvdon 1339,44 Fine

'Settlement by R. Corve'. It is here assumed that printed forms such as *Corston* are scribal or editorial errors for *Corfton.*

Corfton is a township of Diddlebury parish.

COSTON SO 386803 DB Manor

Cozetune 1086 DB

Coston 1255 RH *et freq* with variant spelling *Coston'*
Costan 1255-6 *Ass*
Caston(e) 1272 Cl, *Caston'* 1306-7 *Ass* (p)
Corston' 1271-2 *Ass*

'Cott's estate', *v.* **tūn**. The personal name is not independently evidenced, but is believed to occur in a number of place-names. One of these, Cossal Nth, exhibits a similar early loss of *-t-*. Cossal is *Coteshale* in DB, but *Cozale* c,1200, exhibiting at a later date than Coston the Norman spelling *-z-* for *-ts-*. The single *Corston'* spelling is best treated as an aberration, since names containing W *cors* 'bog' (e.g. Corston So) keep *-r-* in ME and in modern forms. (DEPN mistakenly treats Coston Sa under a modern form *Corston*, but gives the etymology proposed here). The occasional *Caston(e)* spellings exhibit ME unrounding of ŏ, which is a regular dialectal development.

Coston is in Clunbury parish.

COTHERCOTT SJ 420016 DB Manor

Cotardicote 1086 DB
Codarchote 1204, *Codarcote* m.13th, 1464 HAC
Godardecot' 1261-2 *ForProc*, *Codardecote* 1301 SAC
Crodecot c.1291 TN
Cothercote 1549 Pat, *Cothercott* 1675, 1788 *SBL 13454, 6165*, *Cothercot* 1789 *SBL 6582*
Suddercott 1615 *SBL 3466*
Cathercott 1672 HTR
Cuthercote 1674 *SBL 3467*
Coddercott 1688, 1722,8 *SBL 3469A, 3451,3*
Coodercott 1689 *SBL 6058*
Cudercott 1735, c.1790 *SBL 3459, 6579*

'Cottage(s) associated with Cūðheard'. The OE form probably had a connective **-ing-**. The modern pronunciation is [kʌðəkɔt].

Cothercott is a township of Church Pulverbatch parish.

COTON SJ 531349 DB Manor

Cote 1086 DB, 1255-6 *Ass*
Coten' 1255-6 *Ass, Cotten* 1662 *et seq* to 1690 PR(L) 9, *Coten* 1684 *et seq* to 1690 ib
Cotone 1291-2 *Ass* (p), *Cotton* 1586-7 *RentSur et freq* to 1745 PR(L) 9

'Cottages', see Cotton *infra.* Coton is a township of Wem.

COTTON UPON TERN SJ 631278 DB Manor

Ludecote 1086 DB
Cota 1121,38,55 SAC
Coten 1271-2 *Ass,* 1284-5 FA, 1312 Cl, *Cotoun* 1371 Cl, *Coton* 1391 Cl, 1443 *SBL 16167, Cotone* 1395 AD, *Coten iuxta Hodnet* 1425 *SBL 6693, Coton' sup' Terne* 1427 *SBL 6599*
Cotes 1271-2 *Ass*

Eyton (IX, p.359) identified DB *Ludecote* with Cotton upon Tern because one of the two tenants in 1086 was *Thoci,* who is plausibly identified with the *Tochil* who gave this place to Shrewsbury Abbey (SAC, p.33). *Lude-* in place-names is frequently ascribed to OE *hlūd* 'loud' used of noisy streams (see Ludlow), but this seems impossible in the present case, so it is presumably the OE pers.n. *Luda.* This was perhaps a temporary affix to an originally simplex name.

There are six instances of the name Cot(t)on in Sa as well as a Cote House in All Stretton and several instances of Coates. All these are from OE *cot(e)* 'cottage', and probably all of them are plural. The neuter word *cot* had a pl. *cotu,* which could give the form *Cota* cited above for Cotton upon Tern. There was also a feminine form *cote,* pl. *cotan,* from which most of the ME and modern forms can be derived. Forms like *Cotes* represent a new analogical strong plural.

The affix *upon Tern* is not on OS maps. The place is in Stoke upon Tern parish.

COUND SJ 558050 Ancient Parish

Cuneet 1086 DB, *Cunette* 1240 Cl, *Cunet'* 1243 Cl

Cona 1221-2 *Ass*

Conet 1242,3 Pat, 1255 RH, 1271-2, 91-2 *Ass*, 1294 InqMisc, *Conet'* 1243 Cl, *Canet* 1271-2 *Ass* (p)

Cuned 1254 Pat, *Cunede* 1261-2 *ForProc*, 1271-2 *Ass*

Conede 1255 RH *et freq* to 1397 InqMisc, *Gonede* 1255-6 *Ass*, *Conode* 1416 Fine

Cunde 1351 Pat, 1577 Saxton *et freq* to 1750 PR(L) 19, *Cund* 1675 Ogilby *et freq* to 1798 *SBL 3549*, *Cund als Cond* 1690-1 *SBL 5230*

Counde 1397 Pat, 1535 VE, c.1540 Leland, 1750 PR(L) 14 *et freq* to 1809 PR(L) 2, *Counde alias Conede* 1397 Pat, *Cownde* 1535 VE, *Cound* 1571 PR(L) 2 *et seq*

Conde 1421 Fine, 1581 PR(H) 3, 1636 *SBL 5135*, 1705 PR(H) 16, 1768 PR(L) 2, *Cond* 1697 PR(H) 18, 1732 PR(H) 3, 1768 PR(L) 6

The two settlements of Upper and Lower Cound are recorded as *Nether Cound* 1571 PR(L) 2, *Over Cound* 1572 ib. Ogilby shows *Cund* and *Upper Cund*.

The name is that of Cound Brook, transferred to the settlement. There is agreement among philologists that Cound is the same river-name as Kennet Berks/W, Kennett Sf/Ca, Kent We/La, from a British *Cŭnĕti̯ŭ*, of unsolved derivation.

DB *Cuneet* suggests that the *ē* of the British name was preserved for a time in the second syllable. The modern pronunciation of Cound is [kund], and the vowel of the first syllable was probably u but *Counde* 1397 indicates an alternative pronunciation [ku:nd], with a long vowel, for the shortened name. This occasional pronunciation produced the fossilized spelling of the modern form.

CRESSAGE SJ 593040 Civil Parish

Cristesache 1086 DB, *Cristesech'* c.1200 *ForProc et freq* with variant spellings *Cristeseche, Cristeshech', Cristessech, Cristisech, Christesech(e), Cristes Ech(e), Cristeseck', Crysteseht,*

Cristeseht to 1322 Ipm, *Christesech alias Cressedge* 1665 *SBL 9927*

Crissege 1271-2 Ass et freq with variant spellings *Crisseg(g)e, Crishegge, Crysseth, Grissech, Cryssech, Crissech, Crissegh, Cryssegh, Chrissege* to 1627 PR(H) 6

Cristerdech 1284-5 FA

Cristeheggh 1316 FA

Cresseche 1323 Cl, *Cressyche* 1394 Cl (p), 1402 Pat, 1406 Cl, *Cressegge* 1397 Pat, *Cressege* 1416 Fine, 1421,40,70 Cl, 1653 PR(L) 14, 1684 PR(L) 2, *Cressedge* 1590 PR(L) 2, 1723 PR(L) 4, *Cressage* 1535 *SBL 7180*, 1623 PR(L) 2, 1670 *SBL 10144*, 1751 PR(L) 4, *Gressedge* 1577 Saxton, *Cresedge* 1675 Ogilby, *Cressich* 1690-1 *SBL 5230*, *Cressadge* 1693 PR(H) 15, *Cressidge* 1725 PR(L) 20, 1732 PR(H) 3, *Cresseche otherwise Cressedge* 1739 *SBL 4135*

'Christ's oak-tree'. The second element is *ǣc*, dative of **āc**.

The gen. of OE *Crist* occurs as first element in a few other place-names. In Chrishall Ess it is combined with **halh**, and in Crissels in Sandhurst Berks the second element is **hyll**. A lost *Aykcrist* in Culgaith Cu is a precise parallel to the Sa name.

Lady Oak (*Lady Oaks* 1675 Ogilby) is marked on OS maps between the straightened A 458 road and the disused Severn Valley railway line, N.W. of the village. There is an excellent account of this tree in A. Morton, *The Trees of Shropshire* (Shrewsbury 1986), pp.50-3. There is a young oak supporting the hulk of an ancient one, and successive replacements could have been occurring since Saxon times. Morton says that the tree stood beside the original winding road, and it is shown in this position on Baugh's map of 1808. It may have had a crucifix attached, and its position beside the Shrewsbury road would make it a suitable identifying feature for the settlement.

CRUDGINGTON SJ 632180 DB Manor

Crugetone 1086 DB, *Crugeton'* 1231 Cl

Crugeltona 1138 SAC *et freq* with variant spellings *-ton, -ton', -tun'* to 1.14th SAC, *Crudgelton'* c.1260 SAC, *Crugleton'* 1291-2 *Ass, Crugilton'* 1.14th SAC

Crucheltuna c.1140 SAC, *Cruchelton'* 1291-2 *Ass*
Crugeleston 1227 Pat
Crogelton' Hy 8 *RentSur*, c.1550 SAS 1/VI
Crougington 1552 Pat, *Crogenton* 1577 Saxton, *Crogiton* 1585 PR(L) 20, *Cruggington* 1588 ib, *Crogenton* 1589 ib, *Croginton* 1591 *et seq* ib, *Craginton* 1595 ib, *Crudginton* 1606,81 ib, *Chrudgington* 1626 ib, *Cro(d)gington* 1629 ib, *Crugington* 1641,70 ib, *Crudgeington* 1655 ib, *Crodginton* 1662 ib, *Crudgington* 1667 ib *et seq*
Crutchington 1692 PR(L) 20
Chrudson 1674 PR(L) 3, *Crutchson* 1701 PR(L) 9

The etymology suggested in DEPN, OE *crȳc-hyll-tūn* 'settlement by a tumulus-shaped hill', is strengthened by the *Crucheltuna, Cruchelton'* spellings from c.1140 and 1291-2, which were not available to Ekwall. The voicing of [ʧ] to [ʤ] is, as Ekwall comments, unusual in names containing **crūc**, but it now appears that there was another form in occasional use which exhibited the more usual development to Crutch-.

OE **crūc** (or **crȳc**) is a borrowing from PrW, where the word *crūg* was used of a hill, mound or tumulus. The word is frequently used in English place-names of a pointed, abrupt hill which resembles a tumulus in shape. The compound with **hyll** is well-evidenced, and is found again in Sa in Church Hill Wood near Pontesbury; but Crudgington may be the only instance in which the compound is followed by **tūn**. The reference is presumably to one of the small hills outlined by the 200ft contour to the E. of the village. The house called Crudgington Leasows is situated on a small hill, of abrupt outline compared to the surrounding contours.

Crudgington is a township of High Ercall parish.

CULMINGTON SO 494820 Ancient Parish

Comintone 1086 DB
Culmintone 1159-60, 1166 RBE, *-ton* 1195 P, 1756 PR(H) 14, 1772 PR(H) 3, *Culmynton* 1297 ChanR, 1324,49 Ipm, 1350,7 Pat, 1535 VE, *Cullminton* 1672 HTR
Colmiton' 1160 P, *Calmitone* ?c.1250 AD
Colminton' 1162 P *et freq* with variant spellings *-ton* and *-yn-* to

1549 Pat, *Colminton alias Colmyton* 1299 Ipm
Culmiton 1200-4 HAC, 1274 RH, *Culmyton'* 1291-2 *Ass, -ton* 1408 Pat
Culnynton 1347 Pat
Colmyngton 1350 Pat, *-ing-* 1665 PR(H) 15
Comyngton 1552 Pat, *-ing-* 1770 *SBL 10308*
Comyton 1577 Saxton
Culmington 1688 PR(H) 13 *et seq*
Cumington 1695 Morden

Probably 'estate associated with Cūðhelm', OE *Cūðhelmingtūn.* DEPN notes the possibility of a pre-English river-name identical with Culm in Devon, but the forms for Culmington strongly suggest an **-ingtūn** compound, and this makes a personal name the likeliest base.

DAWLEY SJ 687065 Ancient Parish

Dalelie 1086 DB
Dalilea c.1200 *ForProc* (p) *et passim* with variant spellings *Dalileg(h)', Dalile(g), Dalyle(e), Dalileye, Dalylegh', Dalyley* to 1428 Fine, *Dalliley* 1388 Fine, 1399 Pat
Daghele 1228 Cur, *Dahlegh'* 1301 SAC, *Dawley* 1559-60 *Corn.R.O. et seq, Dauly* 1685 PR(L) 14
Dilileg' 1255-6 *Ass*
Daghele 1228 Cur, *Dahlegh'* 1301 SAC, *Dawley* 1559-60 *Corn.R.O. et seq, Dauly* 1685 PR(L) 14
Dilileg' 1255-6 *Ass*
Dadele 1446 Cl
Dalley 1535 *SBL 7180*

'Woodland clearing associated with Dealla', OE *Deallinglēah.* Delley in Yarnscombe D has the same etymology, but Dawley Mx is a different place-name.

Affixes have been omitted from a number of the forms quoted. DB gives two entries for *Dalelie.* These are identified in VCH as referring to Dawley Magna and Dawley Parva, both of which are marked on OS maps to the S. of the modern settlement (the G.R. given above is for Dawley Magna). Dawley Parva was distinguished from 1208-9 *(ForProc) to 1271-2 Ass* by the addition of *Cumbray, Cumbreys, Cumbre, Cumbrey(e)*; and Dawley Magna has the affix *Panton', Pantolf, Paunton, Painton, Panton* from 1255-6 *Ass* to 1271-2 *ib.* These affixes refer to manorial owners. The use of *Parva* is first noted in 1261-2 *ForProc* (p), and that of *Magna* in 1271-2 *Ass.* Dawley Magna is *Great Dawley* 1611 *SBL 8432*, and occasionally in the 18th cent. Dawley Parva is *Litell Dawley* 1611 *ib, Little Dauly* 1685 PR(L) 14.

There is a local pronunciation [douli].

DETTON SO 667796 DB Manor

Dodintone 1086 DB, *Dodinton'* 1242 Fees, *Dodinton* 1272 Ipm, 1316 FA, *Dodynton* 1347 Cl
Dodyton 1255 RH, 1346 FA, 1353,4 Pat, 1416 Fine, *Dodyto'* 1255-6 *Ass, Doditon* 1274 RH (p), 1346 FA (p), 1393 Pat
Dodington 1284-5 FA
Detton 1576 PR(H) 17 *et seq*

Probably 'settlement associated with Doda', *v.* **-ingtūn**; The personal name *Dod(d)a* is well-evidenced in OE. Four other Sa names have the same origin as Detton. These are Ditton Priors, Dodington in Whitchurch, Earl's Ditton and Doddington in Hopton Wafers (two settlements sharing the same name) and Dorrington in Condover. Dorrington (not a parish or DB manor) is *Dudinton* 1255-6 *Ass* (p), *Dodinton'* 1255 RH, *Dodington als Dorington* 1619 *SBL 9078.* The other three names are set out *infra.*

In the country as a whole there are at least 20 instances of place-names deriving from OE *Dod(d)ingtūn* or *Dud(d)ingtūn.* They have the modern forms Dainton, Denton, Derrington, Diddington, Dod(d)ington, Duddington, Dunnington. They were discussed by Dr Gillian Fellows-Jensen in an article 'English Place-Names such as Doddington and Donnington' in *Sydsvenska Ortnamnssällskapets Arsskrift* 1974. Dr Fellows-Jensen argues that significant topographical terms, rather than personal names, are likely to be the basis of these and other recurring -ington formations, and that they do not all contain the connective **-ing-** used to link a place-name generic to a personal name or other first element. For the Doddington group she envisages an OE

dod* 'hill' represented by northern dialect *dod* 'rounded summit', and found occasionally in northern place-names such as Brown Dodd in Cumberland; and she would prefer to interpret the compound as formed by the addition of **tūn to an earlier place-name **Doding* 'place near a *dod* '.

A place-name Dodding is evidenced in Dorset, where Dodding's Fm in Bere Regis has ME forms *la Doddingg', la Doddynge, la Doddinge* (PN Do 3, p.274); but it is doubtful whether this justifies the assumption that it (or a similar **-ing** formation with *dod* as opposed to *dodd*) might occur five times in Sa. There is no evidence for the use of the place-name-forming suffix *-ing* in this county, unless it be assumed to occur in -ington names.

The five Sa names do not share a single characteristic geographical situation. Detton and Ditton Priors are on broad hill-shelves. Doddington and Earlsditton (which represent one instance of the place-name) lie on the steeply but smoothly descending slope of Clee Hill. Dorrington in Condover is on the side of a long, low ridge. Dodington in Whitchurch (now a street name, but formerly that of a township) is in low ground where abrupt small hills occur, and this example is probably the best-suited of the Sa names to Dr Fellows-Jensen's interpretation.

In the interpretation of these names there is a choice of basic assumptions: one, that some personal names, such as *Doda* and *Dunna*, happened to be fashionable at the same time as the practice of forming place-names with a personal name, a connective **-ing**, and the generic **tūn**; the other, that when a first element recurs frequently in a certain type of compound it is more likely to be a significant term than a personal name. These problems are discussed in Chapter 7 of Gelling, *Signposts to the Past*.

Detton is in Neen Savage parish.

DEUXHILL SO 697872 Ancient Parish

Dehocsele 1086 DB
Deukeshull' 1203-4, 55-6 *Ass*, *Dewkeshul* 1255 RH, *Deukeshull* 1271-2 *Ass*, 1342, 58, 89, 90 Pat
Dokeshull' 1291-2 *Ass*
Deuxhull, Dewxhull 1535 VE, *Deuxhill* 1544,92 *SBL 4564, 15767*
Deuxill 1535 VE, 1629 PR(H) 3, *Deuxell* 1633 ib, *Deuxcell* 1693

PRHighley, Deuxall 1725,30 PR(H) 13, *Deuxel* 1727 *PRChetton, Deuxil* 1735 PR(H) 13
Duckshill 1695 Morden
Dukeshill 1743 PR(H) 16, 1748 PR(H) 3, *Duke's Hill* 1764, 1805 ib

Second el. **hyll** 'hill'. The first el. occurs again in Sa in *Diowuces pæð*, a boundary mark in a charter of 963, which can be identified with Pave Lane S. of Chetwynd Aston. This is nearly 20 miles N. of Deuxhill. DEPN suggests that both names contain an otherwise unevidenced OE personal name *Deowuc*, and no other suggestion is available. Duxbury La may also contain *Deowuc*, but the available spellings are not early enough for certainty.

DIDDLEBURY SO 508853 Ancient Parish

Dodeleberia c.1090, 1121 SAC, *Dodelebur'* 1242 Fees, 1271-2 *ForProc, Dodelbur'* 1255 RH, *Dodelbury* 1318 *SBL 5426, Dodelebury* 1357 Pat
Dudeleberia 1138 SAC *et freq* with variant spellings *-beri, -bire, -bur', -byr', -bery, -bury* to 1298 Cl, *Dudlibur'* 1274 RH, *Dudlebury* ib *et freq* to 1549 Pat, *Duddelbyry* 1280 Pat (p), *Duddelebury* c.1291 TN, 1346 FA, *Dudulbury* 1346 FA, 1393 *SBL 15760, Duddelbury* 1346 FA (p), 1409 Pat, *Duddulbury* 1391 Cl, *Duddlebury* 1391, 1421 Cl, *Dudilbury* 1407 Cl, *Dudelbury* 1431 FA, *Duddleybury* 1549 Pat
Dudeneberia 1147-8 SAC
Dudesberia 1155 SAC
Dudelesberia 1194 P, *Dudelesbur'* 1221-2 *Ass, Duddlesbir'* 1230 P
Diddelbir' 1231 Cur, *Didleburie* 1552 Pat, 1626 PR(L) 6, *Dydlebury* 1611 *SBL 6375, Didlebury* 1677 PR(H) 18, 1777 PR(H) 8, *Diddlebury* 1688 PR(L) 4
Duddebir' 1255-6 *Ass, Duddebury* 1291-2 *Ass*
Dedilbury 1500 Ipm, *Dedilbery* 1504 Ipm, *Dedulbury* 1535 VE
Didlesbury 1577 Saxton
Delbury 1796, 1807 PR(H) 15, 1803 PR(H) 18, 1817 PR(H) 17, *Diddlebury or Delbury* 1803 Plymley

'Dudela's manor', *v.* **burh, byrig.** The shortened form Delbury is common in local speech.

DINTHILL SJ 429127 DB Manor

Duntone 1086 DB
Dunthull' 1200 Cur, 1291-2 *Ass*, 1316 FA, 1395 *SBL 16293*, *Dunthull* 1203-4 *Ass*, 1217 (1285) Ch, 1443 *SBL 15752*, *Donthull'* 1291-2 *Ass*
Dynthill 1544, 77 *SBL 4564*, *6473*, 1610 PR(L) 7, *Dyntell* 1618 PR(L) 15, *Dintell* 1620,65 ib, *Dintle* 1642 ib, 1731 *SBL 5296*, 1736 PR(H) 1, *Dinthill* 1672 HTR *et seq*, *Dintal* 1786 PR(L) 20
Dinede 1695 Morden
Dentall 1745-6 PR(H) 7, *Dental* 1748 ib
Dinhill 1767 PR(H) 7

Second element **hyll** 'hill'. The DB form is probably a simple mistake rather than an indication of an alternative name with **-tūn**.

The first element is not identified. The spellings make it clear that *dunt* is the OE form of it. The late development of *u* to *i* before *n* is a frequent occurrence in place-names, so the *y/i* spellings from 1544 onwards do not constitute evidence for the original vowel.

DEPN (s.n. Dinting) associates Dinthill with Dinting Db, and with Dent Cu and YW. Dinting may be a related name, though spellings with *Dint-* are much earlier than for Dinthill. The forms cited in PN Db are *Dentinc* DB, *Dunting(e)*, *-yng*, *-ynk* 1226-85, *Dontyng* 1285, *Dintyng*, *-ing* Hy 3, 1285. The forms for the two places called Dent in Cu and YW, on the other hand, suggest an original *din(e)t* or *den(e)t*.

There seems to have been an element *dunt*, found in Dinting Db and Dinthill Sa, but no suggestion is available about its meaning. The undramatic topography of the country W. of Shrewsbury is quite different from that near Glossop, where the Db place is situated.

Dinthill is in Bicton parish.

DITTON PRIORS SO 608892 Ancient Parish

Dodintone, *Dodentone* 1086 DB, *Dodintun'* 1160 P, *-ton'* 1161 P *et passim* with variant spellings *-ton*, *-ynton* to 1334 SR

Dudintona c.1175 (1348) Pat, *-ton'* 1212 AD, 1214 P, *-ton* 1255 RH, 1262 Ch, *Dudynton* 1271-2 *Ass*
Dodington' 1190 P, *Dodyngton* 1281 (1348), 1329,31 Pat
Dudington' 1230 P
Dodyton' 1334 SR, *Dodyton Prioris* 1346 Pat, *Doditon'* 1349 *SBL 6979*
Prioursduditon 1406 Fine
Ditton Prioris, Priorz Dytton 1535 VE, *Ditton alias Priours Ditton, Dytton* 1549 Pat, *Priors Ditton* 1577 Saxton *et seq, Dytton Priors* 1672 HTR, *Ditton Priors* 1833 OS
Dutton 1552 Pat

This is one of the group of names discussed under Detton. There are early forms with *Dud-* for this example, though *Dod-* spellings predominate heavily. *Dud(d)a* and *Dod(d)a* are regarded as variants of the same personal name, so the distinction is not a vital one.

Priors refers to ownership by Wenlock Priory.

DODINGTON Township S.W. of Whitchurch DB Manor

Dodetune 1086 DB, *Dodyton* 1347 Pat, 1397 InqMisc
Duthinton 1255 RH
Dudinton' 1255-6 *Ass, Dudinton* 1284 Ipm
Dodinton' 1271-2 *Ass et freq* with variant spellings *Dodinton, Dodynton* to 1421 Cl
Dudyngton 1347 Cl
Dodyngton c.1376 AD *et freq*
Dodyngdon 1443 Cl

See the discussion of Detton and Ditton Priors. No G.R. has been given, as it is not possible to say where the settlement stood. The name is shown on the 1863 1" map as that of a township.

DONINGTON SJ 809046 Ancient Parish

Dunnintune c.975 ASWills
Donitone 1086 DB, *Donitum* c.1145 SAC, *Doniton'* 1280 SAC *et freq*

with variant spellings *Doniton, Donyton', Donyton* to 1431 FA
Donnitona 1121 SAC
Donintona 1127,55 SAC, *Donyntona* 1138 SAC, *Donynton* 1190 (15th) SAC, 1315,56 Pat, 1316,46 FA, *Doninton'* 1242 Fees
Dunintona c.1155 SAC
Duniton' 1221 SAC, 1255-6 *Ass, Dunyton'* 1255-6 *Ass*
Donington subt' Brewode 1271-2 *Ass, Donyngton* 1315 Ipm, 1315,43 Cl, 1360,67,74 Pat, - *by Albrighton* 1371 Pat, *Donington* 1771 PR(L) 4
Dunningeton 1556, 1601 PR(L) 3, *Dunnington* 1601,82 ib, 1705 PR(L) 4, 1741 *PRShifnal*
Donnington 1675 PR(L) 4 *et seq*

'Estate associated with Dunna', OE *Dunningtūn.* Dr G. Fellows-Jensen, in the article cited in the discussion of Detton, gives more than 20 instances of this name, which she prefers to derive from an OE *Dūning* 'hill-place' + **tūn**. There are two other instances in Sa besides the one which became a parish. These are Donnington in Lilleshall (*Donnyton* 1271-2 *Ass, Dunnyton* 1577 Saxton, *Dunnington* 1740 *PRLilleshall*) and Donnington in Wroxeter (*Donynton* 1303 Ipm, *Donyngton by Wroxcestre* 1348 Pat). The spellings available for the parish name are much more numerous than for the other two, and the earliest of them is from a contemporary copy of an OE will. The evidence for *-nn-* is strong.

The affix 'under Brewood' refers to a St forest.

DORRINGTON SJ 731409 DB Manor

Derintune 1086 DB, *Derinton'* 1255 RH *et freq* with variant spellings *Derynton', -ton* to 1316 FA
Dorinton 1221-2 *Ass* (p), *Dorynton'* 1334 SR, *Dorrinton* 1600 PR(L) 18
Deriton 1255 RH (p)
Deryngton' 1291-2 *Ass*
Dorrington 1655 PR(L) 18, *Dorington* 1655 SAS I/XLVII

'Estate associated with Dēora'. Derrington in Ditton Priors parish has the same etymology; the forms for that name are:

Derinton' 1255-6 *et seq Ass, Deryton* 1271 *SBL 6973, Durrinton'* c.1275 *SBL 6952, Darrington* c.1612 *SBL 15691, Dorington* 1623-4 *Corn.R.O.*

Besides these two Sa examples, there are three instances of the name in other counties: Dorrington Li, and Durrington Sx and W. Gillian Fellows-Jensen (see the discussion of Detton *supra*) would prefer to derive all the names from an OE *Dēoring* 'deer-place' + **tūn**. A third Sa example taken by Dr Fellows-Jensen from DEPN, "Donnington Sa nr Newport (*Derintune* DB --)", is a ghost name. There is only one *Derintune* in the Shropshire DB, and that is Dorrington near Woore, the name under discussion here.

DUDSTON SO 244975 DB Manor

Dudestune 1086 DB, *Dudistun* 1255 RH, *Dudeston'* 1255-6 *Ass, Dudistone* 13th InqMisc
Dudinton 1233 Pat
Dudesdon' 1242 Fees
Duddeston' 1255-6 *Ass*
Dodeston' 1271-2 *Ass,* 1334 SR, *Dodiston'* 1291-2 *Ass, Dodeston* 1295 Ipm, 1375 Cl
Dudson 1629 PR(H) 8
Dudston 1631 PR(H) 8 *et seq*

'Dud's estate', *v.* **tūn**. Dudston is a township in Chirbury parish.

EARDINGTON SO 708907 Civil Parish

Eardigtun 1012-56 ECWM
Ardintone 1086 DB
Erdinton 1203-4 *Ass et freq* with variant spellings *-ton', -ynton* to 1271-2 *Ass*
Herdinton' 1226 Cur, *Herdington* 1284-5 FA
Erdington' 1228 Cur (p) *et freq* with variant spellings *-yngton, -ington* to 1705 PR(H) 3, *Eardyngton* 1535 *SBL 7180, Eardington* 1746 *SBL 9629*

Erditon 1255 RH, *Erdyton'* 1291-2 *Ass*, 1334 SR
Urdendon' 1261-2 *ForProc*
Yerdington 1594 *SBL 9603*, 1739 PR(H) 16, 1794 PR(H) 3, *Yardington* 1639 SAS 50, *Yeardington* 1672 HTR
Yearton 1631 PR(H) 15, *Yerton* 1743 (copy) *SBL 8894 C*
Eardindton 1695 Morden

'Estate associated with Earda'. Other instances of this **-ingtūn** compound have become Ardington Berks, Erdington Wa, and Yarnton O.

The earliest reference occurs in an account of the eastern boundary of the diocese of Hereford.

EARLS DITTON SO 629756 DB Manor

Dodentone 1086 DB, *Erlesdodinton* 1398 InqMisc
Erles Dytton 1566 *SBL 8384*, *Dytton* 1601 PR(H) 9
Doddington al's Ditton al's Erles Ditton Jas I *Corn.R.O.*, *Earls Ditton otherwise Doddington* 1770 *SBL 10308*

See the discussion of Detton. The affix *Earls*, which refers to ownership from DB onwards by the Mortimer family, is probably mainly for distinction from Ditton Priors.

A village named Doddington is situated three quarters of a mile N.W. of Earls Ditton, higher up Clee Hill, in the same parish of Hopton Wafers. Some early references (e.g. *Dodinton* 1316 FA, *Dodyton* 1431 FA, *Dodington* 1566 *SBL 8384*) could refer to either place. It seems likely that there was a land-unit called *Dodingtūn* which lay between Hopton Wafers and Coreley, and that there were two settlements in this unit bearing the same name.

EASTHOPE SO 567952 Ancient Parish

East hope 901 S 221
Stope 1086 DB
Estope 1166 RBE (p), *Estoppes* 1602 PR(H) 1, *Estop* 1659, 84-5 ib
Esthop' 1208-9 *ForProc* (p) *et passim* with variant spellings *Esthop(e)* to 1535 VE

Hesthope 1292 SAC (p)
Eastop 1577 Saxton
Yestope 1780 PR(L) 2

'East' refers to the position of the settlement in relation to a series of places whose names end in **hop**. It is difficult to give a one-word translation of **hop** in these. The settlements lie between the parallel ridges of Wenlock Edge and the Aymestrey Limestone escarpment. Part of the valley between the ridges is called Hope Dale. The settlement-names are Easthope, Wilderhope, Millichope, Middlehope, Westhope and Dinchope. They lie in funnel-shaped hollows the openings of which run through the Aymestrey Limestone to the R. Corve, except for the southernmost one, occupied by Dinchope, which faces W. through Wenlock Edge. Presthope, at the N. end of the series, is not in a valley now, but overlooks the broad end of an identical feature. Easthope and Westhope are not the most easterly or the most westerly of the settlements. These are Presthope (assuming it once lay in the valley which it overlooks) and Dinchope.

Easthope occupies the most spacious of the funnel-ends in the series, and it is the only one of the settlements to have become a parish, albeit a very small one. Millichope, Middlehope and Westhope, though not parishes, are in DB. Probably all the settlements are ancient ones, but the secluded and constricted sites prevented them from becoming administrative centres.

EATON

Eaton is a recurrent place-name compound which means 'river settlement or estate', from OE **ēa** and **tūn**. DEPN lists 23 examples (with one Eton and one Yeaton). As with other such compounds, Shropshire has more instances than other counties, but the distribution is not Shropshire-centred, as it is for Acton, so no attempt has been made at collecting and mapping the whole corpus. It is natural to suspect that the name refers to an economic function of the place, rather than being a simple statement about its geographical situation. If only the latter were intended it would be difficult to understand why some settlements by rivers have this name and not others to which it would be equally appropriate. It is possible that settlements called *ēa-tūn* had some special responsibility in relation to the river, such as controlling ferry services or organising water-borne transport.

There are six instances of the name *ēa-tūn* in Shropshire. These include four 'major' names, Eaton Constantine, - Mascot, and -under-Heywood, and Yeaton, the evidence for which is set out below. (Little Eton in Pitchford is here included with Eaton Mascot). Two instances of lesser administrative status are Eaton in Lydbury North parish, situated on the R. Onny (*Eton'* 1291-2 *Ass*), and Eaton upon Tern in Stoke upon Tern parish (*Eton'* 1255-6 *Ass*).

EATON CONSTANTINE SJ 599064 Ancient Parish

Etune 1086 DB, *Eton'* 1235 Cl *et passim* with variant spellings *Eton* to Hy 4 AD, *Eton Constantyne* 1535 VE
Catton Constentin 1199 (1265) Ch, *Eatton Constentin* 1217 (1285) ib, *Eatton' Constentyn* 1395 *SBL 16293*
Etton 1221-2 *Ass*, 1290 Ipm, *Ecton Constentin* 1284-5 FA
Eyton Constantyn 1498 Ipm
Eaton Constantyne 1615 PR(L) 20, *Eatonconstardine* 1655 SAS I/XLVII, *Eaton Constantine* 1730 PR(L) 4

Eaton Constantine was a very small parish, sandwiched between the larger units of Wroxeter and Leighton. It is now in the civil parish of Leighton. It was assessed at 2 hides in DB. The village is not beside the R. Severn, but the parish is bounded by the river, and the road S. from Eaton leads to the only road-crossing of the river between Buildwas, 3½ miles E., and Atcham, 4½ miles W.

The family of *(de) Costentin* appear in connection with this estate in the first half of the 13th cent. Many of the *Eton, Eton'* spellings summarized above have the affix, and forms with *Cos-* and *Cons-* are both common.

EATON MASCOTT SJ 538059 DB Manor

Etune 1086 DB, *Etun* 1215-36 HAC, *Eton'* 1242 Fees *et freq* with variant spellings *Etone* to 1583 *SBL 15799, Eton' Marscot* 1255 RH, *Eton Marhcote alias Marhscote* 1295 Ipm, *Eton' Massecote* 1301 SAC, *Eton Mascot'* 1334 SR, - *Marescot* 1346 FA, - *Mascot* 1397 InqMisc, - *Mascote* 1404 Fine, 1431 FA, - *Marescote*, - *Mascote* 1428 FA

Eatune c.1160-72 HAC

Eton' et Marscote 1255-6 *Ass*, *Marscote et Etone* 1291-2 *Ass*

Etton' 1291-2 *Ass*

Massecote 1.13th *ForProc*

Eyton 1583 *SBL 15759*

Eaton Mascott 1648 PR(L) 14 *et freq* with variant spelling - *Mascot*; *Eaton Marscot* 1781 PR(L) 1

Eaton Mascott is one of the four ancient townships of Berrington parish. It was assessed at 3 hides in DB. The Hall overlooks Cound Brook, which must have been considered worthy of the term **ēa** in pre-Conquest times. (It is called *lee Ree* c.1280 HAC and *Rea* in 17th-19th cent. sources, from ME *atter e* 'at the river'). S. of the Hall there are two places where tracks cross the brook.

The lost hamlet "variously known as Eton, Little Eton, and Eton juxta Pitchford" (VCH VIII, p.117) in the adjacent parish of Pitchford may derive its name from an ancient connection with Eaton Mascott rather than being an independent example of the place-name. It was assessed at 1½ hides in DB.

The affix to Eaton Mascott is from a tenant named *Marescot* to whom William FitzAlan granted the manor between 1135 and 1166 (VCH VIII, p.20). Marescot is frequently mentioned in HAC and is listed as a tenant of William FitzAlan in 1166 RBE. He has no surname in this list, but his descendants (e.g. Willelmus *Marescot* 1242 Fees, - *Marscot* 1274 RH) used his name as a surname. The references from 1255-6 and 1291-2 *Ass* suggest that government officials sometimes misunderstood the affix, taking it for another English place-name. A similar misunderstanding about the family name occurs in 1346 FA, in a reference to "Eton Marescot quod Willelmus de Marescot quondam tenuit". It is impossible to say whether the use of *Massecote* for the place in *ForProc* in the late 13th cent. is due to this misinterpretation, or whether it is an early instance of the use of a manorial affix without the place-name which it originally qualified.

EATON-UNDER-HEYWOOD SO 500900 Ancient Parish

Eton 1227 Ch *et passim* with variant spelling *Eton'* to 1747 PR(H) 15, *Eton' Prioris* 1291-2 *Ass*
Etton 1255-6 *Ass, Etton alias Eton alias Eyton* 1551 Pat
Eaton 1631 *et seq* PR(H) 1, *Eatton* 1737 PR(H) 15, *Eaton-under-Haywood* 1737 PR(L) 1

This Eaton is beside a large stream now called Lakehouse Brook, Eaton Brook, and Byne Brook in different stretches, which must have seemed big enough to be termed **ēa** in Old English. The parish is a large one, with several stream-crossings in its area.

Prioris because it was a manor of Wenlock Priory. The affix *under-Heywood* refers to a royal forest mentioned in 1250 Fees as *foresta de Stratton' et Heywode.* This name means 'wood with enclosures'.

EDENHOPE SO 158887 DB Manor

Etenehope 1086 DB
Edenhope 1272 Ipm, 1641 SAS 3/IV
Edenehope 1284 Cl
Ednop 1577 Saxton, 1611 Speed, *Ednopp* 1672 HTR

'Ēada's remote valley', *v.* **hop**. The pronunciation represented by *Ednop* is still current locally.

Edenhope is a township of Mainstone parish. The G.R. is for Upper Edenhope, which is named on the 19th-cent. 1" map, but not on later ones. Lower Edenhope is a mile to the E. Offa's Dyke runs between the two settlements and cuts across the eastern end of Edenhope Hill.

OE **hop** is used in a number of names along the line of the Dyke. Immediately N. of Upper Edenhope the earthwork passes between Hopton and Castlewright (DB *Cestelop*), both in Montgomeryshire.

EDGEBOLD SJ 458111 DB Manor

Edbaldinesham 1086 DB
Edbladenham 1271-2 *Ass*
Egbaldenham 1271-2 *Ass*, 1274 Ipm
Egebaldenham 1291-2 *Ass*, 1301 Cl, 1334 SR, 1336 Pat, *Eggebaldenham* 1365 *SBL 10762* (p)
Egebaldham 1337 Pat, *Edgebaldham* 1535 VE
Edgebould 1599 PR(H) 1, *Egboult* 1628 ib, *Edgbolt* 1649 SAS 4/VII, *Edgbould* 1686 PR(H) 1, *Edgebold* 1732 ib, *Edgboult* 1695 Morden, *Edgebolt* 1797 PR(L) 14

Upper and Lower Edgebold are S.W. of Shrewsbury. This name has to be considered in conjunction with EDGEBOLTON in the parish of Shawbury (SJ 575220) for which the spellings are:
Egebaldesham c.1190-8 HAC, *Egge-* c.1230-5 SAC
Egebaldeham c.1220-40 HAC (p)
Egebaldenham 1271-2, 91-2 *Ass*, - *iuxta Shawebury* 1292-5 *Ass*
Erchaldinham 1284-5 FA
Egbalde(n)ham 1291-2 *Ass*, *Edgbaldeham* R 2 SAC
Egebaldon' 1291-2 *Ass*, *Edgboulden* 1672 HTR
Eggebald 1495 Ipm
Edgebalton 1577 Saxton, *Edgbolton* 1645 PR(L) 12, 1687 PR(L) 20, *Edgeboulton als. Edgebouldenham* 1692 *SBL 5704, Edgebolton or Edgboulton alias Edgbaldon* 1720 *SBL 6536*

This is a double occurrence of the same place-name, applied to places which lie 10 miles apart. The spellings indicate a compound of a personal name *Ecgbeald(a)* with **hām** 'village'. It is surprising that this compound should occur twice in Shropshire, but no other explanation is available.

The two instances of the name have developed differently. Edgebold has suffered the loss of its final syllable. This development, which is specially characteristic of Shropshire, is discussed under Edgmond. In Edgebolton the final syllable was weakened to *-on', -en*, and because of the *-d* of *-bald-* it was possible to re-interpret the name as ending in *-tūn*.

EDGELEY SJ 557402 DB Manor

Edeslai 1086 DB, *Edesle* 1271-2 *Ass*
Eddesl' 1255-6 *Ass, Eddesleye* 1291-2 *Ass*
Edele 1271-2 *Ass*
Eddysley 1581-2 *SBL 5304*

Edgeley is a township of Whitchurch, and the name appears in its modern form on the *TA Map* of 1841, and on the 19th-cent. 1" map. The place is not shown on Baugh.

This is almost certainly the same name as Edgeley in Cheadle, Ch (PN Ch **1**, 248), for which there is an extensive run of early spellings which show the etymology to be 'clearing at or near an enclosed park', from OE **edisc** and **lēah**. There is another Edgeley in Ch (PN Ch **3**, 309-10), near Bunbury, for which the forms are not conclusive, but which probably has the same origin. The sparse early forms for the Sa name could be held to point to derivation from the gen. of a personal name such as *Ēad*, but the development to Edge- is in favour of *edisc-lēah*.

EDGMOND SJ 720195 Ancient Parish

Edmendune 1086 DB, *Edmundona* c.1090, 1138 SAC, *Eadmundona* 1121 SAC, *Edemundone* 1415 Fine, *Edmondon* 1690-1 *SBL 5230*
Eigmendona, Egmundun' 1155 SAC, *Egmendon'* 1167 *et seq* to 1209 P, 1306-7 *Ass, Egmundune* c.1175 SAC, *Egmenton'* 1189 *et seq* to 1200 P, *Egmendune* 1196 P, *Egmundon* 1227 Ch *et freq* with variant spelling *-don'* to 1316 FA, *Egmonden'* 1271-2 *Ass, Egmonden* 1318 Cl, *Egmondoun* 1391 Cl
Eggemendon', Eggemeton' 1177 P, *Eggemendon', Eggemandon'* 1230 P, *Eggementon'* 1230-1 MemR, *Eggemunden* 1317 Cl, *Eggemundoun* 1401 Cl, *Eggemondon* 1422 *SBL 16181*, 1455 Cl, *Eggemonton* 1491 Ipm
Egemendun' 1200 Cur *et freq* with variant spellings *-mendon', -mundun(e), -mundon', -mindon', -mondon, -mundon(e)* to 1535 VE
Cychmundune c.1240 SAC
Egemundesdon', Eggemundesden 1255-6 *Ass*

Hethemendon' 1267 Cl
Edgemundun 1284-5 FA, *Edgmindon* 1287 (1292) Ch, *Edgemonden* 1715 PR(L) 3
Echemundon' 1291-2 *Ass*
Eggmundon' 1294-9 *Ass*
Egremundon 1313 Cl
Egmyngdon 1322 Pat
Egmonde 1535 VE, *Edgemond* 1549 Pat, 1577 Saxton, *Edgemonde* 1596,7 *SBL 3463, 4675, Edgmond alias Edgmonden* 1601 *SBL 3464, Edgmount* 1695 Morden, *Edgeman* 1702 PR(L) 13, *Edgmont* 1706,32 PR(L) 4

Most of the spellings point to a compound of the personal name *Ecgmund* with **dūn** 'hill'. This compound was apparently formed without the genitival inflection; but it is possible that *-es-* dropped out of the name in the pre-Conquest period. The spellings with *-es-* from 1255-6 *Ass* may represent a form in which the gen. was preserved, but the Assize Rolls are not generally a reliable source of local variant forms. A few spellings, including the four earliest, suggest that the name was sometimes considered to contain the much commoner personal name *Ēadmund*.

The development is unusual in two respects. The spellings of the final element, *dūn*, show only occasional signs of the weakening to *-den* which might have been expected in a name of this length. In fact there are spellings with *-doun* in 1291 and 1401. But in spite of the preservation of the long vowel of this element, the name was eventually shortened by dropping the final syllable. This is a development especially characteristic of Shropshire, which has occurred also in Edgebold, Ercall and Fitz. It is probably due to imitation in local speech of the stress-pattern in Welsh names, where the main stress falls on the penultimate syllable. There are other instances in Wales: Borras in Denbighshire (e.g.) is *Borasham, Boresham* in 1315 (NCPW 196-7, cf. also H. Wyn Owen, *Nomina* XI, pp. 99-114).

The **dūn** referred to is the large area enclosed by the 250 ft. contour, on the east edge of which the village stands. This hill is a little higher than the 'islands' made by the 200 ft. contour in the adjacent Weald Moors, for which the word **ēg** is used in settlement-names.

EDGTON SO 387858 Ancient Parish

Egedune 1086 DB, *Egedun'* 1232 Cur, *Egedon'* 1242 Fees, 1291-2 *Ass*, *Egedon* 1271-2 *Ass*, 1397 InqMisc, 1431 FA
Eggedune c.1155 (1348) Pat, *Eggedon'* 1232 Cur, 1255-6 *Ass* (p), 1334 SR, *Eggedun'* 1255-6 *Ass*, *Eggedon* 1327 Pat, 1346 FA
Eggesdon' 1208-9 *ForProc* (p), 1306-7 *Ass*
Exedon 1255 RH, *Exton* 1399 Cl
Egindon' 1255-6 *Ass* (p)
Egeton' 1272 Cl
Heketon' (p), *Eketon'* 1272 Cl
Eggeton 1316 FA, 1327 Pat
Edgeton 1577 Saxton, 1788 PR(H) 14, *Edgton* 1667 PR(H) 17 *et seq*, *Edghton* 1772 PR(H) 8
Edgon 1610 *SBL 8424*, 1714 PR(H) 13, 1730 PR(H) 14, *Edgedon* 1675 PR(H) 2, *Edgedon* 1720 ib
Egdon Jas 1 *Corn.R.O.*
Edgston 1641 SAS 3/IV, 1687 *SBL 8462*, 1770 *SBL 10308*, 1801 PR(H) 2, *Edgeston* 1696 PR(H) 13, *Edgeston otherwise Edston* 1771 *SBL 6212*, *Edgestone* 1798 PR(H) 17
Edgson 1653 PR(H) 2, 1670 PR(H) 18, 1697-8 PR(H) 17
Edson 1676 PR(H) 8, 1727-8 PR(H) 2

'Ecga's hill', *v.* **dūn**. Spellings with *-s-* are heavily outnumbered, but it is noteworthy that they persist, from *Eggesdon'* in 1208-9 to *Edgston* in 1801. There may have been an alternative form derived from *Ecgi*, which is the strong version of the personal name.

The substantive **ecg** 'edge' (which is the source of the personal names) is rather rare in settlement-names. It does not seem a likely first element here as there is nothing distinctive in the topography which would warrant its use.

For the confusion of **dūn** and **tūn**, cf. Abdon.

EDSTASTON SJ 519319 DB Manor

Stanestune 1086 DB
Edistanston', *Edestaneston'* 1255-6 *Ass*, *Edenestanton'* 1291-2 *Ass* (p)
Edstanton 1376 Cl

Hedistaston 1484 Cl
Estaston 1577 Saxton
Edstaston 1672 HTR *et seq, Edsteston* 1674 PR(L) 11

'Ēadstān's estate', *v.* **tūn**. Edstaston is a township of Wem.

ELLERDINE SJ 609208 DB Manor

Elleurdine 1086 DB, *Ellewurd'* 1195 P *et freq* with variant spellings *-wurth', -wurthin', -wardyn, -worthyn* to 1.14th SAC
Ailwarthin 1233 Cl, *Eylwrthin* 1255-6 *Ass*
Elewarthin 1233 Cl, *Elewrthin* 1234 SAC, *Elewurthin'* 1261-2 *ForProc* (p)
Elwrthin 1234 SAC *et freq* with variant spellings *-wrthyn, -worthin, -warthyn, -wardin(e), -wardyn(e)* to 1680 PR(L) 20, *Elwardyng* 1395 AD, *SBL 15760,* 1398 Cl
Elleswrthyn c.1240 SAC, *Elleswrthin* 1255-6 *Ass*
Eldwardyn 1291-2 *Ass* (p)
Ellerdon 1577 Saxton, *Ellerdyne* 1586, 1632 PR(L) 20, *El(l)ardine* 1587 ib, *Ellerdine* 1589 *SBL 6512 et seq, Ellardine* 1655 SAS 1/XLVII, 1782 PR(L) 13
Elverdine 1585 PR(L) 20
Elladine 1653 PR(L) 20, *Ellwadine* 1689 ib
Ellwardine 1661 PR(L) 20, *Ellwerdine* 1705 ib
Edwardine 1722 PR(L) 20

'Ella's settlement', *v.* **worthign**; a township of High Ercall.

ELLESMERE SJ 398349 Ancient Parish

Ellesmeles 1086 DB
Eslesmere c.1150 SAC
Ailesmera 1177 P, *Eylesmere* 1271-2 *Ass* (p)
Ellismera 1177 P, *Ellesmere* 1204 P *et passim, Ellesmare* 1203-4 *Ass,* 1698 PR(StA) 2, *Ellismere* 1259 Pat, 1577 Saxton, 1655 SAS 1/XLVII, 1724,33 PR(L) 12, 1747 PR(StA) 2, *Elism'* 1581 PR(StA) 4, *Elismer* 1614 ib, *Ellismear, Elismare* 1726 PR(StA) 2

Elsemere c.1200 MM, 1601 PR(L) 9, *Elsemeare* 1703 PR(StA) 2
Elesmere 1221 Fees, Cur, 1255-6 *Ass*, 1549 Pat, 1623 PR(StA) 2, 1704 PR(L) 9, 1784 PR(L) 20, *Elesmear* 1714 PR(L) 9
Ellemere 1230 P
Elsmere 1516 (1773) *SBL 17285 et freq* with variant spellings *-mer, -mire, -meere, -meare, -mare* to 1750 PR(L) 10, *Ellsmere* 1760 *PRL.Wenlock*, 1775 PR(StA) 2
Alismore 1702 PR(StA) 2, *Alesmore* 1711 ib
Elmeare 1675 Ogilby

'Elli's lake', second element **mere**. This is the largest of the north-Shropshire lakes.

Ellesmere is much the commonest early spelling. The persistence of the variant *Ellismere* into the 18th cent. suggests that a trisyllabic pronunciation co-existed for some time with the disyllabic form clearly reflected in the spelling *Elsmere*. The name is always disyllabic now.

EMSTREY SJ 526105 DB Manor

Eiminstre 1086 DB, 1256 (1332) Ch, *Eiministram* 1155 SAC
Eministriam c.1090 SAC, Eministra 1155 SAC, *Eministra'* c.1226 Cur, *Eministr'* c.1248 SAC, *Emunstre* 1255-6 *Ass*
Alministra 1138 SAC
Hemenst' 1177 P
Eumistr' 1256 (1346) Ch
Emestre 1271-2 *Ass*, *Emuster* 1275 SAC (p), *Emystre* 1316 FA, *Emustre* 1334 SR, *Emustr'* l.14th SAC
Eymystre Hy 8 *RentSur*
Emstre Hy 8 *RentSur*, 1553 Pat, 1577 Saxton, *Emstry* 1631 *et seq* to 1776 PR(L) 14, *Emstrie* 1655 SAS 1/XLVII, *Emstrey* 1672 HTR *et seq*
Empstree 1553 Pat, *Empstrey* 1716 *et seq* to 1804 PR(L) 14, *Empstry* 1719 *et seq* to 1766 ib, *Empestry* 1721 ib
Yenstwey 1675 Ogilby

'Minster-church on an island site', from **ēg** and **mynster**. The order of elements, with **mynster** as the generic and **ēg** as the qualifier, should mean that the church referred to was at this site, but nothing is known of it. In DB Emstrey is a large estate of 9 hides belonging TRE to Earl Edwin, recently given by Earl Roger to Shrewsbury Abbey. It is in the parish of Atcham.

The 'island' is likely to have been an area of slightly raised ground in the flood-plain of the R. Severn.

HIGH ERCALL SJ 594174 Ancient Parish

Archelou 1086 DB, *Archalou* 1121 SAC, *Archalue* 1155 SAC, *Arcalewe* 1250 Cl
Ercalon c.1090 SAC, *Erkalon* a.1175 SAC, *Ercalewe* 1203-4 *Ass* (p) *et passim* with variant spellings *Erkalow, -loe, -lewe, Ercalu(we), -lowe* to 1.14th SAC, *Magna Ercaluwe* 1315 Ipm, *Ercaluwe Magna* 1316 Cl, *Erkalewe Magna* 1334 SR, *Ercalewe Magna* 1346 FA, *Erkallewe* 1.14th SAC, *Erkelowe* 1427 Cl, *Ercalowe Magna* 1431 FA
Hercalue 13th *SBL 4391*
Erkehale 1255-6 *Ass*
Erkalwe, Ercalwe 13th *SBL 3589,90* (p), *Erkalwe* 1304 Ipm, 1345 Cl, *Ercalwe* 1316 FA, 1332,34,98 Pat, *Ercalwe Magna* 1428 FA
Arcalwe 1323 Cl (p)
Hegh Arkall' 1390 *SBL 4416*, *Arcoll* 1535 VE, 1552 Pat, *High Arcall* 1577 Saxton, 1733 PR(L) 7, *High Arcoll* 1599 *SBL 6003*, 1784 PR(L) 6, *Higharkole* 1654 PR(StA) 4, *Arcol* 1695 Morden
Erkall 1394 Pat, *Miche Ercall* 1535 VE, *High Ercolle* 1546 *Eyton*, *Greate Ercoll* 1548-9 *SBL 4508*, *Ercall* 1549 Pat *et seq*, *Great Ercall otherwise Highe Ercall* 1569 *SBL 4509*, *Magna Ercall* 1669 *SBL 15748*, *High Ercall* 1710 PR(L) 8
Archaule c.1540 Leland, *High Erchal* 1658 PR(H) 3, *Archall Magna* 1703 PR(L) 8
Great Axole 1565 PR(L) 11
Earkall 1714-15 PR(L) 14

CHILD'S ERCALL SJ 665250 Ancient Parish

Arcalun 1086 DB, *Arkeluu* 1198 Cur, *Arkelawe* 1200 Cur, *Arkelun* 1205 Cur
Parva Erkalawe 1242 Fees, *-lewe* 1271-2 *Ass, Childes Erkelewe, -*

Erkalew 1294-9 *Ass, Ercalewe* 1310 Ipm, 1397 InqMisc, *Erkelawe* 1310 Cl, *Erkalow* 1326 Pat, *Ercalewe Parva* 1334 SR
Excalewe 1242 Fees
Hercalwe Parva 1255 RH, *Herkalwe* 1331 Ch
Childes Ercalwe 1333 Cl, *Parva* - 1316 FA, *Ercalwe Parva* 1346, 1428 FA
Childeserchalewe 1339 HAC
Childesarkeslowe, -erkeslowe 1397 Pat
Childes Ercall 1410 Fine, *Little* - 1449 Fine, *Chyles* - 1540 *SBL 6083, Childesercall otherwise Arkelowe* 1440 Cl, *Ercall Parva* 1698 *SBL 10383*
Arcall Parva 1535 VE, 1633 PR(L) 20, *Childes Arcoll* 1577 Saxton, *Childs Arcol* 1695 Morden, *Childs Arcoll alias Arcoll Parva* 1699 *SBL 13071, Little Arcoll* 1722 PR(L) 7
Childs Arkoe 1582 PR(L) 9, *Chields Arkhole* 1695 ib
Erchall Parva 1705 PR(L) 11, *Childs Archall* 1708 ib

High and Child's Ercall are 6½ miles apart. There is no reason to suspect an ancient administrative connection between them, but they share the same place-name, which is extremely well-documented. Its OE form can be reconstructed with a fair degree of confidence from the ME spellings, and it appears likely to have been **Earcaluw.* Many of the spellings show influence from OE **hlāw** 'tumulus, hill', but the *-lue, -luu, -luwe* spellings which occur for Ercall do not appear in names containing **hlāw**. (In a number of forms given above, scribal or editorial misreading has produced *-lun, -lon* for *-luu, -lou*).

The hill called The Ercall, adjacent to The Wrekin, lies 6 miles S.E. of High Ercall, 9½ miles S.S.W. of Child's Ercall. No early spellings exist for it. *Ercal* Wood is shown on the side of the hill on the 19th-cent. OS map, but apart from that the hill-name is not documented. This means that no ancient connection can be proved between the hill-name and the two settlement-names; but it seems likely that Ercall was a district-name used for a large portion of the Shropshire plain with this striking hill at its southern edge, and that the district-name became attached to the hill. It remains a difficult question whether the original reference of the name was to a district or to a settlement.

Ercall has hitherto been considered "an old Welsh name of the district" (DEPN), though Welsh scholars have recognised that it is not explicable in Welsh. M. Richards ('The Lichfield Gospels ---', *Nat.Lib. of Wales Journal* XVIII, no. 1, 1973, p.142) says "Ercal is the Anglo-Saxon form of an earlier Welsh name". Professor Richards was discussing the form *Ercal* which occurs in the cycle of poems known as Canu Heledd, which have been considered to date from c.850, but which may be considerably later. It seems at least as likely that *Ercal* is a Welsh version of an English name whose form is preserved more accurately in the series of records which begin with DB. Cf. what is said above about the references to Baschurch in these poems.

If **Earcaluw* were a hill-name, it would be explicable as a compound of **ēar** 'gravel', ?'mud', and a substantival use of the adjective *caluw* 'bare'. The latter word (modern *callow*) is generally cited as nom. **calu**, dat. *calwe*; but *caluw* is one of the recorded OE spellings. Use of the adjective as a substantive in place-names has given several instances of *Callow(e)*, and the Welsh use of *moel* may be compared. The word *ēar* is only recorded in OE as the name of a rune, and its precise meaning is not known. It is cognate with ON *aurr* 'gravel, loam' and Swedish *ör* 'gravel', and it occurs in the place-names Earith Hu, Erith K and Yarmouth Wt. A compound of a geological term with *caluw* 'bare hill' might suit the settlement-site of High Ercall, which stands among low hills. It may be tentatively suggested that the name was applied originally to this settlement and then became the name of a district bounded by The Ercall. The stanza of Canu Heledd in which the name occurs says that "the sod of Ercall is on brave men", and this could be interpreted as showing that in Welsh tradition Ercall was a district rather than a settlement.

The spelling *Arcall* represents the modern pronunciation. The spellings *Archaule* c.1540, *Erchal* 1658, *Archall* 1703 (H. Ercall) and *Erchall* 1705, *Archall* 1708 (C. Ercall) suggest that there was a variant local form with [ʧ]. (Early ME spellings with *-ch-* have no significance in this respect, as at that date the spelling was occasionally used for [k]).

The loss of the final syllable, first evidenced in the late 14th cent., should be compared with the development of Edgebold, Edgmond and Fitz. The spelling *Ercal* in Canu Heledd suggests that this happened at a much earlier date in Welsh speech.

As regards the affixes used to distinguish High and Child's Ercall, *Magna/Parva* and *Great/Little* are self-explanatory. *High* is synonymous with *Great*, as is *Miche* ('much'). *Child's* has not been explained. The settlement belonged to the Strange family, and ME *child* 'young nobleman' could refer to a junior member of that. The same affix occurs in Childswickham Gl, and there also it is not precisely accounted for.

EUDON BURNELL and EUDON GEORGE

SO 699893, 689890 DB Manors

Eldone (*bis*) 1086 DB
Eudon' 1242 Fees *et freq* with variant spellings *-don(e), -doun* to 1790 *PRChetton, Ewdon* 1416 AD, 1421 Cl, 1624,31 *PRChetton, Ewden* 1592 *SBL 6130*, 1672 HTR, 1787 *SBL 15728*
Euthon 1269 Ch
Yowden 1579 *RentSur*

'Yew hill', *v*. **īw, dūn**. Forms for both settlements have been amalgamated in the above summary, as there is no doubt that these neighbouring villages in the parish of Chetton share the same name. There was probably at one time a single land-unit which took its name from the hill at Eudon George, which is a typical **dūn**.

The surviving affixes, Burnell and George, refer to the families of Robert *Burnel*, mentioned in this connection 1269 Ch, and William *de Sancto Georgio*, who is named as the tenant in 1242 Fees.

Eudon Burnell was earlier *Eudon' Maleseuers* 1242 Fees, -*Maleseveres* 1255 RH, - *Malesoueres* 1272 Cl. The affix *Burnel* first appears in *Eudon Burnel* 1315 Ipm, and is frequent after that.

Eudon George was *Ewdensauvage* c.1270 InqMisc, *Eudone Sauvage* 1301 SAC. This affix, from the family-name which appears also in Neen Savage, overlaps with the later one, which occurs in *Eudon' Sancti Georg'* 1274 RH, *Eudon Jory* 1316 FA, *-Seint George* 1362 Fine, *Ewdon George* 1631 *PRChetton, Eudon George* 1712-13 *ib.*

PRChetton mentions *Nether Ewdon* 1606, *Lower Eudon* 1790 (? E. Burnell), and *Over Ewdon* 1624 (? E. George). There was also a *Eudon' Clement* 1271-2 *Ass.*

EYTON

Shropshire has five instances of this name, which is a compound of OE **ēg** 'island, dry ground in marsh' sometimes 'promontory', and **tūn**. Elsewhere in England, the compound has more frequently given modern Eaton, and care has to be exercised in distinguishing between those Eatons which derive from *ēg-tūn* and those which mean 'river-estate', OE *ēa-tūn*. In Shropshire the distinction is not difficult, as can be seen by comparing the spellings for names discussed under Eaton with those set out here. Two parishes, Baschurch and Lydbury North, contain both an *ēa-tūn* and an *ēg-tūn*, and Eyton on Severn and Eaton Constantine are less than 2 miles apart, so the difference in form and meaning must have been clearly appreciated in this county.

Four of the Shropshire *ēg-tūn* names belong to parishes and/or DB manors, and these are set out below. The Shropshire place with lesser administrative status which bears this name is Eyton in Lydbury North (SO 372876). This is *Eton'* 1251 Fees, *Eyton'* 1255 RH, 1291-2 *Ass*, 1334 SR, *Eyton* 1271-2 *Ass*, 1641 SAS 3/IV, *Eton* 1272 Ipm, 1316 FA, *Etone* 1291-2 *Ass*, *Eyton alias Yeton* 1547 Pat. The settlement here is above the 600 ft. contour, an unusually high position for a name containing *ēg*, but the word is sometimes used for a high promontory between streams, cf. the discussion of Baveney.

Little Eyton in Dawley has not been noted in any source earlier than the 19th-cent. 1" map. It may be a transferred name from Eyton on the Weald Moors. VCH XI, p.120 n.15, says there was a coal-pit here in 1828.

EYTON in Alberbury parish SJ 377140 DB Manor

Etune 1086 DB, *Eton'* 1220 Cur, 1251 Fees
Eyton' 1220 Cur *et passim* with variant spelling *Eyton; Eiton* 1274 Ipm, 1644 PR(H) 6, *Eighton* 1658 ib, *Eaighton* 1659 ib
Itton 1650 PR(H) 6, *Iton* 1695 Morden
Eaton 1661-2 PR(H) 6

The **ēg** is a low promontory jutting out into the flood-plain of the R. Severn. It can be seen clearly from the B 4393 road W.

of the farm. The place is occasionally described as 'near Alberbury' in 13th-14th-cent. references.

A related settlement at Stocksfield, a mile S.E. of Eyton, is *Etune* 1086 DB, *Eytonstok* 1276 Cl, *Eyton Stokkes* 1376 Pat. VCH VIII, p.191, cites a 13th-cent. reference to a path from Eyton to *le Stockes.* The name probably contains **stoc** 'dependent settlement'.

EYTON in Baschurch parish SJ 441229 DB Manor

Hetone 1086 DB
Eton 1203-4 *Ass, Eton'* 1221 SAC, 1271-2, 1291-2 *Ass,* 1334 SR
Eyton 1271-2 *Ass*, 1355 Pat, 1410 *SBL 4454*, 1510 *SBL 4459, Eyton'* 1291-2 *Ass, Eyton juxta Baschirch* 1346 FA

This settlement occupies a raised site in an area of marsh and pools.

EYTON ON SEVERN SJ 573063 DB Manor

Aitone 1086 DB, *Aitona* 1138 SAC
Eitona c.1090, c.1150 SAC, *Eyton* 1190 (15th) SAC *et passim* with variant spelling *Eyton'; Eyton Monachorum* 1271-2 *Ass, Eyton' Abbatis* 1291-2 *Ass,* 1334 SR, *Abbots Eyton* 1371 Cl, *Eyton Abbots* 1404 Cl
Eton 1271-2 *Ass, Eton'* 1291-1 *Ass*
Eaton sup-Sabrina 1577 Saxton

This settlement has a promontory site overlooking the flood-plain of the R. Severn. It belonged to Shrewsbury Abbey, hence *-Monachorum* and *-Abbots.*

EYTON UPON THE WEALD MOORS SJ 653147 Ancient Parish

Etone 1086 DB, *Eton'* 1291-2 *Ass*
Eiton 1200 Cur (p), 1255 RH, *Eyton'* 1231 Cl *et freq* with variant spelling *Eyton; Eyeton* 1517 *SRO 327*
Ayton 1342,9 Pat (p), 1737,40 PR(L) 8
Iton Wilmore 1589 PR(L) 9

This is one of a cluster of names in the Weald Moors which contain **ēg**; see Buttery. The affix appears in several variants, e.g. *Eyton in Wydemore* 1255-6 *Ass*, *Eton' sub Wyldemor'* 1291-2 *Ass*, *Eyton super Wildemore* 1346 FA, *Ayton super le Wildmor* 1342 Pat, *Eyton of Wyldemor* 1346 Pat, *Eyton-in-the-Wildmoors* 1646 PR(L) 6.

FAINTREE SO 662890 DB Manor

Faventrei 1086 DB, *Fawintre* 1278 InqMisc
Feintrie 1204 P (p), *Feyntre* 1271-2 *Ass* (p), *Feyntree* 1629 *PRChetton*
Faentre 1210-12 RBE (p), *Faintr'* 1221-2 *Ass* (p) *et passim* with variant spellings *Faintre(e)*, *Fayntre(e)*, *Faintr(e)y*; *Faintru* 1274 RH
Fagentre 1212 Fees (p)
Fakintrou c.1212-17 RBE (p)

'Variegated tree', OE *(æt) fāgan trēowe.*

The G.R. given above is for Faintree Hall. Lower Faintree is at 657884. The two settlements are *Overfayntry*, *Nether Fayntry* 1595 AD. They are in Chetton parish.

FARLEY SJ 388080 DB Manor

Fernelege 1086 DB
Fereleye 1291-2 *Ass*
Farleye 1291-2 *Ass*, *Farley* 1581,2, Ch 2 *SBL 6786, 6808, 9945*
Fareley 1563 PR(H) 12 *et freq* with variant spelling *-leye* to 1694 *SBL 9955*, *Fairley* 1697 *SBL 3556*

'Fern clearing', *v.* **fearn, lēah**, identical with various examples of Farley, Farleigh, Farnley in other counties, and with Fairlight in Sx. There is another Farley, of identical origin, in Much Wenlock.

There has been a recent change from Fairley to Farley in the modern form of the Pontesbury name. *Fairley* is the form given on the 19th-cent. 1" map, in VCH I p.325 (1908), and in

Bowcock (1923). Kelly's Directory for 1934 has *Farley.*

FARLOW SO 640807 Civil Parish

Ferlau 1086 DB, *Ferlaue* 1206 Cur (p), *Ferlowe* 1399 Pat
Ferulawe (sic print) c.1188 SAC, *Fernlaw* 1203-4 *Ass* (p), *Fernlawe* 1209 For (p), 1221-2 *Ass* (p), 1226-8 Fees (p)
Farnlawe 1221-2 *Ass* (p,), *Farnlowe* 1273 Ipm, 1293 InqMisc
Farlawe 1255 RH (p), *Farlowe* 1273 Ipm (p), 1389 Cl, 1397 InqMisc, 1410 Pat, *Farlow* 1403 Pat, *Farloe* 1688 PR(H) 9, 1700 PR(H) 16, 1719, 36 PR(H) 14
Faierlawe 1577 Saxton, *Farelow* 1727 PR(L) 14, 1732 *SBL 6489, Farela* 1727 *PRChetton*

'Fern tumulus', *v.* **hlāw**. When the present church was built in 1857-8 a seated skeleton was found in a mound. S.C. Stanford, *The Archaeology of the Welsh Marches* (1980), p.71, mentions this along with several other extant or recorded Bronze Age tumuli in the area crossed by the Clun-Clee Ridgeway. The church occupies a very dominating site, with steep falls and splendid views on the N. side.

FELTON BUTLER SJ 394176 DB Manor

Feltone 1086 DB, *Felton'* 1241 Fees *et passim* with variant spelling *-ton*

'Settlement in open ground', *v.* **feld, tūn**. The implied contrast with less easily accessible land may relate in this instance to the marshy area to the W. There are two other Feltons in Sa, one in Bromfield, and the other a parish. The last is West Felton, q.v.

The affix is the surname of Hamo *le Butiler* (also *Pincernator*) who is the tenant 1242 Fees. It is first noted in c.1270 InqMisc (*Felton Buttler*) and is fairly frequent after that, the commonest 14th-cent. spelling being *Botiler.* It usually follows the place-name, but *Botilerfelton* occurs 1397 Pat.

FENEMERE SJ 445230 DB Manor

Finemer 1086 DB, *Finemera* 1121 SAC, *Fynymer* Hy 8 RentSur
Fenemere 1255-6 *Ass, Fenemoore* 1672 HTR
Fennymare 1255-6 *Ass, Fennimare* 1271-2 *Ass, Fenymare* 1291-2 *Ass* (p), *Fenymere* 1361 Ipm, *Fenymer* 1362 Cl, *Fennimeare* 1655 SAC 1/XLVII
Fennyngmer' 1305-6 *Ass* (p)
Venimere 1342 HAC (p)

'Mouldy lake', *v.* **mere**. The first element is probably an adjective ***fynig**, from OE **fyne** 'mould'. The 1121 SAC reference is to "quandam terrulam cum lacu qui vocatur finemera". The name was probably coined for the lake, and transferred later to the settlement(s) in Baschurch parish. The 19th-cent. OS map calls the lake *Fennymere Pool* and shows *Higher* and *Lower Fennymere* as the names of two farms. Only *Lower Fenemere Fm* is named on the 1961 1", and on this map *Fenemere* (without the addition of Pool) is printed in blue lettering as the name of the lake.

FITZ SJ 448179 Ancient Parish

Witesot 1086 DB
Phitesoth 1128 SAC, *Phitesso* 1138 SAC
Fiteshod' 1155 SAC, *Fittesho* c.1175 SAC, 1194,5 P, 1235-45 HAC, 1275 Pat, *Fit(t)esho* 1255 RH, *Fytisho* 1291-2 *Ass*
Futesho 1255-6 *Ass*
Fittes 1255-6, 1271-2 *Ass et freq* with variant spellings *Fyttes* to 1811 PR(L) 12, *Fittus* 1379 Pat, *Fittis* 1478 HAC, *Fyttys* 1498 Ipm, Hy 8 *RentSur*
Fitts 1535 VE, 1648,54 PR(L) 4, 1655 SAS 1/XLVII, 1722 PR(L) 4, *Fittz* 1577, 1686,92 PR(L) 4, 1809 PR(L) 17, *Fitz* 1658 PR(L) 12 *et seq*
Fettys 1535 VE

'Fitt's spur of land', *v.* **hōh**. The two earliest forms from SAC have unusually early instances of *Ph-* for *F-*. The church and manor house at Fitz stand near the tip of a clearly defined, long, narrow spur, which is the *hōh* of the name.

The loss of the final element is to be associated with the same development in Edgebold, Edgmond and Ercall. The spelling *Fittes* in 1255-6 shows that it happened earlier in this name than in the others. The spelling *Fyttys* shows that a disyllabic pronunciation was preserved at least till the 16th cent. *Fittes* spellings continue into the 19th cent., but they are not conclusive evidence for a disyllable at that date. The monosyllabic form is first clearly evidenced in 1535, and the voicing of *-s* to *-z* in 1577.

Fitz is now in the civil parish of Pimhill.

FORD SJ 415135 Ancient Parish

Forde 1086 DB *et passim* with variant spellings *Ford(a), Ford'; La Forde* 1291-2 *Ass* (p), 1453,6 Fine, *La Ford* 1447,54 Fine
Fordes 1252 Ch, 1378 Pat
Furde 1255 RH (p)
Forthe 1322,75 Pat
Fourd 1562 *SBL 13455, Foord* 1600 PR(H) 1 *et freq* to 1672 PR(H) 16, *Foorde* 1620 PR(H) 1
Foard 1703 *SBL 6042*

'Ford'. The reference is most likely to be to a made-up crossing place where the Welshpool road crosses Cardeston Brook, S. of the village. The 6" map has the name Welshman's Ford here.

The variant spellings correspond fairly closely to those given in NED for the noun *ford.* This and the occasional use of the French definite article indicate that the meaning was never forgotten.

FORTON SJ 430161 DB Manor

Fordune 1086 DB
Forton' 1240 Cl *et passim* with variant spelling *-ton(e)*
Forten 1646 PR(L) 4

'Settlement near a ford'. The name occurs also in Ha, La and St. Forton is in the parish of Montford *(infra)*, and both names refer to the crossing of the Severn which was superseded by Montford Bridge.

FOUSWARDINE (lost, in Sidbury parish) SO 675856 DB Manor

Fuloordie 1086 DB, *Fulwardyn* 1397 InqMisc
Fuleswrth 1255 RH, *Fuleswortdin* 1284-5 FA, *Fuleswarthyn* 1291-2 *Ass* (p), *Fullswarden* e.17th SAS 4/III
Foules werwin c.1270 AD
Fouswardine 19th OS 1", - *Coppice* 1902 OS 6"
Fousington 1843 *TA*

Second element **worðign**, a settlement-term especially characteristic of Sa, He and Gl. The first is probably a personal name, most likely *Fugol* (literally 'Bird'). This usually manifests itself in early ME spellings with some instances of *-g(h)-*, but there might have been earlier contraction in this name because the final element had two syllables.

The manor was assessed at ½ hide in DB. There was a building here in the 19th cent. which is called *Fousington* in the *TA* and *Fouswardine* on the 19th-cent. 1" map. The 6" map of 1902 marks only *Fouswardine Coppice*, on the parish boundary, a short distance N.W. of the buildings shown on earlier maps. The 1" map of 1967 shows a path leading to the site of these buildings.

(ENGLISH) FRANKTON SJ 452298 DB Manor

Franchetone 1086 DB, 1166 RBE (p), *Franketon'* 1221-2 *Ass* (p), 1242 Fees, 1255 RH (p), 1272 Cl, 1334 SR, *-ton* 1316, 1428 FA, 1398 Pat, *Francketon* 1490 Ipm
Fronchetone 1166 RBE (p), *Fronketon'* 1261-2 *ForProc* (p)
Francton' 1221-2 *Ass* (p), *Frankton'* 1255-6 *Ass, Frankton* 1730 *SBL 4015*
Fraunketon' 1255-6 *Ass, -ton* 1376 Cl, *Frauncton* 1548 PR(H) 1
Englyshe Frankton 1577 Saxton, *Englishe Franketon* 1590 *SBL 4006, English Frankton* 1656-7 PR(StA) 4

'Franca's estate'. *v.* **tūn**. Eyton's account (X, pp.106-7) of the manorial descent of English Frankton makes it clear that all the references up to the late 14th cent. are to this place, which is in Cockshutt parish, formerly in Ellesmere. The prefix is for distinction from Welsh Frankton, 5 miles W.N.W., on the Ellesmere/Whittington boundary.

The first specific mention noted of the other settlement is to *Franckton'* 1544-5 *RentSur* in Whittington. On Saxton's map of 1577 *Englyshe Frankton* and *Welsch Francton* are both shown. Other references include *Welsh Franckton* 1672 HTR, - *Frankton* 1709 PR(L) 4. Whittington PR (StA 2) gives *Franc(k)ton, Frankton* from 1602-96, with no prefix; these can be taken as references to Welsh Frankton, which is just within the parish. The 19th-cent. OS map shows a hamlet called *Frankton Common*, S. of Welsh Frankton. This appears in Hordley PR (L 7) as *Francton Common* 1706, *Frankton Common* 1794, 1811, and the same register mentions *Lower Frankton* in 1724.

It is possible that English Frankton had an area of pasture on the Whittington/Ellesmere/Hordley boundary, and that Welsh Frankton was one of several small settlements which grew up on this common. Settlement growth must have been encouraged by the coming of the Ellesmere Canal and the G.W.R. station, and an ecclesiastical parish of Frankton was created round Welsh Frankton in 1865.

FRODESLEY SJ 514014 Ancient Parish

Frodeslege 1086 DB *et freq* with variant spellings *-lega, -leg(h)', -ly(e), -ley(e); Frodsly* 1569 PR(H) 2 *et freq* with variant spellings *-ley, -lie* to 1781 *PRCardington*

Froddesl' 1208-9 *ForProc, -leye* 1313 *SBL 3609, -ley* 1431 FA, 1437 *SBL 6690*, 1726 PR(L) 19, 1776 *PRCardington, -ly* 1720 *PRShifnal*

Fredesleg' 1242 Fees, 1255 RH (p), *-ley* 1271-2 *Ass, Fridesleye* 1271-2, 92-5 (p) *Ass, Fredeslegh* 1290 Cl, *-leye* 1297 ChanR

Frodel' 1261-2 *ForProc, -leye* 1271-2 *ib*, 1397 Pat

Frodligh' 1267 Cl

Frenslye, Frendeslye 1271-2 *Ass, Frondesli* 1272 Cl

Fordisley c.1540 Leland

Frodgley 1584, 1731 PR(L) 6, 1707 PR(L) 1, 1710 PR(L) 19,

Frogley 1595, 1673,87 PR(L) 6, *Frodgsley* 1653 ib, *Frodgly* 1667 PR(L) 19, *Frodgeley* 1679 ib, 1705 PR(L) 6, *Frogely* 1700 ib
Fragly 1642 PR(L) 6, *Fragley* 1674,84 ib, *Frageley* 1680 ib, *Fradgley alias Frodesley* 1676 PR(L) 20

'Frōd's clearing', *v.* **lēah**. The development of the vowel of *Frōd* resembles that in Frodsham Ch (PN Ch 3, 221-2), where there are some ME *Fred-* spellings, and a single *Frid-*. In the Ch name, however, *Frad-* spellings are much earlier, starting with *Fradesham* 1245. Frodsham, like Frodesley, has some spellings with *-dd-*.

The *Frodesley, Frodsly* spellings have been grouped together because it is impossible to determine the date at which a disyllabic pronunciation became usual. The *Frodesley* spellings (which persist to today) cannot all represent a trisyllabic pronunciation.

The development to *Frodg(e)ley* has yielded one of the alternative local pronunciations: the name is either [frʌʤli] or [frɔdzli]. There are parallels for this, the closest noted being Mudgley So, for which DEPN gives early spellings *Mudesle* 1157, *Modeslega* 1176. Mudgedown Gl may also be compared: PN Gl 3, 2 gives the spellings *Modelesdon* 1322, *Moddesdone* 1327, *Mudgedown* 1777.

The *Frogley* spellings have been grouped with the *Frodg(e)ley* ones on the assumption that all of them represent a pronunciation with [ʤ]. This consideration applies also to *Fragl(e)y, Frageley, Fradgley.*

GLAZELEY SO 701882 Ancient Parish

Gleslei 1086 DB
Gleseleg' 1221-2 *Ass* (p), *Gleselege* c.1230 SAC, *Gleseleg* 1274 RH (p)
Glasele 1255 RH *et passim* with variant spellings *-ley(e), -leg(h)* to 1710-11 PR(H) 3
Glasleg' 1261-2, 71-2 *ForProc* (p), *Glasley* 1318 Ipm, 1535 VE, 1733 PR(H) 14, 1767 PR(H) 17, *Glaslegh'* 1364-6 *ForProc* (p)
Glasseleye 1284-5, 1316 FA, 1291-2 *Ass*
Glazeleye 1308 Ipm (p), *Glaysley* 1577 Saxton, *Glazely* 1744 *PRChetton*
Glassley 1728 PR(H) 14, *Glasslye* 1728 *PRChetton*

v. **lēah**. The spellings for the first element suggest OE **glæs** 'glass', which might have been used as a stream-name. The large tributary of the Severn called Borle Brook is not likely to be designated, as this is *aqua de Borle* 1271-2 *Ass*; but there are two small streams flowing into Borle Brook, one N. and one S. of Glazeley village, and one of these might have been called *Glass.*

Glaze occurs elsewhere as a stream-name, in Glaze Brook D and La, and in Glaisdale Beck YN. These are usually derived from the British ancestor of Welsh *glas* 'blue, green, grey'. The early forms with *-e-* make the OE word *glæs* seem more appropriate for Glazeley, however. Glasshampton Wo may have the same first element; that name also has some early *-e-* spellings.

There is some evidence in Ess and La for an OE stream-name *Glæsen*, perhaps a derivative of *glæs.*

In 1271-2 *Ass* there is a reference to *Glasel' Parva*, but no confirmation has been noted for this hint that there were two settlements called Glazeley.

GOLDING SJ 545035 DB Manor

Goldene 1086 DB, c.1180 HAC *et freq* with variant spelling *Golden* to 1733 PR(L) 19
Goldeton' 1255-6 *Ass*
Goldyng 1569 *SBL 6621, Golding* 1730 PR(L) 4 *et seq, Goulding* 1597 PR(L) 19, 1620 PR(L) 2, *-inge* 1606 PR(L) 19, 1626 PR(L) 2

'Gold valley'. Golding is situated between two valleys both of which have the narrow, curving shape appropriate to OE **denu**. The first element could refer to yellow-coloured flowers, or to soil. Golding is a township of Cound parish.

GRAVENHUNGER SJ 743426 DB Manor

Gravehungre 1086 DB, 1299 Ipm
Gravinh'ker 1255 RH, *Crauenhungre, Grauenh'nger* 1255-6 *Ass, Gravenhungre* 1267 Cl *et passim* with variant spelling *-hunger*, *Gravinhunger* 1283 Ipm, *Gravenhongre* 1302 Pat, 1392 Cl,

Fine, 1393 Cl, 1411 AD, *Gravonhungur* 1343 AD, *Gravenhanger* 1695 Morden
Granhungre 1327 AD, *Grauhonger* 1436 AD, *Gravhonger* 1437,52 AD, *-hongur* 1452 AD
Grenehongher 1550 Pat, *Grenhanger* 1583 *SBL 5452*, *Gravenhunger alias Greenhonger* 1607 *SBL 1388*
Grosvenhunger 1672 HTR

Probably 'hanging wood with a coppice', from the gen. of OE **grāfa** (variant **grǣfe**) and **hongra** (variant **hangra**). The identity of the first element is not certain, but this interpretation suits the spellings and makes reasonable sense. It is likely that **grāfa** was the OE term for coppiced woodland, and if so the word could have been combined with other woodland terms, such as **lēah** and **hangra**, to denote a part of the area which was managed in this way.

Gran- in 1327 is probably an error for *Grau-*, but it seems clear that there was an alternative form *Gre(e)nhonger* in 16th and 17th cents. The modern pronunciation is [greivənhʌŋə]; this may be due to association with the word *graven.*

The place is in the parish of Woore. The house called Gravenhunger stands next door to the one called Banktop. On the opposite side of the road, behind another row of houses, there is a steep bank running parallel with the road. From the west, a wood on this bank would probably appear 'hanging'.

GREETE SO 577705 Ancient Parish

Grete 1196 P *et passim* to 1577 Saxton
Groete 1278 InqMisc, 1395 AD
Greote c.1291 TN *et freq* to 1431 FA
Grute 1291-2 *Ass* (p), 1391, 1405 Cl
Grote 1366 Ipm
Greete 1552 Pat, *Greet* 1699 PR(H) 13

'Gravel', from **grēot**, or 'gravelly place', from a derivative ***grēote**. There are other instances of this simplex name in Gl, K and Wo. Kelly's Directory (1934) says "The soil is various, principally strong loam and stiff gravel". The presence of the latter must have seemed the dominant feature to the earliest English settlers.

GRETTON SO 514952 DB Manor

Grotintune 1086 DB, *-ton'* 1214 Cur, c.1225 SAC (p), 1261-2 *ForProc*, 1271-2 *ib* (p), *-ton* 1284-5 FA, *Grotynton'* 1334 SR
Gredinton' 1208-9 *ForProc*, 1255-6 *Ass*
Gretiton 1255 RH, 1297 Cl
Gretton' 1255-6 *Ass*, 1301 SAC, *-ton* 1499 Ipm, 1625 *SBL 6390*
Gretinton' 1269 Cl, 1271-2 *ForProc* (p), *-tun* 1302 Ch, *Gretynton* 1397 InqMisc
Grotiton' 1271-2 *Ass* (p), *ForProc*
Grytington', *Gretington* 1271-2 *Ass*
Grodyton' 1291-2 *Ass*
Grotyngton 1375 Pat, 1446 Cl
Grodyngton 1400 SAS 1/XLVII

'Gravelly settlement', *v.* **tūn**. The first element is **grēoten*, an adjectival derivative of **grēot**. The place is situated on a small patch of morainic deposits consisting of clayey gravel (ex. inf. Ann Cole).

Gretton is on the southern boundary of Cardington parish.

GRINSHILL SJ 520235 Ancient Parish

Grivelesul 1086 DB, *Grineleshul* 1242 Fees, *Griuelesul*, *-hul'* 13th *SBL 10731,5*, *Grineleshull* 1255 RH, 1346, 1428 FA, *Griueleshull'* (also *Grimenhull'*) 1255-6 *Ass*, *Gryneleshulle* 1320 *SBL 5410*
Gruneleshull 1182-1200 HAC
Grilleshill' c.1224-32 HAC, *Grileshill* 1308 HAC, *-hul(l)* 1342 HAC, *Grilleshull'* 1414,23,29 *SBL 10741,2,5*, *-hull* 1431 FA
Griuenesh'l 13th *SBL 10734*
Cryneshull 1271-2 *Ass*
Greneleshil 1291-2 *Ass* (p), *-hul* 1320 Ch
Grenehull 1316 FA
Greneshull' 1334 SR, *Grenushull'* 1403 *SBL 15668*
Grulsull' 1354 *SBL 10738*

Greleshull 1397 InqMisc, *Greelsel* 1421 *SBL 3650*
Grilsull' 1411 *SBL 10739*, *Grilshull'* 1516 *SBL 3651*
Grynshill 1577 Saxton, *Grinsell* 1587 *SBL 6883*, 1655 SAS 1/XLVII, 1716 *SBL 5022 et freq* with variant spelling *-el* to 1779 PR(L) 14, *Grynsill* 1667 PR(L) 1, *Grinsoll* 1672 HTR, *Grinshill* 1746 PR(L) 4 *et seq*
Greenshill 1686 PR(L) 7 *et freq* to 1746 PR(L) 1, *Greensell* 1703 PR(L) 4, *Greenshall* 1760 PR(H) 15
Grindshill 1715 PR(L) 14

The OE form is likely to have been **Gryneleshyll*. All *Grivel-*, *Griuel-* forms are assumed to be scribal or editorial errors for *Grinel-*, so they have not been separately presented in the setting-out of spellings. The name is most likely to refer to the irregularly-shaped eminence now called Grinshill Hill, and OE **hyll** is an appropriate term for this. There appears to be no parallel for the first element, a hypothetical OE **grynel*, appearing here in the genitive. A derivative of *grin, gryn* 'noose, snare' might be thought of, perhaps referring to the prevalence of animal snares on the hill (in which case the *-es* would give a collective gen. sing.), or perhaps because the outline of the hill was thought to resemble some sort of snare, in which case **Grynel* would be the name of the hill.

HABBERLEY SJ 398035 Ancient Parish

Habberleg' 1242 Fees, *-le* 1299 Pat, *-leye* 1301,10,53 (p) Cl, 1309 Ipm, *-ley* 1577 Saxton *et seq*
Hatburleg' 1242 Fees
Habrutel' 1255-6 *Ass*
Haberle 1271-2 *Ass et freq* with variant spellings *-ley(e), -legh* to 1774 PR(H) 12
Habburley 1341 Pat
Haburleye 1346 FA, 1354 Fine, *-ley* 1381, 1411 Pat, 1383, 1414 Fine, 1431 FA, 1535 VE
Haberbergh 1347 Cl
Aberleye, Aberelye 1354 Pat

'Heaðuburh's or Hēahburh's clearing', second element **lēah**.

The first element is clearly a feminine personal name, ending in *-burh. Hatburleg'* 1242 Fees was taken by Ekwall (DEPN) to be evidence for *Heaðuburh*, and the form *Habrutel'* from 1255-6 *Ass* possibly supports this, though the *-t-* has been eccentrically placed.

HADLEY SJ 675120 Civil Parish

Hatleye 1086 DB, *Hathlegh'* 1271-2 *ForProc*
Hedleia c.1138 SAC *et freq* with variant spellings *-leg', -leg(a), -ley* to 14th *SBL 4402* (p)
Hetlega 1155 SAC, *Hethlegh'* 1238 Cl, *Hetleg'* 1261-2 *ForProc, -legh'* 13th *SBL 4393* (p)
Hadlega 1191 P (p) *et freq* with variant spellings *-leg', -lee, -ley(e), -legh*
Haddele 1251 Ch *et freq* with variant spellings *-leg', -leye* to 1363 Cl
Heddeleg' 1255-6 *Ass*
Hadelegh' 1291-2 *Ass, -leye* 1325 Ch, 1329 Cl, *-ley* 1346 FA, 1421 Cl, *-leygh* 1421 Cl

'Heath clearing', *v.* **hǣð, lēah**. In other counties this name appears also as Hadleigh, Headley, Heatley, Hedley.

A civil parish of Hadley was formed in 1898; it was formerly part of Wellington.

HADNALL SJ 522200 Civil Parish

Hadehelle 1086 DB
Hedenhale e.13th *SBL 5392* (p), a. 1297 *SBL 5423*
Heddenhale c.1220 *SBL 5396* (p), 13th *SBL 10736*
Adenhal' (p), *Adenhel'* 1221-2 *Ass*
Hadenhale 13th *SBL 10735 et passim* with variant spelling *-hal* to 1431 Cl, *Hadenhall* 1366 Cl
Haddenhal' 1252 Cl (p)
Hadenal(l) 1394 *SBL 5434, Hadenale* 1414 *SBL 10741*, 1428 FA, *Hadenall* 1450 *SBL 4436*
Hadnale 1402 *SBL 5436, Hadnall* 1450 *SBL 4437 et seq, Haddenhall alias Hadnall* 1646 *SBL 5827, Hadnoll* 1672 HTR, 1717 *SBL 3448*

'Headda's nook', with **halh** referring to the slight valley running from E. to W. The parish was formed in 1856 from the parish of Myddle.

HALFORD SO 436834 Civil Parish

Hauerford 1155 BM
Haleford 1221-2 *Ass* (p)
Hancforde c.1260-70 HAC
Halegford 1291-2 *Ass* (p)
Hawkeford 1535 VE
Hawford 1535 VE, 1668 PR(H) 18, 1677 PR(H) 17, 1744 PR(H) 2,
Hauford 1577 Saxton, 1675 Ogilby, 1710 PR(H) 17

Probably 'nook ford', with first element **halh**, in spite of the *Hauerford* spelling of 1155. DEPN, quoting only *Hauerford* 1155 and *Hawkeford* 1535, says 'hawkers' ford', and this has been accepted uncritically by later commentators (including Gelling in *Place-Names in the Landscape*, 1984). VE spellings are, however, particularly likely to be corrupt, and *Hawkeford* might be an error for **Haulcford*. The 1155 and c.1260-70 spellings are very difficult to explain. If the base be indeed *halh-ford*, Norman French confusion of l-n-r may be responsible. The compound *halh-ford* has become Halford in Wa and D, but the early forms for those names do not exhibit such great variation. Names in which **halh** is the first element are not numerous, so there is no great body of material for comparison. It may be seen from the material set out under Haughton that considerable variety occurs in the spellings for names derived from that compound.

A possible position for the original ford is at G.R. 433837, where the 19th-cent. 1" map shows a road crossing the R. Onny. This has dwindled to a footpath on the 1958 1", though the bridge is still shown.

Several meanings of *halh* are possible in this name. 'Hollow' does not seem especially appropriate. Perhaps the 'administrative' sense - 'detached or projecting part of an estate' - is the most suitable, as Halford (together with Dinchope) belonged to Bromfield Priory, 5 miles S.E., and was a chapelry of Bromfield until it was made into a separate parish in 1841. Another possibility is 'land in a river-bend'; there is a broad flood-plain, and there could have been a meander in the R. Onny which embraced the site of the village. At present the river makes a series of squiggles.

GREAT HANWOOD SJ 440095 Civil Parish

Hanewde 1086 DB *et passim* with variant spellings *-wud', -wod(e)* to 1398 *SBL 5435*
Haunewode 1416 Fine
Hamwode 1421 Cl
Hanwode 1535 VE, 1591 PR(L) 14, *Greate Hanwood* 1559 PR(H) 1, *Hanwood* 1597 ib *et seq, - Magna* 1649 SAS 4/VII, 1685 PR(H) 1

v. **wudu**. The first element has generally been interpreted as 'cock', from OE **hana**, which is used in literary sources of the domestic cock, mostly with reference to its crowing; but the combination of this with 'wood' is not altogether convincing. *Hana* could be a personal name. Descriptive terms are, however, the commonest qualifiers in names containing **wudu**, and another possible first element is OE **hān** 'rock'; but some topographical justification would be required before this suggestion could be entertained.

Little Hanwood is a township in the parish of Pontesbury. VCH VIII (p. 248) speaks of "an area of ancient woodland, which presumably gave its name to Great and Little Hanwood", but no surviving records refer to the wood, as distinct from the settlements.

HARCOURT SJ 570250 DB Manor

Harpecote 1086 DB *et passim* with variant spelling *-kote* to 1381 Cl
Harpercote 1271-2 *Ass*
Harecote Park, - Myll 1495 Ipm, *Harescot Park or Harecot Park* 1814 PR(L) 19, *Hare-court Park* 1818 ib
Harcott als Harpcott 1692 *SBL 5704, Harcourt Park* 1808 Baugh, *Harcott Park* 1810 PR(L) 2, *Harcot Park* 1829 PR(L) 19

Second element **cot**. The first element could be OE **hearpe** 'harp', ***hearpa** 'harper', or the gen. pl. of OE **hearpere** 'harper'. These words are well-evidenced in place-names, but this seems to be the only instance in which the activity of harping is associated with the sort of settlement designated by **cot**. The modest implications of this generic are appropriate to the DB assessment of ½ hide, but a church of *Harpercote* is mentioned 1271-2 *Ass*, and from 1495 (Ipm) onwards most references noted are to the manor house, which was known as Harcourt or Harcott Park in the e. 19th cent., rather than to the hamlet. The association of the name with the manor house would assist the change from -cot to -court. Harcourt has always been in the parish of Stanton upon Hine Heath.

HARCOURT SO 700827 DB Manor

Hauretescote 1086 DB
Havekercot 1255 RH *et freq* with variant spelling *-cote* to 1314 Fine, *Hauerekercote alias Hauekercote* 1303 Ipm
Hauekerscote 1293 Ipm
Hakercote 1316 FA, 1317 AD, 1338 Pat
Hagurcote 1334 SR, 1402,3 Cl, *Hagercote* 1357 Ipm, 1358 Pat, 1363 Cl
Havercote 1350 Fine, *Havercote, Hafkercote* 1349 Ipm
Hasketot 1354 Fine, *Haskercote* 1357 Cl, Ipm
Harcourt 1707 *SBL 4071,* *Harcott* 1808 Baugh

'Hawker's cottage', first element OE **hafocere**. Harcourt is one of the townships of Stottesdon, and on the *TA* map Upper and Lower Harcourt are shown as adjacent farms. Only Upper Harcourt appears on the modern 1" map.

HARLEY SJ 597015 Ancient Parish

Harlege 1086 DB, *Harleia* c.1200 *ForProc et passim* with variant spellings *-leg(h)', -ley(e), -le*
Herleia c.1090, 1121,38 SAC, *Herleg'* 1206 Cur (p), *H(i)erleg'* 1221-2 *Ass* (p), *Herle* 1344,5 Fine (p)

Hartl' 1237 Cl
Harelegh' 1255-6 *Ass, -legh* 1276 Cl (p)
Horle 1271-2 *ForProc* (p), *Hoorley* 1780 PR(L) 2

'Rock wood or clearing', from OE ***hær** (only known from place-names) and **lēah**. Harley has hitherto been explained as 'hares' wood/clearing', with OE **hara** as first element; but now that the early spellings from SAC are available it appears much more likely that the first element was **hær**. The spellings for nearby Harnage show a similar alternation of *-a-* and *-e-* (*Harenegga* 1167 P, *Hernegie* 1232 Ch), and this name is likely to contain ***hæren**, an adjective from ***hær**.

HATTON

This name means 'settlement on, or near, heathland', from OE **hǣð** and **tūn**. Examples are fairly widespread, occurring in Db, Li and Mx, but the main concentration is in the west midlands, as is frequently the case with recurrent **-tūn** compounds. There are two Hattons in Ch, one in St, and one in Wa; and Shropshire has four. Three of the Sa places are DB manors, and their spellings are set out below. The fourth is Hatton in Eaton under Heywood, which is *Hetton'* 1167 P, *Hatton'* 1227 Cur. Hungryhatton in Child's Ercall parish is too poorly evidenced in records to be a certain example.

HATTON GRANGE SJ 766044 DB Manor

Etone 1086 DB
Hettun 1189 CartAntiq
Hatton 1212 P *et freq* with variant spelling *-ton'*; *Soldehatton'* 1251 Fees, *Hatton juxta Ideshal* 1271-2 *Ass, Hatton Grange* 1535 VE
Henton' 1226-8 Fees
Haditon 1284-5 FA

Part of Hatton is given to Buildwas Abbey in the 1189 reference; hence - Grange. The *Solde-* form is unexplained. *Ideshal* is the alternative name for Shifnal, in which parish the place lies.

COLD HATTON (in High Ercall parish) SJ 624211 DB Manor

Hatune 1086 DB, *Goldehaton* 1199 (1265), 1265 Ch
Hatton' 1212,42 Fees, *Colde Hatton'* 1233 Cl, 1334 SR, *Coldehatton'* 1255 RH, 1255-6, 91-2 *Ass*, *Colde Hatton* 1346, 1428 FA, 1535 VE, *Goldehatton* 1443 *SBL 15752*, *Coulde Hatton* 1591 PR(L) 13, *Could* - 1604 ib, 1618 PR(L) 20, *Hatton frigida* 1661 ib, *Cold Hatton* 1701 ib
Colde Atton 1285 Ch, *Atton(e) Colde* 1291-2 *Ass*

The affix is 'cold'. The two *Golde-* spellings may reflect a desire for a more attractive name. There are settlements called Cold Hatton Heath and Ellerdine Heath to the E. and N. of Cold Hatton.

HIGH HATTON (in Stanton upon Hine Heath parish) SJ 611248 DB Manor

Hetune 1086 DB
Hatton' 1242 Fees, *Hatton* 1255 RH, 1332 Ch, *Heghe Hatton'* 1291-2 *Ass, Hatton upon Hyneheth* 1300 Ipm, *Heghehatton sur Hyneheth* 1333 HAC, *Hatton Hineheath* 1655 SAS 1/XLVII, 1672 HTR, *Hatton Hine Heath als. High Hatton* 1692 *SBL 5704*
Atton' Onhyneheth' 1291-2 *Ass*

High Hatton is 2½ miles N.W. of Cold Hatton, and the affixes are probably intended to distinguish the two settlements from each other. There is no significant difference in elevation, so 'high' probably means 'more important'. Hine Heath is discussed under Stanton upon Hine Heath.

HAUGHTON or HALTON

The OE compound *halh-tūn* has given rise in Shropshire to four instances of Haughton and one of Halton. In other counties it sometimes takes the additional modern forms Halloughton, Hallaton, Halghton, Houghton. This is not a unitary class of names as **halh** has a variety of meanings in place-names, with a dichotomy between the 'topographical' senses (themselves very diverse) and the 'administrative' one. Only one of the five Shropshire instances qualifies for full treatment here, this being Haughton in Upton Magna, discussed below, which is an excellent example of the 'administrative' use of **halh**.

The other Shropshire names derived from OE *halh-tūn* are:

1) Halton near Ludlow. The name is shared by three settlements, Lady, Hill and Priors Halton. The meaning is probably 'valley settlement'.

2) Haughton in West Felton parish. The meaning of **halh** in this instance may be 'firm ground in marsh'.

3) Haughton in Morville parish. Perhaps an 'administrative' name as the parish boundary makes a detour to the N. of the place.

4) Haughton in Shifnal parish. In this area **halh** has the meaning "hollow'.

Haughton in Ellesmere parish is not sufficiently well-documented to be a certain example.

HAUGHTON (in Upton Magna parish) SJ 552163 DB Manor

Haustone 1086 DB

Halghton c.1220 HAC, *Halhton, Hali(h)ton* 1255 RH, *Halchton* 1284-5 FA, *Halghton'* 1289 *SBL 5844*, 1301 SAC, *Halechton* 13th *SBL 4390* (p), *Halughton'* 1291-2 *Ass* (p), *Halghton* 1301 Cl, 1535 VE, *Halgton'* 1306-7 *Ass, Halghton by Haghemon* 1318 Pat, *Halhton* 1334 *SBL 5790* (p), *Halghton by Haghmon* 1336 Pat, - *under Haumond* 1346 Pat, *Halughton by Haghman* 1430 Fine

Halinton' 1255-6 *Ass, Halencton'* (p), *Haleuthon'* 1261-2 *ForProc, Halentton' sub Haweman* 1271-2 *ib, Halenchton', Holinton, Halenthen, Halenhton, Halinthon* 1271-2 *Ass*

Haleton' 1255-6 *Ass* (p), *Halton* 1271-2 *Ass, Halton'* 1306-7 *Ass*

Aleweȝton' 1271-2 *ForProc* (p)

Halukiton 1271-2 *Ass*

Haughton 1535 *SBL 7180 et seq*

In spite of the variety of the spellings, there is no doubt that this is OE *halh-tūn* 'nook settlement', referring to the position of the farm in a knob projecting from the N. boundary of Upton Magna. Part of the estate known as Haughton was in High Ercall parish.

The 1086 spelling exhibits the well-evidenced DB *-st-* for OE *-ht-*, together with vocalisation of *-l-* to *-u-*. The other spellings have been roughly grouped as follows:

1) Those which show preservation of the OE velar spirant *h*
2) Those in which the spirant has been replaced by ȝ, which was then vocalised to *-u-*. Spellings such as *Halinton'*, *Halentton'* have been included in this group on the assumption that *-n-* is a mistranscription for *-u-*. These are all from *Ass* and *ForProc*, and the letters in question were read as *-n-* by EPNS research assistants. They have not been checked; in any case it may be impossible to say whether the MSS have *-u-* or *-n-*.
3) Those in which the spirant has disappeared, giving Halton, which is a frequent modern development of this compound.

Haughton is descended from type 1.

The affix 'by' or 'under Haughmond' refers to Haughmond Hill. This name is extremely well-documented from 1156 onwards; most of the references are to the Abbey, but a substantial number refer to the Forest. The spellings are:

Hageman 1156 *et passim* to 1320 Pat, *Hagheman* c.1176 CartAntiq *et freq* to 1283 Pat, *Haugeman* 1244 Cl, *Haghman* 1274,84 Cl, 1327,36 Pat

Hagemon' 1141-52 HAC, *Haghmon'* c.1160 HAC *et passim* with variant spelling *-mon* to c.1540 Leland, *Haghemon* 1176, c.1196 HAC, c.1305 APW, *Haughmon* c.1225 HAC, 1398 Pat, 1627 PR(L) 2, *Hagemon* 1235-6 Fees, 1271-2 *Ass*, c.1272 SAC, 1307 *SBL 5425*, *Hagmon'* c.1260, 1339,40 HAC, *Hawghmon* 1559 *SBL 5828*

Haemannia 1172 HAC, *Haman* c.1291 TN

Hagemmanie c.1190 HAC

Hamon 1203-10 HAC, 1291-2 *Ass*, 1439 Cl, 1695 Morden, *Ha(y)mon* 1255 RH, *Haemon'* 1271-2 *Ass*

Hageham 1222 Pat, *Hegham* 1310 Cl

Haweman 1241 Pat *et freq* to 1300 Pat, *Hauman* 1250 Cl, 1322 Pat,

1329 Cl, *Hawman* 1254 Ipm

Hawemon 1255 RH *et freq* to 1.13th *SBL 3582*, *Hawmon* 1261-2 *ForProc*, *Haumon* c.1291 TN, 1340,61,71 Pat, *Haumun* 1.13th *SBL 3581*

Hakeman 1275 Cl

Haghmond 1331,4 Pat, *Haumond* 1346 Pat, *Haghmont* 1397 InqMisc, *Hagmonde* 1406 Cl, *Haughmonde* 1535 *SBL 7180*, *Haghmond(e)*, *Hayghmonde* 1535 VE, *Haughmond* 1553 Pat *et seq*, *Hamond* 1577 Saxton, 1730 *SBL 4015*, *Hamonde* 1628 *SBL 4641*, *Haughmond alias Hamond* 1646 *SBL 5827*

This name is a mystery. The spellings require OE **hagaman*. DEPN suggests that OE *man* 'man' might have been used as a term for a hill, or for a cairn on top of a hill (for which last Ekwall cites the northern dialect use); and that *haga* 'enclosure' or *haga* 'haw' might have been combined with *man* to give a meaning 'hill with enclosures' or 'hill characterized by haws'. There is, however, no known parallel for *man* as a term for a hill in ancient names, so it cannot be regarded as a place-name generic, to be qualified by a first element appropriate to a particular example. If Haughmond does contain 'man' the name should be a meaningful compound, referring to a particular sort of human being. It is not, perhaps, inconceivable that such a compound might be used figuratively to name a hill, but no such term is on record in OE, and speculation about possible compound appellatives would be a hazardous exercise.

The British ancestor of Welsh *mam* 'mother' is believed to have been used as a hill-name in Mamble Wo, Mamhead D, Mansfield Nt and Manchester. All of these, however, have *Mam-*, either to the present day or till late ME, so the regular *-man, -mon* of the Haughmond spellings tells conclusively against the presence of the British word.

The change of *-man* to *-mon* is due to west-midland rounding of ă before a nasal. The *-d* and occasional *-t* which appear from 1334 onwards are probably parasitic consonants. These occur regularly after *-n* in the early modern period, and they develop in the ME period in words of French origin (like *ancient*). There is nothing in the development of Haughmond which is clearly due to popular etymology, and there was probably no association with Latin *mons* or French *mont*. Local speech appears to have preserved this enigmatic name without rationalisation, allowing it to develop on regular phonological lines.

The pronunciation [heimɔn], represented (albeit sparsely) in spellings from 1172 onwards, is still current locally. The Latinisation *Hamonensis* occurs in HAC in the mid-12th cent.

HEATH SO 557856 Civil Parish

La Hethe 1255 RH *et freq* to 1295 Ipm, *Hethe* 1271-2 *Ass et freq* to 1562-3 *SBL 7146, Hethe iuxta Hol(e)godescastel* 1291-2 *Ass, Heth* 1334 Cl
Heythe 1347,53,54 Pat, 1416 Fine
The Heathe 1566 *SBL 8384, Heath* 1559-60 *Corn.R.O., Heathe* 1577 Saxton, *The Heath* 1610 *Corn.R.O.*
Hythe 1416 Fine

OE **hǣð** 'heath', one of several instances in the country in which this word is used as a simplex name for a settlement which later attained some administrative status. In addition to this place, which was a chapelry of Stoke St. Milborough, Shropshire has several minor names from **hǣð**.

HENLEY (in Bitterley parish) SO 543764 DB Manor

Haneleu 1086 DB
Hennele 1242 Fees *et freq* with variant spellings *-leg', -leye* to 1428 FA
Heneleghʼ (p), *-ley* 1271-2 *Ass, -leye* 1291 Ch, *Heneleye alias Henneleye* 1318 Ipm
Henleg 1271-2 *Ass, -leye* 1356 Ipm, *-ley* 1374 Pat *et seq*
Hanley 1291-2 *Ass*

Second element **lēah** 'wood or clearing'. The first is *henna*, gen.pl. of **henn** 'hen', which is usually translated 'wild bird' when it occurs in place-names. There are two more 'hens' woods or clearings' in S. Shropshire: Henley in Acton Scot parish (*Hennel* 1255 RH, *Hennelegh* 1301 SAC) and Henley in Tasley parish (*Henneleg'* c.1143, c.1155 SAC). This recurrence as a settlement-name may indicate that the compound has a meaning more directly related to farming, and 'clearing where hens are kept' might be a better translation than 'wild birds' wood'.

HIGFORD SJ 754007 DB Manor

Huchefor 1086 DB
Hugeford 1203-4 *Ass* (p) *et freq* with variant spelling *-ford'* to 14th *SBL 4409*
Uggeford 1214 P (p), *-ford'* 1230 P (p)
Huggeford 1242 Fees *et freq* with variant spellings *-forde, ford'* to 1428 FA
Hukford 1316 FA
Hugford 1325 Pat, 1431 FA, 1472 *RentSur*
Hygforde 1492 Ipm, *Higford* 1577 Saxton, *Higfort* 1628 PR(L) 3
Hickford 1787 PR(L) 3

Higford (in Stockton parish, on the R. Worfe) has the same first element as Highley, about 10 miles S. on the R. Severn. There is no possible physical feature common to the two places, so the element is presumably a personal name. DEPN postulates **Hugga.* The road-pattern suggests that the ford was immediately adjacent to the village.

HIGHLEY SO 741835 Ancient Parish

Hugelei 1086 DB, *Hugel'* 1233 Cl *et freq* with variant spellings *-leg', -ley(e), -legh'* to 1428 FA
Huggel' 1203-4 *Ass* (p) *et passim* with variant spellings *-legh, -legh', -ley(e), -le* to 1399 Cl
Hugley 1399 Cl, *Hug(h)lye* 1535 VE
Highley 1535 VE, 1720 PR(H) 9 *et seq*
Hig(g)ley 1535 VE, *Higley* 1551 *PRHighley et freq* to 1822 *SBL 4108, Hygleye* 1589 PR(H) 3, *Higgeley* 1720 *PRHighley*

'Hugga's clearing', second element **lēah**. For the first element, cf. Higford. The change from *Higley* to Highley is probably due to popular etymology, High- being appropriate to the situation of the place, near the end of a long ridge. The name is still *Higley* on the 19th-cent. 1" map; it is Highley in the *TAMap*, but *Higley* in the accompanying apportionment.

HINSTOCK SJ 695263 Ancient Parish

Stoche 1086 DB
Hinestok, Hynestok' 1242 Fees, *Hinestock* 1255 RH, *Hynestok* 1281 Ipm, 1283 Cl, InqMisc, *-stoke* 1284-5 FA
Hinstok 1282 InqMisc *et freq* with variant spellings *-stoke, -stock; Hynestoke* 1335 Ipm *et freq* with variant spellings *-stok, -stocke* to 1577 Saxton
Hynnestok', Hinnestok' 1294-9 *Ass*
Henstocke 1685 *SBL 6513*

OE **stoc** 'dependent settlement', to which has been prefixed ME **hine** 'domestic servants'.

When OE **hīgna** (from which ME *hine* is derived) occurs in place-names which are likely to be of pre-Conquest origin, it is likely to be a reference to ecclesiastical ownership. This is clearly the case in Hinton in Stottesdon, the first mention of which (*Hinetona* c.1090) is in SAC. There is, however, no record of ecclesiastical ownership of Hinstock, and DB *Stoche* is probably a correct rendering of the original simplex name. *Stoche* was one of the manors of William Pantulf in 1086, forming part of the Barony of Wem, later held by the Butlers. It is possible that the profits of this manor were assigned to the upkeep of the household servants of the baronial family.

HOBENDRID approx. SO 309766 ?DB Manor

Edretehope 1086 DB
Obbendrif 1272 Ipm
Owendrisse 1272 Cl
Obendrit, Ob(b)endrith 1284 Cl
Howbeurid 1641 SAS 3/IV
Hobendreed 1672 HTR,*Hobendred* 1695 Morden

OE **hop** 'secluded valley' is the second element of the DB name, and probably the first element of the later one (which has the alternative form Hopebendrid). The DB manor was held before his rebellion by Edric the Wild, and it is reasonable to interpret *Edretehope* as containing a slightly corrupt version of his name. It is not likely, however, that the second part of Hobendrid can be considered a more corrupt version of *Edric.* It is more likely to be a Welsh personal name.

The identification of *Edretehope* with Hobendrid is not certain to be correct. Hobendrid is a small area, difficult to locate on modern maps. Kelly's Directory for 1923 says under Clun "Hopebendrid is a hamlet 3½ miles south", but no such hamlet is shown on maps. In the Clun *TA* (1847), Hobendrid is shown as a township on the S. boundary of the parish, with the townships of Purlogue, Menutton, Hobarris and Pentrehodry encircling it on the other sides. It includes the settlement of Chapel Lawn (named from *New chappell* 1611 Speed) and several farms, but no farm or hamlet is named Hobendrid. The DB assessment of 2 hides and 1 virgate for *Edretehope* is too high to refer only to this mountainous area.

If DB *Edretehope* is to be located here, better results could be obtained by considering the claims of Hobarris, the township which adjoins Hobendrid on the N. It is possible that there was an area called *Hop*, known in the late-11th cent. as 'Edric's Hop', which later split into the two townships of Hobendrid and Hobarris, distinguished from each other by the addition of Welsh personal names. The forms available for Hobarris are *Owaris* 1272 Cl, *Obaris* 1272 Ipm, *Obbarrys* 1284 Cl, *Hobarrys* 1381 *SRO 552/1/20, Howbarris* 1641 SAS 3/IV, *Hobarrough* 1672 HTR, *Hopharris* 1847 *TA.*

The two townships form a figure of eight, joined in the centre by the narrow valley of a tributary of the R. Redlake. Both contain mountain land, the proportion of this being very high in Hobendrid. The *TA* map shows that Hobarris has a compact area of arable land around the settlement, with woodland in the narrow centre of the figure of eight. Hobendrid contains long stretches of meadow. Regarded as a single unit, the two townships would be a reasonable equivalent for the DB manor of *Edretehope.* Only Clun (15 hides), Menutton (1 hide) and *Edretehope* (2 hides 1 virgate) are named in DB in the area which was later that of the great manor of Clun.

HOCKLETON SJ 274301 ?DB Manor

Elchitun 1086 DB
Hokelton' 1242 Fees *et freq* with variant spellings *-tun*, *-ton*(*e*) to 1431 FA, *Hoculton'* 1334 SR, *Hocculton* 1370 AD (p), *Hokulton* 1502 Ipm, *Hockleton* 1630 PR(H) 8 *et seq*
Hukelton' 1242 Fees, *-ton* 1250 Ipm
Hokylit(*t*)on' 1291-2 *Ass* (p)
Hugkelton' 1291-2 *Ass*, *Houghleton* 1577 Saxton
Hokeleton 1332 InqMisc
Heccalton 1535 VE

Probably 'estate connected with Hucel(a)', OE *Hucelingtūn*. Hucclecote PNGl 2 147 provides a parallel, though the *Huk-*, *Huc-* forms are more numerous there. The personal name is not on independent record, but both **Hucca* and **Hucel*(*a*) appear to be well-evidenced in place-names.

The DB form probably belongs here; if so, it shows metathesis in the first element.

HODNET SJ 614287 Ancient Parish

Odenet 1086 DB, 1232 Cur (p), 1267 Pat (p)
Hodeneth c.1090, c.1138, 1241 SAC, *Hodenet* 1121 SAC *et passim* to 1398 Cl, *Hodenete* 1231 Cur, *Hodenat* 1284 Pat, *Hodenit* 1361 Cl, 1724,9 PR(L) 18, 1735, 1807 PR(L) 8, *Hodenette* 1374 AD
Hoddenett 1227 Ch (p)
Hodnet 1230 P, 1274 Ipm, 1345 Cl, 1374 AD, c.1540 Leland *et seq*, *Hodnett* 1383 *SBL 15760*, 1535 VE, 1598, 1617, 1716,24,31 PR(L) 9, *Hodnitt* 1684 ib, 1738 PR(L) 14, *Hodnit* 1724,9 PR(L) 18, 1735, 1807 PR(L) 8
Hodenhac 1232 Cur (p)
Hodynet 1284 Ipm (p) *et freq* with variant spelling *Hodinet* to 1398 Cl
Odinett 1690-1 *SBL 5230*

Ekwall's suggestion (DEPN) that this is a British name meaning 'pleasant valley', from the words which became Modern

Welsh *hawdd* and *nant*, has met with general acceptance. Ekwall explains the loss of the second *n* in *nant* as due to dissimilation. It is clear from the voluminous documentation set out above that the letter had disappeared completely by the time of the Norman Conquest.

There are several instances of Hoddnant in Wales. In Cornwall the corresponding name has become Hennett, Henon and Huthnance. Hodnet overlooks the broad valley of the R. Tern. Prees, the adjoining parish on the N.W., also has a British name.

Although *Odenet* is the DB form for the manor, the hundred-name appears there as *Hod(e)net*.

HOLDGATE SO 563897 Ancient Parish

Castrum Helgoti 1109-18 CartAntiq, *Castellum Helgod* c.1200 MM, *Holegot* 1203-4 *Ass*, 1235-6,42,50 Fees, - *Helgoti* 1210 SAC, [*castrum*] *Halegot'* 1212 Fees, *Castelholegode* 1253 Pat, *Castrum Holegod* 1255 RH *et freq* to 1291-2 *Ass* (p), - *Halgod* 1255-6 *Ass, Chastel Holegod* 1291 Ch, *Castrum Holgod* 1291 Ipm, *Castelhelgod* 1317 Cl, *Castle Holgod* 1372 Pat

Hologodescastel 1199 SAS 2/X (FF), *Holgotcastel* (p), *Holdgodescastel* 1271-2 *Ass, Holgotescastel* 1336,48 Pat, *Holgate Castel* c.1540 Leland, *Howgate Castle* 1577 Saxton, *Houldgate Cast* 1695 Morden

Castrum de Holecote 1271-2 *Ass*

Holegod 1294 InqMisc, 1339 Pat, *Holgod* 1301 Ipm, 1346, 1428 FA, *Hologod* 1316 FA, *Holgote* 1346 Cl, 1350 Fine, 1431 FA, *Holcote* 1364-6 *ForProc* (p), 1415 Pat, *Holgot* 1387 Pat *et freq* to 1421 Cl, *Holegote* 1421 Cl, *Holgate* 1549 Pat *et freq* to 1812 PR(L) 4. *Holgat* 1549 Pat, *Holgatt* 1594 PR(H) 18, *Hollgatt* 1621 *SBL 6383, Howgate* 1647 *SBL 6116*, 1748 PR(H) 16, *Holegate* 1672 HTR, 1703 PR(H) 13, *Holl Gate* 1701 PR(H) 13, *Holdgott* 1729 PR(H) 15, *Holdgate* 1732 PR(L) 4 *et seq*

'Helgot's castle'. *Helgot* was the tenant of the estate in 1086. In DB the place is called *Stantune*; and it is *Stantona* 1121-6, c.1140, 1155 SAC. It must at one time have been united with the neighbouring estate of Stanton Long, *q.v.*

The tendency to regard the Norman personal name as a place-name seems to have started in the late 13th cent. *Hol-* instead of *Hel-* may be due to scribal error. There is surprisingly little popular etymology - only a single *-cote* form - until the 16th cent., when the final element was perhaps assumed to be the word *gate.* The parasitic *-d-* of *Holdgate* appears late and infrequently. The modern pronunciation is that which is clearly represented by the 1672, 1702 spelling *Holegate*; but this pronunciation may also have obtained for *Holgate*, which is the most frequent 16th-20th cent. form, and appears on the 19th-cent. OS map and on the *TA*. Kelly's Directory for 1934 calls the place *Holdgate or Holgate.*

Goodrich in He was *castellum Godric* in 1102, and this is an exact parallel. Godric, like Helgot, appears in DB.

HOPE

This name is from the dat. (*hope*) of OE **hop**, for which the most recently-suggested translation is 'remote enclosed place'. The word is not used exclusively of valleys, but that is its characteristic sense in He and Sa. The densest concentration in the whole country of names in which **hop** means 'valley' is probably in Sa S. of the R. Severn. The valleys are of varied shapes and sizes, but most of them offer settlement-sites with restricted access. Most of the Sa names in which **hop** is the generic have a qualifying first element, but there are some simplex examples, three of which are names of parishes. These are set out below.

HOPE BAGOT SO 589740 Ancient Parish

Hop' 1242 Fees *et freq* with variant spelling *Hope* to 1301 Cl
Hope Baghod 1255 RH, *Hopelagard* c.1270 InqMisc, *Hope Bagard* 1291-2 *Ass et freq* to 1431 FA, *Hopebaggard* 1397 Pat, *Hope Bagar* 1546 *SBL 6100,* - *Bagotte* 1595 AD, - *Baggott* 1728 PR(H) 16, - *Bagot* 1763 ib
Hobaggard' 1291-2 *Ass* (p)
Baggoteshope 1577 Saxton, *Bagshope* 1675 Ogilby, *Hope Baggot alias Baggoteshop* 1803 Plymley

The affix is from the surname of Robert *Bagard*, who is the tenant in 1242 Fees. The material available suggests that this was corrupted to *Bagot* in the second half of the 16th cent.

HOPE BOWDLER SO 476924 Ancient Parish

Fordritishope 1086 DB
Hop' 1201 Cur, 1242 Fees, 1255 RH, *Hope* c.1240 (1292) Ch, 1271-2 *Ass*, 1285 InqMisc
Hope Bothelers, Hup Budlers 1255 RH, *Hopebul(l)ers, Hope Budlers* 1255-6 *Ass, Hopebulers* 1261-2 *ForProc*, 1274 Ipm, 1376 Pat, *Hope Boillers, - Boyllers* 1271-2 *ForProc, - Bowelers* 1276 Cl, *- Boulers* 1284-5 FA *et freq* to 1428 FA, *Hopebudlers, Hope Boutlers* 1285 InqMisc, *Hope Bulers* 1286 Pat, *- Budlers* c.1291 TN, *- Boudlers* 1291,4 Ipm, 1301 SAC, *Hopeboudliers* 1315 Ipm, *- boudelers* 1385, 1421 Cl, *Hope Bowdelers* 1431 FA, *- Bowdler* 1535 VE
Hoppebuleers 1261-2 *ForProc*
Boudlereshope 1291-2 *Ass*

It may seem perverse to consider this as a simplex name, since the DB form has a prefix and most spellings from 1255 onwards have a suffix; but there are enough *Hope* forms to make this classification defensible. The affix which stuck is the surname of Robert *de Bullers*, who is one of tenants 1201 Cur. The DB prefix is probably the OE pers.n. *Forðræd*, but no owner of this name is on record; the TRE holder is Edric the Wild.

HOPESAY SO 389833 Ancient Parish

Hope 1086 DB, c.1200 *ForProc*, 1254 Pat, 1272 Ipm
Hope de Say 1255 RH, 1255-6 *Ass, Hop Say* 1294 Pat, *Hope Say* 1302 Ipm *et passim* with variant spellings *Hopesay(e)*; *Hopsaye* 1607 PR(H) 1, *Hoopsaye* 1632 PR(H) 9, *Hopes Saye* 1661 PR(H) 11, *Hopsay* 1661 PR(L) 19, *Hopesea* 1750 PR(H) 18

Picot *de Say* is the holder in DB.

HOPTON

There are six settlements in Shropshire named from this compound of **hop** and **tūn**: Monkhopton, Hopton near Hodnet, Hopton near Ness, Hopton Cangeford, Hopton Castle and Hopton Wafers. Hopton near Ness, the only one which does not qualify for full treatment here, is well-recorded from 1271-2 *Ass* onwards. In this name, and in Hopton near Hodnet, **hop** seems likely to have the meaning 'enclosure in waste'. In the others, which are S. of the R. Severn, **hop** refers to valleys.

HOPTON (in Hodnet parish) SJ 593267 DB Manor

Hotune 1086 DB
Hopton' 1242 Fees *et passim* with variant spelling *-ton*; *Hopton by Hodenet* 1340 Pat, 1397 InqMisc, *Hopton by Lye* 1395 AD

This name is associated with nearby Hope Wood. The places are on the S. and E. side of a narrow hill. The names could refer to recesses in the hill; but modern maps mark rough ground in the area, and 'enclosure in waste' seems the likeliest meaning for **hop**.

- *by Lye* refers to Lee Brockhurst.

HOPTON CANGEFORD SO 548804 Ancient Parish

Hopton' 1255-6 *Ass et passim* with variant spelling *-ton*; *Hopton Cangefot* 1271-2 *Ass*, 1291, 1315 Ipm, 1316 Pat, *Hopton Kandivant alias Candyvant* 1318 Ipm, *-Candivant* 1336 Ipm, *-Cangeford* 1356 Ipm, *-Candyvaucz* 1385 Cl
Opton' 1271-2 *Ass* (p), *-ton* 1264 Cl
Hopton in the Hole 1647 *SBL 6116 et freq* to 1740-1 PR(H) 15, *Hopton Caingeford or Hopton in the Hole* 1803 Plymley

The village lies near the head of a deep valley. Eyton (V, p. 13) notes that Herbert *Cangefot* is mentioned in 1199 in connection with Clee St Margaret. The connection of his family with Hopton does not seem to be clearly documented, but there can be no doubt that this distinctive surname is the origin of the place-name affix.

HOPTON CASTLE SO 367780 Ancient Parish

Opetune 1086 DB, *Oppetune* c.1155 (1348) Pat
Hopton' 1242 Fees *et passim* with variant spelling *-ton*; *Hoppton'* 1306-7 *Ass, Hopton by Clone* 1397 InqMisc, *Hopton Corbet* c.1540 Leland, *Hopton Castle* 1577 Saxton

The village lies in a deep valley. Leland's *-Corbet* may be a mistake for *-Castle.*

HOPTON WAFERS SO 637763 Ancient Parish

Hopton 1086 DB *et passim* with variant spelling *-ton*; *Hopton' Wafr'* 1271-2 *Ass, Hopton Waffre* 1284-5 FA, - *Wafre* 1302, 1394 Pat, 1577 Saxton, - *Wafers* 1535 VE, *Weavers Hopton* 1704 PR(H) 13
Upton Wafre 1316 FA

The village lies in a very deep valley. Robertus *Wafre* de Hopton' is mentioned 1255-6 *Ass.* He is called Robertus *le Wafre* 1255 RH.

HORDLEY SJ 382308 Ancient Parish

Hordelei 1086 DB *et passim* with variant spellings *-leia, -leg, -leg(h)'*, *-lee, -ley(e)* to 1535 VE
Hordileg' 1197-1203 HAC (p), *Hordylee* 1271-2 *Ass, Hordyleye* 1306-7 *Ass* (p), *Hordileye* c.1307 APW
Horderle, Hordesleg' 1271-2 *Ass* (p)
Hordley 1577 Saxton

This name has previously been interpreted as 'wood or clearing of hoards', from OE **hordalēah.* A Roman coin-hoard has been found in the parish in modern times, and such a name would be appropriate as a reference to others which were discovered in the Anglo-Saxon period. Some doubt arises, however, from the series of spellings beginning with *Hordileg'* 1197-1203. An adjectival derivative of *hord* formed with *-ig* is theoretically possible, but does not seem convincing.

HORTON

Shropshire has four examples of this fairly common name, which means 'dirt settlement'. The first element is either OE **horu** 'dirt' or **horh** 'phlegm', or perhaps a conflation of these two related words. Two of the Sa examples are treated fully here. The others are Horton (now surviving as Hortonlane) S.W. of Shrewsbury, which is well-recorded from 1242 Fees onwards, and a lost *Horton* in Ellesmere, only mentioned in 1284 Pat.

HORTON SJ 683145 DB Manor

Hortune 1086 DB *et passim* with variant spellings *-ton', -tun', -ton*

This settlement is in the Weald Moors, and *horu* may reasonably be considered a reference to muddy soil. It is in Hadley parish.

HORTON SJ 490298 DB Manor

Hortune 1086 DB *et passim* with variant spellings *-ton', -ton*; *Horton' iuxta Wemme* 1291-5 *Ass*
Haughton 1695,6 PR(L) 9, *Houghton* 1695 ib

Here, also, wet ground is the obvious explanation of the name. The 1695,6 forms are inverted spellings, due to *Horton* and *Haughton* being pronounced similarly. The settlement is in Wem parish.

HOWLE SJ 691234 DB Manor

Hugle 1086 DB, *Huggel'* 1255-6 *Ass*
Hulle 1221-2 *Ass, Hull'* 1291-2 *Ass, Hull* c.1291 TN
Howle 1250 HAC *et seq, Howele* 1271-2 *Ass*, 1281 Ipm, 1283 InqMisc, *Houle* 1271-2 *Ass et freq* to 1586 *PRChetwynd, Howelye* 1284-5 FA, *Howel* 1301 SAC
Hulam' 1253 Ch, *Hule* 1255-6 *Ass, Hul'* 1331 Ch
Whole 1655 SAS 1/XLVII

This name and Howle He (S.E. of Ross) are considered to constitute evidence for an OE word ***hugol** 'small hill'. A related term ***hygel** is found in Hile Do and Hoylake Ch, and probably in some minor names and field-names in La and Ch. Both terms are rare, and in view of this rarity it is noteworthy that forms for the Sa name show only occasional confusion with **hyll**.

On 19th-cent. maps (Baugh, OS and *TA*), Howle is the name of the site which modern maps call Howle Manor. The hachuring on the 19th-cent. 1" shows this as occupying a small hill-spur. A settlement S. of Howle Pool is shown, but not named, on this map; this presumably grew into the place now called Howle. The area is in Chetwynd parish.

Howle He is in much more dramatic country than the Sa place.

HUGHLEY SO 565980 Ancient Parish

Leg' 1203-4 *Ass* (p), (*La*) *Legh'* 1231 Cur, *Leye* 1331 (1348) Pat
Huleye, Hewelege c.1291 TN, *Hughleye* 1334 SR, *Hulegh* 1493 Ipm, *Hugh(e)lye* 1552 Pat, *Heowlye* 1557 AD, *Hygley* 1548 Pat, *Hewlee* 1577 Saxton, *Hughlie* 1608 PR(H) 1 *et passim* with variant spellings *-ly(e), -ley, -lee, -leigh*; *Huley* 1664-5 PR(H) 3, *Hugley* 1672 HTR, *Hugh Lee, - Leigh* 1730,33 PR(H) 18, *Hewlee* 1743 PR(H) 16

'Clearing' seems the most appropriate translation for **lēah** in this instance. The eponymous *Hugh* occurs in the earliest reference noted (1203-4 *Ass*), which is to *Hug' de Leg'*.

HUNTINGTON SO 537710 DB Manor

Hantenetune 1086 DB
Huntiton 1255 RH *et freq* with variant spellings *-ton', -yton'* to 1318 Ch
Huntington' 1255-6 *Ass* (p), *-yngton* 1329 Pat, 1415 AD
Huntindon c.1270 InqMisc, *-yndon* 1334 SR
Huneketon' 1291-2 *Ass*
Hontyton 1337 AD
Hunteton 1292 *SBL 15760*

Most of the spellings suggest 'estate associated with a huntsman' or 'with a man named Hunta', from OE **Huntingtūn*. There is some interchange of **tūn** and **dūn**. Huntington in Little Wenlock has a similar run of forms, but in that name **dūn** may have been the original second element.

IGHTFIELD SJ 595385 Ancient Parish

Istefelt 1086 DB, *Istefeld', Iftefeld'* 1230 P, *Istefeld* 1308 Ipm
Hichtefeld' 1175 P (p), *Hictefeld'* 1177 P (p), 1200 Cur (p), *Hichtefeud* 1255-6 *Ass* (p)
Ychtefeld 1210-12 RBE (p), *Yhtefeld* 1214 P (p), *Ichtifeld'* 1228 Cur (p), *Ihttefeld* 1230 P (p), *Yhtefelt* (p), *Ihttefeud* 1255 RH
Yttefeld 1235-6 Fees (p), *Ittefeld* (p), *Ythefeld* 1271-2 *Ass* (p), *Ittefeld'* 1306-7 *Ass, Ithtefeld* 1317 Ipm, Cl, *Ithefelde* 1392,3 Cl, *-feld* 1392 Fine
Hittefeld (p), *Hythefeld* 1235-6 Fees, *Hittefeld* 1255 RH
Ichefeud 1242 Fees, *Ichefeld* 1255-6 *Ass* (p), *Ychefeld* 1316 FA
Huchefeld', Hutefeld' 1271-2 *Ass* (p)
Ychtesfeld 1271-2 *Ass, Yttesfeld'* 1291-2 *Ass*
Ightefeld 1284-5 FA *et freq* to 1363 Pat, *Ightfelde* 1376 Pat *et freq*; *Yghtfeld* 1399 AD, *Ightfield* 1703 PR(L) 4
Ythfeld 1331 Ch
Hightfeld 1374 AD, c.1540 Leland, *Higthfeld* c.1540 Leland
Eighfild 1675 Ogilby, *Eitfield* 1677 PR(L) 9, *Eightfield* 1764 PR(L) 4, *-fields* 1765 *SBL 4264*

'Open land by the River *Giht*'.

Scribal and editorial renderings of *-c-* and *-t-* may not always be correct in the above spellings, but the nature of the first element is clear enough. The forms closely resemble those for the first element of Islip in Oxfordshire, which contains a river-name spelt *Gent, Giht* in OE sources, *Ychte* in 1185. The name did not survive - the river is now called Ray - but Ekwall, *English River-Names* 209, lists it under the hypothetical form *Ight.* There can be little doubt that Ightfield contains another instance of this river-name. The village is near the source of a long tributary of the Tern (called Bailey Brook lower down its course). The river-name has not been satisfactorily explained; it is presumed to be pre-English.

The last set of spellings suggests a pronunciation as in *eight,* but in modern usage *Ight-* has the pronunciation usual for this spelling.

INGARDINE SO 629814 DB Manor

Ingewyrthe ?c.975 ASWills, *Yngewurthe* 1188 P (p)
Ingurdine 1086 DB, *Ingwrdin* 1199 P *et passim* with variant spellings *-wurdin, -wirthin, -wrtin, -wortin, -wardyn, -wardin, -uardin* to 1271-2 *Ass, Ingwrithdin* 1284-5 FA
Inggeuardin' 1271-2 *Ass* (p)
Igguardyn 1346 FA (p)
Engwarden 1535 VE
Ingardine 1713 *SBL 6309*

Probably 'Inga's enclosure'. The second element appears to have been **wyrð**, a variant of **worð**, with alteration to **worðign**, the derivative of **worð**, which is a place-name generic characteristic of Sa and He.

DEPN suggests that the first element is OE ***ing** 'peak', a term believed to occur in a number of place-names, including Ingon Wa, Inkpen Berks and Ingleton YW; but the situation is probably not dramatic enough to warrant this assumption.

The farm called Ingardine on modern maps lies at the bottom of a low spur extending from the eastern edge of the Clee Hills. The 19th-cent. 1" map calls this place *Lower Ingardine,* and *shows Upper Ingardine* higher up the slope. The places lie in Farlow parish.

ISOMBRIDGE SJ 611138 DB Manor

Asnebruge 1086 DB, *Anebrig* 1198 Fees
Esnebrugg 1249 Ipm *et freq* with variant spellings *-brug(g)e, -brige* to 1328 *SBL 4477, Esenebrugge* c.1326, 1415 *SBL 4475, 4491, -brugg* 1328 Pat (p), *Esenbrugge* 1359 Fine, *Ezen-* 1359 Ipm, *Esonbridge* 1548 *SBL 4508, Esen-* 1569 *SBL 4509, Esyn-* 1584 *SBL 4469*
Isnebrug 1255 RH *et freq* with variant spellings *-brigge, -brugge* to 1315 Fine, *Isenbrigg* 1301 Pat *et freq* with variant spellings *-brugg(e)* to 1396 Cl, *Isynebrugge* 1329 Cl, *Isonbridge* 1548-9 *SBL 4508*, 1740 *SBL 5120*
Eselbrige, Essebrug' 1255-6 *Ass*
Esembrugg 1362 Fine, *Esumbrugge* 1397 Cl *et freq* with variant spellings *-bregge, -bridge* to 1559 *SBL 5105, Esembrugge* 1398 Pat, *Esomebrigge* 1535 VE, *Esombridge* 1581 *SBL 4466*
Isumbrygge 1395 Pat, *-brigge* 1418-19 SAS 52, *Isembrugge* 1437 Cl, *Isombridge* 544, 82 *SBL 4564, 4520 et seq, Ysembrydge* 1564 *SBL 5106, Isombridge or Esombridge or Esonbridge* 1614 *SBL 4895, Izombridge* 1615 *SBL 15755*

'Bridge of the servants'. The bridge was probably on the R. Roden, between Isombridge and Allscott. The first element is the gen.pl. of OE **esne**, which has various meanings, including 'servant' and 'young man'. Groombridge K and Knightsbridge in London are similar place-names, perhaps referring to bridges where young men were in the habit of meeting.

The local pronunciation is [izdʌmbridʒ], with short I-. The change of *-nb-* to *-mb-* is frequent in place-names. The settlement is in the parish of Rodington.

KEMBERTON SJ 730045 Ancient Parish

Chenbritone 1086 DB
Cambristona 1121, 55 SAC
Kebrinton' 1208-9 *ForProc*
Kembricton' 1242 Fees *et freq* with variant spellings *-brytton', -brighton', -bri(t)hton', -bryghton', -brighton* to 1387 Pat
Kenbricton' 1242 Fees, *-bryghton* 1428 FA

Kemp'ton 1255-6 *Ass*
Kembirton 1284-5 FA, *Kemburton, -berton* 1397 Pat, *Kemberton* 1431 FA *et seq*
Kymb'ton' 1291-2 *Ass* (p), *-brighton* 1369 Pat, *-berton* 1397 InqMisc, 1470 Fine, *Kimberton alias Kemberton* 1610 *SBL 15757*
Kemerton 1316 FA

'Cēnbeorht's estate'. This is another instance of the absence, or perhaps early loss, of the *-s* of the genitive in a compound of **tūn** with a personal name in *-beorht.* The phenomenon is discussed under Albrighton near Shrewsbury.

KEMPTON SO 360830 DB Manor

Chenpitune 1086 DB
Kempeton 1255 RH, 1271-2 *Ass,* 1302 Ipm, 1327 Pat, *Ke'peton'* 1291-2 *Ass*
Kempiton' 1271-2 *Ass, -ton* 1272 Ipm
Kempton' 1291-2 *Ass, -ton* 1327 Pat *et seq*
Kym'ton 1291-2 *Ass*

'Cempa's estate'; the original form may have been **Cempingtūn,* with connective **-ing-**, rather than **Cempantūn,* with the personal name in the genitive. *Cempa* ('Warrior') is not on independent record as a personal name.

Kempton is a township of Clunbury parish.

KENLEY SJ 560004 Ancient Parish

Chenelie 1086 DB, *Kenele* 1203-4 *Ass* (p), *-legh'* 1209 For, 1231 Cur
Kenleg' 1203-4 *Ass* (p) *et freq* with variant spellings *-legh', -lye, -ley(e)*
Kinelege 1214 Cur
Kennel' 1261-2 *ForProc*
Kendly 1724 PR(L) 20, 1761 PR(L) 19, *-ley* 1763 PR(L) 14, 1775 PR(L) 2, 1787 *PRCardington*
Kinley 1737 PR(L) 19

'Cēna's clearing'; the name occurs also in Sr.

KINLET SO 719803 Ancient Parish

Chinlete 1086 DB, *Kinlet* 1242 Fees, 1703 PR(H) 3, *Kynlet* 1255 RH *et passim* to 1577 Saxton, *Cynlet* 1334 SR, *Kynlett* 1535 VE *et freq* to 1591 PR(H) 3, *Kinlett* 1587 *PRHighley*, 1677 PR(H) 3, 1701 PR(H) 16, 1773 PR(H) 1, *Kinlat* 1752 PR(H) 9
Killet 1193,4,5 P (p), *Kylet* 1251 Ch
Kunlet 1309 Cl
Kenlet 1450 Fine
Kindlet 1666 PR(H) 3
Kinglett 1730 PR(H) 13

This name is explained in DEPN as 'royal portion', OE *cyne-hlēt*, contrasting with Shirlett Forest, 11 miles N.W., which means 'shire portion'. The spellings suit this etymology perfectly; but *hlēt* is not certainly evidenced in place-names except for these two Sa examples, and the situation which would give rise to such names can only be a matter for conjecture. In DB Kinlet is said to have belonged before 1066 to 'Edith', who may be Queen Edith.

KINNERLEY SJ 339210 Ancient Parish

Chenardelei 1086 DB, *Kenardeleye* 1308 Cl
Kinardesle 1223,8 Pat, 1240 Cl, *Kynardesl'* 1249 Cl, 1291-2 *Ass*, *-leye* 1299 Ipm, *-lee* 1397 InqMisc, *-legh* 1397 Pat, *-ley* 1398 Pat
Kynardel' 1230 Cur (p), *-ley* 1283 Ipm, 1394-5 *SBL 9777*, 1427 *SBL 4028*, *-legh'* 1291-2 *Ass*, *-leye* 1308 Ipm, 1335 Pat, *Kinardeleye* 1308 Cl, *Kynardley* 1412 Pat, *Kynnardly* 1681 *SBL 8492*
Kinardinlhe 1254 Norwich, *Kynardynllef* c.1291 TN, *Kinnerdinlle* 1307 LCA
Kenardesle 1277 InqMisc
Kynnerley 1575 AD *et freq* to 1726 *SBL 4156*, *Kinnerley* 1577 Saxton *et seq*, *Kinerley* 1655 SAS 1/XLVII, 1696 PR(StA) 5, 1779 PR(StA) 2, *Kynerley* 1685 *SBL 10258*, 1695 PR(StA) 5, 1752 PR(L) 4, *Kynnarley* 1713 PR(StA) 2

Kynersley 1763 PR(StA) 2, *Kinnersly alias Kinnerley* 1803 Plymley

'Cyneheard's clearing', *v.* **lēah**. There were alternative forms with and without the genitive inflection. The latter form is the commoner, but it is interesting to note that the tradition of a form with -*s*- persisted down to the 19th cent.

The Welsh form of the name, *Cinerdinlle* (ex. inf. R. Morgan), is taken back to 1254 by the spelling in *The Valuation of Norwich*. This shows association with the Welsh words *din* 'fort' and *lle* 'place'.

KINNERSLEY SJ 673168 Ancient Parish

Chinardeseie 1086 DB, *-eia* 1138, c.1144, 1155 SAC, *Kinardeseia* c.1138 SAC, 1223 Pat, *Cin-* c.1144 SAC, *Kynardeseye* 1255-6 *Ass* (p), 1303 Cl, 1317 Ipm (p), 1.14th SAC, *- in Wyldemor* 1261-2 *ForProc, Kinnardsy* 1694 PR(L) 3, *Kynnardsey in ye Wildmoors* 1697 PR(H) 16
Kinardesheye c.1175 SAC, *-heia* 1185 SAC, *Kynardesheye* 1256 (1332,46) Ch, 1256 SAC, *Kinardesh'* c.1270 SAC
Kynardesleye 1291-2 *Ass*
Kynnashey 1535 VE
Kynnersey c.1550 SAS 1/VI
Kynesley 1577 Saxton, 1672 HTR, *Kinesley in the Moor* 1611 PR(H) 1, *Kinesly* 1694 PR(L) 8
Kinersley 1655 PR(L) 9, *Kinnersley* 1687 PR(L) 8 *et seq*

'Cyneheard's island, enclosure, and woodland clearing'. Topographically, this is a perfect **ēg** site, the village being on the southern edge of a large, oval-shaped island in the Weald Moors made by the 200 ft. contour. But the *-hey*(*e*) forms are sufficiently frequent to be evidence for an alternative name with **(ge)hæg**, which is used in place-names for an enclosure in woodland. A full collection of spellings also makes it clear that *-ley* is not a modern corruption; there was apparently a third name in which the generic was **lēah**. It seems necessary to assume that the belt of woodland attested by -ley names between Wellington and Oakengates extended northwards over this part of the Weald Moors. There was perhaps a tongue of woodland running between Eyton and Preston, which ended on this raised patch of ground.

KNOCKIN SJ 334223 Ancient Parish

Cnukin 1195-6 MemR, 1196,7 P, *Knukin* 1198 FF, *Knukun* 1199 FF, *Cnucin* c.1200 MM, *Knukyn* 1291-2 *Ass*, 1309 Cl, *Knuckin* 1622 PR(H) 6 *et freq* to 1799 PR(L) 7, *The Knuckin* 1741 PR(StA) 3

Knokin 1221-2 Ass (p) *et freq* to 1276 Ipm, *Knokyn* 1255 RH *et passim* to 1470 Cl, *Le Knokin* 1276 InqMisc, *Le Knokyn* 1303 Pat, *Knoken* 1402 Cl, *Knockyn* 1616,37 *SBL 5365, 6434*, *Knockin* 1681 PR(StA) 3 *et seq*

Knoukyn 1305-6 *Ass*, *Knookin Castle* 1577 Saxton

Knokyng 1351 Cl, *Knoking* c.1540 Leland, *Knocking* 1672 HTR, 1685 PR(StA) 3, *Ye Knocking* 1739 ib, *Knocking pronounced Nuckin* 1803 Plymley

Knuckinge 1609 PR(H) 6, *Ye Knucking* 1677 PR(StA) 3, *Knucking* 1713 PR(StA) 2 *et freq* to 1744 PR(H) 18, *Nucking* 1777 PR(L) 7

This has been generally explained as Welsh **cnycyn** 'little mound', a diminutive of **cnwc**. The only other instances of this word noted in English place-names are two field-names in Cheshire, *Knukyn* 1307-23 in Irby, and *Kneckyn* 1454 in Caldy, both in the Wirral (PN Ch 4, 266, 286). **cnwc** is the source of Knook, W. The full collection of spellings for Knockin set out here suggests that there was association both with OE **cnocc** 'hillock' and with Welsh **cnwc** (to which the long vowel of *Knoukyn* 1305-6 and *Knookin* 1577 might be ascribed). The addition of *-g-* from 1351 onwards is a common occurrence in words and names ending in *-in* or *-en*. Plymley's "pronounced Nuckin" is a fair representation of the modern spoken form.

The 1in. map shows small oval-shaped hills at the E. and W. ends of the village. The occasional use of definite article from 1276 to 1741 suggests that the name was felt to refer to a visible feature.

KYNASTON SJ 354202 DB Manor

Chimerestun 1086 DB

Kineuerdeston' 1198 FF

Kynemereston 1.13th APW (p), *Kynfriston* 1292 BBCS 13 (p)
Kinardeston 1308 Cl
Kynarston 1346 SRO *103/1/5/1*
Kynaston 1421 *SBL 3650 et seq, Kinaston* 1679 PR(StA) 3,
Kinnaston 1687 ib, *Kinneston* 1789 ib

'Cyneweard's estate', *v.* **tūn**. The Welsh name, Tregynferdd, is a translation. It is recorded as *Tregynborth* 1542, *Drigenverth* 1623 *MorganTs.*

Kynaston is a township of Kinnerley parish.

LACK SO 266938 DB Manor

OE **lacu** 'watercourse'. The DB entry, which refers to a tiny holding of 1½ virgates, is the only early documentation noted for this name.

The 19th-cent. OS map shows Lack and Lack Sarn on either side of the Church Stoke - Newtown road, in Church Stoke parish. The building there called Lack (also on *TA* map) is shown without a name on the 1947 1in. map. The name probably refers to the tributary of the Caebitra Brook which is the boundary between Brompton and Rhiston parish and that of Church Stoke, and also the Shropshire/Monmouthshire boundary.

LACON SJ 539326 DB Manor

Lach 1086 DB, *Lak'* 1255-6 *Ass* (p), *Lack'* 1271-2 *Ass*
Lakene 1271-2 *Ass et freq* to 1397 Cl, *Laken* 1284-5 FA *et freq* to 1529 *SBL 5450, Lacken* 1695 Morden
Lakoun 1439,40 Cl (p), *Lacon* 1577 Saxton *et seq, Lakon* 1652 PR(L) 1, *Lackon* 1701 ib
Laketon 1597, 1601 PR(L) 9
Leacon 1783 PR(L) 10

This is the dative plural of OE **lacu,** which is used in place-names in the senses 'small stream', 'side-channel of a river' and 'drainage channel'. The last seems the appropriate one here.

Lacon is a township of Wem parish. The 1" map shows

Lacon at the GR given above, also Upper and Lower Lacon and Lacon Hall, these places being spread over 1½ miles of low-lying, wet country.

LANGLEY (HALL) SJ 539002 DB Manor, Civil Parish with Ruckley

Languelege 1086 DB
Langelega 1191 P (p) *et freq* with vriant spellings *-leg(h)'*, *-ley(e)* to 1377 Fine
Longeleg' c.1248 SAC *et freq* with variant spellings *-ley(e)*, *-lye*, *-legh'*, *-leie* to 1499 Ipm
Langlegh 1249 Pat, *-leg* 1253 Ch, *-ley* 1577 Saxton *et seq*
Longleye 1428 FA, *-ley* 1598 PR(L) 19

'Long clearing', *v.* **lang**, **lēah**; a fairly common place-name.
The "confused" parochial status of Ruckley and Langley is discussed in VCH VIII, p.141. Langley had a Hall, a Chapel and a few houses. The affix 'little' occurs in PR(L) 2 (1581,2,94, 1652) and PR(L) 19 (1585, 1673), and the township is marked LITTLE LANGLY on the 19th-cent. OS map. This is presumably for distinction from Langley in Stanton Lacy, though that place is not much larger.

LAWLEY SJ 668086 DB Manor

Lauelei 1086 DB, *Lauele* 1177 P (p) *et passim* with variant spellings *-leg(h)'*, *-leye* to 1302 Ipm, *Lauley* 1392,6 AD, 1517 *SRO 327*
Laweleg' 1271-2 *Ass*, *Lawelegh* 1381 Cl, *Laweley* 1391 Cl, *Lawley* 1494 Ipm *et seq*
Laley 1577 Saxton, 1695 Morden, 1735 PR(L) 18

'Lāfa's clearing', *v.* **lēah**. The last set of spellings may indicate that there was an alternative development to a pronunciation [leili]. This is found in some comparable names, such as Stayley, PNCh **1**, 317-8, from OE **stæfa-lēah*.
Lawley is a township of Wellington parish.

LEATON SJ 468185 DB Manor

Letone 1086 DB, *Letona* 1243-8 HAC *et freq* with variant spellings *-ton', -ton(e)* to 1404 Fine
Leeton' 1250 Fees (p), 1255 RH (p), *Leeton* 1397 Cl
Leytun' 1250 Fees (p), *Leyton* 1609,11 PR(L) 4
Letton 1552 Pat
Leaton 1577 Saxton, 1602 PR(L) 4 *et seq*
Leighton 1613, 1772 PR(L) 4
Leiton 1614 PR(L) 4

This name is unexplained. OE **lēa(h)-tūn* would suit the spellings, but the weight of place-name evidence is overwhelmingly against the use of **lēah** as first element of a compound. DEPN suggests either **(ge)læt** or **hlēo**. The first of these words, though said in DEPN to mean 'water-course' (as in modern *leet*), is as least as likely to mean 'road-junction'. This would suit the position of Leaton quite well, but **(ge)læt** is only noted in ancient names well to the S. of Shropshire, and it seems unlikely that this rather rare southern term should be used just once in this county. A compound of **(ge)læt** and **tūn** might also have been expected to give more spellings with *-tt-*. *hlēo* 'shelter', would probably have given some spellings with *Lu-, Lew-*.

The modern pronunciation is [leitən]. Leaton is in the civil parish of Pimhill.

LEDWYCHE, UPPER SO 555792 DB Manor

Ledewic 1086 DB, *Ledewich* 1221-2 *Ass* (p) *et freq* with variant spellings *-wyz, -wyce, -wis, -wiche, -wiz, -wych* to 1398 Pat, *Shireuesledewyche* 1291-2 *Ass, Schirreuesledewych* 1292-5 *Ass* (p)
Ledwic 1203-4 *Ass, Ledwiz* 1242 Fees (p), *Ledwich'* 1261-2 *ForProc* (p), *Ledwyche* 1409 Pat, *Ledwych* 1492 Ipm, *Ledwedg* 1641 PR(H) 16, *Leadwitch* 1803 *SBL 6111*
Ludwych 1255-6 *Ass* (p)
Leddewych 1255-6 *Ass*
Lodewych 1311 Pat (p), *Lodewich* 1346 FA (p)
Lettwich 1672 HTR

Forms for Lower Ledwyche, situated three miles lower down Ledwyche Brook, are: *Lodewik'* Hy 2 (1261-2) *ForProc, Ledewich* 1155 BM, *Presteledwych* 1255 RH, *Ledewyz* 1271-2 *Ass, Presteledewych'* 1291-2 *Ass, Low Ludwich* 1695 Morden.

Forms for Ledwyche Brook are: *Aqua de Ledewych'* 1255-6 *Ass, Ledewik Broke, Lidwik Brooke* c.1540 Leland, *Ledwiche Flu* 1577 Saxton, *brooke called Ledwick* 1675 Ogilby.

The first element of Ledwyche is the river-name of British origin which is found in its full form, OE *Ledene*, in Leadon, the tributary of the Severn which gives name to Ledbury He. In Ledbury, as in Ledwyche, the river-name has lost its *-n*. The same river-name is found in Lodden and Lydden, two tributaries of the Stour in Dorset. The British name was **litano-* 'broad', which became OE *Ledene* (in Leadon) or *Lydene* (in the Do names). Some of the Ledwyche spellings suggest that the latter development is in part the relevant one for the Sa name.

Ekwall, RN p.246, does not associate Ledwyche with Leadon, Lodden, Lydden on account of some 13th-cent. spellings *Lotwys, Lotwych*: but these actually refer to Lutwyche, *q.v.*

The second element of Ledwyche is OE **wīc** 'dependent hamlet, dairy farm'. The *-s, -z* spellings are due to a regular Norman French sound substitution.

It is not likely that Upper and Lower Ledwyche were ever parts of a single large estate. They are probably two settlements of independent origin both with names meaning 'dairy farm by the river called *Lede*(*n*)'.

Lower Ledwyche (in Ludford parish) belonged to Bromfield Priory, hence *Presres-*. Upper Ledwyche (in Bitterley parish) belonged to William FitzAlan, who was sheriff of Shropshire 1190-1201.

There is a local pronunciation [ledidʒ].

LEEBOTWOOD SO 476988 Ancient Parish

Botewde 1086 DB, 1189 CartAntiq, *Bottewode* 1163-6 HAC, *Botewd* 1189 Templars, *-wude* 1227 Ch

Lega in Bottewode c.1170-6, 1253 HAC, 1.13th *ForProc, - apud Bottewode* 1179 HAC, *Lega* 1204-10, 1215-c.30, 1243-55, 1273

HAC, *Leg' de Bottewud'* 1212 Fees, *Leg' Bottewode* c.1240 SAC (p), *Leybotwood* 1255 RH, *Lega, - in Botwod'* 1255 *Ass, Leg' Bottewud'* 1261-2 *ForProc, Leye Bottewode* 1271-2 *ib, Legh' Bottewode* 1291-2 *Ass, Leye* 1316 FA, - *in Botwode* 1320 Ch, - *in Bottewode* 1334 SR, *Lebotwood* 1577 Saxton, *Leebottwood* 1647 PR(H) 12, 1730 PR(L) 4, *-botwood* 1713 PR(L) 14, *Leabotwood* 1730 ib, *Le Botwood* 19th OS

Lyebottewode 1372, 1458 HAC, *Lye, Liobottewode* 1400 HAC, *Lye(e) Botwood* 1535 VE, *Libot Wood* c.1540 Leland, *Lybotwood* 1549 Pat *et freq* to 1744 PR(H) 8, *Libotwood* 1552 Pat, *Liebottwood* 1612 PR(L) 14

Botwood is 'Botta's wood', and Lee is OE **lēah** 'clearing'.

The DB manor of *Botewde* was assessed at ½ hide and was held since before the Conquest by a man named Auti, who also held a 1-hide estate at Lydley Hays, which is in Cardington parish but adjacent to Leebotwood. The next references to Botwood occur in two sources, the cartulary of Haughmond Abbey and the records of the Knights Templars. The Templars were granted assarts "apud" Botwood in 1189 (the Templars and CartAntiq references, and that of 1227 Ch, concern this grant). The tenor of the document, which lists assarts "apud" a number of places, suggests that Botwood may be the name of a settlement as well as the name of the wood which was assarted. The Templars' estate here is, however, called *Bot(t)elegee* in the 1185 survey in Templars, where it is closely linked with Lydley, both having been donated by Herbert de Castello of Castle Holdgate.

The Haughmond estate at Botwood is first recorded in 1163-6, when Henry II granted "duas landas in Bottewode et terram in eandem forestam --" to the abbey. Subsequent deeds in HAC record a vigorous policy of assarting by that house. A chapel was given rights of baptism and burial in c.1170-6, before which the settlement had been parochially dependent on Condover. The chapel is called "capella de Lega in Bottewode", and this is the first certain appearance of the name Lee in connection with this place. After this, the settlement is called 'Lee' or 'Lee in Botwood' or 'Leebotwood'.

A very careful study would be required before an opinion could be formed concerning the relationship between the DB settlement of *Botewde*, the place where Haughmond Abbey built a chapel, and the Templars' estate of *Bot(t)elegee.* Another DB estate of 2 hides in the vicinity, which is called *Lege*, seems to be the place later known as Longnor, adjoining Leebotwood to the north. The impression given is that there were several small settlements in the wood, all called *Lege*, and that the name of the wood was sometimes used for these.

Bot(t)elegee is one of a number of place-names related to Botwood. In 1255 RH the Templars are said to have a house at Lydley in the wood called *Bottewde* on *Bottestrete.* The last name clearly refers to the southward continuation of Watling Street, which is called *Bottestret* 1185 HAC in this stretch, and in 1301 SAC, at a point 7 miles further south. Botvyle in Cardington parish (G.R.477962) is *Botefeld* 1185 Templars, *-feld'* 1190 P, *Botesfeld'* 1201 Cur, *Bottefelt* 1255 RH, *-feud* 1261-2 *Forroc*, 1301 SAC, *-feld'* 1271-2 *Ass.* The reference to *Bottestret* in 1301 SAC occurs in the bounds of Bushmoor Hay, and these also mention *Bottelowe*, which is probably to be equated with Botleymoor Wood in Wistanstow, which adjoins the road.

Botwood is probably the earliest of these names. The southward extension of Watling Street, which ran through the wood, was probably called **Bottanwudustrǣt*, which would become ME *Bottestrete* by the normal process of dropping the middle element in a three-element compound. Botvyle is probably a shortened version of **Bottanwudufeld*, referring to open land south of the wood. Botley(moor), earlier *Bottelowe*, is probably a shortened version of **Bottanstrǣthlāw*, 'tumulus by the Roman road called *Bottan(wudu)strǣt'.* The Templars' manor of *Bot(t)elegee* is probably a shortened form of a ME **Bottewodelege*, which would be a sort of forerunner of the eventual name Leebotwood.

LEE BROCKHURST SJ 549268 Ancient Parish

Lege 1086 DB *et passim* with variant spellings *Legh'*, *Legh*, *Ley(e)* to 1392 Fine, *Legh' sub Brokhurst* 1271-2 *Ass*, *Leye subtus Brochurst* 1284-5 FA, - *Brockhurst* 1316 FA

Le 1203-4 *Ass* (p), *Lee* 1318 *SRO 2821/1*, c.1540 Leland, 1577 Saxton, 1675 Ogilby, *Leebrockhurst* 1608 PR(L) 20, *Lee Brockhurst* 1665 *SBL 8383*

Lyegh, Liegh subtus Brochurst 1331 HAC, *Lyghe under Brokhurst* 1414 Fine
Lye subtus Brochurst 1336 HAC, - *Brokehurst* Hy 6 *SBL 6173*

Lee is from OE **lēah** 'woodland clearing'. Brockhurst means 'wooded hill frequented by badgers', and this name occurs also in Wa.

The wood called Brockhurst was mainly in Wem Parish. Preston in Moreton Corbet was also 'sub(tus)' Brockhurst, i.e. on its outer fringes. The 13th- and 14th-cent. references are to the wood. There is a settlement called Brockhurst in Wem parish, on a hill for which the word **hyrst** is appropriate, but no references to this have been noted earlier than 1748 PR(L) 10.

LEEGOMERY SJ 664128 DB Manor

Lega 1086 DB *et freq* with variant spellings *Lege, Legh'* to 1202 P, *Lega Aluredi* 1167 P, *La Legh'* 1208-9 *ForProc, Lege Cumbray, -Cumbrei* 1249 Ipm, *Leg' Cumbray* 1251 Cl, 1261-2 *ForProc, Lega Cumbrey* 1255 RH, *Legh Cumbrey* 1258 Cl, *-Combreys* 1301 SAC, *-Cumbreye* 1349 Ipm, *-Combray* 1409 Pat, *Leygh Combrey* 1492 Ipm
Leycumbre 1271-2 *ForProc, Leye Cumbray* 1284-5 FA *et freq* with variant spellings *-Cumbre, -Combrey* to 1334 SR
Lye Cumbre 1271-2 *ForProc* (p), *Lycombray* 1455 Cl
Cumbreyeslegh' 1291-2 *Ass*
Lee Gomery 1760 PR(L) 20

'Clearing', OE **lēah**. The G.R. is for Leegomery House.

The affix is from the family of Alfred de Cumbray, who was the owner c.1180 (VCH XI, p.114). It is presumably his Christian name which appears in the form from 1167 P.

OE **lēah** gives rise to several simplex names in the county, in addition to Leebotwood, Lee Brockhurst and Leegomery. Alternative spellings are Leigh and Lye.

Leegomery is a township of Wellington parish.

LEIGHTON SJ 611055 Ancient Parish

Lestone 1086 DB
Lecton' 1198 FF *et passim* to 1271-2 *ForProc*
Lehton' c.1200 *ForProc* (p), *Lechton* 1203-4 *Ass* (p), 1255 RH, 1284-5 FA, *SBL 4389, Le(c)hton* 1253 (1292) Ch, *Leghton'* 1253 Cl (p) *et freq* with variant spelling *-ton* to 1577 Saxton
Leihton 1212 P (p), 1255 RH, *Leichton, Leyc(h)ton* 1255-6 *Ass* (p), *Leygthton'* 1.13th *ForProc, Leighton* 1318 *SBL 5427* (p) *et seq, Leyghton* 1431 FA
Lethon 1253 (1292) Ch
Leyton 1255-6 *Ass*
Leton 1271-2 *Ass*, 1318 *SBL 5427, Leeton* 1409 Pat
Laighton 1679,80,86 PR(L) 14
Layton 1683 PR(L) 8 *et freq* to 1761 *PRLittle Wenlock*
Lyton 1717 PR(L) 8

OE **lēac-tūn**, 'leek enclosure, herb garden', later 'kitchen garden'. There are settlements called Leighton from this source in Ch, Hu, and La, and several instances of modern Laughton have the same origin. It has also become Lacton K, Latton Ess, W, Letton He.

LILLESHALL SJ 728154 Ancient Parish

Linleshelle 1086 DB
Lileshelle Canon' 1167 P, *Lyleshul* 1172 (e.14th) HAC, *Liļeshull'* 1200 Cur *et freq* with variant spellings *-hul(l), -hill* to 1737 PR(L) 20, *Lilishull* 1255 RH, *Lylyshull* 1513 AD
Lilleshull' 1198 Cur *et passim* with variant spellings *-hill', -hell', -hull(e), -hul, -hil* to 1660 *PRLilleshall, Lillushull'* 1219 Cur, *Lylleshull* 1245 Cl *et freq* with variant spellings *-hulle, -hyll, -hill* to 1549 Pat, *Lillushull* 1305 Pat, *Lillesulle* 1394 Cl, *Lyllushill* 1494 AD
Lillelshull' c.1229 SAC
Lulleshull 1230 Cur, 1299, 1329,47 Cl, *-hull'* 1255-6, 71-2, 91-2 *Ass*, *-hulle* 1265 Cl, *Lolleshul* 1268 Cl, *Lulleshule* 1308 Pat
Lilshull 1316 FA, 1380 Pat (p), *Lylselle* 1438 Cl, *Lylsyll* 1505,6 AD, *Lilsell* 1608 PR(L) 20, *Lillshill* 1742 ib

Lulshill 1462 Cl
Lysley 1535 *SBL 7180*
Lincel c.1540 Leland, *Linshull* 1637 PR(L) 3, *Linshall* 1704 PR(L) 19, *Lilleshall alias Linsell* 1708 PR(L) 8, *Lindsil* 1741 ib, *-sill* 1741,2,5,9 ib, *-sall* 1743 ib, *Linsill* 1747 ib, *Lineshall* 1759 *PRShifnal*, *Linsell alias Lilleshull* 1773 PR(H) 15
Lillshall 1655 SAS 1/XLVII, *Lylleshall* 1673 PR(L) 7, *Lilleshall* 1684 PR(L) 8 *et seq*, *Lillishall* 1783 PR(L) 20

'Lill's hill'. second element OE **hyll**, first element a personal name. The boundary survey of the neighbouring estate of Church Aston in a charter of A.D. 963 mentions *Lilsætna gemære* 'boundary of the Lilleshall people'.

There was a local form *Linshull*, *Linshall* which developed a parasitic *-d-* and became *Lindsill*, *Lindsall*. The *Lins-* form, in which the first *-l-* had been dissimilated to *-n-*, was probably heard by Leland, causing him to write *Lincel* in his travel notes. The change from *-hill* or *-hull* to *-hall* is shown by the spellings to be 17th-cent. There was a disyllabic form (*Lilshull*, *Lylsyll*, *Lillshill*) in the 14th - 18th centuries, but the modern pronunciation is trisyllabic.

LINLEY SO 687985 Ancient Parish

Linlega c.1135, 1138 SAC (p), 1177 P (p), c.1200 *ForProc* (p), *Linleia* c.1165 SAC (p), 1203-4 *Ass*, *Lynlee* 1261-2 *ForProc*, *Linley(e)* 1272-3 Ipm, *Linleye* l.13th *ForProc*, 1316 FA, 1331 (1348) Pat, *Lynlegh* 1301 SAC, *Lynle* 1320 Ch, *Lynlege* 1334 SR, 1362 Ipm, *Lynley* 1495 Ipm, *Lynlege* 1577 Saxton
Linglea 1167 P, *Ligleg'* 1255 RH
Lindleg' 1203-4 *Ass* (p), *Lyndleg'* 1261-2 *ForProc*
Lylleye 1291-2 *Ass*

Probably 'lime-tree wood', OE **lind-lēah*. The occurrence of 13th-cent. forms with *Lind-*, *Lynd-* tell against the etymology 'flax clearing', OE **līn-lēah*. This last name sometimes becomes modern Lindley, but in these instances the parasitic *-d-* makes its appearance at a much later date.

There is another Linley in the parish of More, and for this

also there is an early 13th-cent. spelling with *-d-*: *Lindele* 1208-9 *ForProc.* There is also a form with *-g-*, *Lingl'* 1255-6 *Ass*, which parallels the spellings for the parish name in 1167 P and 1255 RH.

LLANFAIR WATERDINE SO 241763 Ancient Parish

Watredene 1086 DB, *Waterdene* c.1155 (1348) Pat, *Watirden* 1331 (1348) Pat
Thlanveyr 1284 Cl, *Llanvaire* 1672 HTR
Lanweyrwaterden 1376 Pat, *Llanvaier-* 1577 Saxton, *Llanfair Water Dene* 1614 PR(StA) 4, *Llanverwaterdine* 1625 PR(H) 2, 1670-1 PR(H) 17, 1751 PR(H) 14, *Llanvairwaterden* 1641 SAS 3/IV, *Llanvair Waterdine* 1808 Baugh

The OE name was *wæter-denu*, 'water valley'. Another example of this compound has become modern Waterden in Nf, and Watercombe Do is analogous. **wæter** sometimes means 'lake' in place-names (as it does in the Lake District), and there are pools in the small valley from which the Nf place is named. No pools are to be found in the side-valleys of the Teme in Llanfair Waterdine, however, and the meaning here is probably 'wet valley'.

The Welsh affix, Llanfair, is 'Mary church'. The gift to Wenlock Priory of St Mary's church here is the subject of the Patent Roll references given above. The process of replacing an older name by a 'church' name was widespread in Wales but rare in England, and this use of both names is an interesting compromise between Welsh and English practice. Llanfair is a common Welsh name.

LLANYBLODWEL SJ 239229 Ancient Parish

Blodwelle c.1200 MM, *-vol* 1254 Norwich, 1407 Pat, *-vell* 1483 *SBL 3637*, *-wall* 1577 Saxton, 1627 PR(StA) 4, *-well* 1598 *et seq*, *Blodwell Vechan*, *- Vaure* 1634 *SBL 6058*
Blodewell' 1272 Cl, *-uel* 1277 Pat, *-walle* 1303 Pat, *Blodewal Vaghan* 1307 Pat, *Blod(e)voel* 1377 Pat
Bledewell Vaghan, *Bledewelle Vaur* 1302 Ipm
Blodwoll Vaur, *- Vechan* 1393 Slack

Llanblodwell 1535 VE, 1666 PR(StA) 4, *Llan Blodwall* 1579 PR(StA) 4, *Llanablodwell* 1687, 1735 ib, 1798 PR(L) 7, *Llanyblodwell* 1728 PR(StA) 5 *et seq*

Llanymblodwell 1576 PR(StA) 1, *Llanyemblodwell* 1602-3 PR(StA) 4, *Llannamlodwall* 1609-10 ib, *Llanymlodwall* 1614 ib, *-llodwall* 1618 ib, *-lodwell* 1639 ib, 1687 PR(StA) 5, *Lanymlodwell* 1707 PR(L) 20, *Llanumblodwell* 1686 PR(StA) 3, *Llanimblodwell* 1711 ib

Blodwell is probably 'blood spring'. The first reference occurs in a list of "aquae dulces" in Shropshire, in which the other items are the rivers Severn, Tern, Meole and Cound. The tributary of the R. Tanat which encloses Llanyblodwel is much smaller than these others, and it is likely that the stream, or the spring at its source, had a special quality which caused it to be known outside the immediate vicinity. OE **blōd** occurs in Bloody Beck in Hackness, PN YN 113, which is *Bludebec* 1268. Both names may refer to a superstition.

The Welsh affix means 'church of -'. It is interesting that the grammatically correct form, Llanymlodwel, occurs in parish registers, albeit sometimes with *-b-* in addition to *-m-*. Several spellings have WMidl *-wall* for *-well.*

Vaur and *Vechan* are Welsh 'Great' and 'Little'. The modern settlement has two foci, one at the church and the other are Blodwell Hall, a mile to the E.

LLANYMYNECH SJ 267208 Ancient Parish

Llanemeneych' 1254 Norwich, 1272 LCA, *Llanymenych* 1310 LCA, *Llanymeneth* 1404 Pat, *Lannemenagh* 1474 Cl, *Llanymynech'* 1483 *SBL 3637, Llanamonach* 1577 Saxton, *Llanymynych* 1583 PR(StA) 4, *-mynech* 1614 ib *et seq, -minich* 1628-9 ib, *Llanomonech* 1655 SAS 1/XLVII, *Lanamynech* 1668 PR(StA) 2, *Llanaminecke* 1688 PR(StA) 3, *Lanamunough* 1714 PR(StA) 2, *Llanymynych* 1716 ib

Lanmenagh' 1272 Cl, *Thlanmenygh* 1307 Pat

'Church of the monks', a wholly Welsh name. DEPN notes that the early spellings preserve the old plural of *mynach*, which was *myneich*. The precise significance of the reference to monks is unexplained.

LONGDEN SJ 442063 DB Manor

Langedune 1086 DB, *-don'* 1251-2 Fees, 1271-2, 91-2 *Ass*, *-done* 1291 InqMisc, *-don* 1364 Ch, 1385 Pat
Longedun', *-don'* 1235-6 Fees *et freq* with variant spellings *-dun*, *-don*, *-doun* to 1421 Cl, *Longedon' Botereus* 1271-2 *ForProc*
Langesdon' 1242 Fees, *Longesdon* 1367 Cl
Lungedon, *Lundgedon* 1284-5 FA
Longdon 1294 InqMisc, 1546 *Eyton et seq* to 1764 PR(L) 20, *Longden* 1615, 1783 PR(H) 12

'Long hill', OE *Langandūn*, one of two Sa examples of this name, which has become Langdon or Longdon in several other counties. There is a 400ft-high ridge athwart the north-south road here, which presents a smooth, whale-back profile when approached from Shrewsbury. This is a distinctive feature, as many of the nearby hills have a 'sugar-loaf' shape. VCH VIII, p.261, mistakenly says 'long valley', but it is clear from the spellings that -den only appears in the 17th-cent., and is due to a modern weakening of the final syllable, not to partial derivation from **denu** 'valley'.

Botereus from the Boterel family, frequently mentioned in the 13th cent. Longden is a township of Pontesbury parish.

LONGDON UPON TERN SJ 623155 Ancient Parish

Languedune 1086 DB, *Langedon'* 1203-4 *Ass*, 1221 SAC, 1271-2 *ForProc*, 1291-2 *Ass*
Longedon 1217 (1285) Ch, 1255 RH, 13th *SBL 3592*, *-don'* 1291-2 *Ass*, *Longedon supra Tyren* 1491 *SBL 4560*
Longdon uppen Tyren 1516 *SBL 4561*, *Longdon* 1592 PR(L) 20, 1692 PR(L) 8, - *upon Tearne* 1631 *SBL 4573*, *Longden* 1739,78 PR(L) 8
Longchappel 1577 Saxton, *Longe* 1610 PR(L) 20, *Long super Tearne* 1658 ib, *Long* 1755, 86, 89 PR(L) 8, 1769 (PR(L) 20, 1808 Baugh, *Long otherwise Longdon upon Tern* 1767 *SBL 5739*

Langton 1655 SAS 1/XLVII, *Longton super Tearne* 1672 HTR

Another 'long hill'. Longdon upon Tern is raised above the Weald Moors by a ridge and two islands made by the 175 ft. contour. It does not have so typical a **dūn** as Longden in Pontesbury. The shortening to *Long* is an unusual development. Baugh's map of 1808 calls the village *Long*, and the wood to the N. of it *Longs Wood*; but he marks *Longden Waste* to the N.W.

LONGFORD SJ 726184 Ancient Parish

Laganford 1002-4 Burton, *Langanford* 1004 ib
Langeford 1086 DB, 1194,5 P, 1198 Cur, 1316 Cl, *Langafordia* 1155 SAC, *Langeford'* 1193,4 P, *-forde* 1201-2 RBE
Longeford c.1182 SAC (p) *et passim* with variant spellings *-forth*, *-forde* to 1428 FA
Longford 1199 P, 1577 Saxton *et seq*, *-ford'* 1301 SAC, *-forde* 1445 Cl, 1535 VE, *-fort* 1598 PR(L) 3
Longheford, *Lonhkeford* 1255 RH
Lungeford' 1306-7 *Ass* (p)
Glongoford 1397 Pat

It is impossible to discuss this name without reference to the road called The Longford, which runs through Newport, just over a mile to the east of Longford village. It is not, however, certain that the settlement is named from the road, as Longford parish does not extend much to the east of the village, and the parish of Church Aston lies between it and Newport. The village and parish of Longford could be named from a crossing-place on Strine Brook, well to the west of the road which has the same name.

The settlement in Moreton Say parish called Longford (*Langeford'* 1232 Cur) is much more likely to be named from the road, as there is no settlement between it and The Longford, though this place also lies a mile from the road. Three early references to the road have been noted. In 1319 and 1322 Pat there are grants of pontage for a bridge across the R. Tern, and in these the road is described as the causeway of *Longeford* between the towns of Bletchley and Newport. In 1331 Ch, *Le Longford* is mentioned in some boundaries in Moreton Say.

OE **ford** frequently occurs in place-names in geographical contexts which make 'causeway' the best translation, and this usage is probably found in the road-name. A hypothetical crossing of Strine Brook in Longford parish would also have required a causeway. Longford or Langford is a frequent recurrent place-name throughout the country.

LONGNER HALL SJ 528112 DB Manor

Languenare 1086 DB, *Langenore* 1267 Ch
Longenhalre c.1203, c.1227-36 HAC, *Longhenhalre* 13th *SBL 4391* (p), *Longenholre* 1283 Ipm, *Longenolre* 1328 Pat, 1363 *SBL 3818* (p), 1380 Pat (p), *Longnolre* 1377 Cl (p), *Longenorle* 1378 Cl (p)
Longenore 1367 Cl, *Longnore* 1451 *SBL 6171, Longnour* 1549 Pat, *Severnes Longnor* 1566 *SBL 5793, Longnor on Severn* 1688 *SBL 6236*
Longner 1679 PR(L) 15 *et seq*
Logner 1697 PR(L) 15, *Longer* 1705 ib, *Lonnor* 1716 ib

OE **Langanalre*, literally '(place at) the tall alder tree', but DEPN conjectures very reasonably that the tree-name is used collectively, and that the meaning may be 'long alder-copse'. There are three examples of the name, the other two being Longnor 7 miles S.S.W., which is discussed below, and Longnor 3 miles W. of Penkridge, St.

Longner Hall is in Atcham parish.

LONGNOR SJ 487006 Ancient Parish

Langanara 1121 SAC, *Langanarra* 1155 SAC
Longenalra 1155 SAC, *-alre* e.13th, c.1233 HAC, *-alr', -olre* 1261-2 *ForProc* (p), *-olre* 1271-2 *Ass et freq* to 1338 Pat (p), *-olr* 1334 SR, *-holre* 1322 Pat, *Longnolre* 1431 FA
Longelorn' 1242 Fees
Longenour' (p), *Longenore* 1255-6 *Ass, Longnore* 1569 *SBL 6621, Longnor* 1587 PR(L) 19 *et seq*
Langenolre 1291-2 *Ass* (p)

Longner 1672 HTR, 1675 PR(L) 6, *Logner* 1675 Ogilby

See the discussion of Longner above. Some early-13th-cent. bounds of woodland in Longnor (HAC p.144) mention a thick alder ("ad grossam alnum"), but this probably only an indication of the persistence of alders in the parish, not an indication that Longnor is named from a single tree.

A DB estate called *Lege* is considered to be Longnor (see discussion of Leebotwood above). *Longenorlegh'* 1291-2 *Ass* and *Longnorley* 1586 *SBL 6699* may preserve the DB name, with Longnor as prefix.

LONGSLOW SJ 655354 DB Manor

Walanceslau 1086 DB
Wlankeslaw' 1200 Cur (p), *-lawe* 1214 P, 1271-2 *Ass* (p), *-lauwe* 1221-2 *Ass* (p), *-lowe* 1290 (p), 1314 Ipm
Wlonkeslawe 1212 Fees (p) *et passim* with variant spellings *-lowe, -lauwe* to 1431 FA, *Wlonckeslawe* 1235-6 Fees (p), *Wlonkislow* 1255 RH, *Wloncuslowe* 1334 SR
Wancleslawe 1235-6 Fees (p)
Wlonkelawe 1271-2 *Ass* (p)
Wronkeslowe 1271-2 *Ass*
Wlongeslowe p.1362 *SBL 6594*, 1410 Fine
Lonkeslowe 1489 Ipm, *Lonkslow* 1717 PR(L) 4
Longslowe 1672 HTR, *-low* 1712 PR(L) 4

'Wlanc's tumulus'. The personal name, which means 'stately, proud', would be appropriate to an aristocratic Mercian of the late 6th - early 7th century, when barrow-burial was in fashion among the Anglo-Saxons. Shropshire names of this type are discussed under Beslow.

Longslow is in Moreton Say parish.

LOPPINGTON SJ 471293 Ancient Parish

Lopitone 1086 DB, 1210-12 RBE (p) *et freq* with variant spellings *-ton, -tun', -ton'* to 1452 *SBL 4525*

Lopinton' 1199 P *et passim* with variant spelling *-ton* to 1397 *SBL 16293*, *Lopynton'* 1334 SR *et freq* with variant spelling *-ton* to 1535 VE
Loppinton' 1203,5,6 P, 1255 RH (p)
Lopi(n)gton' 1230 P (p), *Lopyngton* 1395 Pat, *Loppyngton* 1431 FA, *Loppington* 1535 VE *et seq*
Lupinton' 1255-6 *Ass* (p), *Luppynton'* 1291-2 *Ass*
Luppeton', Loupton' 1306-7 *Ass*
Lappington 1656 PR(L) 20, 1672 HTR, 1732 PR(L) 9, 1770 PR(L) 12, *Lapinton* 1678 PR(L) 11, *Lapington* 1769 PR(L) 12

Probably 'estate associated with Loppa', OE **Loppingtūn*. The personal name would be from *loppa* 'spider'. It would be desirable to have more early spellings with *-pp-* to support this etymology, however.

LOTON SJ 356147 DB Manor

Luchetune 1086 DB
Lohton 1255 RH, *Lochton* 1274 RH, *-ton'* 1291-2 *Ass, Loghton* 1301 Cl, 1302 Ipm
Luton' 1271-2 *Ass*
Loton 1334 Pat, 1715 PR(H) 6
Lughton 1414,30 Fine, Hy 6 *SBL 6173*, 1613 *et seq* to 1661 PR(H) 6
Loughton 1474 Cl, 1661 PR(H) 6

The forms for this name, and those for Loughton (below), indicate an OE **luh-tūn*, 'lake-settlement'. OE **luh**, which is only recorded once outside place-names, is considered to be a borrowing from Welsh *llwch*. It is a rare place-name element, Lutton Li being probably the only settlement-name containing it apart from these two Shropshire examples. There might have been a lake in the great loop of the R. Severn N. of Loton Park.

Loton is in Alberbury parish.

LOUGHTON SO 616830 Civil Parish

Loketona 1121 SAC

Lochetona 1138,55 SAC
Luchton' c.1143, c.1248 SAC, *Luhtune, -tone* c.1230 SAC, *Luchton* 1255 RH, *Lughton'* 1291-2, 1306-7 (p) *Ass, -ton* 1327 Pat, 1803 Plymley
Lucton' c.1275 SAC
Lohton' 1291-2 *Ass, Loghton* 1327 Pat
Louhton', Lowchton' 1.14th SAC, *Loughton* 1405 *SBL 6990 et seq, Lowghton* 1575 PR(H) 3
Lowten 1675-6 PR(H) 15, *Lowton* 1696 *PRBurwarton*, 1744 *PRChetton*
Loton 1786 *PRChetton*, 1795 *PRBurwarton*

See the discussion of Loton, above. Loughton stands on a hill-spur between two small streams, and modern maps show no pool; but there must have been a water-supply to attract settlement.

In 1327 Pat the name has an affix which the Calendar renders "under the Clee". This was perhaps to avoid confusion with Loton, similarly spelt at that date.

Both names are pronounced [loutən].

LOWE FARM SO 631805 DB Manor

Lau 1086 DB
La Lawe 1203-4 *Ass* (p) *et freq* to 1271-2 *Ass*
La Lowe 1255 RH (p) *et freq* to 1428 FA, *Lowe* 1291-2 Ass *et seq, Louwe* 1305 Ipm (p)

'Tumulus', OE **hlāw**. This term occurs as a simplex name in Alveley and Wem, also.

A nearby tumulus gave name to the parish of Farlow, in which Lowe Farm is situated.

LUDFORD SO 513741 Ancient Parish

Ludeford 1086 DB, 1242 Fees, 1255 RH, 1346, 1401 Cl
Lodeford 1271-2 *Ass* (p) *et freq* to 1350 Pat
Ludford 1346 Cl, c.1540 Leland *et seq, -forde* 1535 VE

Lutford 1792 *PRChetton*

Ludford and Ludlow both have as first element OE **hlūde** 'loud one', referring to the R. Teme in this stretch. Ludford is on the south bank of the Teme, where the north-south road crosses it to enter Ludlow.

LUDLOW SO 512747 Ancient Parish

Ludelaue 1138 Hunt *et passim* with variant spellings *-lawa, -lawe* to 1347 *SBL 3817* (p), *Ludelow* 1255 RH *et passim* with variant spelling *-lowe* to 1414 Fine, *Ludelaghe* 1318 Cl
Lidielawe 1212 Fees
Lodelawe 1242 Fees *et passim* to 1347 *SBL 3817* (p), *Lodeloue* 1272 Pat *et passim* with variant spellings *-low(e)* to 1438 Fine
Ludlowe 1372 Cl (p), 1408 Pat *et freq* with variant spelling *-low*; *Ludlo* c.1540 Leland
Luddelowe 1394 Cl, 1405 Pat, 1460 Fine
Loudlowe 1535 VE, *Loodlowe* 1603-4 SAS 4/III

'Tumulus by the torrent', see the discussion of Ludford above. The **hlāw** is considered to be a large tumulus demolished in 1199 when the parish church was enlarged. There is an excellent account of this in T. Wright, *The History of Ludlow and its Neighbourhood*, Vol.I (1841), pp. 13-14.

Lude, which precedes Ludford in the Herefordshire section of DB, has sometimes been considered to be Ludlow, but it is Lyde, He.

LUTWYCHE SO 557947 DB Manor

Loteis 1086 DB
Lotwich 1203-4 *Ass* (p), 1255 RH, *-wyche* 1271-2 *Ass, Lot Wyht* (p), *Lotwych'* 1291-2 *Ass*
Lotewich' 1261-2 *ForProc* (p), *-wych'* 1301 SAC, *-wyche* 1401 Cl
Lutwich 1651 *PRAston Botterell*, *-which* 1672 HTR
Luttidg 1662 PR(L) 12

This name has a parallel in Wo, where a lost place near Droitwich called *Lootwic* is mentioned in a charter of 716-7 (S 102). This is described as a place where salt is made.

The second element is OE **wīc**, often 'dependent farm' in Sa, but 'salt-making establishment' in the Droitwich area of Wo. The only available suggestion for the first element of Lutwyche and *Lootwic* is an OE word **lōt*, conjectured from Continental parallels to be a term for a sort of shovel. Ekwall (*Old English wīc in Place-Names*, p.24) suggested that it was an implement specifically used in salt-making, and it may be relevant that there were salt springs in the nearby parish of Preen, and "a bog designed for a salt-work" is shown on a map of Preen Common, c.1730 (*SRO 283/1-2*).

Lottage in Aldbourne W (PN W 292) is probably a different name, as the earliest spelling is *Luttewyk* 1249 *Ass*, though later spellings are similar to those for Lutwyche.

The name Lutwyche Hall on the 19th-cent. 1" map has been replaced by Wenlock Edge School on modern maps. Lutwyche Hall and House are in the parish of Rushbury.

LYDBURY NORTH SO 353861 Ancient Parish

Lideberie 1086 DB, *-bir'* c.1150-60 HAC, *-bery, -bury* 1179-80 HAC, *Northlidebiry* 1254 Pat, *Lidebur' Nor(h)t* 1255 RH, *Lydebyr'* 1271-2 *Ass*. *-bury* c.1291 TN, 1334 SR, 1385 Fine, 1394 Pat
Ledebir' 1208-9 *ForProc et freq* with variant spellings *-bur', -byr, -bury* to 1306-7 *Ass, Ledebir North* 1221-2 *Ass, Ledebur North* 1241 Ch, *Ledebirynorth* 1258 Pat
Ludbir' 1221-2 *Ass* (p), *Ludbury* 1747 PR(H) 18
Leddebyr 1255-6 *Ass*
Liddebury 1271-2 *Ass* (p)
Lidbur' North 1291-2 *Ass, Lydbery, -bury* 1535 VE, *Lidbury* 1672 HTR *et freq* to 1800 PR(H) 12, *Lydbury North* 1641 SAS 3/IV
Ludebury 1306-7 *Ass*
Luddebury 1384 Fine
Libury 1727 PR(H) 17, 1728 PR(H) 3, 1753 *PRHope Bowdler*

Probably 'manor-house by the stream called *Hlȳde*'. The cond element is OE **byrig**, dat. of **burh**. The alternation of *Lid-* ,

Led-, Lud- spellings indicates a first element with *-y-*. The well-evidenced stream-name **Hlȳde** ('loud one') would suit, and this might have been an early name of the R. Kemp. Lydbury has previously been associated with Lydham, but a full run of spellings for both names suggests that they are of independent origin.

North is for distinction from Ledbury He, a different name ('manor-house on R. Leadon') but with similar ME spellings.

LYDHAM SO 336910 Ancient Parish

Lidum 1086 DB, *Lidam* 1271-2 *Ass. Lydoum* 1290 Ipm, 1441 Cl, Fine, *Lydom* 1290 Cl *et freq* to 1687 *SBL 5348, Lydum* 1290 Cl *et freq* to 1327 Pat, *Lydam* 1291-2 *Ass, Lidom* 1327 Pat, *Lidome* 1672 HTR, 1759 PR(H) 8

Lideham 1250 Ipm, 1253,66 Cl, 1255 RH, 1256 Pat, *Lydehum'* 1265 *SBL 3992, Lidham* 1255 RH (p), 1272 Pat, 1701 PR(H) 13, 1746 PR(H) 18, *Lydham* 1258 Pat *et freq, Lydhum, Lidhum 1291-2 Ass, Lydeham* 1292 Cl

Liden 1254 Pat, *Lidun* 1255-6, 91-2 Ass, 1267 Ch, 1272 Ipm, *Lydon, Lydun* 1271-2 *Ass, Lydon* 1306-7 *Ass, Lydoun* 1316 FA

Lydenham 1258 Pat

Lythom 1431 Fine

Ledom 1447 HAC, 1596 PR(H) 3, 1659 *SBL 6236, Ledum* 1497 Ipm

Ledon 1535 VE, *Ledon alias Leedham alias Lyddam, usually written Lydham* 1803 Plymley

Lyddum 1577 Saxton, *Liddam* 1641 SAS 3/IV, 1664 PR(H) 6, *Lyddom* 1664 *SBL 6236*, 1691 PR(H) 3, *Lyddam* 1733 PR(L) 4

Leddom 1659 *SBL 6236*

Leedham 1728 PR(H) 3

This is clearly a simplex name with the dative plural ending *-um*, not a compound with **-hām** as second element. The OE vowel must have been *-i-*. The *Ledom, Ledon* forms from the 15th cent. onwards, and the occasional later *Leedham*, exhibit the development of OE *-i-* in open syllables seen, e.g., in *week* from OE *wicu*, and *weevil* from OE *wifol*. The alternative development, with a short vowel, is occasionally indicated by *-dd-*.

Lydham may be the dative plural of OE **hlid**; if so, it would be identical with Lydd K, for which there is an OE spelling *Hlidum.* **hlid** in these names has been explained as a side-form of **hlith** 'hill-slope'; but this is topographically improbable for the Kent place, which is in Romney Marsh, and seems unlikely for the Sa name because **hlith** is fairly frequent in this county. The only recorded OE word *hlid* is the ancestor of modern *lid.* In OE it is sometimes extended to mean 'door' or 'window-shutter', but it does not mean 'gate', and it is difficult to envisage a topographical use. Lydham overlooks a marshy area.

LYDLEY HAYS SO 485983 DB Manor

Litlega 1086 DB, *Litlegh* 1222 SAS 3/VII
Lidlegee 1185 Templars *et freq* with variant spellings *-lega, -leg', -leye, -le* to 1397 Pat, *Lydleg'* 1261 Cl *et freq* with variant spellings *-ley*(*e*), *-legh', -le*
Liddeleg, Lydeleg 1222-c.1230 HAC, *Lidel* 1255 RH, *Lydely* 1271-2 *Ass et freq* with variant spellings *-ley*(*e*) to 1416 Fine, *Lideley* 1331 Pat
Lidsley 1251 Fees
Lichlehey 1271-2 *Ass*
Lydley Hayes 1573 *SBL 8403, Lydlowes Heyes* Jas I *Corn.R.O., Lydlies Hayes* 1672 HTR, *Lydleys Hayes* 1741,86 *PRCardington, Lydley Hayes* 1745 *ib*

DEPN says 'small *lēah*', taking the first element to be OE *lӯt*(*el*); but only the DB form and the one from 1222 support this. Most of the spellings suggest another occurrence of the mysterious term **hlid**, which is discussed under Lydham. There was a *hlīdlēah* in Berks, the name of which was incorporated in that of Littlewick Green in White Waltham (PN Berks 72).

Lily Farm in Charmouth, Do was *Lidleghe* 1240, *Lydlege* 1327 (Mills p.98). The sense of the compound is obscure.

The **lēah** ('clearing') of Lydley was one of a number in this neighbourhood, see the discussion of Leebotwood. Hays is from OE **(ge)hæg**, ME *hey*, 'woodland enclosure'.

The settlement (in Cardington parish) hardly exists on modern maps. The 19th-cent. 1" shows the name adjacent to Day House, but only the latter is marked on the 7th-series 1". There seem nevertheless to have been two settlements in the 16th century. *Lydley, Inferior Lydley* occur 1535 *SBL 7180*, and *Lydley, Neyther Lydley* 1566 *SBL 8384*.

LYE SO 337758, 333757 DB Manor

Lege 1086 DB
The Lye 1658, 1734 *PRBucknell*

'Clearing', OE **lēah**. In spite of the sparse later documentation this was a one-hide estate in DB. Two settlements on either side of the R. Redlake are shown, but not named, on the 7th series 1" map. The 19th-cent. 1" calls these *Upper Ley* and *Lower Ley*. The *TA* map of Bucknell parish, however, shows *The Lye* S. of the R. Redlake a short distance to the W. from these houses.

The simplex name *Lēah* has similarly become Lye in Morville and in Quatt in this county, and in He and Wo, and the common spelling Leigh sometimes has this pronunciation. In Sa, however, the more frequent development is to Lee.

MADELEY SJ 696041 Ancient Parish

Madelie 1086 DB, *Madelega Prioris* 1167 P, *Madeleg'* 1224 Cl *et freq* with variant spellings *-legh, -lye, -legth, -ley(e), -le*; *Madeleye Prior's* 1350 Pat
Maddeley 1190 (15th) SAC *et passim* with variant spellings *-leg', -le, -leye, -legh'* to 1331 Pat, *Maddele Priors* 1346 Pat
Meddeleye 1291-2 *Ass*
Madley 1695 Morden, 1708 PR(H) 13

This name, and two instances of Madeley in St, have been interpreted as 'Māda's clearing', while Madingley Ca is considered to be 'clearing of Māda's people'. A full collection of spellings for the Sa place reveals, however, that *-dd-* predominates heavily over *-d-*. The double consonant is also very frequent in the spellings for Madingley. A personal name *Madda* would suit these forms better, and such a personal name could be a hypocoristic derivative of the postulated *Māda*.

The modern pronunciation of Madeley reflects the spelling which was usual from c.1350 onwards, but *Madley* in 1695 and 1708 may indicate an alternative development, with a short vowel, from ME *Maddeleye*.

The place belonged to Wenlock Priory (hence *Prioris*), and it is considered to be the estate named *Magdalee* listed in the document known as the Testament of St Mildburg. The place-name spellings in this document do not go back to St Mildburg's time, and probably *Magdalee* is not of sufficient authority to outweigh the numerous ME spellings which are summarised above.

MAESBROOK SJ 297216 DB Manor

Meresbroc 1086 DB
Maysbrok' 1271-2, 92-5 *Ass* (p), *-brook* 1397 InqMisc, *Maesbroc* 1427 *SBL 4028*, *-brooke* 1578 AD, 1709 *SBL 5324*, *-bruck* 1587 PR (StA) 4, *Maesbrock Ucha* 1607 *SBL 5929*, *Maysbrocke* 1608,16 *SBL 5937, 5905*, *Maisbrocke Ucha* 1618 *SBL 5934*, *Maesbrook Issa*, *- Ucha* 1730 *SBL 4015*
Masbroke 1455 Cl *et freq* with variant spellings *-broock*, *-brouke*, *-brook(e)* to 1738 PR(L) 20, *Masbrocke Ucha* 1620 *SBL 5936*, *Lower, Upper Masbrooke* 1672 HTR, *Booth Masbrooks*, *Masbrook Ucha*, *- Issa* 1673 *SBL 3382*, *Higher Masbrook* 1731 PR(StA) 3, *Massbrook* 1741 ib
Marsbrooke 1602 (copy) *SBL 3382*
Mesbrooke 1602 Slack
Upper, Lower Macebrook 1762,3 PR(StA) 3

The DB form suggests 'brook of the boundary', with the gen. of **gemǣre** as first element. But the other spellings point to a hybrid Welsh/English name, with Welsh *maes* 'open field, plain'. In the unfortunate absence of 12th-cent. spellings it is impossible to say whether an original **Mǣresbrōc* was transformed by association with the Welsh word, or whether the DB form should be dismissed as erroreous.

The G.R. given above is for Maesbrook House, not necessarily the site of the earliest settlement. *Maesbrook Ucha* and

Issa are two townships of Kinnerley parish in the *TA*. The 'lower' settlement is shown on modern maps as Maesbrook Isaf. The hamlet at Maesbrook Green corresponds roughly to the 'higher' place of the *TA*. The 'brook' rises near this settlement.

MAESBURY SJ 309257 DB Manor

Meresberie 1086 DB, *-byr'* 1271-2 *Ass*, *-bury* 1294, c.1320, 1337 HAC, 1302 Ipm, 1307 Pat
Mersbir' 1272 Cl, *-buri* 1272 Ipm
Mersshbury 1306-7 *Ass* (p)
Mesbury 1392-3 Slack, *Mesburie* 1588 PR(StA) 4 *et freq* with variant spellings *-bur(e)y* to 1706 PR(StA) 3, *Messbery* 1600 PR(StA) 4
Measburie 1582 PR(StA) 4 *et freq* with variant spelling *-bury* to 1805 PR(StA) 3, *Measebery* 1681 PR(StA) 5
Maesbury 1602 Slack, 1669,75 PR(StA) 5, 1730 *SBL 4015*, 1755 PR(StA) 6, 1811 PR(StA) 3, 1839 *TA*
Masbury 1674 PR(StA) 5

'Manor' or 'fort of the boundary', from the gen. of OE **gemǣre** and the dat. of **burh**.

The spellings suggest very occasional confusion of the first element with OE **mersc** 'marsh'. The substitution of Welsh **maes** 'plain' appears, however, to be late, and it did not gain general currency until the 19th cent. The development of *Meresbury* to *Maesbury* can be paralleled, as in Eastbury Wo (*Eresbyrie* DB, *Esebire* 13th, PN Wo 129) and Fazeley St (*Faresleia* c.1142, DEPN). The Welsh form of the name, Maesbwrch, derives from the forms in which *-r-* has been lost.

The spellings for Maesbury contrast with those for Maesbrook *supra*, and this strengthens the case for considering the two names to have different first elements. It will be seen from the forms set out above that there can be no question of Maesbury being identified, even as regards the first element, with *Maserfelth*, the name given by Bede to the battle of A.D. 642 in which King Oswald was defeated and killed by the forces of King Penda.

The seven-hide estate with five dependent settlements which DB describes under the name *Meresberie* is considered to be the later manor of Oswestry. DB records the building at *Meresberie* of a castle called *Lvvre.* This is *castellum de Osewaldestr'* c.1180 SAC (the earliest occurrence of the name Oswestry), but the DB name may have been remembered to reappear as *Castrum Leorv', Leouv, Leorud* in *SBL 9777*, a document dating from 1394-5. This is presumably French *l'oeuvre*, 'the work'.

The town of Oswestry was a post-Conquest creation at the northern edge of the parish. *Meresberie*, later Maesbury, survived as the name of a township in the southern half of the parish. The location of the township, and of the settlements to which the name Maesbury is attached, seems to preclude association of *byrig* with the great prehistoric fort called Old Oswestry which is north of the town. *byrig* probably means 'manor house' in Maesbury.

Mersete Hundred, said in DB to belong to *Meresberie*, has a name which means 'boundary dwellers'. Both Offa's Dyke and Wat's Dyke run through the parish of Oswestry, but 'boundary' in these names is probably a general concept, rather than a precise reference to the earthworks.

See the discussion of Oswestry, *infra*.

MAINSTONE SO 275876 Ancient Parish

Meyneston 1284 Cl, *Meynston* 1333 *SRO 552/1/2r*
Maynstan 1336 *SRO 552/1/2r*
Maynston' 1344 *SRO 552/1/10, Maynston* 1381 *ib/20*, 1577 Saxton, 1672 HTR, *Maynestone* 1599 PR(H) 18, *The Mainstone* 1640 PR(L) 15, *Maynstone* 1641 SAS 3/IV, *Mainston* 1695 Morden, *Mainestone* 1711 PR(H) 13

A compound of OE **mægen** 'might, strength, power' with **stān** 'stone'. The spellings suggest that there was no association of the first element with Welsh **maen** 'stone'.

The same place-name occurs in D, Db, He and Sr, and the phrase is used for boundary marks in Anglo-Saxon charters in Co, D, W and Berks. At Mainstone in Chobham, Sr, the reference is considered to be a block of ironstone, and in the Berks boundary-mark (in Woolstone) it is to a large sarsen.

The name has always been interpreted as 'great stone', but a paper in SAS I/VII (1884) suggests another possibility, at least for the Shropshire example. This states (p.127):

"The stone from which the parish seems to have taken its name lies outside the west gate of the Church. It is a small granite boulder of an irregular shape, weighing about 230 lbs. Of its history nothing could be learned from the two persons who, at our visit, seemed to compose the population of the place. It is now used by the young men of the neighbourhood as an instrument whereby to try their muscular development ---. The trial is made by lifting it up to the height of their faces, and then casting it over the left shoulder. The difficulty involved in getting a sufficient grip of it enhances the danger as well as the credit of making a satisfactory cast."

The stone is now installed in the church. Its surface is extremely smooth and shiny, as if from much handling, and this explains the remark in the quotation about the difficulty of obtaining a grip. It is not granite, but may be dolorite.

It is possible that *mægen* in this compound has the sense which it retains in the phrase 'might and main'. This accords better than 'big' with most of the examples which occur in Old English literature. There is one instance of *mægenstān* in a text. This refers to a stone which fell down a mountain, and a metrical version of the text substitutes *micel stan* for *mægenstan.* This has seemed to justify the translation of the Mainstone place-names as 'great stone', but it does not outweigh the numerous instances in which *mægen* means 'strength'. The compound *mægen-byrðen* in Beowulf could fairly be interpreted as referring not simply to a large burden but rather to one which required great strength in the bearer.

MARCHAMLEY SJ 597296 DB Manor

Marcemeslei 1086 DB
Merchemeslege 1185 P (p), *Merchemeslega* (p), *Merchemelesga* c.1190-4 HAC
Marcemeleg' 1206 Cur, *Marchemeleg* 1227 Ch, 1278 Ipm, *-leg'* 1271-2 *Ass, Marchemnlegh* 1271-2 *Ass*
Marchamlegh 1229 Ch, *Marchumleg'* 1242 Fees *et passim* with variant spellings *-legh, -le(g), -ley(e), -leie* to 1796 *SBL 5374, Marchumeleg* 1252 Ch, *Marchameleg'* 1255-6 *Ass* (p),

Marchomelegh' 1271-2 *Ass, Marchomley* 1307 HAC *et freq* to 1672 HTR, *Marchamleye* 1316 FA, c.1320 AD, *-ley* 1374 AD *et seq, Marchumelegh* 1378 Pat
Merchimeleg' c.1230-40 HAC (p)
Merchomleg' 1242 Fees, *Merchomel', -hamel* 1255-6 *Ass* (p), *Merchumleg'* 1276 Ipm
Marchimleg 1255 RH, *-lega* 1256 HAC, *-leye* 1318 Cl
Marchunley 1283 Ipm, 1397 InqMisc, *-legh'* 1291-2 *Ass, -le* 1324 Fine
Marhamlee 1291-2 *Ass*
Marshomley 1695 Morden

This name has been discussed together with Mortomley in YW and Barthomley in Ch. In PN YW Part 1, pp. 247-8, A.H. Smith suggests that Mortomley was originally **Mōrtūnhǣmelēah* ('wood of the dwellers at a place called *Morton*') and Barthomley was **Beretūnhǣmelēah* ('wood of the dwellers at *Barton*'). This is accepted by J. McN. Dodgson in PN Ch Part 3, pp. 5-7. Both scholars appear to be assuming that in Shropshire a place-name **Merchām* gave rise to a name **Merchǣmelēah*, which is the suggested source of Marchamley. This would not be exactly parallel to the solutions they are proposing for Mortomley and Barthomley, as the *t-* of *tūn* is needed to account for the recorded forms of these names. The postulated **Merchǣmelēah* could be assumed to derive from the more usual process of adding **-hǣme-** 'dwellers' to the first element of a pre-existing place-name, not to an abbreviated version of both parts of a dithematic name.

The three place-names have in common a preponderance of forms with *-um-* and *-om-*. Barthomley, like Marchamley, has *-em-* in DB. There are no *-em-* spellings for Mortomley, but this may be because the series only starts in 1190. Smith and Dodgson do not discuss the problems of deriving ME *-hum-* (for which *-hom-* is a characteristic spelling variant) from OE **-hǣme-**. These must be formidable, perhaps insoluble. But the main objection to their suggested etymologies is perhaps the improbability of **-hǣme-** being used to form place-names in the counties of YW, Ch and Sa. The detailed West Riding survey produced no other possible examples, and the few suggested instances in Cheshire are unconvincing. When A.H. Smith discussed **-hǣme-** in *English Place-Name Elements* he concluded that it was not found in the north country.

He accepted Ekwall's view that it occurs in Marchington, which would take it into north St; but that is a far from certain instance. The suggestion that our three names are formations with **-hǣme-** 'dwellers' must, with regret, be abandoned.

The likeliest source of *-um* in ME place-names is the OE dative plural inflection. In names which certainly belong in that category, inorganic *-h-* often gives *-hum* in ME spellings, and DB *-em, -en* are well-evidenced; so the forms for Mortomley, Barthomley and Marchamley fit the general pattern well enough. (A useful collection of spellings for such names is provided in N. Wrander, *English Place-Names in the Dative Plural*, Lund 1983). It is worth considering whether these three **-lēah** names could be 'wood or clearing at the **mortas*, **bertas*, **merce*', whatever those objects might be.

A place-name element ***mort** is postulated, though unexplained, for a number of names listed under it in Elements. The first component of Barthomley might be a contracted form of *Beretūnum* 'at the granges'. What are the possibilities for Marchamley?

Marchamley cannot contain **mearc** 'boundary', as that gives Marc- or Mark-, as in Marcle He and Markham Nf. Modern English *march* 'boundary' is a borrowing from French. Marchamley could, however, contain *Mierce* 'Mercians', which is believed to be a derivative of **mearc**. *Mierce*, though properly the name of the people, is used of the kingdom, as in "Tha feng Æthelbald to rice on Mercium". A compound meaning 'wood at the Mercians' is perhaps not a totally impossible place-name. This is the north-east of Shropshire, and the Sa/St/Ch border may correspond roughly to the division between the *Myrcna land* of the Tribal Hidage and the *Wreocensætna land* which follows it in that list.

The only other possibility seems to be the plant-name **merece** 'smallage'. This is well-represented in place-names, but would not lend itself to a dative plural formation.

It seems necessary to assume that the OE had *Merc-*, since there is no doubt about the palatalisation of *-c-* in this name. The *Marc*-spelling in DB, and other early sources is due to Norman substitution of *a* for *e*, and this would be supported at a later date by the early Modern English change of *-er-* to *-ar-*.

The *-s-* of the earliest forms can probably be disregarded, since there is no sign of it in the large number of later spellings.

This *-s-* caused Ekwall to propose an etymology 'Merchelm's clearing', but the massed evidence of the spellings is against this.

Marchamley is a township of Hodnet parish.

MARCHE HALL SJ 335105 DB Manor

Mersse 1086 DB, 1255 RH, 1255-6, 1271-2 *Ass*, *Merse* 1209 For (p), 1220 Cur (p), 1255-6 *Ass* (p), *Mershe* c.1221, 1390 HAC, 1285 Pat, *Mers* 1242 Fees (p), 1255-6 *Ass* (p), *La Mersse* 1242 SAS 4/VI (FF)

Messe 1086 DB

Marshe 1221-2 *Ass*, *Marsse* 1255 RH, *Marse* 1.13th *SBL 3585* (p), *The Marshe* 1618, 1621 *SBL 6775, 6770*, *The Marsh* 1654, 1706 PR(H) 6, 1764 *SBL 4207*

Merche 1242 Fees (p), 1346 FA (p)

March 1681 PR(H) 6

'Marsh', OE *mersc*. The name should have developed normally to *Marsh*, which is the form in the *TA* and on the 19th-cent. OS map, and is still current locally. The substitution of *March* may be due to the position, near the Welsh border. *Marsh and Wigmore* is shown on the 19th-cent. map as a township of Westbury parish. Both names refer to the flat, wet ground adjoining the northern end of the massif which includes the Long Mountain.

There were two DB holdings, one of 2 hides, the other (*Messe*) only 3 virgates. In spite of its modest assessment, this last had been held TRE by three men "as three manors".

MARKET DRAYTON SJ 675340 Ancient Parish

Draitune 1086 DB, *-ton* 1203-4 *Ass* (p) *et freq* with variant spelling *-ton'* to 1452 AD, *Drayton'* 1271-2 *Ass et passim* with variant spelling *-ton*

Dreitona c.1138 SAC, *-ton'* p.1256 SAC, *Dreyton'* 1276 SAC, *-ton* 1593 PR(L) 20

Draton 1577 Saxton, 1726,31 PR(L) 9

Dreton 1659,61 PR(L) 9

A Drayton (OE *drægtūn*) is a settlement where dragging takes place. The name is considered to refer to a portage on a river in some instances, and to a steep slope in others. In this instance the likeliest reference seems to be to the use of sledges, rather than wheeled vehicles, on marshy ground. The same name has become Dryton in Wroxeter parish.

There were two settlements, Market and Little Drayton, and they have separate entries in DB. Little Drayton is *Minor Draitona* 1121 SAC, and this affix is used in SAC till the mid-13th cent. The place is *Parva Drayton* 1271-2 *Ass*, 1540 *SBL 6083, Drayton Parva* 1517 *SRO 327, Little Drayton* 1672 HTR.

Market Drayton is *Magna Drayton'* 1271-2 *Ass, Magna Drayton, Muche* - 1529 *SBL 5441, 5450, Great Drayton* 1549 Pat, *Drayton Magna* 1661 PR(L) 4. The earliest use of *Market* noted is *Draiton Market* c.1540 Leland. Leland also used *Drayton upon Terne.* The commonest affix, however, is - *in Hales.* This occurs 1290 Cl *et freq*, with variant spelling - *in Halys. Drayton in Le Hales* occurs 1316 FA, *Drayton' in Le Halys* 1334 SR, and there is one instance of - *under Hales,* 1701 *SBL 4244.* This affix and 'great' are frequently combined, as in *Magna Drayton in Hales* 14th *SBL 9892, - in le Halys* 1407-8 *SBL 9905. Drayton in Hales otherwise called Markett Drayton* occurs 1680 *SBL 4547*, and *Drayton-in-Hales* is given as an alternative name in Kelly 1934.

Hales is a district-name covering lands on both sides of the St/Sa border. There is a settlement called Hales in the St parish of Tyrley, which adjoins Market Drayton, and the name occurs as an affix in Norton in Hales, *infra*, three miles N.E. of Market Drayton. This is the plural of OE **halh**, a place-name element which is used in a variety of senses.

The commonest sense of **halh** in Shropshire is a broad, shallow depression, a valley which is not sufficiently well-defined to be a **cumb**, a **denu** or a **hop**. Other well-attested senses are 'tongue of land between rivers', 'land in a river-bed', and 'piece of land projecting from, or detached from, the main area of its administrative unit'. None of these senses is obviously appropriate for this district-name. Another suggested meaning is 'raised ground isolated by marsh'. This is evidenced in north Shropshire, Whixall near Wem being a good example. It seems reasonably appropriate to the area east and north-east of Market Drayton.

MARRINGTON SO 272975 DB Manor

Meritune 1086 DB, *-ton'* 1203-4, 1271-2 *Ass* (p), *Meryton'* 1271-2 *Ass*
Merinton' 1242 Fees, *Merynton* 1277 InqMisc
Maritun 1255 RH, *Mariton* 1299, 1323 Ipm, 1361 Cl, 1535 VE, *Maryton* 1312 Pat, *-ton'* 1334 SR
Marinton 1255-6 *Ass*
Merington' 1271-2 *Ass* (p)
Marington 1629 PR(H) 8, 1672 HTR, *Marrington otherwise Marriton* 1780 *SBL 3398*

Probably 'estate associated with a man named Mere', OE **Meringtūn.* A Welsh name, *Hafodwen,* is used in 16th- and 17th-cent. Welsh sources. This means 'white summer dwelling'. The place is a township of Chirbury parish.

MARSTON (lost) SO 532862 DB Manor

Merstun 1086 DB, *-ton* 1255 RH, 1271-2 *Ass*
Meryston 1255 RH
Mersshton' 1306-7 *Ass, Merssheton in Corvedale* 1394 Fine, *Mersshton* 1413 Fine (p), 1491, 1500, 1504 Ipm
Marshton 1317 Pat

'Marsh settlement', OE *mersc-tūn.* The name is incorporated in a field-name, *Marstons Meadow,* in the Tithe Award of Broncroft and Lower Parks Township in the parish of Diddlebury; and a site noted on air photographs at the G.R. given above is believed to be that of the settlement.

MARTON SJ 288025 DB Manor

Mertune 1086 DB, *-ton* 1228 Lib, *-ton'* 1242 Fees, 1255-6, 1271-2 *Ass*
Marton 1255 RH *et passim* with variant spelling *-ton'*
Martine c.1540 Leland, 1695 Morden

'Settlement by a mere', a well-evidenced name which sometimes has the modern forms Marten, Martin, Merton. This

Marton is a township of Chirbury parish. There is a lake called Marton Pool near the village, and the reference in Leland is to that: "Martine Poole, meately large and plentiful of Fische". There are two other Shropshire Martons, in Ellesmere and in Myddle.

MAWLEY SO 689753 DB Manor

Melela 1086 DB
Melleleg' 1242 Fees
Malleye 1255-6, 1274, 1291-2 *Ass*, 1346, 1428 FA, *Mallegh'* 1291-2 *Ass*, *Malley* 1431 FA
Mauleye 1305 Ipm, *Maueley* 1399 Cl, *Mauley* 1666 *SBL 6387*

Probably 'dappled clearing', from **lēah** and an adjective **mǣle**, which has been noted in several south-country names. The first *-l-* has been vocalised, cf. Dawley *supra*.

The G.R. is for Mawley Hall, which is so named 1659 PR(H) 9. Half a mile N. of this is Mawleytown Fm, which is *Mawley Town* 1770 PR(H) 17. The places are in Cleobury Mortimer parish.

MEADOWLEY SO 668925 DB Manor

Madolea 1086 DB
Medeweleg' c.1235 SAC *et freq* with variant spellings *-leye, -legh'* to 1301 SAC, *Medowele* 1242 Fees, *Medweleg'* ib, 1261-2 *ForProc* (p), *-le* 1255 RH, *-legh* c.1270 InqMisc, *Medueleg* 1274 RH, *Medeueleye* 1284-5 FA, *Meduleye* 1301 Ipm, *Medueleye* 1317 Cl, *Meduweleye* 1.14th SAC, *Medoley* 1577 Saxton, *Meadowley* 1650 *SBL 9573*

'Meadow clearing', from OE **mǣd** (dat. *mǣdwe*) and **lēah**. Meadowley is in Morville parish.

MELVERLEY SJ 334167 Ancient Parish

Meleurlei 1086 DB, *Melewerleye* 1291-2 *Ass*

Melwardleye 1271-2 *Ass* (p), *Mulverdeleg* (p), *Mel-* 1286 Cl, *Maluerdelegh'* 1291-2 *Ass, Meluerdeley* 1394-5 *SBL 9777*
Mulewerleye 1291-2 *Ass*
Meluerlegh', -leye 1291-2 *Ass, Milverlegh* 1311 Ipm, *Melverly* 1357 Pat, *-ley* 1455 Cl, *Milverley als' Melverley* 1635 *SBL 10293*
Melvard 1770 *SBL 10308*

Probably 'clearing by a mill-ford', though this etymology postulates a lost crossing-place on the R. Severn. There are several place-names in which **ford** has been reduced to *-ver-* in a triple compound.

There was a Welsh form *Melwern*, recorded 1400 *SRO 103/1/6/145*, which shows association with *gwern* 'swamp'.

MENUTTON SO 304775 DB Manor

Munetune 1086 DB, *-tone* 1272 Ipm
Moneton' subtus Porteloke 1272 Cl, *Meneton, Moneton* 1284 Cl
Mynuttyn 1641 SAS 3/IV, *Minuton* 1695 Morden
Manutton 1672 HTR

A hybrid Welsh/English name, from **mynydd** 'mountain' and **tūn**. The settlement lies just below the 1000 ft. contour, by a spur of the massif which includes Clun Hill. The reference to *Porteloke* (Purlogue, 1½ miles S.W.) is probably for distinction from Minton in Church Stretton, *infra.* There was also a lost *Muneton* in Worthen. The preservation of the middle syllable in Menutton will be due to the stress pattern of Welsh speech. The pronunciation is [menʌtən].

Menutton is a township of Clun parish.

MEOLE BRACE SJ 486106 Ancient Parish, now part of Shrewsbury

Mela(m) 1086 DB, *Mele(s)* 1221-2 *Ass, Mele* 1255-6 *Ass* (p), 1261-2 *ForProc, Melesbracy* 1274 Ipm, *Melebracy* 1301 SAC, *Bracemele* 1577 Saxton
Moles 1203-4 *Ass*, 1208 Cur, *Mole(s)* 1206 Cur, *Mole* 1235-6 Fees,

Moles Bracy 1276 Cl, *Molebracy* c.1291 TN, *Mole Brase* 1777 PR(L) 20
Meola 1221-2 *Ass, Meoles* 1305 Ipm, *Meole Bracy* 1334 SR, 1346, 1428 FA, *Meole Brace alias Brace Meole* 1586 *SBL 7065, Meole Brace* 1633 PR(H) 1 *et freq*
Mueles 1238 Cl, *Meules* 1254 Pat, *Meulesbracy* 1296 Pat
Meeles 1242 Fees, *Brasemeele* 1589 PR(L) 6, *Meele* 1597, 1615 PR(H) 1 *et freq* with *Brace* - to 1716 PR(L) 4, *Meelbrace* 1685 PR(L) 8
Moeles 1281 Ch, 1305 Ipm, *Moelbraci* 1326 Pat, *Moelesbracy* 1397 Cl
Mulebracy 1352 Ipm, 1385,99 Cl
Mylbrace, Mil- 1535 VE, *Milbrace alias Brace Meole* 1803 Plymley
Bracemeale 1670 PR(H) 17, *Brace Meale* 1675 Ogilby, 1687 PR(H) 17, *Bracemeal* 1749 PR(H) 7

Meole Brace is situated by Meole Brook (now known as the Rea Brook), which joins the Severn at the English Bridge, Shrewsbury. The brook is *Mola(m), Meolam* c.1130 Ordericus, *Mele* c.1200 MM, *aqua que vocatur Meola* 1215-40 SAC, *aqua de Meole* 1234 SAC, *Meole Broke* 1508 AD. Ekwall (RN 287) suggests that the river-name is a back-formation from the settlement-name, and that it was originally a hill-name from Primitive Welsh *mę̄l*, Welsh *moel*, 'bare hill'. He acknowledges that the Welsh name would have had to survive in Welsh speech until quite late, perhaps the 9th century, in order to have the form which would give the pronunciation [ø] indicated by the spellings. In this discussion (as elsewhere) Ekwall assumed a continuance of Welsh speech in Shropshire which is not supported by the fuller place-name material now available. This phonological difficulty, and the absence of a conspicuous hill of the sort usually described by Welsh *moel*, render an alternative explanation desirable.

The spellings bear a remarkable resemblance to those for Meols Cheshire and a series of names (Raven Meals, *Argarmeles*, North Meols) along the Lancashire coast near Formby and Southport. The main differences are that forms with *-s* predominate very heavily in the Ch and La spellings, whereas they are in a minority in the Sa forms, and the Ch name has some forms with *-ll-*.

The Ch and La names are explained as deriving from Old

Norse *melr* 'sandbank'. J. McN. Dodgson (PN Ch Part 4, p. 297) explains the rounded vowel [ø] as due to the *-s* of the English plural being attached to the Norse name. He suggests that this caused some degree of vocalisation of *l*, which affected the vowel.

Derivation from ON **melr** is not an available option for the Sa Meole, and the resemblance of the spellings should probably be regarded as a coincidence. The Sa name is likely to have been an Old English name for Meole Brook. It may derive from the word *meal*, OE *melo, meolu*. Water with a cloudy appearance could have suggested an association with flour.

The plural forms could be due to the existence of several manors. DB describes holdings belonging to the Bishop of Chester and to Ralph de Mortimer, and a virgate belonging to the Abbey in the Mortimer manor. The Mortimer holding passed to Adolf *de Braci* at the beginning of the 13th century, and there was litigation lasting from 1203 to 1211 about the rights of his son, who had the same name. Eyton (VI, pp. 350ff.) gives a detailed account of this. Nothing is heard of Shrewsbury Abbey's holding after the DB entry. The Bishop of Chester's manor was given to Buildwas Abbey. It is called *Meola* in the charter confirming the grant (1189 CartAntiq). Later it appears as *Monkemoel* 1334 SR, *Monkmeole* 1349 *SBL 3786*, *Monkemeole* 1430 Fine. Eyton (VI, pp. 359-60) calls this manor *Monk Meole and Crow Meole.* The latter name is *Crowmehill* 1535 VE, *Cromyle* 1549 Pat, *Crowmeole* 1577 *SBL 3649*, *Cromeale* 1582 *SBL 4022*, *Crawmel* 1695 Morden. A ded of 1672 (*SBL 4021*) speaks of *Crowmeale alias Crowmyle alias Munckmeale alias Munckmyle*, and the two names are given as alternatives in deeds of 1730 and 1731 (*SBL 4015, 1460*). Crowmeole is shown on the 19th-cent. OS map at G.R. 469119. It was a township of Shrewsbury in *TA*. The building is shown, but not named, on modern maps. This must have been the western extremity of the area called Meole, and it is some distance from the river. The affix is probably 'crow'.

Cruck Meole in Pontesbury parish is a separate settlement, on the headwater of Meole Brook called Rea Brook. The affix to this name, and the first element of nearby Cruckton, may be *cruck* 'curved building timber'. This word is poorly documented in literary sources and has not been recognised as a place-name element. Full discussion must await the treatment of names of lesser administrative status than those included in the present volume.

MERRINGTON SJ 472209 DB Manor

Muridon c.1220-30 HAC, 1320 Ch, 1348 Pat, 1478 HAC, *-done* 1274 RH (p), *Murydon* 1334 SR
Muryden 1535 VE
Meryden 1572,7 *SBL 6665, 6670, Meryden, Myriden* 1586 *SBL 6022*
Meriton 1577 Saxton, *Merriton* 1695 Morden
Merington 1655 PR(L) 9, 1778 PR(L) 10, *Merrington* 1694 PR(L) 4
Mariton 1710 PR(H) 6

'Pleasant hill', from OE **myrig** and **dūn**. This name replaced an alternative, earlier-recorded name, which was

Gellidone 1086 DB
Gulidona 1155 SAC *et freq* with variant spellings *-dun(e), -don'*, *-don* to 1277 HAC, *Guledon'* 1271-2 *Ass, Gulydon'* 1291-2 *Ass*
Gilydon' 1291-2 *Ass*

This also has **dūn** as second element, but the first element appears to be unique to this name, and it is obscure.

There was a considerable period of overlap between the two, and the earlier name survived as a surname after it ceased to be used for the settlement: in 1325-46 HAC, John son of Thomas *de Gulidon* is a tenant in *Muridon*.

The village has a typical **dūn** site, at one end of a low hill. It is within the area of Pimhill civil parish.

MIDDLEHOPE SO 498886 DB Manor

Mildehope 1086 DB
Midelhop' 1203-4 *Ass*, 1255 RH, *Middelhope* 1204 Cur *et passim* with variant spellings *-hop, -hop'* to 1360 Ipm, *Middilhope* 1255-6 *Ass*, 1271-2 *ForProc*, 1311 Pat, 1495 Ipm, *Myddelhop'* 1261-2 *ForProc, Midlehope* 1672 HTR
Midlinghope 1291 Ch
Mydlop 1577 Saxton

The use of **hop** in a series of names between Wenlock Edge and the Aymestrey Limestone escarpment is discussed under

Easthope. Although designated 'middle', Middlehope is actually well in the southern half of the series, with only Westhope and Dinchope to the south west, and four *-hop* names to the north east. The settlement occupies a very constricted site. It is a township of Diddlebury parish.

MIDDLETON

Shropshire has four examples of this common name, three being of sufficient administrative status to be set out here. The fourth is Middleton in Oswestry, which is first recorded 1272 Cl. Middleton Prior has a different etymology.

A country-wide study of the whole corpus (including those with the modern form Milton) might elucidate the precise significance. Middleton may sometimes denote a settlement which performed some central function, e.g. that of a market-place, for a group of communities, rather than one which is roughly equidistant from two others.

MIDDLETON (in Chirbury parish) SO 297990 DB Manor

Mildetune 1086 DB
Middelton 1228 Lib, 1316 FA, *-tun* 1255 RH, *-ton'* 1255-6 *Ass*, 1334 SR, *Midelton* 1281 Ipm, 1317 Cl, *Middleton* 1361 Cl, *Mydelton* 1431 FA

This place is on the eastern edge of the group of settlements in Chirbury which are named in DB. It is half-way on the road between Rorrington and Priest Weston.

MIDDLETON (in Bitterley parish) SO 540770 DB Manor

Middeltone 1086 DB, *-ton* 1255 RH *et passim, Middelton' iuxta Ludelawe* 1291-2 *Ass, Midilton* 1346, 1428 FA, *Middelton Hugforde* 1421 Cl, *Hykford Middelton* 1525 AD, *Myddylton* 1535 VE
Meddelton 1431 FA, *Hygforde Medilton* 1492 Ipm

This is not an obvious 'half-way' place. The affix, which persisted into modern usage, is from the family of Walter de *Hugeford*, mentioned 1255 RH.

MIDDLETON SCRIVEN SO 681876 Ancient Parish

Middeltone 1086 DB, *-ton'* 1167 P, *-ton* 1255 RH *et freq, Midleton'* 1271-2 *Ass. Middleton* 1284-5 FA, *Myddelton'* 1334 SR, *Midelton by Briggenorth* 1403 Pat, *Skrevensmyddleton* 1577 Saxton, *Midelton Screeven* 1737 *PRChetton*
Mitletone c.1291 TN, *Myttleton'* 1291-2 *Ass*

This, also, is not obviously 'half-way'. *Scriven* is probably a family name.

MILLICHOPE SO 522893 DB Manor

Melicope 1086 DB
Myllincheope c.1175 (1348) Pat (p), *Milinchope* 1249 Ipm, *Myllynchehope* 1301 Ipm, *Millynchope* 1334 SR, *Millinchop* 1550-1 *RentSur,* 1637 PR(H) 15
Millinghope 1199 P (p), 1221-2 (p), 1255-6 *Ass*, 1301 SAC, 1316 FA, 1346 Cl, *-hop* 1268 Cl, 1294 InqMisc, *Millynghop'* 1271-2 *Ass, Myllynghope* 1291-2 *Ass, Millynghope* 1322 Pat, 1421 Cl
Millingehop' 1221-2 *Ass* (p), *-hop* 1255 RH, *-hope* 1271-2, 91-2 *Ass,* 1331 (1348) Pat, *Myllyngehope* 1402 Cl, 1418 Fine, *Millyngehop* 1416 AD, *-hope* 1421 Cl
Milinghop' 1255 RH, *-hop* 1294 Ipm
Milingehop' 1255-6 *Ass*
Molynghop' 1271-2 *Ass*
Mileshope 1332 Cl
Millyngeshope 1360 Fine
Millichop 1535 VE, 1632 PR(H) 15, *-hope* 1551 Pat *et seq*
Millichere, -cherr 1551 Pat
Myllychape 1577 Saxton, *Millichapp* 1575 PR(H) 15, *Milchap* 1695 Morden
Mellychop 1672 HTR

There are two settlement-sites, half a mile apart. The 19th-cent. 1" map calls them Millichope and Millichope Park, the 1952 1" has Upper Millichope and Millichope Park. DB describes a single one-hide manor, but 1255-6 *Ass* mentions "vil' de Millinghop' et altera Millinghop'". In 1301 SAC the two places are *Parva Millinghope et Millinghope Superior.* Lower Millichope is called - *Minor* 1301 Ipm, and in 1550-1 *RentSur* the two places are - *Magna* and - *Parva.* Upper Millichope, which has a very constricted site, contains the Forester's Lodge, a building of the 13th-14th centuries. The places are in Munslow parish.

Millichope is one of a group of similar names in the Welsh Marches, in all of which *-inghop*(*e*) has been modified by palatalisation or assibilation of the *-g-* of *-ing-*. The names are Bullinghope He, Burlingjobb and Evenjobb Rad, Dinchope, Millichope and Ratlinghope Sa. Palatalisation has produced the -j- of Burlingjobb and Evenjobb and is seen in the modern pronunciation of Bullinghope. Assibilation produced the -ch- of Dinchope and Millichope and the old pronunciation - Ratchop - of Ratlinghope.

Except in the case of Bullinghope He, these names use *hop* in the sense 'remote valley', which is its standard one in this region; and Dinchope and Millichope are items in the series of *-hop* names discussed under Easthope.

The complex problems associated with the *-ing*(*e*)- of these names were discussed in a paper in the Journal *Nomina* for 1982. The explanation put forward there, that *-ing-* in these names is the connective particle which is used to link a landowner's name to a word which describes his estate, is offered again here with the recognition that it has not met with any substantial measure of acceptance. If this syllable is indeed the connective **-ing-**, then the *-inge-* spellings must be considered as representing a palatalised pronunciation. This seems to be the only available explanation which is congruous with the likely date of origin of these names - the late 7th or the 8th centuries - and with the nature of the settlements.

Bullinghope, Burlingjobb, Dinchope, Evenjobb and Ratlinghope can be derived from OE personal names, and it is probable that the first element of Millichope is to be explained in the same way. **Milla* would be a possible short form of compound names in *Mild-*. 'Remote valley associated with Milla' is the suggested etymology.

MILSON SO 640728 Ancient Parish

Mulstone 1086 DB, *Mulston'* 1221-2, 55-6 *Ass*, 1242 Fees, *Mulston* 1284-5 FA *et freq* to 1431 FA
Mulestone 1210-12 RBE (p), *Muleston'* 1242 Fees (p), 1255-6, 71-2, 91-2 *Ass, Mulestun* 1255 RH (p)
Mullestona 1255 RH, *Mulleston'* 1255-6, 91-2 (p) *Ass*
Mulnestone 1291-2 *Ass*
Milston' 1291-2 *Ass, Milston* 1535 VE, 1683-4 PR(H) 9, *Mylston* 1577 Saxton
Mulson 1316 FA
Millson 1672 HTR, 1702 *et seq* to 1743 PR(H) 13, *Milston, usually written Milson or Milsom* 1803 Plymley

The forms suggest derivation from *mylenstān* 'millstone'. This has not been noted as a place-name element, and there is obviously a problem concerning its relevance as a settlement-name. The parish is watered by Mill Brook, a large tributary of the R. Rea, and in 1291-2 *Ass* there is mention of the mill of *Muleston'* in connection with an incident in which a man from this village fell into *aquam de Mullebrok'*. All mills have millstones and these are normally concealed in a building, but there may have been some peculiarity of construction here which caused the grinding stones to be visible.

If the derivation be not 'millstone', then the name must be interpreted as a compound of **tūn** with a personal name. DEPN suggests *Myndel*.

MINSTERLEY SJ 374050 Civil Parish

Menistrelie 1086 DB
Musterleg 1203-4 *Ass*
Munstreleg 1246 Ch, *Munsterleg'* 1255 RH *et passim* with variant spellings *-ley(e)*, *-le(i)e, -legh* to 1396 Fine, *Munstrele* 1291-2 *Ass, Munsturley* 1301 Ipm, *Munstreleye* 1313 Pat
Monesterlye 1271-2 *Ass* (p), *Monsterleye* 1306-7 *Ass*, 1322 Ipm

Menstreleye 1294 Pat
Minstreley 1333 Cl, *Mynsterley* 1403 Cl, 1577 Saxton, 1613 PR(H) 6, *Minsterly* 1628 PR(H) 1, *-ley* 1667 *SBL 9945*

'Wood or clearing belonging to a minster church'. Minsterley was in the ancient parish of Westbury, for which DB records two priests. Mention of more than one priest is considered to be evidence for a minster church.

MINTON SO 431907 DB Manor

Munetune 1086 DB, *-ton* 1198 Fees *et passim* with vriant spellings *-tone* to 1329 Ipm, *Muniton'* 1255-6, 91-2 *Ass* (p), *-ton* 1276 Cl, *Munyton'* 1291-2 *Ass*
Miniton' 1198,9, 1200 P (p), *Minetone* c.1212-17 RBE (p), *-ton'* 1250 Fees (p)
Minneton' 1208-9 *ForProc* (p)
Monetonia 1250 Fees, *Moniton* 1255-6 *Ass* (p), *Moneton'* 1268 Cl (p) *et freq* with variant spelling *-ton*(*e*) to 1376 Pat
Menethon' 1260 Cl (p), *Meneton* 1284 Cl, *-ton'* 1291-2 *Ass*
Munton 1463 HAC
Mynton 1535 VE, 1577 Saxton, 1601 *SBL 6485*, 1665 PR(H) 8, *Mintown* 1686 PR(H) 8

This is the same name as Menutton, referring in this instance to the Long Mynd. Minton is in Little Stretton parish.

MONKHOPTON SO 626935 Ancient Parish

Hopton 1255 RH *et passim* with variant spelling *-ton'*, *Hop'ton' Monachorum* 1291-2 *Ass*, *Hopton Priors* 1302 Pat, *Munkehopton* 1577 Saxton, *Monke-* 1664 PR(H) 1, *Munk Hopton* 1697 PR(H) 18, *Monk Hopton* 1711 PR(H) 1, *Munk Hopton* 1767 *PRDitton Priors*

'Valley settlement'; other instances of this compound are discussed under Hopton. The present site of Monkhopton, at the mouth of the valley, is more open than is usual for names containing **hop**. The affixes refer to Wenlock Priory.

MONTFORD SJ 419148 Ancient Parish

Maneford 1086 DB, *Manaforda* 1121 SAC, *Maneford'* 1241 Cl, 1255-6 *Ass, Manford* 1272 Ipm, *-forde* 1617 PR(H) 6
Moneford 1203-4 *Ass* (p) *et passim* with variant spellings *-ford', -fort'* to 1695 PR(L) 7, *Monford* 1381 Pat *et freq* to 1740 PR(H) 18
Muneford 1255-6 *Ass, Munford* 1326 Ipm, 1695 Morden
Muntford 1255-6 *Ass* (p)
Moleford 1271-2 *Ass*
Mundeford 1386 Cl
Mountfort 1412 Pat, *-ford* c.1540 Leland, 1775 PR(L) 7
Monyford 1431 FA
Montford 1601 *SBL 12706 et seq, -fort* 1741 *et seq* to 1768 PR(L) 4, 1741 *et seq* to 1793 PR(L) 7
Mondford 1672 PR(L) 4

Many of the references are to the bridge, e.g. *pons de Muneford* 1255-6 *Ass, Monfordbrigg* 1374 Pat. A bridge here was a traditional meeting-place for English and Welsh potentates when negotiations were required. The bridge presumably superseded the ford of the place-name. Forton in this parish (for which spellings are given *supra*) also refers to the ford.

The nature of the first element of Montford is uncertain. A word which would suit the spellings is OE *gemāna*. This had a number of meanings, the two which seem most relevant here being 'common property' and 'fellowship, association, society'. The related adjective **gemǣne**, 'common', which occurs quite frequently in place-names, does not suit so well, as there are no forms with *Men-*. If *gemāna* were the first element, the *-ā-* could be assumed to have been shortened in the compound. The spellings would then be appropriate, as *ă* regularly becomes *ŏ* in the west midlands, and *u* is a regular occasional spelling for *ŏ* The meaning may be 'ford where people gather'. The use made of the place for negotiating with Welsh princes in the thirteenth century might have been carrying on an ancient tradition.

DEPN suggests a personal name *Manna* or the gen.pl. of

mann 'man', but either of these should have given some spellings with *-nn-*.

The development of *-t-* is probably due to association with French **mont** 'hill'. The fame of Simon de Montfort in the thirteenth century may have assisted this association, though evidence for the final element of the place-name being corrupted to *-fort* is relatively slight. The use of the *Montfort* spelling in the parish register for some time after 1741 is explained by a note:

> "1741 May. Memorandum, in the beginning of this Month His Majesty was pleased to create Henry Bromley, Esqr., Lord of this Mannor, a Peer of Great Britain, by the Stile and Title of Lord Montfort, Baron of Horseheath in the County of Cambridge, and my Lord at that time by word of Mouth, gave me Orders to alter the name of the Parish in this Register according to his Title."

MORE SO 336910 Ancient Parish

La More 1199 SAS 2/X (FF), 1226-8 Fees (p) *et passim* to 1401 Cl, *The More* 1515 *SBL 6236, The Moore* 1566 AD, 1601-2 PR(H) 2, *Ye Moor* 1681 PR(H) 3

Mora 1226-8 Fees, 1255 RH (p), 1271-2 *Ass* (p), *More* 1291-2 *Ass*, 1293 Cl, 1334 SR, 1356 Pat, 1535 VE, *Moore* 1721 PR(H) 14, *Moor* 1766 PR(H) 15

OE **mōr** 'marsh'. The church overlooks the wide valley of the River West Onny. In 1291-2 *Ass* the place is called *La More in valle de Lydom* (i.e. Lydham *supra*).

MORETON

Shropshire has four examples of this common name, which can mean either 'marsh settlement' or 'moorland settlement'. In Shropshire **mōr** consistently means 'marsh'. In addition to referring to geographical situation, the name may denote the function of these settlements in larger estate units, for which they perhaps supplied the vital hay crop.

Two of the Shropshire places are ancient parishes and one is a DB manor; these are set out below. The other example is Moreton in Cound.

MORETON CORBET SJ 559232 Ancient Parish

Mortone 1086 DB *et passim* with variant spellings *-ton(a), -tuna, -ton'* to 1719 PR(L) 9, *Morton' Corbet* 1255-6 *Ass et freq, Mortoncorbet* 1577 Saxton
Moorton' 1334 *SBL 5413, -ton SBL 5415, Mourton* 1347 Cl, *Moorton Corbett* 1586 *SBL 7065, Mourton* - 1655 PR(L) 9
Moreton 1381 Fine, 1398, 1476 Cl, - *Corbett* 1734 PR(L) 4

There would be a great deal of meadow by the R. Roden. The Corbet family is frequently mentioned in connection with this estate in the 13th cent. An alternative affix appears 1271-2 *Ass*, (*Morton' Turet*) and 1322 Pat (*Morton Teret*); this is from an earlier owner called *Toret* (VCH I, p. 299).

MORETON SAY SJ 630345 Ancient Parish

Mortune 1086 DB *et freq* with variant spellings *-ton', -ton* to 1719 PR(L) 8, *Morton' de Say* 1255 RH, *Morton Say* 1284-5 FA, 1336 Ipm, 1389 Cl, - *Se* 1601 PR(L) 9, *Sea* 1660 ib, 1707 *SBL 5335, Morton Sey al Morton Sew* 1696 *SBL 4992, Morton Sey* 1713 PR(L) 4
Mourton Say 1349 Ipm
Moreton Say 1394 Cl, 1744 PR(L) 8, *Moreton* 1577 Saxton, - *Sea* 1655 SAS 1/XLVII *et freq* to 1834 *SBL 5652*, - *Sey* 1708,12 PR(L) 4

The village lies among the headwaters of the R. Duckow, and there would be an area of meadow where the streams unite. The affix is from the family of Robert de *Say*, who had a tenancy in *Morton' de Say* in 1255 RH. *Sea* would be an acceptable spelling-variant for *Say* in the 17th and 18th centuries.

MORTON SJ 291243 DB Manor

Mortune 1086 DB, *Morton* c.1230 HAC, 1277 InqMisc, 1302 Ipm, 1577 Saxton *et seq*
Mortyn 1600-1 PR(StA) 4, *-tin* 1627 ib
Moreton 1615 PR(StA) 4, 1721 PR(StA) 2, 1724 PR(StA) 5
Moorton 1702 *SBL 6188*
Mertin 1633 PR(StA) 2, *Merten* 1716 PR(StA) 3

The township lies between two tributaries of the R. Morda, and the area may have been the main source of hay for the great manor of Oswestry. The spellings show occasional 'Welshification' of *-ton* to *-tyn*.

MORVILLE SO 670940 Ancient Parish

Membrefelde 1086 DB
Momerfeld' c.1138, c.1218, 1256 SAC, *-feld* 1155, 1226-7, 1268,80 SAC, 1289, 1327,68, 1405 Pat, 1334 SR, 1382 Cl, Pat, *-feud* c.1255 SAC (p), *-felt* 1258-9 SAC (p), *Mommerfeld* 1377 Pat
Mamerfeld c.1138, c.1194 SAC, 1201-2 P (p), 1256 SAC, 1269 Pat,
Mainerfeld' 1235 Cl
Menneresfeld' 1235 Cl, *Minnersfeld* 1383 Pat
Momerefeld 1255 RH, *-feud'* 1261-2 *ForProc*
Momeresfeud 1255-6 *Ass, Mom'sfeld'* 1291-2 *Ass, Momersfeld* 1317 Pat, *Mommersfeld* 1377 Pat
Moum'feld c.1291 TN
Mumerfeld 1306,98 Pat, 1310 Cl
Mambirfeld 1331 (1348) Pat
Munersfeld 1398 Pat
Mumervill 1443 (copy) *SBL 15752* (p)
Morfelde 1464 AD, *Morfeld, -vilde* 1535 VE, *Morfeild(e)* c.1540 Leland, *Morveld* 1554 *SBL Ms 292 et freq* to 1614 PR(H) 1, *Morvild* 1573 PR(H) 3, 1661 PR(H) 1, *Morvill* 1577 Saxton *et freq, Morveille, -vile* 1635 PR(H) 1, *Morvell* 1662-1703 ib, *Morveild* 1661 *SBL 9574A, Morville* 1704 PR(H) 13, *Morvield* 1722 PR(H) 17
Moorvild 1669 PR(H) 1
Marvel 1704 PR(H) 1, *Marvele* 1713 ib, *Marvill* 1741 PR(H) 17,

Marvil 1746 PR(H) 16

This full collection of spellings indicates that the usual OE form was **Mamerfeld*, probably with an alternative **Mameresfeld*. The prevalent ME spellings with *Momer-* are due to the normal WMidl rounding of ă There is surprisingly little sign of intrusive *-b-*. The 18th-cent. *Mar-* forms have the unrounded ŏ which was fashionable at that date. The transformation of the final element results mainly from the voicing of *-f-* to *-v-*.

So what is a *mamer*? DEPN takes the first element to be the old name of Mor Brook. This is a reasonable conjecture, but Ekwall did not have a large collection of spellings, and he thought the stream-name was **Me(o)mere*, which he compares with R. Mimram in Hrt. This is no longer valid since the two names have different vowels; and there is no other river-name which is a possible parallel. **feld**, 'open land', refers to an area rather than to a point, and the first element could be the name of the nearest hill. This is Aston Hill, S.W. of Morville, which rises to 726 ft. A British hill-name **Mam* is thought to occur in Mam Tor Db, Mamhead D, Mansfield Nt, Mamble Wo and Manchester, but it seems improbable that the OE suffix *-er* should be added to this. The name must be regarded as unsolved for the time being.

MOSTON SJ 561265 DB Manor

Mostune 1086 DB *et passim* with variant spellings *-ton', -ton*
Mosseton 1520 AD

'Moss settlement'; the wood to the E. of the hamlet is called Top Moss. This name is on the southern edge of the area in which **mos** (which means 'moss' the plant as well as 'bog') is regularly used for boggy areas. There are a few instances in southern England, and one Sa example, Mose in Quatford, is further south than Moston, but **mos** is only common in counties N. of Shropshire. The compound with **tūn** recurs in Ch and La.

Moston is a township of Stanton upon Hine Heath parish.

MUNSLOW SO 522877 Ancient Parish

Mosselawa 1167 P, *-lawe* 1242 Fees
Musselawa 1187 P, *-lawe* 1255 RH (p), 1261-2, 71-2 *ForProc*, *Muselawa* 1190,1 P
Munselowe 1252 Cl *et freq* to 1334 SR, *-lawe* 1261-2 *ForProc*, *Muncelawe* 1255-6 *Ass* (p), *Munsselowe* 1271-2 *Ass*
Monselawe 1261-2 (p), 1271-2 *ForProc*, *Monsselowe* 1284-5 FA, *Monselowe* 1291-2 *Ass et freq* to 1394 Fine
Moneslawe 1291-2 *Ass* (p)
Monslouwe 1305-6 *Ass*, *-lowe* 1492 Ipm *et freq* to 1730 PR(H) 14
Mounselawe 1331 Fine, *-lowe* 1337 Cl *et freq* with variant spelling *-low* to 1571 PR(H) 15
Mounslowe 1549 Pat *et freq* to 1750 PR(H) 1
Munslow 1577 Saxton, 1581 PR(H) 15, 1732 PR(H) 14 *et seq*
Maunslow 1632 *SBL 8631*
Mountslow 1749 PR(L) 19

It seems best to disregard the spellings *Mulslaye, Mulsleie* which occur in a document printed in Eyton III, pp. 232-3. This is an inspeximus dated 1348 of a document of c.1110-15. Several of the place-name spellings are corrupt, and there may have been mistranscriptions in the inspeximus. The only other evidence noted for *-l-* in the first element of Munslow is a reference to the hundred as *Mulselawahundr* in 1187 P; the same entry has *Musselawa*. It is likely that these spellings either result from mistranscription of *-s-* or are due to interchange of *-n-* and *-l-*. The spellings for Munsley He, which DEPN brackets with Munslow, show similarly slight evidence for *-l-* in the first element. Ekwall's suggestion of a personal name *Mundel* for both place-names, while offering a welcome solution, receives little support from a full collection of spellings.

Spellings for Munsley He, though similar in some respects to those for Munslow, do not exhibit metathesis of *-es*, and the two place-names should probably be dissociated as regards both first and second elements (the second element of Munsley is **lēah**). The OE form of Munslow seems likely to have been **Munsehlāw* or **Munselhlāw*. The first element is entirely obscure. The tumulus (OE *hlāw*) might have been the marker for the meeting-place of Munslow Hundred. As with all tumuli mentioned in Shropshire place-names it seems to have disappeared without trace.

A form with a long vowel (spelt *-ou-*) in the first syllable was in use in the 14th-18th cents. *Mun-* or *Mon-* may have been associated with words like *hound* and *pound*, in which regular lengthening took place before the combination *-nd*. But (as so frequently in Shropshire) the obscure name Munslow was hardly affected by popular etymology; there is only one spelling with *Mount-*.

MYDDLE SJ 468237 Ancient Parish

Mulleht 1086 DB
Muthla 1121 SAC, *Mhutle* 1242 Fees
Mudla 1155 SAC, *Mudle* c.1220 FFW *et passim* to 1450 Cl, *Mudley* 1291-2 *Ass*
Mudele 1234, 1315,37,98 Pat, 1251,72, 1373 Cl, 1291-2 *Ass*, 1316, 1431 FA, 1381 HAC, *Mudell* 1379 Pat
Midele, *Mydele* 1255-6 *Ass* (p)
Middell 1272 Ipm, *Middle* 1535 VE *et freq*, *Myddle* 1554 *SBL 3606 et seq*, *Mydle* 1615 *SBL 15755*, *Midle* 1672 HTR, 1721 *SBL 6521*, *Middle alias Mudhall* 1646 *SBL 5827*
Modle c.1291 TN
Muddle 1303,40 Pat, 1346, 1428 FA
Medle 1308 Strange
Mytley 1421,2,36 Fine
Meddyll 1499 Ipm, *Medill* 1539 AD

Myddle has been explained as a compound of **gemȳðe** 'stream-junction' and **lēah** 'wood, clearing'. A full range of spellings supports this derivation for the first element, but it is not possible to accept **lēah** as the generic. The spellings for Alveley (*supra*) may be compared. Alveley is OE *Ælfgȳðelēah*, which offers a close parallel to the postulated **gemȳðelēah*, but there is no sign of reduction of *lēah* to *-la*, *-le* in the earliest spellings, and it is usually *-lei*, *-ley*(*e*), *-leg*(*e*) even in the later ones.

Myddle may derive from a diminutive of *gemȳðe* formed with the suffix *-el*. A name meaning 'miniature stream-junction' may have suited the site in the Dark Ages. It is necessary to postulate some alteration in drainage in order to derive the name from *gemȳðe* or **gemȳðel.*

DEPN discusses the name under the form Middle, which is the spelling used on Baugh, on the 19th-cent. 1", and in the *TA.*

MYNDTOWN SO 391896 Ancient Parish

Munete 1086 DB, *Muneta* 1166 RBE (p)
Munede 1242 Fees *et freq* to 1397 InqMisc, *La Munede* 1255 RH *et freq* to 1431 FA
Meind' 1272 Cl
La Munde 1316 FA
La Mende 1414 Fine (p)
Mynde 1431 FA
Myntowne 1577 Saxton, 1641 SAS 3/IV, *The Mintowne* 1633 PR(H) 2, *Mintown* 1695 Morden *et freq* to 1808 PR(H) 15
Myndtoon 1608 PR(H) 1, *Mindtown* 1803 Plymley, 1808 Baugh
Mine Town 1672 HTR

Primitive Welsh **mönith**, Welsh **mynydd**, referring to The Long Mynd, against the western edge of which the settlement is situated. Modern *-town* is a late addition. Minton (*supra*), also named from The Long Mynd, is a compound name with OE **tūn**.

The settlement is tiny and the resources listed in DB are small; but the area of the parish is quite large, and the use as settlement-name of the pre-English name of the massif may indicate that the place was once of greater importance.

MYTTON SJ 453170 DB Manor

Mutone 1086 DB
Mitton' c.1220-30 HAC, *-ton* 1498 Ipm *et freq* to 1809 PR(L) 4, *Mytton* 1577 Saxton *et seq*
Mutton 1255-6 *Ass et freq* with variant spelling *-ton'* to 1383 *SBL 3770*

OE *gemȳðtūn*, 'river-junction settlement', referring to the confluence of R. Perry with R. Severn. Elsewhere this compound has become Mitton and Myton.

NASH SO 604717 Civil Parish

Fraxinus 1210-12 RBE (p), 1274 RH (p)
Esses 1211-12 RBE (p), 1255 RH
La Esse 1242 Fees (p), *Esse* 1271-2 *Ass*, 1346 FA (p)
Asses 1255-6 *Ass*
Frene 1255-6 *Ass* (p), 1274 RH (p)
Assche, Assh 1308 Ipm, *Asshe* 1334 SR, 1391 Cl, *Asshe Stormy* 1371 Fine
Magna Aske 1291-2 *Ass*
Nazsche 1391 AD, *Nasshe* 1395 AD, *Nassch* 1440 AD, *Nashe* 1577 Saxton, *The Nashe* 1575-6 *et freq* PR(H) 17, *The Nash* 1654, 1701 PR(H) 16, *Nash* 1701 ib

'Ash-tree', OE æsc. When used as a surname, the place-name was occasionally translated into Latin (*Fraxinus*) or French (*Frene*). The late-appearing *N-* suggests that the place was referred to locally as *atten ashe*, 'at the ash-tree', though *Asshe* was considered the correct written form till the late 14th cent.

There are two settlements, Ash (presumably *Magna* -) and Lower Ash. One or both must have belonged to the *Stormy* family, a member of which held the nearby Whatmore in 1346 FA.

NEEN SAVAGE SO 675774 Ancient Parish

Nene 1086 DB, 1242 Fees *et passim, Nena* 1193,4 P (p), *Nene Savage* 1255 RH *et freq, -Sauvage* 1255-6 *Ass et freq, Hun(d)esnene* 1256 Pat, *Houndenene* 1577 Saxton
Niene 1195 P (p), 1221-2 *Ass, Niensauvage* 1346 FA, *Nien Savage* 1362 Fine, Ipm, 1428 FA
Nenne 1255-6 *Ass*
Neen 1256 Pat, *-Savage* 1305 Cl, 1495 AD, 1535 VE, *-Sauvage* 1334 SR, 1346 FA, *-Monell* 1535 VE, *-Salvage* 1686, 1701 PR(H) 13, *Over Neen* 1690 PR(H) 17, *Upper Neen* 1704 PR(H) 13, 1781 PR(H) 1
Neyn Savage 1431 FA, 1440 AD
Nyende Savage 1535 VE, *Nyend Savaige* 1602 *SBL 6468, Niend Savage* 1796 PR(H) 9
Houndes Nyne 1586 PR(H) 18

Neend Savage 1760 PR(H) 17

Neen is the ancient name of the R. Rea, beside which Neen Savage, Neen Sollers and Neenton are situated. It is identical with the Nth/Hu/Ca/Nf/Li R. Nen(e), and is a pre-English name of obscure etymology. In an OE survey of land in Knighton-on-Teme Wo, near the junction of R. Rea and R. Severn (S 1185), the bounds run "in thære ea Nen". This provides both a pre-Conquest form for the river-name and an indication of how it was displaced by the use of the phrase *æt/in thære ea*, which, by misdivision, gave Rea. The later name appears in the surname of Ade *de La Re* 1271-2 *Ass* (in Neen Sollers), but *aqua de Neene* occurs c.1275 *SBL 6968* (in Middleton Priors).

The forms for the three Sa names are consistent with derivation from OE *Nēn*. Names from OE *cwēn-tūn* (e.g. Quinton, Gl, Nth) show a similar mixture of spellings with *-e-*, *-i-*, *-ei-*, *-ey-*. The *-ie-* forms can be paralleled in the Berks name Speen (OE *Spēne*), which is *Spienes* 1199, 1201 P. The earliest manifestation of this - *Nientona* c.1090 SAC for Neenton - is by no means certain to be the spelling of the original document.

There were two estates at Neen Savage in 1086, and the manorial history of these is traced in Eyton IV, pp. 230ff. One belonged to *Huni* TRE, and Eyton takes this personal name to be the source of the affix *Hun(d)es, Hounde(s)*. The more usual affix is from the family of *Le Savage*, who were heirs of Ingelram, the DB tenant. The other DB estate is identified by Eyton with the property called *Neen Monell* which appears in VE as belonging to Wigmore Abbey. The source of this affix has not been identified.

The 19th-cent. 1" map calls the place Neen Savage or Upper Neen. 'Upper' is for distinction from Neen Sollars, lower down the river. 'Over', however, in the reference from 1690, may not be a synonym for 'Upper'. Foxall's Gazetteer gives Over and Lower Neen as parts of Neen Savage. These names do not appear on *TA*.

NEEN SOLLARS SO 660723 Ancient Parish

Nene 1086 DB, 1211-12 RBE, 1242 Fees, - *Baudwin'* 1242 Fees, - *Baudewyn* 1255-6 *Ass*, - *Bauwyn* 1255 RH, *Solers Nene* 1271-2

Ass, Nene Solers 1284-5 FA *et freq* to 1320 Pat, *Nenesalers* 1577 Saxton

Nensolers 1271-2 *Ass* (p), 1309 Cl, 1348 Ipm, *Nen Solers* 1274 RH (p), 1308 Ipm

Neen Solars 1305 Cl, - *Baldewyn* 1346, 1428 FA, - *Soliers* 1361 Pat, *Neensolers* 1385 Pat, *Lower Neen* 1720 PR(H) 17

Soliers Nient, Solers Nyen 1341 Pat, *Nynesolers* 1361 Fine, 1362 Ipm, *Nyen Solers* 1399 Cl, *Neyn* - 1399 Pat, *Solerisnien* 1431 Fine, *Nien Solers* 1431 FA, *Solersnyen* 1442,53 Fine

Solas 1535 VE

Nyend Solas 1743 PR(H) 16

See Neen Savage *supra*, for distinction from which this place is called *Lower*. The manorial history is given in Eyton IV, pp. 291ff. *Baldwin* le Poer acquired the manor a.1185, Roger *de Solers* acquired it between 1190 and 1196.

NEENTON SO 638878 Ancient Parish

Neweniontone 1086 DB, *Newenton* 1221-2 *Ass*

La Nientona c.1090 SAC, *-ton'* c.1200 *ForProc, Nyenton* 1325 Pat, 1535 VE, *Nienton* 1400 SAS 1/XLVII

Nenton' 1242 Fees *et freq* with variant spelling *-ton* to 1346 FA

Neynton 1255 RH, 1399 Cl, 1431 FA, 1577 Saxton, *-ton'* 1271-2 *ForProc*

Nynton' 1291-2 *Ass, -ton* 1495 Ipm, 1579 PR(H) 3

Neenton 1362 Ipm, 1388 Cl, 1408 Pat, 1691 PR(H) 13 *et seq*

Nineton 1607 PR(H) 3, 1695 Morden

Neen Town 1724-9 PR(H) 14

'Estate on R. *Neen'*, *v.* **tūn** and see Neen Savage *supra*. There is some confusion of the first element with **nīwe** 'new'.

GREAT NESS SJ 398190 Ancient Parish

Nessham 1086 DB, *Nessa* c.1090, 1121 SAC, 1167,70,75 P

Nesse 1154 Strange *et passim* to 1341 *SBL 6298, Nesse Extraneus* 1271-2 *Ass, Ness le Estraunge, Ness Magna* 1311 Strange,

Straungeness 1318,38 Pat, *Nesse Extranea* 1334 SR, *Erlusnesse* 1345 *SBL 3611, Straungenesse* 1382 Cl, 1401 Fine, *Nesse Lestrange* 1428 FA, *- Le Straunge* 1431 FA, *Straunge Ness* 1439 Cl, *Greatenesse, Nestrange* 1553 Pat, *Nesse Magna* 1577 Saxton, *Nesse Strange* 1657 *SBL 6397 et freq* with variant spelling *Ness* - to 1782 *SBL 4149, Great Nesse* 1672 HTR *et seq*

Nasse 1291-2 *Ass* (p)

Neysse Le Straunge 1305-6 *Ass*

Nesse alias Nessehome 1323 Ipm

OE **ness** 'ness', which is used in place-names for coastal promontories and for dry ground jutting into marsh, only occasionally for striking inland hills, like Totnes D. The ridge of Nesscliff may have been thought of as a promontory jutting into marsh, or it may have seemed to deserve this special term because of its short, 'nose-like' shape, which contrasts with the longer ridges characteristic of central Shropshire.

The place is frequently referred to as *Great Ness(e) otherwise Ness(e) Strange* in 18th-cent. sources. The *Lestrange* family obtained the manor in the mid-12th cent. In 1086 Earl Roger of Montgomery held Great Ness in demesne, and *Erlus-* in 1345 may refer to this. *Nesham* in DB is here treated as an oblique case of the Latinised form *Nessa.* The *alias Nessehome* of 1323 Ipm is probably not to be connected with the DB form. There is some evidence in Shropshire for the addition of *-home* to names of parishes which consist of scattered hamlets.

LITTLE NESS SJ 407197 Civil Parish

Nesse 1086 DB, *Nesse Alayn* 1271-2 *Ass, - Parva* 1284-5 FA, *Little Nesse* 1635 *SBL 10293 et freq, - Ness* 1782 *SBL 4149*

See Great Ness *supra. Alayn* from the family of *Fitz Alan.*

NETLEY SJ 474017 DB Manor

Netelie 1086 DB, *-legh'* 1208-9 *ForProc et freq* with variant spellings *-lega, -leye* to l.13th *ForProc*

Netleg' 1208-9 *ForProc, Netley* 1419 *SBL 6688 et seq, Nettley* 1587 PR(L) 6, 1672 HTR, *Nettle* 1675 Ogilby
Nethelegh 1301 SAC

'Nettle clearing', *v.* **netel, lēah.** The presence of nettles may have been noted as indication of a deserted habitation site.

Netley is the southern half of Stapleton parish. Settlement is scattered, and VCH VIII, p. 163, states that this has been so since the Middle Ages. The 19th-cent. 1" map shows Higher and Lower Netley, Netley Hall, and a cluster of buildings simply called Netley. The version of the map which shows townships also gives NETLEY in the print used for township names, but the area was included without distinction in the Stapleton *TA.* Lower and Upper Netley are so named 1807 PR(L) 1.

NEWPORT SJ 745190 Ancient Parish

(*de*) *Novoburgo* 1136-c.1139 SAC *et passim,* in this form or as *Novus Burgus,* to 1322 Ch
Neuport 1221-2 *Ass* (p) *et passim* to 1501 *SBL 16170, Le Neuport* l.13th *SBL 16198, Nyweport' 1306-7 Ass, Neweport* 1319 Pat *et freq* to 1494 Ipm, *Newport* 1443 *SBL 16167 et seq*
Neweburg' 1232 Cl, *Newborough, Newburgh* 1317 Cl
(*de*) *Nova Villa* 1266 Pat

This 'new market town' is believed to have been founded by Henry I within the royal manor Edgmond. Eyton (IX, 129ff) gives an excellent account of the materials available for an appraisal of its early history.

DEPN quotes a mint signature of c.1050 as the earliest reference, but it is very doubtful whether this belongs to the Shropshire Newport. Two relevant coins are listed in *A Catalogue of English Coins in the British Museum: Anglo-Saxon Series,* Vol II (1893), p. 418. Both are of Edward the Confessor, and one has the mint inscription SIRED ON NIWEPORTE, the other SIRED ON NIPEPO. There are two Newports which were in existence at the time of the Domesday Survey, Newport in Cambridgeshire and Newport Pagnell in Buckinghamshire. Both are called by the English name *Neuport* in DB, and either would be a likelier candidate for a pre-Conquest minting-place than Newport in Shropshire.

The English and Latin names for the Shropshire Newport coexisted till the 14th century, and there appears to have been a rival Anglicisation, *Newbury.*

NORBURY SO 364928 Ancient Parish

Norbir' 1236 SAS 4/IV(FF), *Norbur'* 1255 RH, *Norbury* 1316 FA, 1515 *SBL 6236 et seq, Norberye* 1586-7 PR(H) 2, *-berie* 1655 PR(H) 6

Northbur' 1242 Cl, *-byr'* 1255-6 *Ass* (p) *et freq* to 1349 Ipm

'North manor-house', *v.* **burh, byrig**, probably named from its position in relation to Lydbury.

NORTON

Shropshire has seven examples of this name, which means 'north settlement'. One is a parish and three others are named in DB; the material relating to these four is set out below. The three which do not qualify for detailed treatment here are Norton in the northern part of Stockton parish, which is first recorded 1271-2 *Ass*, Norton north of Wroxeter, which is first mentioned 1155 HAC, and Tong Norton, immediately north of Tong, first noted 1284-5 FA.

NORTON IN HALES SJ 703387 Ancient Parish

Nortune 1086 DB *et passim* with variant spellings *-ton(a)*, *-ton'*

'North' in this Norton may refer to the position of the settlement in the district called Hales, which stretched at least as far as Hales in Tyrley St, three miles south.

Affixes include *sub Limam* 1225 Cur, *subtus Lymam* 1292-5 *Ass, under Lyme* 1313 Pat, referring to the southern extremity of the district called Lyme. In 1121-6 SAC the place is described as "Nortona que sita est iuxta nemus quod lima dicitur". *v.* PN Ch **1**,

2-6, for a discussion of Lyme.

A much more frequent affix is *in Hales*, which occurs 1271-2 *Ass et freq* with occasional variants such as *in Halys, in Halles.* The district-name is discussed under Market Drayton. Both affixes are used in 1291 *Ass* where the place is called *Norton' in Hales subtus Lyme.*

NORTON SO 639827 DB Manor

Nortone 1086 DB, *-ton* 1263 Ch, 1274 RH (p)

This Norton is in the southern part of the parish of Aston Botterell, so the significance of 'north' is not obvious. If it is named from its relationship to Farlow, the administrative districts were presumably differently divided when the name was coined.

NORTON SJ 495058 DB Manor

Nortune 1086 DB *et freq* with variant spelling *-ton*
Northton' 1255-6 *Ass*, l.13th *ForProc*

This Norton is north of Condover, and is described as a "member" of Condover 1255-6 *Ass.* The affix *by Conedovere* is used 1315 Ipm, *by Condore* 1416 AD. An alternative affix is *iuxta Beystan* 1301 SAC; this refers to Bayston *supra.*

NORTON SO 461817 DB Manor

Nortune 1086 DB *et freq* with variant spellings *-ton', -ton*
Northton 1520 AD

This Norton is in the northern part of the parish of Onibury.

OAKENGATES SJ 695110 Civil Parish

Okynyate 1535 VE, *Okenyate* 1577 Saxton, 1695 Morden

Oaken yates 1655 PR(L) 20, *Okenyeats* 1679 *PRShifnal, Oakenyats* 1686 *ib, -yates* 1688 *ib, Okenyates* 1688 *ib, Oken Yeats* 1693,8 *ib, the Oaken Yates* 1735 PR(L) 8
the Oaken Gates 1707 PR(L) 8, *Oakengates, Oaken Gates* 1735 *PRShifnal, ye Oaken Gates* 1772 *et freq* PR(L) 8
Oakengate 1765 *PRShifnal*, 1801,8 PR(L) 17

The name is traced back to 1414 in VCH XI, p. 286: the precise spelling is not quoted there, but Dr. G. Baugh informs me that it is *Okenȝate juxta Wombrygge.* The hamlet is of late medieval origin, but the name is probably older. It means 'pass characterised by oak trees', from the OE adjective **ǣcen**, and **geat** 'gate, gap, pass between hills'. The settlement lay on Watling Street, at the mouth of a narrow valley running to the south, which was followed by railways and canals. The topography is shown clearly on the 19th-cent. hachured maps. The plural form and the substitution of modern *gate* for *yate* are relatively late developments.

VCH XI gives an account of the evolution of the place. There were a few cottages here in 1535-6, owned by Wombridge Priory. Settlement grew with industry and mining between the 16th and 19th centuries, and Oakengates assumed an urban role in the mid-19th century when a market was established and the railways arrived. It became an urban district in 1898 and a civil parish in 1934.

There is not likely to be a connection between this name and that of *Uxacona*, the nearby Romano-British settlement.

OAKS SJ 424047 DB Manor

Hach 1086 DB
Akes 1199 SAS 2/X, 1209-10 MGS (p), 1255 RH, 1255-6 *Ass*
Okes 1271-2 *Ass et freq* to 1713 *SBL 5343, des Okes* 1283 InqMisc, *La Okes* 1306-7 *Ass, Oakes* 1565 PR(H) 12 *et freq* to 1702 *SBL 13394*
Oke 1316 FA
Hockes 1319 Ch

'Oak tree', probably originally singular, but with the inorganic *-s* which was frequently added to monosyllabic names after the Norman Conquest. Simplex names from OE āc are fairly common, but they more frequently have modern forms such as Nock, Noke or Rock, Roke because they were preceded in ME speech by *atten* or *atter*, 'at the -'. Rock in Ludlow is 'at the oak tree'.

Oaks was a township of Pontesbury parish.

OBLEY SO 327778 DB Manor

Obelie 1086 DB
Obbeleg' 1255-6 *Ass*. *-le* 1272 Ipm, *-le(ye)* 1283 Cl
Owele 1272 Cl
Hobale, Hobale Seison 1381 *SRO 552/1/20*
Obley 1619 PR(H) 2
Obleads, -leyds, -leids 1625 PR(H) 2

'Ob(b)a's wood or clearing'. The 1381 form suggests a Welsh pronunciation with stress on the middle syllable of three. *Seison* is 'English', a meaningful distinction in this corner of the county. The 1625 forms are unexplained, but the rarity of *lēah* in this area may have led to various corruptions of the final element. The 1272 form may be mistranscribed.

Obley was a township of Clunbury parish.

OLDBURY SO 710920 DB Manor

Aldeberie 1086 DB *et passim* with variant spellings *-beria, -bur', -byr', -bury* to 1291-2 *Ass*
Audebir' 1255-6 *Ass*
Oldebur' 1261-2 *ForProc et passim* with variant spelling *-bury* to 1535 VE, *Holdebury* c.1291 TN, *Oldbury* 1535 VE
Hadeburie 1284-5 FA
Owdburye 1575-6 PR(H) 3
Wowbury 1576 SAS 1/XLVI, *Woberye* 1600 ib, *Wobury* 1577 Saxton
Olbury 1748 PR(H) 1

'Old fort', a fairly common name which sometimes becomes Aldb(o)rough, Albury or Aldbury. These names can sometimes be shown to refer to prehistoric fortifications, for which **burh**, dat. **byrig**, was the standard OE term. In Oldbury near Bridgnorth the reference may be to the earthwork called Panpudding Hill, which is called *le Tirrett alias le Old Castle* 1571 *SBL MS 292.* The date of this earthwork has not, however, been ascertained, and the use of the unusual term 'turret' in the 16th cent. and the modern name Panpudding (presumably an inversion of pudding-pan) both suggest that its shape was felt to be unusual; and this might have prevented the application to it of the standard term *ealdan byrig.*

There is no reason to suppose that the Anglo-Saxon fortification discussed under Bridgnorth was located at Oldbury.

ONIBURY SO 456792 Ancient Parish

Aneberie 1086 DB, 1121 SAC
Onebur' 1247 Cl *et freq* with variant spellings *-byr', -bari, -buri, -bury* to 1769 *SBL 8158*
Onnebur' 1255-6 *Ass, Onnibury* 1727 PR(H) 14
Onyebur'. -bir' 1255-6 *Ass* (p), *Onybury* 1334 SR *et freq* to 1766 PR(H) 2, *Oniberry* 1675 Ogilby
Honnebur', Honibur' 1255 RH

'Manor house by the R. Onny'. Spellings for the river-name are *Onie* c.1250 HAC, *Oneye* 1301 SAC, *Oney* c.1540 Leland, *On*(*n*)*y* 1577 Saxton, *On*(*e*)*y* 1675 Ogilby.

The river-name Onny has hitherto been derived from British **Onnīo*, explained as the Primitive Welsh word for ash-trees plus the suffix *-īo.* Discussion in RN (p. 310) and LHEB (p. 612) concentrates on the vowel *O-*, and it is agreed that this is possible if the name was taken into English c.650. RN regards the *A-* of the two earliest spellings as confirmation for this derivation, comparing the Hampshire river-name Ann, in the spellings for which *A-* is universal, and which Ekwall derives from *onn* 'ash-trees' without a suffix. RN offers as an alternative to **Onnīo* a compound of Welsh *onn* with OE **ēa** 'river'. This suits the spellings better than the Celtic suffix *-īo.*

A more serious difference between the spellings for Onny and the Hampshire Ann than that of the vowel, however, is the single *-n-* of the former and the universal *-nn-* of the latter. A full collection of spellings for Onibury makes it clear that the OE form had *-n-*, and (despite the modern form) the single consonant is universal in early spellings for the river. It seems necessary to dissociate Onny from Ann.

Onny may be an English name meaning '(at the) single river', OE **ānan īe.* The salient feature of the R. Onny is that it has two headwaters of equal size, now known as R. East and West Onny. These unite about three miles upstream from Onibury. The united stream could have been called **āna ēa*, 'single river', and the dative of this would be a possible source for the ME spellings. The compound **ānstiga**, 'single track', is used in place-names for a short stretch of road into which several tracks merge at either end, and this use of *ān*(*a*) is similar to that proposed for Onny. The vowel of *āna* would be shortened, and ă before a nasal would become o in west-midland speech.

Matters are complicated by the possible occurrence of another R. Onny near Leominster He. A large tributary of the R. Lugg now called Pinsley Brook is *Oney* 1577 Saxton, and a form *Onye* dated 1250 was assigned to it in a paper by W. St. Clair Baddeley, from which it is cited in RN. Unfortunately Baddeley did not give a source for this spelling, so the identification cannot be checked.

ONSLOW SJ 437129 DB Manor

Andreslaue 1086 DB, *-lawa* c.1177 *SBL 5403* (p)
Andrelau 1086 DB
Hondreslowe c.1200 (1292) Ch (p)
Ondeslawe c.1230 SAC *et freq* with variant spellings *-lauwe, -loue, -lowe* to 1454 *SBL 4526*
Hundeslawe 1271-2 *Ass* (p), *-louwe* 1306-7 *Ass* (p), *Undeslowe* 1421,2 Fine
Oudredeslowe 1276 Cl (p)
Oneslowe 1393 *SBL 4534*, 1478 *SBL 4446*, 1638 PR(H) 1, *Ouneslow* 1431 FA, *Onneslowe* 1436 Fine, 1496 Ipm, *Onyslow* 1510 *SBL 4459*, *Oneslo* c.1540 Leland, *Onislowe* 1600 AD
Onnslowe 1442 *SBL 4483*, *Onslow* 1577 Saxton

Probably 'Andrǣd's tumulus'. The name has previously been

interpreted as containing a personal name *Andhere*, but the form from 1276 Cl suggests *Andrǣd*. *On*(*n*) was sometimes mistranscribed as *Ou*(*n*). Neither personal name is on independent record, but both would be regular OE formations.

This is one of several Shropshire names in which **hlāw** 'tumulus' is associated with a person, and it is possible that there were aristocratic barrow burials of the 7th century, though no burial mound has been identified at any of the places.

Onslow is now the name of a single large house in the parish of Bicton. The parkland between the house and the A 458 road is marked by a number of low, drumlin-like mounds. One of these, crowned by an oak, is higher than the others, and commands a fine view. It is the sort of vantage point on which a tumulus would be sited, and the eye of faith can see the top of it as a ploughed-out or worn-down barrow.

OSBASTON SJ 323228 DB Manor

Sbernestune 1086 DB
Osbertune 1172 HAC
Osberneston c.1230, 1248 HAC
Osberston' 1292-5 *Ass*, *-ton* 1297 Strange
Osbaston 1397 InqMisc *et seq*, *Osbeston* 1655 SAS 1/XLVII, *Osboston* 1672 HTR

'Ōsbeorn's estate'. A Welsh form, *Treosberne*, is recorded in 1611 (*Morgan Ts*); this has **tref** for OE **tūn**.

OSWESTRY SJ 295295 Ancient Parish

Blancmonasterium 1160,1,2,3,4 P, *Blancmustier* 1170 P *et freq* with variant spellings *-muster, -moster, -mustir* to 1272 Cl, *Album Monasterium* c.1200 SAC *et freq* to 1304 Cl, *Blauncmuster* 1244 Cl, *Blanmouster* 1317 Cl, *Blankmonstier* 1342 Strange, *Blaunkmonster* 1344 ib
Osewaldestr' c.1180 SAC, *Oswaldestroe, id est Oswaldi arborem* 1191 Gir, *Oswaldestr'* e.13th SAC *et passim* with variant spellings *-treo, -tre*(*e*) to 1500 Cl, *Osewaldistre* 1255 RH, *Osewaldestre*

1282 Pat *et freq* to 1437 Cl, *Osewoldestre* 1282 ChanR, *-try* 1394-5 *SBL 9777, Osswaldstree* 1665 PR(StA) 4, *Oswaldstrey* 1670 PR(StA) 2

Croesoswald 1254 Norwich, *Croes Hyswallt, Croes Oswallt* l.13th Brut y Tywysogyon, *Crassawald'* 1306-7 *Ass*

Osolvestre 1277 Pat

Oswoldestrete 1294 Cl, *Oswaldestrete* 1299 Cl, 1322,4 Pat, *Osewaldestrete* 1322 Cl

Osewastre 1324 Ipm, 1398 Pat, *Oswastre* 1389,98 Pat, *Osewestre* 1399 Pat, *Oeswestrie, Oasewestre* 1427 *SBL 4028, Oswester* 1451 Fine, *Oswestr'* 1483 *SBL 3637, -tre* 1535 VE *et seq, -try* 1701 PR(L) 9 *et seq*

Oswalstr' l.14th SAC, *Osswellstre* 1703 PR(L) 15, *Oswalstery* 1708 ib, *Oswelstrey* 1713 ib

Osoestri 1612 PR(H) 6, *Ossestrie* 1638-9 PR(H) 3, *Ossistree* 1718,19 PR(L) 16

Ostwestry 1672 PR(L) 14

The French and Latin names in the first set of forms mean 'white minster'. Oswestry means 'Oswald's tree', and *Croes Oswald* is a Welsh translation of this, interpreting 'tree' as 'Christian cross', which was one of its senses in OE and ME.

Although it is not recorded till c.1180, there is no doubt that Oswestry is an OE name. In its first appearance in SAC it occurs in the phrase *castellum de Osewaldestr'*. In Domesday Book the castle had a French name, *Luvre* 'the work' (which reappears in *SBL 9777*, dated 1394-5, as *Castrum Leour'*). The manor in which the castle stood in 1086 is called *Meresberie*. This last survives as modern Maesbury, a hamlet 2½ miles S. of Oswestry, and it means 'manor of the boundary'. The estate later acquired the French and Latin names *Blancmuster* and *Album Monasterium*, and these were displaced after 1300 by Oswestry, though a Welsh translation, *y fynachlog wen*, occurs as late as 1440-93 (*Morgan Ts*)). Maesbury is well-documented in the late 13th and early 14th centuries as one of the settlements in this large estate, and it seems clear that the centre of administration shifted from Maesbury, in the southern part, to the place on its northern edge where the Norman castle was built.

If there had been no question of an association with King Oswald of Northumbria, who was killed in battle by the pagan King

Penda of Mercia in 642, Oswestry would have seemed a normal specimen of a well-evidenced type of place-name in which the genitive of an Old English personal name (frequently dithematic) is combined with the word *tree.* Thirty-eight examples which are either settlement-names or names of meeting-places are known, and an uncounted number is to be found in the boundary clauses of Anglo-Saxon charters. Situation on a boundary is a marked characteristic of these names, and it is probable that the original *Oswaldestrēow* was a boundary-marker on the northern edge of Maesbury. The Welsh and English traditions which made this the site of the battle of 642 may have been encouraged by a superficial resemblance between *Maserfelth*, the name by which Bede refers to it, and *Meresbyrig.* There was a similar tradition at a place called Oswald's Tump in Marshfield in Gloucestershire, *v.* PN Gl 3, 61.

When the centre of administration had shifted to Oswestry and the collegiate church was built there it was probably dedicated to St Oswald because the place-name suggested him as the appropriate saint. Parallels to this process are discussed under Atcham. The association was doubtless fostered by the priests who served the church. The first reference to the dedication occurs in SAC in 1121, where the church is called *Ecclesia Sancti Oswaldi.* If it be accepted that the dedication arose from the place-name, this carries the place-name back earlier than c.1180.

The interpretation of Oswestry as 'cross of St Oswald' becomes explicit probably in the late-12th cent., when Gerald of Wales translates it as 'the tree of Oswald', and certainly in the 13th cent., when the Welsh form *Croes Oswallt* appears in records. But the battle of 642 is called *Maserfelth* by Bede and *Maes Cogwy* in Welsh poetry, and nothing corresponding to those names is to be found in this neighbourhood. There can be no way of demonstrating that the battle did not take place at Oswestry, but there is no firm evidence to show that it did. The occurrence of the personal name Penda in Penley, Fli, some 10 miles from Oswestry, is sometimes cited in this connection, but this is of doubtful relevance. Penda is the first element of other names, such as Pinbury Gl, Pinley Wa, Pinvin Wo, and it is probable that other Mercians were called by it besides the king. Oswald was a common OE name.

Local pronunciations include [ozəztri] and [odʒəztri].

OVERS SO 393963 DB Manor

Ovre 1086 DB
Houeres, Oueres, Oures 1250 Fees (p), *Overes* 1251 ib (p), *Oweres* 1255 RH (p), *Oures* 1291-2 *Ass* (p), *Overes* 1353 Ipm
The Overs 1676 *SBL 6207, Overs* 1690-1 *SBL 5230*

OE **ofer** is used in settlement-names to describe a place poised on the end of a flat-topped ridge, and there is such a ridge here, overlooking the R. East Onny. The place is in Wentnor parish.

There is a hundredal division called Overs in the S.E. of the county. The meeting-place has not been located but must have been at a place also called *Ofer.*

OVERTON SO 666868 DB Manor

Ovretone 1086 DB, *Overton'* 1232 Cl (p) *et passim* with variant spellings *-ton(e)*

Probably 'higher settlement', OE *ufera tūn*, but there is no way of distinguishing this from a hypothetical compound of **tūn** with the word discussed under Overs, except for the few instances of Overton and Orton which have pre-Conquest spellings. This Overton is a township of Stottesdon parish. There is another Sa Overton, in Richard's Castle parish, which is first recorded in c.1180.

OXENBOLD SO 594920 DB Manor

Oxibola 1086 DB, *Oxebald'* 1194,5 P, *-bolde* 1255 RH
Oxenebold', -bode 1205 Cur, *-bold* 1251 Ch, *Oxenbold'* 1261-2 *ForProc et freq* with variant spellings *-bold(e)*; *Oxnebolde* c.1291 TN, *-bold* 1327 Pat
Axenbold 1251 Ch
Oxebowde, Oxne- 1255 RH, *Oxebaud* 1255-6 *Ass*
Oxbolde 1413 Fine

'Building for oxen'. **bold** is the WMidl form of a word which occurs as *bōðl* in the north, and as *bōtl* in the north and in the east midlands. The manner in which this term is used in place-names suggests that it refers to a building of unusual size or importance. It is best-evidenced in the compound with **nīwe** 'new', which occurs three times in Shropshire (Nobald in Meole Brace, Nobold in Baschurch and a lost *Newbold* in Cound). Oxbode Lane in Gloucester may preserve a second reference to an 'oxen building', but none of the other compounds in which the word occurs suggest specific agricultural uses.

Oxenbold is a township of Stanton Long parish. There are two farms, a mile apart, called Great and Little Oxenbold. Both are shown on the 19th-cent. OS map. The G.R. given above refers to Great Oxenbold, which is probably the *Old Oxenbold'* of 1550-1 *RentSur.*

PATTON SO 584950 DB Manor

Peattingtune 901 S 221
Patintune 1086 DB *et freq* with variant spellings *-ton', -ton* to 1291-2 *Ass* (p), *Patunton c.1220-30 HAC (p), Patynton* 1271-2 *Ass* (p), 1284-5 FA, 1329 Ipm (p), 1396 Cl
Patiton' 1255 RH (p), 1255-6 *Ass* (p), *Patyton* 1276 Cl (p) *et freq* with variant spelling *-ton'* to 1419 Fine, *Patiton* 1300 SAC, 1411 Cl
Patton 1443 AD, *-ton'* 1550 *RentSur*

'Estate associated with Peatta', an **-ingtūn** formation. The personal name is not on independent record but is believed to be evidenced in several place-names. Patton is a township of Stanton Long parish.

PEPLOW SJ 627247 DB Manor

Papelau 1086 DB, *-lawe* c.1155 SAC
Pepelawe c.1138 SAC, 1255-6 *Ass, -lowe* 1374 Fine *et freq* to 1520 AD
Pippelawe 1255-6 *Ass, Pyppelowe* 1294-9 *Ass*
Peppelawe 1255-6 (p), 1291-2 *Ass, -lowe* 1284-5 FA *et freq* to 1366 Fine

Peplow 1562 PR(L) 11, *-loe* 1615,92, 1730 ib, *-lowe* 1616 ib
Puplow 1690-1 *SBL 5130*

'Pebble tumulus', from OE ***pyppel** and **hlāw**. There can be no question of a natural hill, but in the field opposite Peplow Hall and Chapel one of the oak trees stands on a mound which might be the remains of a tumulus. On the occasion when this was noted (20th June 1987) a ploughed field near Peplow Grange had extremely pebbly soil.

Peplow Grange is not on 19th-cent. maps, so may not be an ancient settlement, but the reference in 1255-6 *Ass* is to *Parva Pippelawe, Parva Pepelawe,* so there do appear to have been two foci. Peplow is a township of Hodnet parish.

PETTON SJ 437265 Ancient Parish

Pectone 1086 DB *et freq* with variant spelling *-ton(a)*, *-ton'* to 1306-7 *Ass*
Peton' 1230 Cur (p), 1259 Cl, *Peton* 1300 Pat, *Petone* 1307,17 Pat
Petton' 1255 RH (p) *et freq* with variant spelling *-ton*

'Peak settlement', v. **pēac, tūn**. The site is much more striking than appears from maps. The church and the motte stand on a conical hill which commands wide views all round, and the name would be a perfect description for a settlement either on or beside this hill.

PICKTHORN SO 669843 DB Manor

Pichetorne 1086 DB, *Piketorn Tome* 1194,5 P, *Pikethorn Tome* 1199 P, *Pikethorn* 1200 P *et freq* with variant spellings *Pyke-, -thorne* to 1369 Ipm, *Pichethorn* 1204 P, *-torn* 1214 P, *-thorn'* c.1240 SAC
Pickthorne 1535 VE, *-thorn* 1627 *SBL 4071*

'Spiky thorn-tree', from OE **pīc** 'point' and **þorn**. The affix *Tome* presumably refers to a 12th-cent. tenant.

The name is given to a single house on the 19th-cent. OS

map. This house is shown but not named on the modern 1" map. The manor was assessed at ½ hide in 1086. The place is called *Pickthorn Hamlet* in the Stottesdon *TA*.

PIMHILL SJ 487212 Civil Parish

Pimenhull' 1255-6 *Ass, Pymenhull* 1302-7 APW
Pemehull 1358 *SBL 5850*
Pemenhull' 1371 *SBL 4489*
Pymehull 1415 *SBL 4491*

The hundred-name is:

Pebenhull' 1221 Fees, *Pebenhul* 1271-2 *Ass*
Penbenhull, Pendenhull 1255 RH, *Penbemhull'* 1255-6 *Ass*
Pemenhull' 1255-6 *Ass*
Pymenhulle 1271-2 *Ass, Pimmenhull* 1282 ChanR, *Pymenhull* 1316, 46, 1428,31 FA
Pimehull 1284-5 FA, *Pymehull* 1290 Ipm
Pymele 1305-6 *Ass*

There are numerous early spellings for Pimley, 4½ miles S.E. of Pimhill, and it is clear from these that the two names have the same first element, the OE form of which appears likely to have been **pymba.* The *-b-* is more frequently preserved in the Pimley spellings. Pimley (*Pimelega* 1138 SAC, *Pimbelega* 1182-95 ib) may have been a wood named by the addition of **lēah** to Pimhill, with the loss before the earliest record of the middle element; this is a common way of shortening such names. The second element of Pimhill is **hyll**, and the name is that of a pointed eminence which was presumably the site of the hundred meeting-place. The G.R. given above is for the top of this hill. There was probably a district named from the hill which formed the basis for the 13th-cent. hundred. Pimley may have been on the southern boundary of this district.

It is tempting to associate the first element of Pimhill with a place-name element **pimp,* found in Pimp's Court (in E. Farleigh) K and in Pimperne Do; *v.* PN Do 2, 110-11 for a full discussion. **pimp* is plausibly explained as a term for a hill, related to ModE *pimple.* It must be noted, however, that names in which this term occurs have regular *-mp-* or *-np-* spellings, whereas the Shropshire names demand a term with *-mb-*.

It is not clear whether there was a settlement called **Pymbanhylle.* The nearest ancient settlement to the hill is Lea Hall, which is recorded from 1199 (1265) Ch (*La Lya*). A member of the family whose surname this became is described in 1358 (*SBL 5850*) as Joh. *de La Lee de Pemehull.*

The large civil parish of Pimhill is a modern creation, composed from parts of Baschurch, Fitz, Montford and Shrewsbury St Alkmund, and the whole of Preston Gubbals. It came into existence in 1934.

PITCHFORD SJ 528043 Ancient Parish

Piceford 1086 DB, *Pichefort* 1160-72 HAC, *-ford* 1194 P *et passim* with variant spellings *-forde, Pyche-* to 1583 *SBL 15759, Piccheford* 1235-6 Fees (p), *-ford'* 1252 Cl (p), *Pyccheford* 1285 Pat (p), 1312 Cl (p)
Pikeford 1177 P (p)
Pichford 1189 CartAntiq *et freq* with variant spellings *-ford'* and *Pych-* to 1577 Saxton, *Picford* 1242 Fees (p), 1274 RH
Pichesford 1203 P (p)
Pygford' 1261-2 *ForProc* (p)
Pechford' 1271-2 *Ass. Pecheford* 1488 Ipm
Pitcheforde 1579 *Eyton, Pitchford* 1593 *SBL 6713*

'Pitch ford'. There is a pitch well 250 yards N.E. of Pitchford Hall (VCH VIII, p. 116), and the road from Shrewsbury used to cross the Row Brook near this well. It was diverted eastwards in 1833. The G.R. given above is for the Hall. The village of Pitchford is ¼-½ mile S. of this, and there is a farm called Little Pitchford ½ mile N.

PLAISH SO 529965 DB Manor

Plesc, Plæsc 963 S 723
Plesham 1086 DB, *Plesse* 1255-6 *Ass*, 1274 RH, *Plese* 1261-2

ForProc, 1284-5 FA, *Plesshe* 1294-5 *Ass* (p), *Plehssh* 1301 SAC
Playsse 1255 RH, 1508 *SBL 4425*, *Plaishe* 1590 *SBL 4006*
Plessye 1291-2 *Ass*
Plasse 1291-2 *Ass* (p), *Plashe* 1304 Pat, 1577 Saxton, 1602 *PRCardington*, *Plasshe* 1306-7 *Ass* (p), 1316 FA, 1322 Cl (p), *Plash* 1695 Morden, 1740 *PRCardington*

OE **plæsc** is only recorded in the 963 reference for this name, but it occurs in a few other place-names which have post-Conquest spellings, and the word *plash* is recorded in literary sources from 1400 onwards. The accepted translation is 'shallow piece of standing water'.

A. Morton, in *The Trees of Shropshire* (Shrewsbury 1986) gives an excellent description of a spring near Holt Fm, ¼ mile E. of Plaish, which issues from beneath the roots of a giant pollard oak. The water from this spring was stored in underground stone chambers and pumped from there to supply the village with drinking water until 1984, when Plaish was put onto mains water supply. It is possible that in pre-Conquest times the overflow from this spring formed a pool with special characteristics, for which this rare term seemed appropriate.

An alternative suggestion by H.P.R. Finberg (SAS 56, p. 30) refers the name to "an area of wet grass and sedge --- enclosed within a semicircular stone wall --- projecting from the garden wall of Plaish Hall". Finberg says that in wet weather this pool has been known to flood the roadway.

Plaish is in Cardington parish. *Plash* 1695 represents the modern pronunciation.

POLMERE SJ 411094 DB Manor

Pole 1086 DB
Poulemere 1255-6 *Ass* (p), 1308 Ipm
Poulmere 1271-2 *Ass* (p), 1274 RH (p), 1276 Ipm, *Powlmer* 1553 PR(H) 12
Porlemare 1291-2 *Ass*
Polmer 1490 Ipm, 1601 *SBL 12706*, 1615 PR(H) 12
Pomoore 1672 HTR

The identification of DB *Pole* with Polmere is generally accepted, though VCH VIII (p. 264) refers to it with caution.

Assuming that *Pole* in 1086 is short for *Polemere*, the name appears to be a unique compound of **pōl** 'pool' and **mere** 'pond'. The first is most frequently used in place-names for a pool connected with a larger body of water, such as a harbour on the coast or a wide place in a river. It is possible that in earlier times a small stream ran through the pond at Polmere to the Rea Brook. If the flow was intermittent the meaning of the name might be 'pond which is sometimes a pool'.

Polmere is a township in Pontesbury parish.

PONTESBURY SJ 400060 Ancient Parish

Pantesberie 1086 DB, *-buri* 1217 Pat (p), *-bur'* 1255 RH, *-byry* 1312 Cl
Pontesbir' 1203-4 *Ass* (p) *et passim* with variant spellings *-biri, -bur', buri(e), -byr', -bury*; *Pontisburi* 1310 Ipm, *-burie* 1602 *SBL 13450, -bury* 1722,6,34 PR(L) 20
Pauntesbir' 1221-4, 71-2 *Ass*
Pantebur' 1242 Fees
Pauntebir' 1266 Cl
Ponsepre 1454 Fine, *Ponspery* 1619 PR(StA) 4, *Pomspry* 1752 PR(StA) 6
Ponsburye 1495 Ipm *et freq* with variant spelling *-bury* to 1746 PR(L) 14, *Ponsbrey* 1643 PR(H) 6, *Ponsburie alias Pontesburie, Ponsburie upon the Hill* 1615 *SBL 6845*
Pontsburye 1571 PR(H) 12 *et freq* with variant spelling *-bury* to 1775 *PRCardington*
Ponstbury 1631 PR(H) 1, 1715 PR(L) 20
Ponsborough 1649 SAS 4/VII
Punsbury alias Pontesbury 1667 *SBL 9945*

Pontesbury alias Ponsbury occurs fairly frequently in the 17th cent., but in modern times the longer form has prevailed, with trisyllabic pronunciation. *Ponsburie upon the Hill* (1615) refers to the squatter settlement outside the village which is described in VCH VIII, pp. 253-4.

Pontesford has the same first element as Pontesbury, and so

does *Ponteslithe*, the old name of Pontesford Hill. In all these three names the element is in the genitive, and this caused DEPN to express a preference for derivation from the OE personal name *Pant*. The alternative is to consider *Pant* to be the British river-name which is evidenced in Essex and (in the form Pont) in Northumberland and Durham. A tributary of the Rea Brook curves round Pontesford Hill, and it is a crossing of this tributary which is referred to in Pontesford. Pontesbury, on the other hand, is a mile away from the stream. It is likely that Pontesbury was originally coined as the name of the village, since the road layout suggests the presence of a pre-Conquest enclosure, which would be the **byrig** ('fort'). Welsh *pant* in the sense 'valley' (as opposed to being used as a river-name) is not appropriate to the situation, and on the whole the OE personal name offers the most satisfactory solution.

POSENHALL SJ 657015 Civil Parish

Bodeshal' 1167 P
Posenhal' 1203-4 *Ass* (p) *et freq* with variant spelling *-hale* to 1331 (1348) Pat, *Posanhale* 1291-2 *Ass*, *Posenhall* 1535 VE
Pesenhal (p), *Passsnhal'* 1255-6 *Ass*
Possenhal' 1261-2 *ForProc*, *-hale* 1271-2 *Ass*
Posenall 1672 HTR, 1733 PR(H) 16

'Possibly 'hollow shaped like a bag'. There is an OE word *pusa*, *posa*, 'bag, scrip', and the gen. of this would be a suitable first element for a compound with **halh** 'nook'. The topography of the area is much broken. DEPN cites the form *Pesenhale* from 1255-6 *Ass* in support of a derivation from **peosu** 'pease', but the *-e-* in this form may be a scribal error for *-o-*.

The local pronunciation is [pɔznəl].

POSTON SO 549823 DB Manor

Possetorn(*e*) 1086 DB, *-thorn* 1194 P *et freq* with variant spelling *-thorne* to 1322 Pat
Posthorn 1255-6 *Ass*, 1316 FA, *-thorne* 1402 Cl
Porsthorn 1418 Fine

Postern 1418 Fine, 1695 Morden, *-torne* 1499 Ipm, 1600 PR(H) 15, *-terne* 1694 ib
Postenne 1552 Pat, *Poston* 1631 PR(H) 15, *Posten* 1696 ib

'Possa's thorn-tree'. This was perhaps a boundary-mark before it became a settlement-name.

Two holdings, each of one virgate, are noted in DB, and there are now two farms, Greater and Lesser Poston. In 1292-5 *Ass* the two settlements are *Netherposthorn et Ouerposthorn'*. They are distinguished as *Littel* and *Muchel Posthorne* 1402 Cl, *Great* and *Little Postern* 1695 Morden. They are townships in Hopton Cangeford parish.

POYNTON SJ 570178 DB Manor

Peventone 1086 DB
Peuinton 1221-2 *Ass et passim* with variant spelling *-tone* to c.1272-84 HAC, *Peuynton* 1284-5 FA, 1336 *SBL 5429*
Peuyngton' 1271-2 *Ass, Peuyncton* 1276 Cl, *Peuington* 1376 Pat
Peinton' 1291-2 *Ass, Peynton* 1379 Pat (p) *et freq* to 1672 HTR
Peuyton' 1306-7 *Ass*
Paynton 1585 PR(L) 20 *et freq* to 1751 ib, *Painton* 1587 ib, *Payneton* 1671 ib, *Paineton* 1686 ib
Peington 1587 PR(L) 20
Pyonton 1590 PR(L) 20
Pointon 1737 PR(L) 20, *Poynton* 1790 *SBL 5536*

'Pēofa's estate', probably an **-ingtūn** name. In a number of spellings in the first and second series, the form has been printed as *Peninton* etc., but it is clearly permissible to emend to *Peuin-*, *Peuyng-*. *Poynton* was possible current as an alternative form to *Paynton* earlier than appears from the material set out here.

Poynton is a township of High Ercall parish.

PREEN, CHURCH SO 541984 Ancient Parish

Prene 1086 DB *et passim* with variant spelling *Prena* to 1557 AD
Prune 1208-9 *ForProc et freq* with variant spelling *Pruna* to 1462 HAC

Prona 1255 RH
Preone c.1291 TN, 1334 SR
Preene 1316 FA, *Preen* 1552 Pat
Preyn 1692 PR(H) 13, 1750 PR(H) 14

OE **prēon** 'brooch', presumably used of some as yet unidentified landscape feature.

There are two settlements, Church and Holt Preen, the latter shown on modern maps as Holt. They are *Pruna Magna, Parva Prona* 1255 RH, *Chircheprene, Holtprene* 1255-6 *Ass, Chyrcheprene, Parua Prene* 1271-2 *Ass.*

PREES SJ 557335 Ancient Parish

Pres 1086 DB *et passim* to 1327 Pat, *Ppres* 1271-2 *Ass*
Pratis 1255-6 *Ass*
Preess 1259 Ch, *Prees* 1316 FA *et freq, Preese* 1608 PR(L) 9 *et freq* to 1766 PR(StA) 3, *Prese* 1782 PR(L) 14
Prez 1271-2 *Ass,* 1294 Pat, 1307 Ch, 1322,49,98 Pat
Preez 1352 Pat, 1363 Ipm, 1722,3 PR(L) 9
Prys 1362, 1413 Pat, *Pryse* 1416 Fine, *Pris* 1429 ib
Price c.1540 Leland, *Pryce* 1590 PR(L) 20
Prece 1603-4 PR(StA) 4, 1673,81 PR(L) 9, *Preece* 1655 PR(L) 9 *et freq* to 1778 PR(L) 4, *Priece* 1702 PR(L) 11

There is no reason to doubt Ekwall's (DEPN) derivation of this name and of Preese La from PrW **prês,* Welsh *prys,* though Jackson (LHEB p. 343) only accords it a "perhaps". Both authorities translate the term as 'brushwood', but the modern Welsh word means 'copse, grove'. The corresponding Cornish word is also used as a simplex name. The last set of spellings represents the modern pronunciation.

ME spellings with *-e-* and *-ee-* have been listed separately, but they may be taken as representing the same sound. This must be an original long vowel, as there is nothing in the form of the name to cause lengthening. LHEB cites Prees and Preese as possible instances of English adoptions in the 7th century, after vowellengthening had occurred in monosyllables in Welsh.

The *Prys, Pris* spellings are not evidenced for the La name. They probably represent a separate development influenced by that of the Welsh word. Prees is only a few miles from the boundary of the detached portion of Flintshire.

ME *Pre(e)s* would suggest to a French speaker the plural of French *pré* 'meadow'. This has caused the false Latinisation *Pratis* in 1255-6 and it may be responsible for the fairly frequent *-z* forms. Delapre Abbey in Nth is *de la Preez* 1316 FA.

PRESTON

There are five Prestons in Shropshire; as frequently with recurrent **tūn** names this is more than in any other county. The name means 'estate of the priests'. It is likely to refer to the use of revenues for the upkeep of a group of clerics serving a minster church. The church would probably not be situated at the place called Preston.

Four of the Shropshire examples are treated here. The fifth, Preston in Upton Magna, is first recorded 1121 SAC.

PRESTON BROCKHURST SJ 539248 DB Manor

Preston(e) 1086 DB, *Preston'* 1255 RH (p), 1334 SR, *Preston T(h)oret* 1255 RH, *Preston' Turet* 1255-6 *Ass*, *Preston* 1284-5 FA, 1302 Ipm, 1395 AD, *Preston' Taret, - Corbet, - subtus Brokhurst* 1291-2 *Ass*, *Preston Brokhurst* 1385 Fine, 1494 Ipm, *- Brakhurst* 1655 PR(L) 15, *- Brockhurst* 1669 *SBL 15748 et seq*, *- Brockall 1675 Ogilby*, *- Brockas* 1747 PR(L) 7
Presin Brockhouse 1684 PR(L) 11, *Presson Brokust* 1697 PR(L) 19

Neither of the DB estates was in ecclesiastical ownership, so the use of the estate for the upkeep of priests was presumably pre-Conquest. The affix Brockhurst refers to the position of the settlement on the fringes of the wood of that name. This is discussed under Lee Brockhurst. The affixes *Corbet* and *Toret* are discussed under Moreton Corbet (Preston Brockhurst is in Moreton Corbet parish).

PRESTON GUBBALS SJ 493196 DB Manor

Prestone 1086 DB, *Preston* 1217 (1285) Ch, *Preston Gubald* 1255 RH, *Preston' Gobald* 1271-2 *Ass,* 1343 *SBL 10760, - Gobaldes* 1292-5 *Ass, Preston Gubbales* 1654 PR(L) 9, *Gubballes* 1655 ib, *- Gubbolds* 1671 *PRLilleshall et freq* to 1801 PR(L) 4, *- Gubballs* 1694 PR(L) 4, *- Gubbals* 1756 PR(L) 1 *et seq, - Gobalds* 1802 PR(L) 4, *- Gubbalds* 1811 PR(L) 6
Preeston Gubbals 1654 PR(L) 9
Ibalds 1695 Morden
Presson Gobolls 1751 PR(L) 10

The manor was held in 1086 by *Godebold,* a priest who was a tenant of St Alkmund's church in Shrewsbury. The parish is now included in the civil parish of Pimhill.

PRESTON MONTFORD SJ 432142 DB Manor

Prestone, -tune 1086 DB, *Preston juxta Muniford* 1217 (1285) Ch, *Preston'* 1255 RH, 1255-6 *Ass,* 1334 SR, *- de Ponte de Maneford'* 1255-6 *Ass, Preston* 1316 FA, *- by Moneford* 1317 Ipm, *- iuxta Moneford' Brughe* 1361 *SBL 3610, Preston Monford* 1612 PR(L) 7, 1686 PR(H) 6

One of the DB manors belonged to St Alkmund's church in Shrewsbury. For Montford *v. supra.*

PRESTON UPON THE WEALD MOORS SJ 682153 Ancient Parish

Prestune 1086 DB, *Preston'* 1238 Cl *et freq, - in Wyldemor* 1261-2 *ForProc, - sub Wyldemor* 1291-2 *Ass, - sup' Wildemor* 1294-9 *Ass* (p), *- super Le Wyldemor* 1305-6 *Ass, Preston upon Wyldemore* 1392 Pat, *- de Wildmore* 1657 PR(L) 20, *- on the Wild-Moores* 1709 ib, *- of the Wildmore* 1749 ib, *- in the Wildmoors* 1782 PR(L) 14

Here, as for Preston Brockhurst, DB offers no clue about

the ecclesiastical ownership evidenced by the name.

Weald Moor means 'wild, uncultivated marsh'.

PULESTON SJ 734224 DB Manor

Plivesdone 1086 DB
Pivelesdon' 1200 Cur, c.1240,8 SAC (p), *-dun'* 1241 SAC (p), *Pyuelesdon'* 1255 RH (p), 1271-2, 91-2 *Ass* (p), 1334 *SBL 5413* (p), *Pywelesdon'* 1255-6, 91-2 *Ass* (p), *Pyuelesdon* 1285 Ch (p), *Pyvelesdon* 1284-5 FA, *Pywellesdon* 1348 Pat (p)
Piulesdone c.1271 *SBL 16196* (p), *Pyullesden* 1271-2 *Ass* (p), *Pyulesdon* c.1275 SAC (p), *Pywlesdon'* 1291-2 *Ass* (p), *Piulesdon'* e.14th *SBL 16197*
Puwelesdon 1271-2 *Ass* (p), *-don'* 1306-7 *Ass* (p)
Pulesdune c.1275 SAC (p), *-den* 1332 Cl (p), *-don* 1436 Fine
Pewelesdon' 1306-7 *Ass* (p), *Pevellesdo'* 1320 *SBL 4531*
Peulesdoune 1313-14 *Ass* (p), *-don* e.14th *SBL 16201*, 1331 Cl, 1342 Cl (p), e.17th SAS 4/III
Pyllesdon' 1314 *SBL 9894*
Puyllesdon 1346 Pat (p)
Pulston 1586 *PRChetwynd*
Pilston 1587, 1605 *PRChetwynd*, *Pylston* 1596 *SBL 3463*, 1605 *PRChetwynd*, *Pilston alias Puleston* 1601 *SBL 3464*
Peilsone 1639 *PRChetwynd*

Probably 'Peofel's hill'. The second element, **dūn**, is likely to refer to the level raised area which has the smaller summit of Puleston Hill on its S.E. edge. The nature of the first element is open to question. There is a similar run of spellings for Puesdown in Hazleton, Gl (*Peulesdon'* 1236, *Piwelesdon* 1302, *Pewelesdon* 1322, PN Gl **I**, 174), and this is probably a coincidence, but it could be held to suggest that **Peofel* or **Peowel* was a hill-name. The spellings for Pewsham W (PN W 14) have been considered to indicate the existence of a river-name **Pewe*, to which a term **Peowel* could be related. On the whole, however, it seems best to accept Ekwall's derivation (DEPN) from a personal name. *Peuf*(*a*) is on record, so **Peofel* is not an entirely unsupported conjecture.

There is an alternative local form Pilson, and Ekwall discusses the name under this heading. It is *Puleston* 1808 Baugh,

Pilston on the 19th-cent. OS map. It is in Chetwynd parish.

PULLEY SJ 475092 DB Manor

Polelie 1086 DB, *-leye* 1271-2 *ForProc*, 1378 Pat (p), *-ley* 1430 Fine
Pulileg' 1198 Fees *et freq* with variant spellings *-leg, -legh', -leye* to 1346 Cl, *Pullileg'* 1261-2 *ForProc, Pullyley* 1419 *SBL 5798, Pulliley* 1421 Cl
Polileg' 1249 Ipm *et freq* with variant spellings *-ley(e), -legh', -leg* to 1394 Pat, *Polylegh'* 1271-2 *ForProc et freq* with variant spellings *-lee, -ley(e), -leygh* to 1336 Ipm, *Pollylye* 1350 *SBL 3904* (p)
Pullid 1304 Cl
Puleley 1321 HAC, *Pulleleye* 1339 Pat, *-ley* 1377 Cl (p), 1416 AD, 1421 Cl, 1429,45 Fine
Polesleye 1363 Pat
Pulley 1535 VE *et seq, Pulley otherwise called Pulleley* 1567 *SBL 6736A, Pulley alias Pullely* 1598 *SBL 6745, Pully* 1812 PR(L) 14

The second element is **lēah**, 'wood, clearing'. The first appears to be unique to this name. There is no recorded word *pulig*, which is the form suggested by the spellings.

Upper Pulley is *Hoverpolile* 1255 RH. There were two manors, one situated in Meole Brace and the other in Shrewsbury St Julian. They are called *Pulley Vetus* and *Pulley Foreign* in the Land Tax Assessments of 1763.

PULVERBATCH SJ 431029 Ancient Parish

Polrebec 1086 DB, *-beche* 1242 Fees, 1342 Pat, *-bache* 1291-2 Fees, *-bach* 1346 FA
Pulerebege c.1180-6 HAC (p), *-beche* 1186 ib (p), *Pullerbach'* 1255-6 *Ass et freq* with variant spellings *-beche, -bache* to 1421 Cl, *Pullurbeche* 1359 Pat
Pulrebeche 1180-9 HAC (p) *et freq* with variant spellings *-bec(h), -bache* to 1361 Pat, *Pullrebache* 1255-6 *Ass, -beche* 1294 Cl
Phurebek 1226 Cur
Puluerbach' 1261-2 *ForProc, Pulverbech* 1284-5 FA, *Pulverebache*

c.1291 TN, *Pulverbeche* 1339 Pat, *-bache* 1383 Pat, *-bach* 1561 PR(H) 12, *-batch* 1605 PR(L) 14, *-beach* 1635 PR(H) 6, 1688 PR(H) 18

Purlebach' 1261-2 *ForProc*, 1292 Ipm

Puldrebatl' 1271-2 *Ass*

Polerebach 1316 FA

Pollerbache 1359 Pat, *Poler-* 1428 FA

Pullerbache 1395 Pat, 1421 Cl

Powdurbach 1535 VE, *Pulverbatch als Powderbach* 1590 *SBL 6671*, *Powderbach(e)* 1602 *SBL 13450, 6907 et freq* to 1739 *PRLudford*, *Powderbach alias Pulverbach* 1730 *SBL 4051*, 1803 Plymley

Poulderbech 1551 PR(H) 12, *-bache* 1601 *SBL 6848B*, *-batch* 1608 PR(L) 14, *Polderbach* 1615 PR(H) 12, 1799 Townson, *Poulder-*, *Powlderbatch* 1672 HTR

Powtherbech 1591 PR(L) 6

Pulverbache alias Pulderbache 1616 *SBL 6817A*

Second element **bæce** 'stream-valley'. The first appears to be an otherwise unnoted **pulfre*. The *-v-* of *Pulver-* must have developed from an original component of the first element, despite its relatively late appearance in the spellings, as it is not a consonant which would be inserted parasitically. This rules out Ekwall's (DEPN) suggestion of an onomatopoeic stream-name **Purl*, and disqualifies Pulverbatch for its listing in Elements under ***polra** 'marshy land'. (This last is in any case not appropriate topographically). The element **pulfre* is unexplained. Church Pulverbatch stands on a hill between two streams, both of which have **bæce**-type valleys.

The later development of the name shows insertion of parasitic *-d-*, and association with the word *powder*.

The two settlements of Church and Castle Pulverbatch are ½ mile apart. They are distinguished as 'Castle' and 'Church' from the late 13th cent. (e.g. *Chyrche Pulrebach* 1271-2 *Ass*, *Castell Poleredech* 1284-5 FA, *Castel-*, *Chirchpolrebache* 1301 SAC). *Church-* and *Castle-* are frequent in the 16th-18th cents.

Church Pulverbatch is locally called Churton. Early spellings for this are *Chirchetona de Pulrebeche* 1221 HAC, *Cherton* 1535 VE, *Chorton* 1667 *SBL 9945*, *Church Pulverbatch alias Churton* 1697 *SBL 9960*, *Churton or Powderbach* 1742 PR(L) 14. This is 'settlement with a church', a name which sometimes becomes Cheriton or Cherrington, but which has developed to Churton in one other instance, in Ch (though PN Ch **4**, 70-71, questions the derivation from **cirice**).

PURSLOW SO 360810 DB Manor

Posselau 1086 DB, *-lawe* 1242 Fees, *-low* 1327 Pat (p), *-lowe* 1397 Pat
Pusselawa c.1200-10 HAC, *-lawe* 1255-6 *Ass*, *-lowe* 1271 Cl, 1327 Pat, 1346, 1431 FA
Puslowe 1449 Fine
Purslaw 1577 Saxton, *-low* 1641 SAS 3/IV

'Pussa's tumulus', *v.* **hlāw**, referring to a vanished burial-mound which was probably the marker for the meeting-place of Purslow Hundred. This type of name is discussed under Beslow. There is a reference in 1272 Cl to *Pusselowe Superior*, which suggests that there was more than one settlement. Purslow is in Clunbury parish.

The late insertion of inorganic *-r-* is paralleled in Marsworth Bk, which was *Masseworth* or *Messeworth* till the 18th cent. Also in Bk is Drayton Parslow, in which Parslow (a surname) shows a corresponding development from *Passelowe.*

QUATFORD SO 739908 Ancient Parish

Quatford 1086 DB *et passim*, *Quhatford* 1221-2 *Ass*, *Quattford* 1595 PR(H) 3
Quateford 1271-2 *Ass*, c.1540 Leland

'Ford in a district called *Cwat*(*t*)', see the discussion under Bridgnorth.

QUATT SO 757883 Ancient Parish

Quatone 1086 DB

Quatte 1208-9 *ForProc* (p) *et passim* to 1581-2 PR(H) 3, *Qwatt* 1550-1 *RentSur*, *Quatt* 1661 PR(H) 13
Quatoe 1316 FA
Quat 1320 Pat, 1417 Fine, 1577 Saxton, 1682 *PRAlveley*, 1730 *PRChetton*, 1802 PR(H) 3
Cutt 1604 *PRAlveley*, *Cutes* 1616 ib, *Cuts* 1628 ib

The OE form was *Cwat*(*t*), and the name is unexplained: see the discussion under Bridgnorth. Ekwall suggests that Quatt represents a shortening of *Quatton*, but it seems likely that the DB form is aberrant.

Kelly's Directory for 1934 says that the parish comprises the townships of Quatt Malvern and Quatt Jarvis. *Quat Jervis* and *Quatt Malborne* are listed 1672 HTR. Malvern is from the Wo priory of Great Malvern to which this manor was granted before 1127 (Eyton III, 174). Eyton gives a detailed account of the descent of Quatt Jarvis down to 1423, but there is nothing in this to account for the affix.

RATLINGHOPE SO 404969 Ancient Parish

Rotelingehope 1086 DB, 1255-6, 71-2 *Ass*, *-hop'* 1261-2 *ForProc*, 1267 Cl, *Rotelyng'hope* l.13th *ForProc*
Rodelingehope 1208-9 *ForProc*
Rotchchop 1255 RH
Rothinchop' 1255 RH
Rotelinghop' 1255 RH, 1261-2 *ForProc*, 1267 Cl, *-hope* 1255-6, 71-2 *Ass*, 1301 SAC, *-hop* c.1291 TN, *Rotlynghope* 1551 Pat
Rothelinghop' 1267 Cl, *-hop* c.1291 TN
Rolynghope 1271-2 *Ass*, *Rollynghope* 1535 VE
Roderhope 1272 Ipm
Rotelynch'hope 1306-7 *Ass*
Rothinthorp 1316 FA
Rotlinchope 1334 SR
Rotlichap 1577 Saxton
Ratlenhope 1639 PR(H) 12
Ratlinghope 1641 SAS 3/IV *et seq*, *Rattling-hope* 1672 HTR, *Rattleing Hope* 1750 PR(H) 14
Rustlinghope 1649 SAS 4/VII

Ratchop 1737 PR(H) 7
Rattinghope 1754 PR(L) 14
Rathlinghope 1788 PR(StA) 3

'Secluded valley associated with Rōtel'. This is one of a group of names which are discussed under Millichope.

The shortened form *Ratchop* survived within living memory, but appears to have fallen out of use.

RHISTON SO 259952 Civil Parish (with Brompton)

Ristune 1086 DB *et freq* with variant spelling *-ton(e)*; *Ryston'* 1291-2 *Ass. -tone* 1346 AD, *Riston alias Ruston* 1611 *SBL 8475, - otherwise -* 1780 *SBL 3398*
Russeton' 1242 Fees
Rushton 1271-2 *Ass, Russheton* 1394 Pat
Rustone 1315 APW, *-ton* 1318 InqMisc, 1334 SR, 1342 Pat

'Rush settlement', OE **rysc-tūn.* The spelling Rhiston appears on the 19th-cent. OS map.

RICHARD'S CASTLE (SALOP) SO 496697 Ancient Parish

Castellum Ricardi c.1180-86 HAC, 1235-6 Fees
Castrum Richardi 1211-12 RBE *et freq* with variant spelling *-Ricardi*
Chastel Richard 1321 Pat (p)
Richardescastel 1349 Pat *et freq* with variant spellings *Ricardes-* and *-castell; Richarduscastell* 1394 Pat, *Riccards Castell* 1577 SAS 4/III, *Rickerds Castle* 1726,7 PR(H) 14, *Rickards Castle* 1727 ib

The Shropshire parish is part of the land-unit attached to the castle and failed borough in the adjacent part of Herefordshire. The Richard from whom the castle is named is generally stated to be Richard Scrope, whose son, Osbern, held the castle in 1086. Richard himself is said in DB to have been the earlier holder of the land which formed the castlery, but the statement does not necessarily imply that the castle dates from his time.

Editors frequently translate the name, only giving the modern form, and for this reason no final dates have been given for types of spelling which occur *freq.*

RODINGTON SJ 589145 Ancient Parish

Rodintone 1086 DB *et freq* with variant spellings *-ton', -tun, -ton* to 1751 PR(L) 8, *Rodynton'* 1334 SR *et freq* with variant spelling *-ton* to 1559 *SBL 5105*
Radinton 1228 Pat
Roddington 1254 Pat, 1601 *SBL 4622 et freq* to 1809 *SBL 5542*
Rodyngton 1359 Fine *et freq* to 1535 *SBL 7180, Rodington* 14th *SBL 4411 et seq*
Radyngton 1535 *SBL 7180*
Roydyngton 1535 *SBL 7180*
Ruddington 1539-40 *RentSur*
Roditon 1577 Saxton
Rhodinton 1668 *SBL 6039*

This cannot be a straightforward compound of the river-name Roden with **tūn**, as that would not have produced the universal *-in-, -yn-, -ing-, -yng-* spellings. Possibly the name as recorded from 1086 on is a shortening of an earlier **Rodeningtūn*, with **-ing-** as a connective syllable. It does not seem likely that an original **Rodentūn* was interpreted as an **-ingtūn** type by influence of neighbouring names. Hunkington and Withington are nearby settlements, but neither is an original **-ingtūn** name.

The river-name is *Rodene* 1249 *SBL 5409 et freq.* The settlement called Roden (in High Ercall parish) is *Hrodene* l.10th S 1534 (with inorganic *H-*, as in *hlafe* for *lafe* in the same document), *Rodene* 1242 Fees *et passim.* Rodenhurst, between Roden and Rodington, is *Rodenhurst* 1255-6 *Ass.*

Roden derives, via PrW, from Romano-British *Rutunium*, probably meaning 'swift-flowing river'.

ROMSLEY SO 782833 Ancient Parish

Rameslege 1086 DB, *-leg'* 1203-4 *Ass* (p)
Rammesleg' 1203-4 *Ass* (p), *Rammesl'* 1271-2 *Ass*
Remesleg' 1255 RH, *-leye* 1334 SR, 1357,81 Fine, 1366,9 Ipm
Romesleg' 1271-2 *Ass, -legh* 1315 Ipm
Remmesleg' 1274 RH (p), *-ley* 1363, 1421 Cl, 1364 Ipm, *-leye* 1367 Cl
Rommesleye alias Rumisley 1287 Ipm, *Rommesleye* 1291 Ipm, 1387 Fine, *-leygh* 1308 Ipm, *-leigh* 1309 Cl, *-legh* 1316 Cl
Roumesleye 1294 Ipm
Rummesle 1348 Ipm
Ramseley 1649 *PRAlveley, Ramsley* 1695 Morden
Romsley 1672 HTR

This place is probably the *Hremesleage* of Wulfric Spot's will (S 1536, Burton), dated 1002-4. There are apparent inconsistencies in the spellings of the first element. The vowel is variously *-e-* and *-a-*, and there is an unusually even balance between *-m-* and *-mm-*. These inconsistencies may derive from the various forms of the OE word for a raven, which appears in OE texts as *hræfn, (h)refn, hremn, (h)remm, (h)ræm.* Probably 'raven's wood', second element **lēah**. *Ram-* (from *(h)ræm*) has become *Rom-* by the rounding of *a* before a nasal consonant, which is a regular feature of WMidl dialect.

RORRINGTON SJ 301008 DB Manor

Roritune 1086 DB, *-ton'* 1261-2 *ForProc, Roryton'* 1271-2 *Ass, Roriton* 1299 Ipm, 1316 FA
Rorinton' 1255-6 *Ass, Rorynton'* 1334 SR
Roryngton 1535 VE, *Rorington* 1629 PR(H) 8, 1693 *SBL 3547*

'Estate associated with Hrōr', an **-ingtūn** formation. Rorrington is a township of Chirbury parish.

ROSSALL SJ 468152 DB Manor

Rosela 1086 DB, *Rosall'* c.1210 SAC (p), *Rosale* 1428 FA
Roshala 1170 P *et passim* with variant spellings *-hal', -hal(e), -hall*

to 1397 InqMisc, *Roshell* 1654 PR(L) 4
Rushal' 1209 For (p), 1221-2 *Ass* (p), *-hale* 1271-2 *Ass*, 1272 Cl (p), *Rushall alias Russall* 1583 *SBL 15759*
Russhal' 1231 Cur (p)
Rossale 1255-6 *Ass et freq* to 1431 FA, *Rossall* 1577 Saxton *et seq*, *Rossell* 1653,81 PR(L) 4, 1672 HTR, 1695 Morden
Rosshall 1628 PR(L) 15, 1723 PR(H) 1, *Ross Hall* 1808 Baugh
Rowshall 1497 Ipm

There is another instance of this name in La. It means 'horse nook', OE **hros-halh*, **halh** being used in the Sa name in the sense 'land in a river-bend'.

Two estates are described in DB, one of which is the *Roshal' Parva* of 1255 RH (also *parua Rossale* 1255-6, - *Roshale* 1271-2 *Ass*). This was alternatively called *Dun* ('down') *Roshale* 1271-2 *Ass*, by contrast with *Up Roshale ib*; and *Dun* (later *Doun*, *Down*) and *Up* occur as affixes until modern times. In 1349 Ipm the two settlements are *Over-*, *Netherrosale*. Down Rossall is the Rossall of modern maps. The settlement was dominated by a large house (*Rossall Hall* 1934 Kelly), and this will have encouraged interpretation of the second element as 'hall'. Up Rossall is the settlement now called The Isle, which is enclosed by a great bend of the Severn to the north. It was also known as Rossall Superior or Great Rossall. The places are in the civil parish of Bicton.

ROWTON SJ 365124 DB Manor

Rutune 1086 DB, *Rutone* c.1210-12 RBE (p) *et freq* with variant spellings *-ton'*, *-ton* to 1374-7 Pat
S(t)unton' 1251 Fees. *Runton* 1255 RH
Routon' 1255-6 *Ass* (p) *et freq* with variant spelling *-ton* to 1714-15 PR(H) 6, *Routone alias Rouhton* 1319 Ipm, *Routon Castle* 1675 Ogilby
Rughton' 1291-2 *Ass*, *Roughton* 1346 Cl
Rutton 1363 Pat
Rowton Castle 1577 Saxton, *Rowtton* 1679 PR(H) 6

'Settlement in rough ground'. The same name has become Roughton (Worfield) in another Sa instance. DEPN suggests that

rūh is here a noun rather than an adjective.

Rowton in Stokesay and Rowton in High Ercall are different names: see below for the latter.

The G.R. is for the hamlet of Rowton, which is a mile S.W. of the large house called Rowton Castle. Rowton is a township of Alberbury.

ROWTON SJ 614199 DB Manor

Routone 1086 DB
Rowelton' 1195,6 P, 1221-2, 71-2 *Ass, -ton* 1255 RH, 1268 AD, 1284-5 FA, l.14th SAC, *Rouelton'* 1271-2 *Ass, Rouwelton* 1291-2 *Ass* (p)
Ruelton' 1212 Fees, 1255-6 *Ass* (p), *-tun'* 1234 SAC
Rughelton' 1221-2 *Ass* (p)
Reulton' 1223 Cur (p)
Roulton' 1233 Cl, *-ton* 1281 Pat *et freq* to 1590 *SBL 6511A*
Rewelton' 1255-6 *Ass*
Ruwelton 1255-6 *Ass*
Rouilton' 1255-6 *Ass*
Roelton 1275 SAC
Roton 1520 AD
Rowton 1569 *SBL 4509 et seq*
Rooton 1587 PR(L) 20
Ruton 1719 PR(L) 20

Perhaps 'settlement at a small rough place'. If there was a noun *rūh* (see Rowton above), there might have been a diminutive **rūhel.* Otherwise it seems necessary (as in DEPN) to interpret this name as a triple compound, from **rūh** adj, **hyll** and **tūn**.

The DB form is out of step with the rest of the ME spellings.

Rowton in Broseley may be the same name, but only one spelling is available. *Rouweleton'* l.13th *ForProc.*

This Rowton is a township of High Ercall.

RUCKLEY SJ 534002 Civil Parish (with Langley)

Ruclee 1221-2 *Ass*. *Ruckley* 1576 PR(L) 19 *et seq*
Rockel' 1231 Cur, *Rokele* 1249 Pat, *-leg'* 1261-2 *ForProc*, *Rokkeleye* 1266 Pat, *Rokeleye, Rocheley* 1271-2 *Ass*, *Rokeleye* 1297 Pat
Rocley 1251 Cl *et freq* with variant spellings *-le(ye)*, *-legh'* to 1291-2 *Ass*, *Rokleye* 1269 SAC, *-ley* 1271-2 *Ass*, *Rockley* 1655 PR(L) 19
Rouckley 1658 PR(L) 19

'Rook wood or clearing', from OE **hrōc** and **lēah**. Ruckley Grange near Tong has the same origin.

RUDGE SO 811975 Civil Parish

Rigge 1086 DB
Rugge e.13th HAC *et passim* to 1535 VE, *La Rugge* 1296 InqMisc, 1297 Cl
Ruge 1242 Fees, 1274 RH
Ridgelodge 1695 Morden
Rudge 1706 *SBL 14416*

'Ridge'. Rudge is the normal WMidl development of OE **hrycg**. The reference is to the high ground followed by the road from Claverley to Pattingham St.

RUSHBURY SO 514919 Ancient Parish

Riseberie 1086 DB, *Risseberia* c.1200 *ForProc*, *Rysebur'* 1271-2 *Ass*, *Ryssebury* c.1291 TN
Rusberia c.1158 SAC (p) *et freq* with variant spellings *-bir'*, *-bur'*, *-bury(e)*, *-burg*, *-burie*, *-berry* to 1723 PR(H) 14, *Russbury* 1346, 1428 FA
Risberi 1200 Cur (p), *-biri* 1208-9 *ForProc*
Russeberi 1200 Cur (p) *et freq* with variant spellings *-bur'*, *-bur*, *-bir'*, *-bury* to 1318 Ch
Russhebur 1283 Ch *et passim* with variant spelling *-bury* to 1549

Pat, *Ruschebury* 1306-7 *Ass*
Ruyshebury 1316 FA
Rysh-, *Rishbury* 1327 Pat
Rushbury 1577 Saxton *et seq*, *Rushbry* 1745 *PRCardington*

'Rush manor', from OE **rysc** and **byrig**, dat. of **burh**. The name would be appropriate to a prehistoric fort, but there is no record of such a feature here. **rysc** occurs with other habitative terms, particularly **tūn**.

RUTHALL SO 599899 DB Manor

Rohalle 1086 DB, *Rohale* 1167 P, c.1275 *SBL 6953*, 1284-5 FA, *Rohal* 1203-4 *Ass* (p), *Rohal'* 1207 P (p)
Rothal 1203-4 *Ass*, *-hale* 1249 Ipm *et freq* to 1359 Cl, *Rothhale* 1255-6, 71-2 *Ass*, *Rothehale* 1313 Pat (p)
Rodhale 1255 RH
Roughale 1291-2 *Ass*
Routhale 1291-2 *Ass*, 1334 Cl, InqMisc, 1359 Cl, *Rowthall* 1500 Ipm, 1549 Pat
Ruthall c.1612 *SBL 15691*

Second element **halh** 'nook'. The first appears to have the form *rōt*. The adjective **rōt** 'cheerful' occurs in a few place-names, but spellings for these (e.g. Ratley Wa, Roothill Sr) have the medial *-e-* which represents the inflection proper to an adjective, and there is no sign of this in the earlier forms for Ruthall. A noun would suit better. The word *root* (late OE *rōt*) might be considered.

The early forms without *-t-* are unexplained.

Ruthall is in Ditton Priors parish.

RUYTON OF THE ELEVEN TOWNS SJ 395222 Ancient Parish

Ruitone 1086 DB, *Ruitona* c.1155 SAC, *Ruytone* 1318 Ipm, *Ruyton* 1330 HAC *et seq*, *Ruiton* 1611 *SBL 8476 et freq* to 1750 PR(StA) 2, *Ruyton otherwise Ryton* 1770 *SBL 10308*
Ruton' 1242 Fees *et passim* with variant spellings *-tun'*, *-ton(e)* to 1416 Fine, *Reutun* c.1272 SAC, *Rueton* 1326 HAC

Ryton 1497 Ipm *et freq* with variant spelling *Riton* to 1777 *SBL 16874, Ryton als Ruyton* 1635 *SBL 10293, Ryton of the Eleven Towns* 1784 PR(StA) 3
Royton 1577 Saxton, *Royton of the Eleven Towns* 1758 PR(L) 20
Written 1616 *SBL 8481, Writon* 1801 PR)StA) 3
Righton 1704 PR(L) 1, 1732-2 PR(StA) 6, *Wrighton* 1731 PR(L) 7

'Rye farm', from OE **ryge** and **tūn**. This compound more frequently becomes modern Ryton, as in the name set out below, and another Sa example in the parish of Condover.

The affix refers to the eleven townships into which the parish was divided; a number of these are now in the parish of West Felton.

Old R(u)yton, presumably a distinct part of the settlement, is mentioned in 1635 and 1698 (*SBL 10293, 10259*).

The Welsh name for Ruyton (ex. inf. R. Morgan) is *Croes-Faen*. This is recorded in the 16th cent. It means 'cross stone', and it has no connection with the English name.

RYTON SJ 761029 Ancient Parish

Ruitone 1086 DB, *Ruyton* 1316,46, 1428,31 FA
Ruton' 1203-4 *Ass* (p) *et passim* with variant spellings *ton*(*e*) to 1325 Pat
Rutton 1271-2 *Ass, -ton'* 1291-2 *Ass*
Routon' 1306-7 *Ass*
Ryton 1535 VE *et seq, Righton* 1610 *SBL 15757, 1720 PRShifnal, 1765 PR(L) 18*
Royton 1577 Saxton, 1695 Morden

'Rye farm'. In this instance the DB entry includes the information that the manor has "a mill which pays 8 sesters of rye."

ST MARTIN'S SJ 323264 Ancient Parish

Capella de Sancto Martino c.1222, c.1235 SAC, *Capella de Martineschirch'* e.13th SAC, *Ecclesia Sancti Martini* c.1238 SAC,

Ecclesia de Sancti Martini 1254 Norwich, *Ecclesia de Martineschirch'* c.1265 SAC, *M artinchirche* 1307 Pat, *Martyneschirche* 1332 Ch, *St Martyne* 1560 PR(StA) 1, *St Martins* 1562 ib *et seq*

'Church dedicated to St Martin'. The Welsh name is *Llanfarthin*: early forms for this are *Llanvarthin* 1495 Charles, *St Martins alias Llanwarthin* 1653 *RentSur.* This interchange between Llan- and -church is common in He.

SAMBROOK SJ 714246 DB Manor

Semebre 1086 DB
Sambroc 1255-6 *Ass* (p) *et passim* with variant spellings *-brock*, *-brok(e)*, *-brook(e)*

Probably 'sand brook', though some spellings with *San(d)-* might have been expected. Sambourn Wa has *Sam-*, *Sand-* and *Som-*.

Sambrook is a township of Chetwynd parish.

SANDFORD SJ 583340 DB Manor

Sanford 1086 DB *et freq* with variant spelling *-ford'* to 1214 P (p)
Saunford 1203-4 *Ass* (p) *et freq* with variant spelling *-ford'* to 1356 Cl
Samford' 1204 Cur
Saneford' 1212 Fees
Sonford 1235-6 Fees (p), 1346, 1428,31 FA, 1415 Fine
Sontford 1235-6 Fees (p), 1241 SAC, 1249, 1316 FA, 1347 Ipm
Saumford' 1251-2 Fees (p)
Santford 1255 RH (p)
Somford 1272 Ipm
Sandford 1284-5 FA, 1368 Ipm, 1672 HTR *et seq, Sandeford* 1575 *SBL 7068*
Sondford 1308 Ipm, 1334 SR

'Sand ford'. The 'ford' names along its course suggest that

Bailey Brook was more of an obstacle than its modern size would indicate.

There are several other instances of the name Sandford in the country, one of them in Sa, in West Felton parish. The Sandford discussed here is a township of Prees.

SELATTYN SJ 266340 Ancient Parish

Sulatun 1254 Norwich, *Sullatton* 1358 Pat, *Sulatton* 1377 Pat
Solatton 1383 Cl
Salatyne 1552 Pat, *-tin* 1701 PR(StA) 2 *et freq* with variant spellings to 1773 PR(L) 4
Sylattin 1564 PR(StA) 4 *et passim* with variant spellings to 1808 PR(StA) 3, *Shillatine* 1662 PR(StA) 2, *Scilatin* 1693 PR(StA) 5, *Scyl-* 1697 ib
Selattyn 1577 Saxton *et passim* with variant spellings; *Sellatton* 1621 PR(StA) 1
Slattynt 1750 PR(StA) 6

Possibly 'settlement of the ploughs', from **tūn** and *sūla*, gen.pl. of **sulh**. But the ground is much broken, and it is possible that **sulh**, which means 'ploughland' as well as 'plough', is used in a transferred sense such as 'gullies'. Such a meaning is required in a number of place-names, and would be highly appropriate here. Cf. Soulton.

The development is parallel to that of Prestatyn, Fli, from OE *prēosta tūn*; though *-tt-* is a development peculiar to Selattyn. The *-a-* of the gen.pl. has been preserved because the name was pronounced with Welsh stress on that syllable. *-tyn* is the regular Welsh development of **tūn**, cf. Sychtyn. The occasional *Sh-*, *Sc-* spellings may be English attempts to represent a Welsh pronunciation of *Syl-*.

No attempt has been made to summarise the variant spellings in parish registers of the *Salatin*, *Sylattin*, *Selattyn* series of forms. They include every possible combination of *-l(l)*, *-t(t)*, *-y-* and *-i-*.

SHAVINGTON SJ 636388 DB Manor

Savintune 1086 DB, *-ton'* 1219 SAC, 1284-92 HAC (p)
Savigton' 1230 P (p)
Shauenton, Schauinton 1255-6, *Schauynton* 1271-2, *Shauynton'* 1291-2 *Ass* (all (p)), *Shavynton* 1303 Pat (p), 1315 Ch, 1419 Fine
Sahinton' 1271-2 *Ass*
Schauyngton' 1291-2 *Ass, Shavyngton* 1337 Pat, *Shavington* 1618 *SBL 9943 et seq*
Shaffyngton 1339 Cl
Sharington or Shenton 1695 Morden, *Shenton* 1731,60 PR(L) 4
Shevington 1748,91 PR(L) 4

'Estate associated with Scēaf(a)', *v.* **ingtūn**. The same name occurs in Ch. There also it has the modern form Shavington, which survived in spite of competition from a shortened form *Shenton.* The Ch name had an alternative shortened form *Sheynton*, which is not evidenced for the Sa example.

Shavington is in Moreton Say parish.

SHAWBURY SJ 558214 Ancient Parish

Sawesberie 1086 DB, *Sagesbury* c.1170-6 HAC, *Scagesburie* c.1177 *SBL 5403*
Shaburia 1130-47 HAC, *Scabir* 1204 P, *Schabury* 1306-7 *Ass, Shabury* 1535 VE, *et freq* with variant spellings *-biry, -burie, -berie, -ber(r)y* to 1747 PR(StA) 2, *Shabrie* 1571 *SBL 5853, Shabre* 1577 Saxton
Sauberia, -buria c.1135 SAC (p) *et freq* with variant spellings *-beri, -buri* to 1255 RH
Shawberia c.1165 SAC (p) *et freq* with variant spellings *Shau-, Schaw-, Schau-* and *-bir', -bury, -bery, -burie, -berry*
Sagheburi c.1190 SAC, *Sagebir, Scafberge* 1203 P (p), *Sachebur'* 1212 Fees
Schagebir' 1201 P (p), *-buri* 1227 Ch, *Shagebyr'* 1237 Cl, *Schayebur'* 1242 Fees, *Schauebyr* 1255-6 *Ass et freq* with variant spellings *Shawe-, Schawe-* and *-bury* to 1439 Fine
Siageb'i 1203-4 *Ass* (p)

Sawebyr' 13th *SBL 5405, -biry* 1253 Pat
Soghbir' 1237 Cl
Chabur' 1255 RH, *Chaubury* 1285 Ch
Shaghburi c.1273 Ipm
Sheawbury 1702 PR(H) 13

'Manor-house by a small wood', from OE **sceaga** and **byrig**, dat. of **burh**. The earliest instance noted of the modern spelling is 1376 *SBL 5433*.

SHEET SO 532743 DB Manor

Setham 1086 DB, *La Sethe* c.1270 InqMisc
La Scete Hy 3 AD
Sete 1242 Fees *et freq* to 1514 AD, *La Sete* 1274 RH *et freq* to 1328 AD
Cete 1271-2 *Ass*
Seete 1291-2 *Ass*, 1328 (p), 1457 AD, 1552 Pat, *La Seete* 1337,40 AD (P), 1399 Cl, 1457-8 FA, *Seote* 1431 FA
Sheete 1672 HTR, *Sheet* 1828 *PRLudford, The Sheet* 1847 *TA*

In spite of the heavy predominance of *S-* over *Sc-*, and the absence till 1672 of *Sh-*, this is probably OE **scēat**, 'corner, projection'. The *S-* spellings may be ascribed to Norman influence.

scēat is mainly a minor name and field-name element, and it is frequently found (as here) with the definite article. It is also mainly a southern English element, and it may in this instance represent West Saxon influence in the southern fringe of Shropshire.

Nether Seete is mentioned 1462 AD. Sheet is in Ludford parish.

SHEINTON SJ 611040 Ancient Parish

Sc(h)entune 1086 DB, *Shenton'* 1242 Fees, *Schenton* 1255-6 *Ass* (p), 1284-5 FA, *-ton'* 1291-2 *Ass, Shenton* 1305 Cl *et freq* to 1765 PR(L) 2
Seinton' 1200 P, 1207 P (p), *Seynton* 1255 RH, 1262 Pat
Sheinton 1221-2 *Ass* (p) *et freq* with variant spellings *Sheyn-* and

-ton', Scheynton 1253 HAC (p) *et freq* with variant spellings *Schein-* and *-ton'* to 1348 Ipm, *Sceynton'* 1261-2 *ForProc, Sheyinton'* 1271-2 *ib* (p)
Sweynton' 1242 Fees (p), *Swynton* c.1270 InqMisc
Shainton 1255 RH (p), *Schainnton, Schanyton* 1271-2 *Ass* (p), *Shaynton* 1439 Cl
Shynnton' 1255-6 *Ass* (p), *Schinton' ib, Schinnton* 1271-2 *Ass* (p), *Shinton* 1686 PR(L) 14, 1737 PR(L) 2
Sineton' 1261-2 *ForProc, Syneton* 1271-2 *ib*
Seyton 1294 InqMisc
Shienton 1630 PR(H) 1
Shineton 1687 PR(L) 8, 1725-6 PR(H) 16, 1775 PR(L) 2, 1833 PR(L) 14

Sheinton has hitherto been explained as 'beautiful settlement', from OE *scēne* and *tūn*, but in all other occurrences in place-names *scēne* has yielded the modern form Shen-. Neither the modern pronunciation of this name, which is indicated by the last series of spellings, nor the early *-ei-*, *-ai-* are easily explained by reference to *scēne.* If *scēne* were a personal name, however, **Scēnantūn* and **Scēningtūn* might have interchanged, and *Shein-* might be a contraction of *Scēning-*. Quainton Bk provides a parallel, with early *Quen-, Quein-, Queyn-, Quin-* forms. This has been variously explained as from *cwēne-tūn* or *Cwēningtūn*, but in fact both forms may be required to account for the spellings.

The modern pronunciation of Sheinton, represented in the last set of forms, may be due to association with the word *shine. Shainton* would have been the normal development from the ME *-ei-*, *-ai-* forms.

Sheinwood in this parish (*Sheynewud', Sheinwode* 1261-2, 1271-2 *ForProc*) is probably 'Sheinton wood', abbreviated by dropping the middle element.

SHELTON SJ 466135 DB Manor

Saltone 1086 DB
Sheldon 1221-2 *Ass*
Shelfton 1221-2 *Ass* (p)
Shelton 1221-2 *Ass* (p) *et freq* with variant spellings *Schel-* and *-ton'*

Shulton' 1271-2, 94-5 *Ass*
Scholton c.1300 *SBL 3623, Sholton'* 1334 SR

'Shelf settlement', from OE **scylfe** and **tūn**. Shelton is situated on level ground which ends abruptly with a sheer cliff on the W. bank of the R. Severn. It is on the western fringe of Shrewsbury.

There are a number of instances of this name in other counties, sometimes in the modern form Shilton.

SHELVE SO 335990 Ancient Parish

Selva c.1225 SAC, *Selue* 1255 RH, 1291-2 *Ass*
Shelve 1261 Ch *et passim* with variant spelling *Schelve*

'Shelf'. This name is probably from OE **scelf**, rather than the variant **scylfe** which is indicated by the spellings for Shelton.

One of the meanings of 'shelf' in place-names is 'level area among hills'.

SHERIFF HALES SJ 758120 Ancient Parish

Halas 1086 DB
Hales c.1125-38 HAC *et passim*
Schirrenghales, Schirrenchal' 1271-2 *ForProc* (p), *Schirreuehale(s)*, *Shirreueshales ib, Schyreueshale, Sireuehales* 1291-2 *Ass*, *Shiruehales* 1301 SAC, *Shirevehalys, Shirrevehales* 1367 Pat, *Sherreyf Hales* 1398 Pat

'Nooks'. This one of a cluster of names containing **halh**, situated around Shifnal and Albrighton. The affix refers to Reginald of Balliol, the sheriff of Shropshire, who was the holder in 1086 (when the manor was entered in the Staffordshire section of DB).

No attempt has been made to present all the spellings of the affix.

SHIFNAL SJ 750076 Ancient Parish

Scuffanhalch '680' (12th) S 72, *Shuffenhale* 1315 Ch *et freq* to 1459 Fine, *Shuffenale* 1394, 1408 Pat, *Shufenall alias Idsall* 1553 Pat
Shifnael 1212 P, *Schyf(f)nall* 1547 Pat, *Shiffnall* 1600 PR(H) 6 *et freq* with variant spelling *Shif-*; *Shifnol als Shiffenhall* 1651 *SBL 6315, Shifnal* 1713 PR(L) 7
Chaffenhale, Suffenhale, Scharuehale 1271-2 *Ass*
Schophenale 1271-2 *Ass, Shoffenhale* 1291-2 *Ass*, 1342 *SBL 6298*, 1369 Ipm, 1377 Pat, *Shofenhale* 1402 Pat, *Shoffenale* 1416 Fine
Shuffnall 1414 Fine, 1637 *SBL 6341*, 1657 PR(L) 4, *Shuffnull* 1535 VE
Scheffenhale 1450 *SBL 3057, Sheffenhall'* 1552 *SBL 16296, -hall* 1724 PR(L) 14
Shefnall 1535 VE, 1577 Saxton, *She(i)ffnall* Ed 6 *SBL 16296, Shefnel* 1687 PR(L) 4, *Shefnal* 1727 ib
Shiffenhall alias Idsall 1548 Pat
Sheuffnoll 1561 PR(H) 3

Shifnal is almost certainly the place called *Scuffanhalch* which is listed in some forged documents as one of the original possessions of Peterborough Abbey; S 72 is the least corrupt of these documents. The spelling of this name indicates that the forger had a pre-Conquest record to draw on.

The first element is not otherwise noted in place-names. It may be a personal name **Scuffa.* The second element is **halh**, referring to the large shallow depression in which the town lies.

Forms for the alternative name, Idsall, are:

Iteshale 1086 DB, 1282 Pat (p), *Ithessala* 1121, *Iteshala* 1155, *Itessala* c.1155 SAC
Idessala c.1145 SAC, *Idesale* c.1175 SAC, 1282 ChanR, 1285 Pat, 1446 Cl, *Ydeshal'* 1198 P *et passim* with variant spellings *Ides-* and *-hal(e)* to 1431 FA, *Iddeshal'* 1230 P, *Ydeshall'* 1235-6 Fees, *Ydishall* 1255 RH, *Ydesale* c.1291 TN, *Iddsale* 1433 *SBL 6085, Yddessel* 1535 VE
Hideshal' c.1200, 1208-9 *ForProc, -hale* 1210-12 RBE, 1255-6 *Ass*

(p), *Hydeshal'* 1219 SAC, c.1225 *SBL 16288*
Edeshale 1325 Pat
Idsall 1553 Pat *et freq, -alias Shiffenall* 1657 PR(L) 20, *Idshall* 1672 HTR, *Idsoll* 1683,5, 1728 PR(L) 8, *Idsell* 1685,8 ib, *Idsal alias Shiffnall* 1733 PR(L) 7, *Idsall alias Shifnall* 1765 *SBL 9642*
Itsall 1738 PR(L) 8

It has been generally assumed that Idsall is the place called *Iddeshale* which is mentioned in a charter of A.D. 836 as part of the price paid to King Wiglaf of Mercia by the monastery at Hanbury Wo in return for privileges in the Hanbury estate. But this charter is preserved in a contemporary copy, and the *-dd-* of the spelling is inconsistent with the forms for Idsall, which are overwhelmingly indicative of an original *-d-*. *The Iddeshale* of the charter is probably a lost place in Wo.

Idsall is '*Idi's nook', with the same second element as Shifnal. DB and SAC *Ites-* have an Anglo-Norman substitution of *-t-* for *-d-*. Occasional *H-* forms are a regular feature in names with *I-*. The personal name **Idi* is a strong form of the recorded *Ida.*

The alternating use of Idsall and Shifnal over several centuries may be a unique phenomenon. Eyton (II, p. 265) conjectured that the names originally applied respectively to the districts lying E. and W. of the stream which divides the town.

SHIPLEY SO 809959 DB Manor

Sciplei 1086 DB, *Shiple* 1242 Fees, *Schipleg'* 1255 RH (p), *Schyp-* 1274 RH, *Shiplegh'* 1291-2 *Ass, Shippleye* 1334 SR, *Shipley* 1577 Saxton *et seq*
Schepleg' 1271-2, *Shepple* 1291-2 *Ass, Schepleye* 1305 Ipm, *Shepley* 1599 PR(L) 3
Shyppele(ye) 1291-2 *Ass, Scipelegh* 1295 Pat, *Shippe-* 1316 FA, *Shipeleye* 1399 Cl
Sheppele 1291-2 *Ass*

'Sheep clearing or pasture'; **lēah** may have its late OE sense 'pasture' when compounded with words for farm animals. The name occurs in several other counties.

Reference books give *scēp* as the Anglian form of OE **scēap** 'sheep', and *scȳp, scī(e)p* as West Saxon forms, but the spellings quoted above, like those for Shipton *infra*, suggest that *scȳp, scī(e)p* had currency outside the West Saxon dialect area.

Shipley is in Claverley parish.

SHIPTON SO 562919 Ancient Parish

Scipetune 1086 DB
Sip(p)ton 1255 RH, *Sibton, Sipton, Supton* 1271-2 *Ass*
Schipton' 1255-6 *Ass, Shipton'* 1271-2 *Ass et freq* with variant spellings *Shyp-* and *-ton, Schypton* 1283 Pat, *Schip-* 1287 Cl
Parvum Scopton' 1271-2 *Ass*
Shupton 1360 Cl
Shepton 1607,14 PR(H) 1

'Sheep estate', a name which, like Shipley, occurs in a number of counties.

Modern maps show only one settlement, in spite of the 1271-2 reference to 'Little Shipton'.

SHRAWARDINE SJ 400153 Ancient Parish

Saleurdine 1086 DB
Seraordina 1121, *Sera(w)ordina* 1155 SAC, *Serewardin* 1272 Ipm
Scrawardin 1166 RBE, 1195 P, *Shrawurthin* 1240 Cl, Lib, *Scrawrthin* 1255-6 *Ass, Schrawardyn* 1308 Ipm, 1345 *SBL 3611, Shra-* 1381, 98 Pat, 1443 Fine, *Scra-* 1535 VE, *Shrawardine* 1637 PR(L) 7 *et seq*
Screwrdin 1204 P *et freq* with variant spellings *-wrðin, wardin(e), -worthin, -wardyn, -wyrdin'* to 14th *SBL 3583, Shrewardin'* 1215 Cl *et passim* with variant spellings *-wardin, -wrthin, -wordin', -wardyn, -werdine* to 1763 PR(StA) 3, *Schrewardin* 1274 RH, *-wardyn* 1284 Cl, 1284-5 FA
Scawrðin 1205, *Scha-* 1207 P, *Scawardyn* 1320 *SBL 8396, Shawardine* 1813 PR(StA) 1
Srawurthin 1212 Fees, *-worthin* 1210-12 RBE, *-wrðin* 1214 P
Srathwardin c.1212-17 RBE, *Sretwrthin, Strawrthin* 1255 RH, *Shretwardyn* 1291-2 *Ass, Strawardyn* 1397 Pat

Srewardin 1220,50 Fees, 1251 Cl, *-wardyn* 1254 Pat, *-wrthin* 1255 RH, *-worthin* 1271-2 *Ass*
Shewardin 1241 Cl, *-warthyn, -wurthyn* 1255 RH
Shrewworthin 1245 Strange
Seworthin 1255-6 RH (p)
Schyreveworthdin 1292 SAC
Schirewordyn 1302 Ipm
Scerardin 1302 Ipm, *Scherwardon* 1318 *SBL 5427, Sheraudyn* 1397 Pat, *Sharwardyn* 1490 Ipm
Shrowardyne 1397 Pat
Shrauwurdyn 1398 Pat
Shrawardine als Shradon' 1601 *SBL 12706, Shraden* 1609 PR(H) 6 *et freq* to 1692 PR(L) 20, *Shrarden* 1624 PR(L) 7, *Shrawden* 1633 PR(H) 6, *Sraden* 1656 PR(StA) 4, *Shradden* 1780 PR(H) 7
Shrewdon 1689, *Shredon* 1723 PR(H) 6

A few eccentric forms which may be suspected of being misreadings have been omitted from the above list of spellings.

Second element **worðign**, 'enclosed settlement'. The first is uncertain. It is probable that a final consonant has disappeared in the compound with **worðign**. This could be *-f*, as assumed by Ekwall in his derivation of Shrawardine from OE **scræf**, **scref**, 'cave, den, hollow'. It could equally well be *-w*, however. If the qualifying element is **scræf**, **scref**, the reference may be to some landscape feature now obscured by Shrawardine Pool. If the lost consonant were *-w*, the first element would be **scrēawa** 'shrew'. This is not likely, in a compound with **worðign**, to be a reference to the animal, but it might have been used as a personal name or nickname.

The earliest forms show the characteristic Norman-French insertion of a vowel in the simplified initial *Sr-*, and the Domesday form has the equally characteristic confusion of *-r-* with *-l-*. At the end of the 13th cent. there may have been occasional association with *sheriff* and *shire*, but as usual there is remarkably little trace of popular etymology. As in other Shropshire names, the short form *Shraden*, though common in parish registers in the 17th cent., failed to oust the longer form. It is, however, still current locally.

Little Shrawardine, on the opposite bank of the R. Severn, is *Parva Shretwardyn* 1291-2 *Ass* (p), *Little Shrawardine* 1684 PR(H)

7. The main settlement is *Shraden Magna* 1609, *Shrawden* - 1633 PR(H) 6.

SHREWSBURY County Town

(*in*) *civitate Scrobbensis* 901 S 221
Scrob 924-39, 978-1016, 1042-66 Coins, *Sfrobbes* 959-75 ib, *Zcrob* 1016-35 ib, *Screob, Scobe, Srob*(*i*), *Srop, Srobb', Seob,* 1042-66 ib, *Zrobb* 1066 ib, *S*(*c*)*rvb* 1066-87 ib, *Scrv* 1087-1100 ib, *Srob* 1135-54 ib
(*at*) *Scropesbyrig* 1006 ASC, (*into, on*) *Scrobbesbyrig* 1016, 1102 ASC, *Shrobesbury* 1327 Pat (p), *Shrobbesbyri, Schrobbesbury, Shrobsbyri* c.1540 Leland
Saropesberia Wm I CartAntiq, Hy I (1267) Ch, *-berya* 1100-23 (1332) Ch, *Serropesbyria* Hy I (1267) Ch, *Sarropesbir'* 1258 Cl
Scyropesberie Wm I (1267) Ch, *Scir-* 1086 DB
Salopesberie 1094-8 (1332) Ch *et passim* with variant spellings *-beri*(*a*), *-bire, -biri, -bury, -biry, -byry, -bery* to 1377 Pat, *Saloppesbury* 1208-9 *ForProc, -biry* 1226,7 Pat, *Salopisbur'* 1255 RH
Solopesbir' 1214 P, *-bur'* 1255 RH
Salopie 1221 Fees *et freq* with variant spelling *Salopia* to 1267 Cl, *Sallop* 1265 Cl, 1416 AD, *Sallopia* 1267 Cl, *Salop* 1308,47 Cl, 1315 Ipm, 1524 *SBL 3809 et freq* with variant spelling *Sallop*(*e*) to 1746 PR(StA) 3
Salopbr' 1237 Cl, *-bir'* 1241 Cl, *Salopebr'* 1250 Fees. *Salopbyry* 1257 Pat, *-birs* 1326,39 Pat, *-boure* 1376 Cl
Salopsbr', -bir' 1237 Cl
Srovesbroc 1271,82 APW, *Shrovesbury* 1331-5 ib, 1346,51, 1406 Pat, 1453 Fine, Cl, 1459 HAC, 1461 Cl
Saloburs c.1320 FFW
Shrofbury 1339 Pat
Shrousbury 1339,43 Cl, 1349 Fine, 1468, 1503,7 SAS 4/III, *Schrousbury* 1486 AD, *Shrowsbury* 1515 SAS 4/III *et freq* to 1755 PRStA) 2, *Schrowsbury* 1537 *SBL 6291, Shrousbyri* c.1540 Leland
Shrouesbury 1347 Cl *et freq* to 1491 SAS 4/III, *Shrowesbury* 1373 Pat, 1464 HAC, 1644,70 PR(L) 9, *Schrowesbury* 1391 Cl, *Shrouisbury* 1475,82 SAS 4/III, 1567 *SBL 6736A, Shrouysbury*

1477 *et freq* to 1487 SAS 4/III, *Schrouesbury* 1491 ib, *Shrowysbery* 1517 *SBL 5799, Shrowesburye* 1552 *SBL 16296,* 1577 Saxton, *Shrowisbury* 1559 SAS 1/VI

Shrosbury 1364 Cl (p), 1664,90 PR(L) 9, *Schrosbury* 1538 *SBL 6293, Shrosbery* c.1540 Leland, *Srosbury* 1600 *PRAlveley*

Shrewesbury 1384 *SBL 6296,* 1386 Pat, 1395 AD, 1438 Fine, c.1540 Leland, 1567 *SBL 6736A,* 1599 *SBL 6003, Shrewisbyri* c.1540 Leland, *Shrewysburie* 1577 *SBL 3649*

Sherewesbury 1396 AD, *Shereusbury* 1580 *SBL 6586, Shyrosburie* 1593, 1616 PR(StA) 4, *Sherosburie* 1599 ib, *Shewrosbury* 1603-4 ib, *Shorousbury* 1605 PR(StA) 1, *Sherosbury* 1613 PR(StA) 2, *Sherowsbury* 1633 ib, *Shirosbury* 1638 PR(StA) 4, *Sheresburie* 1653,6 PR(H) 6, *Shirosbery* 1663 PR(StA) 2

Shrewsbyri, Shreusbiry c.1540 Leland, *Shrewsbury* ib *et seq, Shreusbury* 1659 *SBL 5883*

Shroisberye 1575 *SBL 4663, Sroesbury* 1695 PR(L) 9

Shresburye 1604,7 PR(L) 7, *Shresbury* 1688 *SBL 3469A*

Shroasbury 1655 *SBL 6046*

Shroosbury 1729 PR(L) 8

The coin forms given above are those published in A.J.H. Gunstone, *Sylloge of Coins of the British Isles 17: Ancient British, Anglo-Saxon and Norman Coins in Midland Museums* (British Academy 1971). Material from Vols. 1-20 of the *Sylloge* is summarised in Veronica Smart's *Cumulative Index* (1981, Vol. 28 of the series), pp. 104-5. Dr Smart says that *Scrobe* or *Scrobr* are the usual forms on coins from Æthelstan to Canute, and that *Srob* becomes extremely common t. Hy 1 - t. Hy 2. She suggests that forms with *eo,* such as *Seob, Sreob,* which occur t. Hy 1 and t. Ed 3, are perhaps more frequent than can be explained by confusion between E and square C. She notes that *Srvb, Scrvbs, Scrv* appear t. Wm 1 and t. Wm 2.

The OE name is established as *Scrobbesbyrig* by the combined evidence of the Latinisation in S 221, the coin spellings and the 1016 ASC form.

A plausible etymology for *Scrobbesbyrig* is 'fortified place of the scrubland'. Modern English *scrub* in this sense is a variant of *shrub.* Both words are connected with OE *scrybb,* a word only recorded once, in a boundary description, where the context suggests the meaning 'belt of scrubland'. Spellings such as *Shrib* and *Shreb* are rather rare in the evidence for minor names like Shrub Fm, The Shrubs, and it has been suggested that there was an OE form **scrubb*, as well as the recorded *scrybb.* The forms for Shrewsbury require a third variant **scrobb*, and this also is suggested by some minor-name spellings. Scrubcut Wood in Tenterden K is *Srobescot* 1240 *Ass, Shrobecote* 1292 *Ass*, and Shrubs in Hatfield Broad Oak Ess is *Schrobbes* 1297 *ForProc* (p). Shrob Lodge in Passenham, Nth, has equal numbers of ME spellings with *-o-* and *-u-*. There are no circumstances which would promote the use of *-o-* as a spelling convention for *-u-* in these names, and it seems necessary to assume that **scrubb* and **scrobb* existed as variants and gave rise to alternative forms of some place-names. It is interesting that there are a few Shrewsbury coin spellings with *-u-*.

Ekwall considered that *Scrobb* was a personal name, and he defended this view by introducing into the discussion in DEPN the curious red herring of the surname of Richard Fitz Scrob, a Norman settler who was established in north Herefordshire in the reign of Edward the Confessor, and who is commemorated in the place-name Richard's Castle. The origin of *Scrob* in Richard's surname is open to debate; but it should not be used as evidence that there was an OE personal name *Scrobb* which could, at a much earlier date, have entered into the name Shrewsbury.

OE *Scrobbesbyrig* became *Shrovesbury* by an interchange of the letters *p, b* and *v* which is documented in other place-names. Pebmarsh Ess has l.13th and e.14th cent. spellings with *-v-*; Bobbingworth Ess has an alternative modern form *Bovinger* ; in Pavenham Bd the *-v-* form prevailed over earlier *Pabenham, Papenham*; and Baverstock W is OE *Babbanstoc.* In all these names except Pebmarsh the change is recorded a good deal later than the date at which it appears in Shrewsbury, where the tendency may have been encouraged by dissimilation from the *-b-* of *-bury.* In Cobham Sr there has been the reverse process, OE *Covenham* becoming *Cob*(*b*)eham in the 15th cent.

Shrovesbury became *Shrousbury, Shrowsbury* by vocalisation of *-v-*. Parallel processes are seen, e.g., in Daventry Nth with its alternative form *Daintry*, Launder's Fm in Watlington O, which is ME *Lauenore*, and Bowcombe Wt, ME *Bouecumbe.* Cf. also Poynton *supra* and Woore *infra.* Normal developments from ME *-ou-* are represented by the spellings *Shroosbury* and *Shrosbury*, with long or shortened vowel. *Shroosbury* is a modern local pronunciation.

There was another form in which the *-es-* of the genitive was fully preserved, and in this the *-v-* of *Shrovesbury* became *-w-*. This form persisted into the late 16th cent., evidenced by such spellings as *Shrowisbury, Shrewysburie.*

The *Shrew-* forms probably result from association with the word *shrew*, which was sometimes spelt *shrowe* in the 16th cent. Further confusion probably arose because of words like the verb *sew*, which had alternative forms *sow(e)* from the 14th-18th cents; and the perception that *-ew-* could be pronounced [ou] presumably lies behind the typically upper class pronunciation [ʃrouzbəri].

The *Saropes-*, *Salopes-* spellings are classic examples of Norman French influence. French speakers found the initial consonant cluster of *Scrobbesbyrig* difficult, so they simplified *Sc-* to *S-*, and separated *Sr-* by inserting a vowel. In Norman pronunciation *-r-* was liable to confusion with *-l-*, and this caused *Sarop-* to become *Salop-*.

The desire for a parasitic vowel between *Sh-* and *-r-* was apparently felt again in later centuries, and resulted in the series of spellings beginning with *Sherewesbury* 1396. Most of the later forms in this series are from parish registers of St Asaph diocese, and it may be to some extent a Welsh-influenced development.

The two forms from t. Wm 1 which have *Scyr-*, *Scir-* may reflect association with the word *shire.*

It remains to consider the Welsh names for Shrewsbury. A place called *Pengwern* appears in early Welsh poetry as the central place of the kingdom of Powys. Giraldus Cambrensis, writing in 1191, identified this with Shrewsbury: "locus, ubi nunc castrum Slopesburiæ situm est, olim Penguern, id est Caput alneti vocabatur" (*Description of Wales* Book I, Ch.4). Giraldus's translation of Pengwern is correct - the name probably means '(place at) the end of the alder swamp' - but there is no firm evidence that this is Shrewsbury.

The modern Welsh name for Shrewsbury is *Amwythig*, and this is well-evidenced. Mr R. Morgan has found it in a late 14th-cent. Welsh source, and in a work of c.1455-85. Mr Morgan suggests derivation from *am* 'about, around', *gwŷdd* 'woods, trees' and the adjectival suffix *-ig*, and thinks it may be a rough translation of the English name.

John Leland, writing about 1540, knew these two Welsh names. He speaks of "Shrewesbury --- commonly called now in

Welsh Moythike. Writers in Welsh called Penguerne, id est, caput Alneti. Schrobbesbury is the very English word truly written, not much dissonant from Penguerne, and Salopia in Latin goeth farre from the Welsh name." This suggests that Leland was puzzled by the *Salop-* forms, but that he believed the first element of *Scrobbesbyrig* to be a word for some kind of woodland.

SIBDON CARWOOD SO 413832 Ancient Parish

Sibetune 1086 DB, *-ton* c.1155 SAC *et freq* with variant spellings *-tun, -ton', -tone* to 1346 FA, *Sybeton'* 1291-2, 94-9 *Ass,* 1334 SR
Sibbedune c.1155 (1348) Pat
Sibbetone 1166 RBE (p) *et freq* with variant spellings *-ton', -ton* to 1431 FA
Sibiton' 1271-2 *Ass, Sybyton'* 1291-2 *Ass*
Sibton 1367 (p), 1391 Cl, 1395 *SBL 15760,* 1500 Ipm, 1647 PR(H) 2, *Sybton* 1396 AD
Sybedon 1397 InqMisc
Cipton 1502 *SBL 7136*
Shepeton Corbet c.1540 Leland
Siddom 1631 PR(H) 18
Sipton 1641 SAS 3/IV, - *Carswood* 1672 HTR, 1695 Morden, - *Carwood* 1737-8 PR(H) 16
Sibdon Carwood 1705 PR(H) 13, *Sibdon* 1714 PR(H) 18, 1751 PR(H) 14

'Sibba's estate', *v.* **tūn**. The change of *-ton* to *-don* is unusual, the reverse process being much more likely to occur, cf. Abdon.

The affix is the name of a wood which apparently lay to the north; the farms called Lower and Upper Carwood are in Hopesay parish, 1½ - 2 miles from Sibdon. The name is very poorly documented. It is *Carwod'* 1306-7 *Ass, Carwood* 1672 HTR, and is apparently a compound of **wudu** with the rare place-name term **carr**, 'rock'. Leland's - *Corbet* is probably a mishearing of Carwood.

SIDBURY SO 684857 Ancient Parish

Sudberie 1086 DB, *-b'i* 1203-4 *Ass*, *-byr* 1255-6 *Ass*, *-bury* 1291-2 *Ass* *et freq* to 1788 PR(H) 17, *-buri* 1342 FA
Suthbery 1208-9 *ForProc* (p), *-bir'* 1255-6 *Ass*
Sodbyr' 1242 Fees, *-bur'* 1274 RH
Sutbur' 1242 Fees. *-bur'* 1316 FA
Sudebur', *Suddebiry* 1271-2 *Ass*, *Sudebury* 1399 Cl
Soudbury 1305 Ipm, Cl
Sidbury 1577 Saxton, 1665 *et freq* PR(H) 1, 1672 HTR, 1704 PR(H) 13

'South manor-house', *v.* **sūð**, **byrig**. It is directly south of Middleton Scriven.

SIEFTON (or SEIFTON) SO 483830 DB Manor

Sireton 1086 DB
Siditonia 1177-86 HAC
Cineton 1200-4, c.1240-8 HAC, *Cyneton* 1274 RH, *Cyvyton* 1337 Pat
Scitheton ?c.1250 AD, *Schitheton'* 1255-6 *Ass*
Siveton 1257 Ch, *Syneton'* 1271-2 *ForProc*, 1301 SAC, *Siuetton'*, *Syuet(t)on'* 1291-2 *Ass*
Shiveton' 1260 Cl
Siuington' (p), *Siuiton'* 1271-2 *Ass*
Cyvynton 1343 InqMisc
Seueton 1343 InqMisc, *Seveton'* Hy 8 *RentSur*
Syffeton 1549 Pat, *Syfton* 1583 *SBL 6377*, *Sifton* 1674-5 PR(H) 17
Sefferton 1577 Saxton
Seefton 1695 Morden

The first element is unusual, and it appears to have been unfamiliar to the earliest clerks who wrote the name down; but the likely OE form which emerges from the spellings is **sifen*. Forms with *Cine-*, *Cyne-*, *Syne-* may fairly be emended to *Ciue-* etc. Some interchange of *-f-* and *-th-* is normal. Evidence for initial *Sc-* is very slight, and should probably be disregarded.

The first element might be the name of the brook on which Siefton stands. This is a fairly substantial tributary of the R. Corve, though it has no name (apart from Siefton Brook or Batch) on modern maps. There is a R. Seven in Yorkshire (YN), for which early spellings are *Sivene, Syvene,* and the stream at Siefton may have had the same name. This is discussed in RN (p. 358), but with only tentative comments on its possible etymology. Leaving that problem aside, 'settlement on a stream called *Siven'* seems a convincing etymology for Siefton.

DEPN does not associate Siefton with the Y river-name. The suggestion given there is for a compound of **tūn** with a feminine personal name, perhaps *Sigegifu.* The forms do not suggest a first element of that length, however.

The alternative spelling Seifton is now the usual one in official publications within the county. The place is in Culmington parish.

SILVINGTON SO 621799 Ancient Parish

Silvinton 1228 Pat, 1647 PR(H) 3, *Silvynton* c.1291 TN, *Sylvynton* 1535 VE
Silvetone 1255 RH, *-ton* 1271-2 *Ass,* c.1291 TN, 1334 SR
Silviton c.1261 Ipm
Selveton' 1267 Cl
Silventon 1319 Ipm
Silvington 1573 *SBL 8403*, 1577 Saxton, 1672 HTR *et seq* with variant spelling *Syl-*
Silverton 1655 PR(H) 17

Probably an **-ingtūn** formation with a dithematic personal name such as **Sigelāf* or *Sigewulf.* DEPN takes the base to be OE **scylfe** 'shelf', but in Shropshire this should have given more variety in the vowel of the first syllable, and at least a few spellings in *Sh-*. The series of forms begins rather late, however, and no certainty is possible.

SLEAP SJ 486267 DB Manor

Eslepe 1086 DB
Slep' 1221 SAC *et freq* with variant spellings *Slep, Slepe* to 1744

PR(L) 9
Sclepe 1255 RH
Slaype 1526-7 *SBL 2000*, *Slape* 1703 PR(L) 9 *et freq* to 1764 PR(L) 10
Sleape 1577 Saxton *et freq* to 1702 PR(L) 9, *Sleepe* 1607 PR(L) 9, *Sleap* 1657 ib *et freq*

'Slippery place', OE **slǣp**. There is another Sleap, of identical etymology, in High Ercall parish. *Slape* represents the modern pronunciation.

The 19th-cent. OS map shows Sleap and Sleap Hall a short distance apart on either side of a brook, in the parish of Myddle. One of the two settlements is *Parua Slepe super Bilemers* 1291-2 *Ass*, the other is *Grett Slepe* 1556 *SBL 345*, *Slepe Magna* 1555 *SBL 346*, *Great Slepe*, *Sleape Magna* 1641 *SBL 329*. The affix *by Bilemersche* qualifies *Slepe* also in 1404 Cl, Pat. Bilmarsh is now the name of a settlement one mile to the S.E.

SMETHCOTT SO 449994 Ancient Parish

Smerecote 1086 DB
Smethecot' 1203-4 *Ass et passim* with variant spellings *-cotes*, *-cot(e)* to 1421 Cl
Smethcot' 1255 RH, *-cote* 1255-6, 71-2 *Ass*, 1416 AD
Smithecote 1376 Pat
Smircote 1577 Saxton, *Smyrcoat* 1722 PR(L) 1
Smythcott 1649 SAS 4/VII

'Cottages of the smiths'. OE *smið* had in Anglian dialects a gen.pl. *smeoða*, which accounts for the *-e-* of most of the spellings and of the modern form. The *Smircote*, *Smyrcoat* variants are curious. There can hardly be a direct connection between them and the DB *Smerecote*, which is probably a simple mistake. A possible explanation is mooted below.

The parish of Smethcott contains the two townships of Picklescott and Betchcott, making an interesting concentration of names with **cot** as generic.

There is another Smethcott in Hadnall parish, first recorded c.1220. The spellings are similar to those summarised above, except that there is no sign of the *-r-* form. Smethcott in Wroxeter parish is not recorded till 1535, but is probably an ancient name of the same origin.

Both the Smethcotts which are recorded in ME have a few forms in which *þ* is written for *-th-*. This happens in 1255 and 1261-2 for the parish, and in some not-precisely-dated 13th-cent. forms for the Hadnall name. It is possible that *þ* was seen in ancient documents and was mistaken for a long *r*, and that this gave rise to the *Smircote* variant.

SOULTON SJ 544303 DB Manor

Suletune 1086 DB, *-ton'* 1200 Cur, 1255 RH
Soleton 1271-2 *Ass*, 1284-5 FA
Sulton' 1271-2, 91-2 *Ass*, *-ton* 1431 FA, 1470,84 Cl, 1703,18 PR(L) 9
Solton' 1334 SR
Sowton 1577 Saxton, 1695 Morden, *Soughton* 1672 HTR
Soulton 1677 PR(L) 9 *et seq*

Like Selattyn, this name is a compound of **tūn** with **sulh** 'plough', perhaps 'gully'. Evidence for the gen.pl. is slighter in the Soulton forms, and the base may have been **sul(h)-tūn*. Immediately to the east of Soulton Hall the stream called Soulton Brook runs in a gully which is a notable event in this hummocky, but generally flat, terrain. Soulton is a township of Wem.

SPOONLEY SJ 662360 DB Manor

Sponelege 1086 DB, *-ley* 1430 Cl
Sponle(e), *-leye* 1291-2 *Ass et freq* with variant spelling *-ley* to 1577 Saxton
Spooneley 1655 SAS 1/XVII, 1672 HTR, *Spoonley* 1693 PR(L) 4 *et seq*, *Spoonly* 1712 PR(L) 8
Spoondley 1750 PR(L) 4

The same compound occurs as a minor name in Gl (PN Gl **2**, 27) and, in the modern form Spoonlets, in K. OE **spōn-lēah* may mean 'wood where material for shingles is obtained', though **spōn** is only recorded in the senses 'chip, shaving'. Spoonley is a township of Adderley.

STANTON

Shropshire has five examples of this name, which means 'stone settlement'. Four are parishes (including Cleastanton *supra*), the fifth is Stanton in Shifnal, which is first recorded 1219 SAC. Elsewhere the name sometimes characterises a settlement by reference to an ancient megalithic structure, but in this county it seems likely to refer in all instances to stony soil.

STANTON LACY SO 496788 Ancient Parish

Stantone 1086 DB *et freq* with variant spellings *-ton', -tun', -ton*
Staunton' 1241 Cl *et passim* with variant spellings *-tun', -ton* to 1790 *PRChetton*
Stounton 1350 Cl

The affix *Lacy* is first noted 1255 RH, and appears in that spelling or as *Lascy, Lacye* in most subsequent references. Roger *de Lacy* was the DB holder.

STANTON LONG SO 572907 Ancient Parish

Stantune 901 S 221, 1086 DB, *-ton'* 1167, 94,5 P
Staunton c.1215 HAC, 1287 Cl
Longa Stantona c.1235 HAC, *Longestanton* 1255 RH, 1315 Ipm, 1316 Pat, *Longstanton* 1577 Saxton, 1605 PR(H) 1, *Lang Stanton* 1690-1, 1738 PR(H) 15, *Long Stanton* 1729 PR(H) 18 *et freq* to 1833 PR(L) 20
Longa Staunton', -tun' 1250 Fees (p), *Longestaunton* 1271-2 *Ass* (p), 1301 InqMisc, *Longstaunton* 1548,52 Pat, *Long Staunton* 1590 *SBL 6333 et freq* to 1753 PR(H) 8
Longeston' 1251 Fees
Lungestainton 1255-6 *Ass*

Staunton Longe 1577 PR(H) 18, *Stanton Long* 1698 PR(H) 15 *et seq*

The village straggles along a road, and this contrasts with the compact shape of Stanton Lacy at the other end of Corve Dale. In 1255-6 *Ass* the affix *templi* 'of the Templars' is used once. In 17th-cent. parish registers the place is occasionally called - *in Cordale. Dirty Stanton* 1685 *PRClee St Margaret,* 1703 PR(H) 13 appears to be this place.

STANTON UPON HINE HEATH SJ 568240 Ancient Parish

Stantune 1086 DB, *-ton'* 1201 P (p) *et freq* with variant spellings *-ton(a)*
Staunton' 1242 Fees *et passim* with variant spelling *-ton* to 1720 *SBL 6517*
Standon 1284-5 FA

The earliest instance noted of the affix is in the form *Stanton upon Hyne Heth* 1327 Pat. Other forms include - *in Hynehet* l.14th SAC, - *upon Hindheath* 1720 *SBL 6517.* The same affix was used for High Hatton, *supra.*

Independent references to the heath are *bruera de Hynehethe* 1291-2 *Ass, Highnehethe* 1421 Cl, *Hyne Heath* 1552 Pat, *Hind Heath* 1796 *SBL 5374.* The first element is the word discussed under Hinstock which usually means 'monastic household' in pre-Conquest place-names, but is likely to mean 'domestic servants' in names of later origin. The exact significance is not clear in this instance.

STANWARDINE IN THE FIELDS SJ 414240 DB Manor

Staurdine 1086 DB, *Stawurdin'* 1177 P (p), *-wurthin* 1213 Cur, *-woryn* 1399 Cl
Stanwardin 1194 P (p) *et passim* with variant spellings *-worthin, -warthin, -worthyn, -worthyng', -wardyn, -wardine*
Staneworthin 1242 Fees, *-wrthin* 1255-6 *Ass*
Stannarton 1616 *SBL 8485, Stannerton, Stannardyne, Stannarden* 1635 *SBL 10293*

'Enclosed settlement on stony ground', OE **stān-worðign.*

The affix appears first in *Staneworthyn Alchamp, Stanwarthin in Le Felde* (p) 1271-2 *Ass.* It is *Stanworthyng' in La Feld, Stanwordyn in Campo* 1291-2 *Ass, Stanworthin ythefeld* 1316 FA. After that it is mostly 'in the field', but *Stanwardine of the Feild* occurs 1649 SAS 4/VII. The modern plural form is found on the 19th-cent. OS map.

feld 'open country' is for distinction from Stanwardine in the Wood, another instance of the same place-name 2½ miles N.E. This is first recorded t. Ric. I and becomes *Stanword' in Bosco* 1231 SAC.

Alchamp and *in Campo* are French and Latin renderings of the affix. The place is in Baschurch parish.

STANWAY SO 527913, 531915 DB Manor

Staneweie 1086 DB *et freq* with variant spellings *-weia, -wey(e), -way* to 1428 FA
Stanwey 1255 RH *et freq* with variant spellings *-weye, -way*
Stanneway 1271-2 *Ass*

'Stone way', a name which occurs in several counties. There are two settlements, Lower and Upper, the latter being called Stanway Manor on modern maps. In 1227 Ch and 1255 RH reference is made to "the two settlements of Stanway". Lower Stanway is *Netherestanweye* 1271-2 *Ass,* and in 1301 SAC the two places are *Overe* - and *Nethere Stanewey.* They are in Rushbury parish.

STAPLETON SJ 472045 Ancient Parish

Stepeltone 1166 RBE (p) *et freq* with variant spellings *-ton', -ton* to 1399 Cl, *Stepleton* 1274 Ipm, 1321 AD, 1584 PR(L) 6 *et freq* to 1785 ib, *Stepulton* 1321 AD (p), 1385 Pat, 1431 FA, 1535 VE, 1569 *SBL 6621,* 1591 PR(L) 6, *-ton'* 1334 SR, *Stepylton* 1492 Ipm, 1730 PR(H) 18
Stapelton 1203-4 *Ass* (p), *-ton'* 1208-9 *ForProc* (p), *Stapleton'* 1204 Cur (p), *-ton* 1577 Saxton *et seq*

Stipelton' 1208-9 *ForProc*
Stepeleston' 1261-2 *ForProc, Stepulston'* (p), *Stepelston'* 1274 RH
Stupelton', -tune 1271-2 *ForProc*
Steppelton 1346 Fine, *Steppleton* 1638 PR(L) 6, 1664 PR(L) 7, 1697 *SBL 9960*, 1716 PR(H) 8
Stappleton 1674 PR(L) 6

Probably 'settlement at a steep place'; OE **stēpel**, modern *steeple*, is thought to have this meaning in place-names. Some of the spellings suggest derivation from *stȳpel*, which is considered to be the West Saxon form. It is curious that Staple- prevailed, although *Step-* is much commoner. The *-pp-* spellings indicate variants with short vowels.

The manor was called *Hundeslit* in DB. This earlier name is probably 'Hund's part of the area called **hlið**', from Lyth Hill in Condover which dominates the landscape.

Stepelwode in this area is probably a shortened form of 'Stapleton wood'.

STEEL SJ 549365 DB Manor

Stile 1086 DB, 1255-6 *Ass, Stiele* 1271-2 *Ass, Style* 1452 Cl
Styghel' 1291-2 *Ass*
Steele 1586-7 *RentSur*, 1655 SAS 1/XLVII, 1672 HTR, *Steel* 1695 Morden

'Stile', OE **stigel**. It has been suggested that this word sometimes means 'steep ascent' in place-names, but this would not be appropriate here. The name probably ceased to be meaningful before the end of the ME period, otherwise it would have become *Stile. The place is a township of Prees.

STEPPLE SO 660780 DB Manor

Steple 1086 DB, 1316 (p), 1428 FA, *La Steple* 1242 Fees, 1306-7 *Ass* (p), 1399 Cl
Steppel' 1271-2 *Ass* (p), *Stepple ib* (p) *et freq, La Stepple* 1305 Ipm *et freq* to 1346 FA (p), *Steppell* 1431 FA

Steeple 1576 PR(H) 17

'Steep place', OE **stēpel**. There is no sign in the spellings of the forms *stȳpel*, which is evidenced in Stapleton *supra*.

There are two settlements, Stepple Hall and Little Stepple. The Hall is *Steple Hall* 1690 *SBL 6335*. There is a reference in 1682-3 PR(H) 17 to "ye new house at Little Stepple". The two places lie on either side of a road over the northern end of the Clee Hills, in the parish of Neen Savage.

STEVENTON SO 522734 DB Manor

Scevintone 1086 DB
Stiventon 1203-4 (p), 1291-2 *Ass*
Stivinton 1255,74 RH, Hy 3 AD, 1306 AD, -ton' 1292-5 *Ass*, *Styvynton'* 1294-9 *Ass*, 1334 SR, *-ton* 1340 AD, *Styvinton* 1346 FA
Stivetun 1255-6 *Ass* (p)
Stevendon 1284-5 FA, *Steventon* 1291-2 *Ass*, 1391 Cl *et seq*
Styvyngton 1291-2 *Ass* (p)
Stevyntone 1318 AD, *Stevinton* 1355 Pat, *Stevynton* 1365,91 Cl, 1416 Fine, 1458 AD
Stiviton 1317 Ch, *Styvyton* 1318 Ch
Stevington 1552 Pat
Stinton 1670 PR(H) 17, *Steaventon als Stynton als Steenton* 1712 *SBL 3377*

Probably an **-ingtūn** formation, 'estate associated with Stīf(a)'. The personal name, which is not recorded, would be derived from the adjective *stīf*, 'stiff'. The spellings for Steventon Berks, Ha, and Stevington Bd, Ess are closely similar. The Sa place is in Ludford parish.

STIRCHLEY SJ 699067 Ancient Parish

Styrcleage 1002-4 Burton, *Stirclege* 1177 P (p), *-legh'* 1208-9 *ForProc*, *Stirclegh*, *Styrclegth* 1271-2 *Ass*
Strichelega 1167 P (p), *Strichleg'* 1280 Ipm, Stricheley 1369 Pat, Hy 6

SBL 6173, *Strycheley* 1535 VE, *Strichley* 1535 *SBL 7180*
Styrch 1199 (1265) Ch, *Stirch* 1217 (1285) Ch
Stirchleia c.1200 *ForProc et freq* with variant spellings *-leg'*, *-ley*, *Styrchle* 1271-2 *Ass*, *-leye* 1284-5 FA
Stirchele 1203-4 *Ass* (p) *et freq* with variant spellings *-legh'*, *-leg'*. *-le*, *-ley(e)* to 1559-60 *Corn.R.O.*, *Styrchel'* 1261-2 *ForProc*, *Styrcheley* 1559-60 *Corn.R.O.*
Stirkele 1203-4 *Ass* (p), *Stirrkeleye*, *Stirkleye*, *Stirkeslegh'* 1271-2 *Ass*
Stireslee 1206 Cur (p), *Stirchesleg'* 1207 P *et freq* with variant spellings *-ley(e)*, *-le*, *-legh'* to 1379 Pat, *Styrchesleye* 1334 SR
Stirlegh' 1209 For
Sturchesl' 1261-2 *ForProc* (p)
Stirichleg' (p), *Styrichleg'* 1261-2 *ForProc*
Stirchull' 1261-2 *ForProc*
Sterchesleg h' 1291-2 *Ass* (p), *-le* 1378 Pat
Stertusley 1378 Pat
Strechley 1577 Saxton, *Stretchley* 1695 Morden
Sterchly 1655 SAS 1/XLVII
Sturchly 1719 *PRShifnal*, *-ley* PR(L) 8
Stritchly 1730 PR(L) 3
Storchley 1808 PR(H) 14

'Stirk clearing'. The OE word which means 'young bullock or heifer' has the forms **stīrc**, **stīorc**, **stȳric**, **stȳrc**, and the spellings for Stirchley suggest that there were variants of the place-name deriving from these different forms. Cf. the discussion of Romsley. The *-ch-* which prevailed is appropriate to *stīrc* and *stȳric*, but there is some evidence for *Stirk-*, which is appropriate to *stīorc*. There is also a persistent metathesised form. **lēah** may have its late meaning, 'pasture'.

STOCKTON

This name is a compound of **stoc**, 'dependent settlement', and **tūn**. The precise meaning has not been ascertained. It occurs at least 17 times in England, some of the examples having the modern forms Stoughton, Staughton. There are three Stocktons in Shropshire. One is a parish, and this is dealt with below. The others are in the parishes of Chirbury (*Stocton'* 1242 Fees) and

Woodcote (*Stocton'* 1201 Cur (p)).

STOCKTON SO 730997 Ancient Parish

Stochetone 1086 DB, *Stoketon'* 1267 Cl
Stocton 1244 Ipm *et freq* with variant spellings *-ton'* and *Stok-* to 1492 Ipm, *Stockton* 1577 Saxton *et seq, Body Stocton* 1392 AD, *Bodystokton* 1420 Cl, *Bodye Stokton* 1492 Ipm
Stocken 1659,60 PR(L) 4

The affix *Body* is from the family of Robert *Body*, who is recorded in 1284 Ch and 1291-2 *Ass* as owner of *Parva Stokton'*. 'Little' may be for distinction from Stockton in Woodcote parish, about 10 miles N.

STOKE

Shropshire has three parishes named Stoke, and one Stoke of lesser status, in the parish of Greet. OE **stoc** is predominantly used as a simplex name, and there are at least 70 examples of this in the country. It occurs fairly frequently as a first element in compounds, mostly with **tūn** (see Stockton *supra*). Its use as a second element is difficult to quantify. There are between 30 and 40 names in *-stoc* which were compounds by the time of DB, but it may be suspected that some of these were simplex when first coined. The term may originally have been used for a dependent settlement which was a component of a large estate; but most of the settlements called **stoc** had become independent centres by 1086.

STOKESAY SO 436817 Ancient Parish

Stoches 1086 DB
Suthstoke 1178-9 HAC *et freq* with variant spellings *Sotstok', Suth Stoke, Southstoke, South Stoke* to 1428 FA, *Suthstoke Say* 1248 HAC
Stoke Say 1255 RH *et passim* with variant spellings *Stok' Say,*

Stokesay(e), Stokesey; *Stoaksay* 1672 HTR
Stoake 1675 Ogilby
Stoke Castle 1719 *PRLudford*, 1724 PR(H) 15

The family surnamed *de Say* held this place and Stoke upon Tern in the 12th and 13th cents., and this place is called 'South Stoke' for distinction from the other property.

STOKE ST MILBOROUGH SO 567823 Ancient Parish

Godestoch 1086 DB
Stok' 1231 Cur, Cl, *Stoke* 1316 FA
Stok' Milburge, Stok' Prioris 1271-2 *Ass, Stoke St Milburgha* 1272 Pat *et freq* with variant spellings - *St Milburg(h)*, - *St Milbridg*, - *St Milburdge*, - *St Milborough*; *Stok Milborowe* 1297 ChanR, *Stoke Milburgha* 1331 (1348) Pat *et freq* with variant spellings - *Mylburg'*, -*Mylberow*, - *Mil(l)borough*, - *Millbrow*, - *Milboro* to 1803 *PRDitton Piors, Stokemilborough'* 1334 SR, *Stokemulburgh* 1405 *SBL 6990, Stoake Milborrough* 1672 HTR
Stok Milburg 1350 Pat, *Stocke Milburne* 1535 VE
Milburghstoke 1389 Pat, *Mylbornstoke* 1577 Saxton, *Milborow Stoke* 1602 PR(H) 18, *St Milburge Stoake* c.1612 *SBL 15691*
Milverstoke 1687 *et freq* to 1700 PR(H) 13, *Stoke Mil(l)vero* 1723 PR(H) 14

This Stoke belonged to the Priory of St Milborough (OE *Mildburh*) at Much Wenlock, and the affixes refer to this, including *Godes-* in DB. The *Milver-* form of the saint's name is noteworthy. The first instance noted of the modern spelling is 1729 PR(H) 15.

STOKE UPON TERN SJ 640280 Ancient Parish

Stoche(s) 1086 DB, *Stoca* 1121 SAC, *Stoke* 1228 Pat, 1255 RH, 14th *SBL 4400* (p), 1371 Cl, c.1540 Leland, *Stok* 1274 Ipm, *Stoake* 1672 HTR, 1702,26 PR(L) 18, *Stoak* 1731 PR(L) 18, 1732 PR(L) 20
Nordestok 1199 SAS 2/X (FF), *Nordstoke* c.1222-4 HAC, *Nortstok'* 1242 Fees, -*stok* 1258 Ch, *North Stoke* 1346, 1428,31 FA

Stok' Say 1255-6 *Ass*, *Stoke Say* 1284-5 FA, 1291-2 *Ass*
Stoke upon Tirne 1309 Ipm *et passim* with variant spellings - *super Tyrne*, - *upon Tyrne*, - *on Tirne*, - *on Tyren*, - *upon Tyern*, - *Uppeterne*, - *upon Tierne*, - *super Te(y)ren'*, - *super Tearne*; *Stoake-super-Tern* 1687 PR(L) 8, - *upon Tearn* 1716 PR(L) 20, *Stooke super Tern* 1717 PR(L) 4

'North' for distinction from the other *Stoke Say.* In 1284-5 FA a place called *Stoke Aubrey* is listed as a 'member' of this *Stoke Say.*

The river-name Tern is from Welsh *tren* 'strong'.

STOTTESDON SO 673829 Ancient Parish

Stodesdone 1086 DB, *-don'* 1162 P *et freq* with variant spellings *-dun'*, *-don* to 1717 PR(H) 9, *-den'* 1174,7 P, *-doun* 1401,33 Cl, *-ton* 1790 *PRAlveley*
Stotesdona c.1090, 1121 SAC *et freq* with variant spellings *-dune*, *-don(e)* to 1804 PR(H) 1, *Stotisdon* c.1143 SAC, *Stotesden* 1303 Pat, 1446 Fine, 1799 PR(H) 9, *-down* 1400,1 Cl
Stotdesdon' c.1155 SAC
Stoddesdone 1159-60 RBE, *-don* 1493 Ipm, 1656 PR(H) 9, 1757, 1807 PR(H) 3, 1813 PR(H) 17, *-ton* 1747 PR(H) 9
Stottesdun' 1160 P *et freq* with variant spellings *-don'*, *-don(e)*; *Stottesden* 1262, 1397 Pat, 1263 Ipm, 1274 RH, 1280 SAC, 1811 PR(H) 9, *Stottisdon* 1348 Pat
Stodeston' 1191 P, *-ton* 1657 PR(H) 9, 1790 *PRAlveley*
Scotedon' 1208 Cur, *Stotedon* 1244 Ch
Stoteresden 1284-5 FA, *Stotteresdon* 1317 AD, *Stoteresdon* 1341 Pat, *Stotyrton* 1535 VE, *Stotterton* 1562,77,92 PR(H) 3, *Stottorton* 1575,6 ib, *Staterton* 1577 Saxton, *Stottesdon alias Stotterton* 1623-4 *Corn.R.O.*, *Stotherton* 1693 PR(H) 17, *Stotesden alias Stoterton* 1711 *SBL 6535*, *Stoderton* 1770 PR(H) 3, 1784 PR(H) 15, *Stotterston* 1800 PR(H) 12
Stotsdon 1699 PR(H) 3

Perhaps 'horseman's hill'. There were variant forms and it is noteworthy that most of them appear early in the records and persist into the 18th or 19th cents.

The *-r-* forms must be taken seriously in spite of the relatively late appearance of the first one in 1284-5. There is no reason why an inorganic *-r-* should have been inserted into an original **Stō-* or *Stŏd(d)esdūn* or *Stō* or *Stŏt(t)esdūn*, so it is probable that these forms represent a local derivative of the original name. There is no record of a term **stō-* or *stŏtere* or **stō-* or *stötere*, but a **stōdere* might well be a man who looked after a herd of horses, OE *stōd.* **Stōderesdūn* could have been shortened to *Stodesdone* by the routine method of dropping the middle element. Alternatively there could have been another version of the name which meant ‘hill of the stud’.

The *-d-*, *-t-* interchange is seen in names from OE *stōdfald* (e.g. Stotfold Bd, which is *Stodfald* 1007, *Stotfalt* DB. In Stottesdon, however, it is perhaps more likely to be a Norman-French change than an English one.

The site is a classic **dūn**, with a whale-back profile when seen from a distance.

STOW SO 311737 Ancient Parish

Stoe c.1200 MM
La Stowe 1255 RH
Stowe c.1291 TN *et freq* to 1672 HTR, *Stow* 1643 SAS 3/IV
Stouw 1294 Ipm, *Stouwe* 1308 Ipm

‘Holy place’. The general meaning of OE **stōw** is ‘venue for a particular activity’. Among its specialised meanings are ‘place associated with a saint’ and ‘monastery’, the latter being a relatively late development.

The reason for choosing the religious sense of **stōw** for this place-name is that the site of the church of St Michael is unreasonable in practical terms and so may be due to an ancient sacred association. It is, as suits the dedication, a "high place", at the very top of its valley, enclosed on two sides but with extensive views in a half-circle. There are three more churches on the south edge of the south-west uplands of Shropshire, Bedstone, Bucknell and Llanfair Waterdine; these are on through routes, but Stow is at the end of a cul de sac. The other chief meaning of **stōw** ‘meeting-place’, is quite inappropriate.

The earliest reference occurs in a list of priories in Shropshire.

STRETTON, CHURCH, ALL and LITTLE

SO 453936, 460953, 444915 Ancient Parish

Stratun(e) 1086 DB, *-tun'* 1159 P, *-ton'* 1190, 1203,4 P, 1221 Fees, *-tone* 1195 P

Strattun' 1156 P *et passim* with variant spellings *-tuna, -ton', -ton, -tune* to 1309 Pat, *Chirch' Stratton'* 1261-2 *ForProc* (p), *Cherchstratton'* 1271-2 *ib*

Stretton' 1195 P, 1272 Cl, *-ton* 1238 *et freq*, *Chirich -, Chirech Stretton* (p), *Magna Stretton* 1261-2 *ForProc, Chyrchestretton', Maugna Stretton'* 1271-2 *ib, Chirchestretton* 1327 Pat, 1337 Ch, 1361 Ipm, *Great Stretton* c.1540 Leland, *Churchstretton* 1577 Saxton, *Church Stretton* 1719 PR(H) 14

Stratton in Strettonedale 1227 Pat, *Strattonedale* 1228,78 Ch, *Strattondal'* 1233 Lib, *Strattune(s)dal'* 1251 Cl, *Strettonesdal* 1253 Pat, *Strettunedal'*, 1253 Cl, *Strat(t)onedale* 1254 Pat, *Strattondale* 1259 *et freq* to 1267 Pat, *Strettondale* 1273 Pat *et freq* to 1434 Cl, *Stretton' in Strettonesdale* 1291-2 *Ass*, 1301 SAC. 1316,27 Pat, *Stretton cum Strettonesdale* 1316 FA, *Strattonesdale* 1397 Pat, *Stretton Le Dale* 1666 PR(H) 8, *Church Stretton En Le Dale* 1694 PR(H) 8, *Stretton en le Dale* 1719 *SBL 6311*, *Stretton in the Dale* 1748-9 *PRLudford*

Startton' 1260 Cl

ALL STRETTON is *Auredestratton', Aluredestretton'* 1261-2 *ForProc* (p), *Aluredes Stratton* (p), *Alurychestretton'* (p), *Aluredestratton', Alvridestratton'* 1271-2 *ib, Aluestretton'* 1291-2 *Ass, Stretton alias Aluestreton* 1395 Pat, *Ould Stretton* c.1540 Leland, *Alstretton* 1577 Saxton, 1636 *SBL 6573, All-Stretton* 1662 PR(H) 8, *Allstretton* 1675 Ogilby.

LITTLE STRETTON is *Parua Stretton'* 1261-2 *ForProc* (p), *-Stratton'* 1271-2 *ib, Little Stretton* c.1540 Leland *et seq.*

Stretton is OE *strǣt-tūn*, 'settlement on a Roman road', which is the source of numerous Strattons and Strettons throughout the country. There is a second Sa example, Stoney Stretton in Westbury.

Church Stretton and the other two settlements are by the Roman road which runs from Wroxeter to Leintwardine. In this section it is following a dramatic valley, the *-dale* of one of the sets of spellings set out above. In all the instances in that set, *Strattondale, Strettonesdale* etc. refer to the manor of Church Stretton, and are presumably to be considered as abbreviations of such forms as *Stretton in Strettonesdale.*

The valley-name also occurs independently as a district-name. In 1261-2 *ForProc* there is an account of the regard of the Long Forest, *Stratton' Dale* and the Long Mynd, in 1291-2 *Ass* there is a reference to pasture "in Stratton' et in Strattonesdale", and Leland calls the valley *Stretton(s) Dale.*

The forms for All Stretton show considerable variety, but there can be little doubt that the affix is the genitive of the personal name *Ælfrǣd.*

The administrative history of Stretton from 1892-1967 is complicated. The present position is that Church and Little Stretton and the village of All Stretton form a civil parish, while the parts of All Stretton outside the village constitute a civil parish in Shrewsbury and Atcham Borough.

SUTTON

Shropshire has seven instances of this name, which means 'south settlement'. The spellings for four major names are set out below. The others are:

1. Sutton in Chelmarsh parish, first noted as *Sutton'* 1271-2 *ForProc.* This is S. of Chelmarsh.
2. Sutton in Claverley parish, first noted as *Sutton'* in 1226-8 Fees. This place is half a mile N. of Claverley, and the relevance of the name is obscure.
3. Sutton in West Felton parish, which is *Sotton'* 1343 *SBL 8387.* This is N.E. of West Felton, and here again the relevance is obscure.

SUTTON MADDOCK SJ 723014 Ancient Parish

Sudtone 1086 DB, *-ton'* 1201 P
Sutton' 1189 P *et passim* with variant spelling *-ton*; *Sutton' Madok* 1255-6 *Ass*
Suton' c.1200 *ForProc*
Sotton' 1242 Fees (p), *-ton* 1274 RH (p), 1284-5 FA

Sutton Maddock is probably the *Suptone* of S 549, dated 949 (13th), and the *Suthtune* of Wulfric Spot's will dated 1002-4; see Burton pp. xxxf. It may be named from its relationship to Brockton, which is a member of the parish, but was an independent manor (albeit a very small one) in DB. The next settlement to the south is, ironically, Norton in Stockton parish, which may be a name of later origin.

Madoc was the first name of members of three generations of the family which held the manor in the 12th and 13th cents. This was a Welsh family whose tenure stemmed from Henry II's gift of Sutton to Iorwerth Goch in return for interpreter services. There are a number of variant spellings of the affix in parish registers. The modern *Maddock* is first noted 1722 PR(L) 7.

SUTTON UPON TERN SJ 667317 Civil Parish

Sudtone 1086 DB
Sutton' 1255-6 *Ass, -ton* 1326 Pat, *Sutton juxta Drayton* 1630 *SBL 5693, - by Drayton* 1661 *SBL 5700, - in Drayton* 1761 *SBL 5739*

This Sutton is S. of Market Drayton, to which parish it formerly belonged. Records of the name are sparse and may not give a full indication of affixes. The modern one, - upon Tern, appears on the 19th-cent. OS map.

SUTTON, Great and Little SO 516830, 513824 DB Manors

Sudtone 1086 DB
Sutton 1208-9 *ForProc et freq* with variant spellings *-tun'*, *-ton*; *Sutton in Corfdale* 1316 Pat

Sotton' 1242 Fees, *-ton* 1284-5 FA

These places are in the southern part of the parish of Diddlebury. The affix for Little Sutton is first noted 1208 *ForProc* (*Parva Sutton*). Great Sutton is *Sutton Major* 1262 Ipm. Most printed calendars translate the affixes as 'Great' and 'Little', so that their forms in the MSS are not easily available. Both places are described in DB.

SUTTON (near Shrewsbury) SJ 499103 DB Manor

Sudtone 1086 DB, *-tona* c.1144, 1155, c.1220 SAC, *-ton* 13th *SBL 6260*
Sutton 1221-2 *Ass et p;assim* with variant spellings *-tune, -ton'*

Probably named from its relationship to Shrewsbury.

SYCHTYN SJ 233272 Civil Parish (now in Oswestry)

Sufton' 1272 Cl, *-tone* 1272 Ipm
Sutton 1302 Ipm
Soghton 1307 Pat, *Soughton'* 1588-9 *RentSur, -ton* 1600,07 Slack, 1672 HTR, *SBL 8404*
Shychton 1591 PR(StA) 4
Sightyn 1602-3 PR(StA) 4, *Sychtyn* 1787 PR(StA) 3
Soughtyn 1717 PR(StA) 5, 1790 PR(StA) 6

The spellings for Soughton in Fli must be compared. They are set out in NCPNW 227. Soughton is *Sutone* DB, *Sutton* 1284-1331, *Syghtyn* 1539, *Soughton* 1653. B.G. Charles gives 'south farm' as the etymology, but this is not certain to be correct for either name, though such an assumed origin may lie behind the *Sutton* spellings. Substitution of *-tyn* for *-ton* is a frequent occurrence in English names in Wales and on the borders, but the development of [x] (spelt *-gh-*, *-ch-*) in names containing *sūð* is not a regular occurrence. There are several Suttons in Wales which show no sign of it.

The first element may be **sōg, *sōh*, the presumed OE form of ME *sogh* 'bog'. A settlement on the same hill as Sychtyn has the Welsh name Wern-ddu, 'black alder-swamp'.

The 1272 spelling *Suftone* is unexplained. It is too early to represent the substitution of [f] for [x] which is common from the 15th cent. onwards.

TASLEY SO 697942 Civil Parish

Tasseleya c.1143 SAC *et passim* with variant spellings *-leg(h)', -l', -le, -ley(e), -leg(h), -lee* to 1443 Cl, *Thasseleg'* 1233 Cl
Tassheley 1416 AD, *Tashley* 1728 PR(H) 16, *Tashley alias Tasley* 1803 Plymley
Tasley 1535 VE *et seq*, *Tasly* 1670,80, 1724 PR(H) 1, 1696 PR(H) 16
Tastley 1743 PR(H) 16
Tarsley 1755 PR(H) 1

There was a place called *Tassewode* in the vicinity, which is referred to by that spelling in 1271-2 *ForProc* (p), 1279 Cl and 1291-2, 1306-7 *Ass*. This could be an abbreviation of earlier **Tasseleyewode*, but it is equally likely that there was a clearing (**lēah**) and a wood (**wudu**) with names which shared the same first element. The identity of this first element is obscure. DEPN suggests *tæsel* 'teazle', but this should have given **Tasel(l)eye* and **Taselwode*. An element **tassa* is required by the forms. Tasburgh Nf has a similar first element, but the evidence in that case is in favour of **tasa* or **tæsa*, and the name is to be compared with *tæsan mæd* in a W charter boundary (S 272). **tæ-* or *tæ̆sa* does not suit the Sa spellings: Tasley and *Tassewode* are unsolved, and apparently unique.

TETSILL SO 662716 DB Manor

Tedenesolle 1086 DB
Tattehal' 1195 P, *Tateshale* 1196 P, *Tet(t)eshale* 1255 RH
Tetenhill' 1200 Cur
Thikeshell' 1201 Cur

Tetneshulle 1211-12 RBE, *-hull* 1287 Ipm, *-hull'* 1291-2 *Ass*, *Teteneshull* 1301 Cl, 1308 Ipm
Tatneshull', Tateneshull' 1271-2 *Ass*
Tetishull' 1291-2 *Ass*, *Tettieshull* 1309 Ipm, *Teiteshull* 1346 FA, *Teteshull* 1348 Ipm, *Teitteshull* 1431 FA
Tettleshull' 1291-2 *Ass*
Temeshull 1309 Cl
Titeshull 1428 FA
Teddestell, Tedstyll 1600-1 *RentSur, Teddestell'* 1602 *ib*
Tetstill 1841 *TA*

Possibly 'Tætel's hill'. *Tātel*, which is on record, is a hypocoristic form of the personal name *Tāta*. There may have been an alternative form *Tǣtel*, which suits this name if allowance is made for Norman French confusion of *-l-* and *-n-*.

Tetstill is beside an eminence called Neens Hill, in the parish of Neen Sollers.

TIBBERTON SJ 680204 Civil Parish

Tetbristone 1086 DB
Tibrihtona 1155 SAC, *Tibricton* 1203-4 *Ass*, *-ton'* 1242 Fees, *Tibrihton* 1255 RH, *Thibrichton'* (p), *Ti-* 1255-6 *Ass*. *Tybrighton'* 1286 *SBL 4127 et freq* with variant spellings *Ti-*, *-brygh-*, *-ton* to 1431 FA (*Tybryghton*), *Tibbrihtonia* 1318 Ch, *Tybrychtoun* 1397 InqMisc
Thibuchton 1199 (1265) Ch, *Tibihiton'* 1208-9 *ForProc*, *Tybuhton* 1285 Ch
Tibrinton' 1208-9 *ForProc*
Tybritun' (p), *-ton* 1236-7 SAC, *-ton* 1271-2 *Ass*
Tibeton 1253 Ch
Tiberton' 1255-6 *Ass*, *-ton* 1331 Ch, 1655 SAS 1/XLVII, *Tyburton* 1428 FA, *Tyberton* 1535 *SBL 7180*, 1672 HTR, *Tybberton* 1535 VE, *Tibberton* 1577 Saxton
Tibriston 1339 HAC
Tibroghton 1346 FA
Tebrighton 1428 FA

'Tīdbeorht's estate', identical with Tibberton Gl and

Tyberton He. The form of the name is discussed under Albrighton near Shrewsbury.

TICKLERTON SO 483909 DB Manor

Tickelevorde 1086 DB, *Ticlewrthin* 1203-4 *Ass* (p), *Tikelewordin* 1221-2 *Ass* (p) *et freq* with variant spellings *Tykele-* and *-wrth', -wrthyn, -wordyn, -worth* to 1291-2 *Ass, Tycleworþin* 1255 RH, *Tykelworthin* 1255-6 *Ass, Tyklward, Tykelwardyn* 1291-2 *Ass, Tyclewardyn* 1301 SAC
Tikelesworth 1203-4 *Ass* (p), *Tykelesworthyn* 1291-2 *Ass* (p)
Tykewarthin' 1231 Cur, *Tigwardin* 1255-6 *Ass* (p), *Tykewurthin'* 1261-2 *ForProc*
Tykelyngworthin, Tyklingwrth' 1271-2 *Ass*
Tyklarden', -dyn' 1550 *RentSur, Tyklerden, Ticklarden* 1551 Pat
Tinklerton 1577 Saxton
Tycklerton 1587 *SBL 1504, Ticklerton* 1654 *SBL 6840A et seq*
Tickleton 1790 PR(L) 11, *Ticklington* 1791 ib

Possibly 'Tycela's enclosed settlement'. The final element is **worthign**. The first might be a hypocoristic derivative of recorded personal names such as *Tuc(c)a, Tic(c)a.*

Ticklerton is in Eaton under Heywood parish.

TITTENLEY FM SJ 647378 DB Manor

Titesle 1086 DB
Tytneleye, -legh' 1291 *Ass* (p), *Tyttenleye* 1305-6 *Ass* (p), *Titenlegh* 1347 DEPN
Tutenlegh 1304 DEPN

'Tytta's meadow', with *lēah* probably in its late OE sense, as in Adderley, in which parish this place lies.

The 1086 reference is in the Cheshire section of DB, and the two spellings taken from DEPN are in Cheshire sources. The place was a detached portion of Cheshire until 1895. It is in Adderley parish.

TONG SJ 795075 Ancient Parish

(*into*) *Tweongan* c.975 S 1543, (*æt*) *Twongan* 1002-4 S 1536, *Twenge* 1221-2 *Ass, Twonge* 1291-2 *Ass*
Tuange 1086 DB, *Twanga* 1167 P
Toenga c.1090, 1121,38 SAC, *Tounga* c.1155 SAC
Tonga c.1145, 1155 SAC, *Tonge* 1221-1 *Ass et freq* to 1733 PR(L) 18, *Tong* 1255 RH, 1533 Pat *et seq, Tongge* 1413 Fine, 1415 Pat, *Tongue* 1568 PR(L) 18 *et freq* to 1728 PR(H) 3
Tang' 1203-4 *Ass* (p), *Tange* 1221-2 *Ass*, 1225 Cur, 1235-6 Fees
Thonke 1212 Fees, *Thonge* 1217 (1285) Ch, 1395 *SBL 16293*
Tunge 1220 Cur, 1280 SAC, 1306-7 *Ass*, 1326 Ipm, Cl, c.1540 Leland
Togge 1284-5 FA
Toong 1401 Pat, *Toung* 1547 Pat, *Tounge* 1689 *PRShifnal*

Twongan is S 1536 has recently been ascribed to Tonge Lei (Burton pp. xxviii), but unless a fuller collection of ME spellings for that place reveals more variety than the two given in DEPN (*Tunge* DB, *Tunga* c.1125) the form fits better with those for the Sa name.

Unlike most of the place-names with modern forms such as Tang, Thong, Thwing, Tong(e), the Sa name cannot be derived from a single OE term. Other names in this group can be assigned to OE *tang, tong* 'forceps' (Tang YN, Tonge K, La), *thwang* 'thong' (Thong K, Nether- and Upperthong YW), or *tunge* 'tongue' (Tonge Lei). Thwing YE is probably ON *thvengr* 'shoe-lace'.

The Sa name, however, appears to have two sources, an OE **tweonga* and *tang, tong* 'forceps'. There may also have been some association with the word *tongue*, but it is not necessary to assume this, as spellings like *Tunge, Toong, Toung(e)* are also found for the word *tongs.*

The topographical reference is almost certainly to the situation between two headstreams of the R. Worfe which unite W. of the settlement. OE *tang* is appropriate to this. The alternative term, **tweonga*, is presumably related to the OE verb *twengan* 'to pinch'. This less common term was probably replaced by *tang, tong.* Tong YW, S.E. of Bradford, is *Tuinc* DB, *Tuenche* 1166, and here also a name derived from an obsolescent **tweonga* may have been refashioned. There may also be a trace of this term, or the related **twang* which is proposed in Elements, in the spellings for Tongham Sr.

TUGFORD SO 557870 Ancient Parish

Dodefort 1086 DB
Tugafort c.1090, 1138 SAC, *-fordia* c.1138 SAC, *-ford* 1155 SAC, *Tugeford* 1274 RH, c.1291 TN, *-fort* 1563 *SBL 7146*
Tuggeford c.1143 SAC *et passim* with variant spellings *-ford'*, *-fort* to l.14th SAC
Taggeford 1284-5 FA
Toggeford' 1291-2 *Ass*, *-ford* c.1291 TN
Togeford' 1306-7 *Ass*
Tugford 1500 Ipm *et seq*
Tuckford 1732 PR(H) 15, 1766 *PRChetton*

'Tucga's ford'. The personal name, which is not on record, is presumed to occur also in Tughall Nb. The village is situated on a tributary of the R. Corve.

There were two settlements, probably adjacent. Entries in 1271-2 *Ass* refer to *Tuggeford et alia Tuggeford* and to *Magna Tuggeford*; 1291-2 *Ass* has *Chyrch' Tuggeford et alia Toggeford'*; *Parva Tuggeford'* occurs c.1275 SAC. In 1563 *SBL 7146* the two places are *Tugefort Superior* and *Inferior*. The 19th-cent. OS map shows Upper House and Lower House on the N. and S. edges of the village.

UCKINGTON SJ 577097 DB Manor

Uchintune 1086 DB, *Uckinton* 1255 RH, 1668 *SBL 6039*, *Ukinton'*, *Huckinton'* 1255-6 *Ass*, *Ukynton'* 1291-2 *Ass*, 1395 *SBL 16293*, *-ton* 1443 *SBL 15752*
Ukington 1217 (1285) Ch, *Uckington* 1669 *SBL 15748 et seq*
Okynton' 1271-2, 91-2 *Ass*, 1334 SR, *Okenton* 1285 Ch
Hokyton c.1280 HAC
Ucketon 1577 Saxton

'Estate associated with Ucca', an **-ingtūn** formation. Uckington Gl is identical.

Uckington is in Wroxeter parish.

UFFINGTON SJ 529138 Ancient Parish

Ofitone 1086 DB
Offinton 1155-62 HAC *et freq* with variant spellings *-tona, -ton'* and *-yn-* to 1462 *SBL 4457*
Uffitun' 1177 P (p), *-tona* 1203-10 HAC, *Uffeton* c.1291 TN
Uffintone 1195 HAC *et freq* with variant spellings *-ton(a), -ton'* and *-yn-* to 1668 *SBL 6039*
Uffington 1535 VE *et seq*
Huffiton 1742 PR(L) 20

'Estate associated with Uffa'. Other instances of the name occur in Berks and Li.

UPPINGTON SJ 600095 Ancient Parish

Opetone 1086 DB, *Opyton* 1291,4 Ipm, *Opiton'* l.13th *ForProc*
Upetuna c.1140 SAC
Oppinton' 1195 P, 1246 Cl
Uppinton' 1208-9, 61-2 *ForProc, -ton* 1259 Ipm, 1271-2 *Ass,* 1577 Saxton, 1658 *SBL 5658,* 1756 PR(L) 8, *Uppynton* 1416 AD
Upton' 1251 Cl
Opinton c.1252 Ipm *et freq* with variant spellings *-ton'* and *-yn-* to 1375 Pat, *Hopinton'* 1255-6 *Ass* (p), *Hopynton* 1316 FA, *Opyntoun* 1397 Cl
Uppiton 1255 RH
Upinton' 1255-6 *Ass et freq* with variant spellings *-ton* and *-yn-* to 1339 Pat, *Hupinton'* 1255-6 *Ass*
Upiton' 1271-2 *ForProc*
Uppiton' 1271-2 *Ass*
Uppington 1284 Cl, 1535 VE *et seq, Uppyn(g)ton* 1421 Cl
Uppyn(g)don 1346 Cl
Oppington 1665 PR(L) 11
Ypington 1695 Morden

The boundary of Uppington is *uppinghæma gemære* in the boundary-clause of S 802, a grant of the adjacent parish of Aston dated 975. This must be the basis for discussion of the etymology. Since OE **-hæma-** 'of the dwellers' is added to the first part of place-names to make this sort of compound, *Uppingtūn* must be presumed to be the OE form. The ME forms accord well enough with this presumption, if allowance is made for the name being sometimes interpreted as OE *Upptūn*, 'higher settlement'.

Uppingtūn might be 'estate associated with Uppa', from a personal name which would be a variant of the recorded *Ubba.* Etymologies involving **up, upp(e)**, 'above, higher', do not seem likely, as the site is not elevated.

UPTON

Shropshire has four examples of this common name, and three of them are ancient parishes. These are set out below. The fourth example, Upton in Shifnal, is first noted in 1247-8 (1292) Ch.

Upton derives from OE *Upptūn* which means 'higher settlement', sometimes referring to elevation and sometimes to position on a river. The former is the relevant sense in all the Sa instances.

UPTON CRESSET SO 656924 Ancient Parish

Ultone 1086 DB
Opeton' 1167 P
Upton' 1201 P (p) *et freq* with variant spelling *-ton*; *Upton Cressett* 1796 PR(H) 3
Opton' 1242 Fees, *-tone* 1290 Ipm, *-ton* 1346 FA
Hopton 1284-5 FA, *- Cressett* 1535 VE
Uppon Cresset 1669 PR(H) 1

The settlement has a high situation. *Cresset* is a family name: Eyton (I, p. 142) says that Thomas *Cressett* married into the family surnamed *de Upton* in the mid-13th cent. Eyton (I, pp. 146-7) quotes two forms with alternative affixes. In 1341 there is a reference to the church of *Upton super Egge* ('on the hill-side'), and in 1354-5 the living is referred to as Upton *Waryn*, possibly from the first Norman sheriff of Shropshire.

UPTON MAGNA SJ 554125 Ancient Parish

Uptune 1086 DB, *Upton'* c.1145 SAC *et freq* with variant spellings *-ton(e)*; *Upton subtus Haghmon'* 1268-71 HAC, *- Undirhamen* 1397 Pat, *Great Upton under Haghmon* 1408 Pat, *Upton Magna, Magna Upton, Upton Mayn* 1535 VE, *Upton Magna alias Upton under Haughmond* 1573 *SBL 5864*
Opetone c.1090, 1138 SAC
Obtone 1121 SAC
Optone c.1138, c.1155, c.1190 SAC, *Opton' subtus Hagemon* 1292 SAC
Hupton sub Hawemon 1261-2 *ForProc*

The position must have appeared elevated by comparison with those of surrounding settlements. *Magna* is for distinction from Waters Upton. The hill-name Haughmond is discussed under Haughton.

WATERS UPTON SJ 634194 Ancient Parish

Uptone 1086 DB *et freq* with variant spellings *-ton', -ton*; *Upton Waters* 1346 AD, *Upton' Parva* l.14th SAC, *Wateres Upton* 1431 FA, *Waters Upton* 1517 *SRO 327 et seq*, *Upton Parva* 1535 VE, 1588 PR(L) 20
Opton' 1242 Fees

The settlement is on a spur of land overlooking the R. Tern. *Parva* is for distinction from Upton Magna, 6½ miles S.W. *Waters* is from the Christian name *Walter*. Walter de Opton' was the tenant in 1242 Fees.

WALCOT SO 264993 DB Manor

Walecote 1086 DB, *-cot* 1247 InqMisc, *-cote* 1255-6 *Ass*, 1274 RH, 1294 Cl
Walcote 1271-2, 91-2 *Ass*, 1280 Ipm, 1334 SR, 1535 VE, *-cot* 1577 Saxton *et seq*

'Cottages of the Britons', OE **Walacotu*, probably denoting a hamlet where Welsh speech was still in use after the general adoption of English. This Walcot, in Chirbury parish, is the furthest west example of the name in the whole country (see map in JEPN 12, p. 35), and is particularly likely to refer to a linguistic rather than an ethnic characteristic of the people concerned.

There are two other Shropshire instances, in the parishes of Wrockwardine and Lydbury North. Neither is in DB, but the Wrockwardine name has numerous 12th-cent. spellings, starting with *Walecote* c.1138 SAC. Walcot in Lydbury North is less well-recorded, but *Walecot*(*e*) occurs from 1255 RH (p) to 1306-7 *Ass* (p).

All three Shropshire Walcots are component parts of large estates.

WALFORD SJ 435206 DB Manor

Waleford 1086 DB, 1255-6 *Ass, -forde* 1307 HAC
Walleforde 1201 HAC *et passim* with variant spelling *-ford* to 1428 FA
Walford 1203 HAC, 1333,75 Cl, 1542 *SBL 4462 et seq*
Welleforde c.1217 HAC, *-ford* 1271-2 *Ass*
Wallford 1609 *SBL 17410*

'Ford by a spring'; **wælla** is the WMidl form of OE **well, wella, welle**, which usually means 'spring' in place-names.

Walford is in Baschurch parish.

WALLTOWN SO 692783 DB Manor

Walle 1086 DB
Waltowne 1526-7, 79 *RentSur, The Wauletoun* 1575 PR(H) 17, *-towne* 1585, 1649 ib, *-toune* 1596 ib, *The Wall Town* 1661 ib

DB *Walle* is listed between Baveney and Catsley, which are nearby, and the identification with Walltown is generally accepted. The gap in records from 1086 to 1526 is unusual, but a good parallel for the later form is provided by Myndtown, which is *Muneta* DB, *Myntowne* 1577. The source could be either **wælla** 'spring', as in Walford, or

wall 'wall'. The latter is probable, with reference to the ancient fort within which the farm has been built.

Walltown is in Neen Savage parish.

WALTON SO 676812 DB Manor

Waltone 1086 DB, 1316 FA, *-ton'* 1255-6 *Ass*, 1334 SR, *-thone* c.1270 AD, *-ton* 1317 AD

Probably 'spring settlement', with the WMidl form of *well* as first element. The farm stands on a watershed between several small streams, one of which may have risen closer to the farm in early times.

In addition to this example in Stottesdon parish, there are five other Waltons in Shropshire. These are:

1. Bridgewalton in Morville (*Waltona* c.1165 SAC)
2. Walton in High Ercall (*Walton'* 1255-6 *Ass*)
3. Walton in Onibury (*Wal(e)ton* 1255 RH)
4. Walton in Wenlock (*Waltuna* 1120 (copy) Eyton (p))
5. Walton in Worthen (*Waleton* 1199 SAS 2/X (FF))

None of these has more than a single occurrence of a *Waleton'* spelling, and this makes it unlikely that they derive from **Walatūn*, 'settlement of Britons'. They are not likely to contain **wald** 'forest' (another possible source of the name in eastern England) as it is very doubtful whether that term occurs as far west as Shropshire. The remaining possibilities are considered to be **wall** 'wall' and **wælle** 'spring'. If the former word is involved in a name (as in Wall Town *supra*) the reason is usually obvious on the ground. 'Settlement by a spring' is probably the safest suggestion for all the Waltons in this county. It should be noted, however, that the *-ll-* of **wælle** is not preserved, as it is in a number of spellings for Walford *supra*.

WATTLESBOROUGH SJ 355126 DB Manor

Wetesburg 1086 DB

Wetlesborc 1242 Fees, *-burh, -bore* 1255 RH
Watelesbur' 1242 Fees. *Watlesbrugg'* 1255-6 *Ass et passim* with variant spellings *-burg', -burgh', -bergh, -burgh, -borugh', -boru, -burugh, -burrough* to 1672 HTR, *Watelesburgh* 1381,2 1474 Cl, *Watlysburgh* 1429 Cl, *Watelesborow* c.1540 Leland, *Wattles-borough* 1621 *SBL 6940*
Watleburg' 1271-2 *Ass, Wathleburgh* 1310 Cl, *Watelborow* c.1540 Leland, *Watleburgh* 1675 Ogilby
Watlestbury 1316 FA

'Wæcel's fort'. second element **burh.** The first is an archaic personal name which occurs in *Wæclingaceaster*, an OE name for St Albans Hrt, Watlington O, and probably Watchfield Berks. The available forms for the O place show that the *-c-* of *Wæcel* had become *-t-* by 1086, so the universal *-t-* of the Wattlesborough spellings is not an obstacle to this derivation. The use of nom. **burh** rather than dat. **byrig** suggests that the reference is to an ancient fort rather than to an Anglo-Saxon manor-house. The use of the nominative in the 'archaeological' sense is particularly common in the west midlands, and there is an obvious contrast with nearby Westbury and Alberbury. It is surprising that the personal name *Wæcel* should appear as far west as this, and there may be a mythological reference.

The G.R. given is that for Wattlesborough Hall, which stands by the tip of a small hill. No prehistoric fortifications are marked on maps. The village called Wattlesborough Heath is on the Shrewsbury/Welshpool road a mile to the S.

Wattlesborough is a township in Alberbury parish.

WELBATCH SJ 459088 DB Manor

Huelbec 1086 DB, *Whelbeche* 1271-2 *Ass*, 1284 Ipm, 1577 Saxton, *-bach* 1316 Ipm *et freq* with variant spellings *-bache, -batch* to 1719 PR(L) 16, *-bech* 1598 *et freq* with variant spelling *-betch* PR(H) 1, *-beatch* 1690,4 ib, *-bitch* 1703 *et seq* PR(L) 15
Welbeg' 1203-4 *Ass, -bach'* 1242 Fees *et freq* with variant spelling *-bache* to 1777 PR(L) 16, *-bech* 1605 PR(H) 1, *-bitch* 1699 *et seq* ib
Wulbech 1255 RH
Wellebech', Wilebache 1255-6 *Ass, Wellebeche* 1280 Cl, *Well Bich*

1718 PR(L) 16, *Wellbeach* 1768 PR(L) 6
Welebache l.13th *ForProc*, *-bach'* 1291-2 *Ass*
Whulbache 1353 Cl
Whellbatch 1605 *SBL 6910*, *Whell Batch* 1610 *SBL 7057*
Wheelbach 1640 PR(H) 1
Wil Bich 1718 PR(L) 16

'Wheel stream', OE **Hwēolbæce*, presumably referring to a mill-wheel. The valley in which Welbatch Brook runs is a typical **bæce**.

Welbatch lies in a detached area of Shrewsbury St Chad parish.

WELLINGTON SJ 650115 Ancient Parish

Walitone 1086 DB
Walintona 1121 SAC, *-yn-* 1138 SAC
Welintun c.1145 SAC *et passim* with variant spellings *-ton(a)*, *-ton'* and *-yn-* to 1455 *SBL 4441*
Weledon' 1177 P
Welington' 1177 P, *-ton* 1286 Cl, c.1540 Leland, 1729 PR(L) 8, *-yngton* 1322 Pat *et freq* to 1455 *SBL 4441*
Weliton' 1192,3,9 P, *Welyton* 1377 Fine
Wolinton' 1195 *et freq* to 1214 P
Wellinton' 1224 Cur, *-ton* 1255 RH, *-ynton* 1284 Cl, 1577 Saxton
Wellington 1244 Ch, 1535 VE *et seq*
Whelynton 1392 Pat
Wyllynton 1535 VE
Walington 1553 Pat
Wollington 1713 PR(L) 8

There are four Wellingtons, one of the others being in Somerset and the remaining two in Herefordshire. The Somerset example occurs in the forms *Weolingtun, Welingtun* in a charter of A.D. 904, and there can be no doubt that *Wē-* or *Wēolingtūn* was the OE form. The etymology has not been ascertained.

An **-ingtūn** formation from a personal name **Wēola* is possible. The occurrence of four examples could be explained in the manner suggested under Detton for the recurring *Dodingtūn*,

Dun(n)ingtūn compounds; but this hypothesis assumes that an otherwise unrecorded personal name was sufficiently common in the west of England to produce four place-names.

In *Notes and Queries* 219 (1974), p. 124, E.J. Dobson discusses a ME adjective *weolie*, suggesting derivation from an OE **wēol* meaning 'artifice'. If there were such a noun, a derivative **wēoling* could have been coined as a term for a mechanical device, and a *Wēolingtūn* could be a settlement where such a device was in operation.

The suggestion in DEPN of an **-ingas** name based on the place-name *Wēohlēah*, 'grove with a heathen temple', is open to serious objections. The spellings of these four names give no indication of **-inga-**, and geographically they are well to the west of the established distribution of place-names which contain references to Anglo-Saxon paganism.

The Sa Wellington was sometimes distinguished by reference to the Wrekin. Forms with affixes include *Welintone sub monte Gileberti* 1232 SAC, *Welynton' subter le Wrekne* 1337-8 *ForProc*, *Welyngton under the Wrekyn* 1489 Ipm, *Wellyngton beneath le Wrekyn* 1547 Pat.

WELSHAMPTON SJ 435350 Ancient Parish

Hantone 1086 DB, *-ton* 1255 RH
Henton 1272,4 Eyton
Hampton 1316 FA *et passim. - by Culmere* 1341 Pat, *Hampton Culmere* 1403 Pat, *Hampton' iuxta Ellesmer'* 1421 *SBL 3650*, *Welch Hampton* 1649 SAS 4/VII, c.1860 Eyton, *Welsh* - 1726 *SBL 5268*
Welch Hamton 1715 PR(L) 9, *Hamton* 1720 PR(StA) 2, 1736 PR(L) 9

'High estate', OE (*æt þǣm*) *hēan tūne*, which sometimes becomes Hempton. The village does not stand very high, but the name may have been understood as referring to the whole estate. The northern part of the parish is hilly.

There are two other examples in Shropshire. Hampton in Worthen is *Hampton'* 1291-2 *Ass* (one estate there is *Hampton Howel*, a form wrongly cited in DEPN under Welshampton). Hampton in Chelmarsh is *Hempton'* 1255-6 *Ass*, and the *Hemp-*

forms persist in that name till the 17th cent.

Affixes to Welshampton are probably for distinction from the Worthen name. 'Welsh' refers to the proximity of a detached part of Flintshire.

WEM SJ 515290 Ancient Parish

Weme 1086 DB, 1367, 1500,4 Ipm, 1586 *et freq* to 1638 PR(L) 9
Wemme 1228 Cl *et passim* to 1727 PR(L) 10
Wem 1577 Saxton *et seq*

There is general agreement that the source of this name is OE **wemm** 'filth'. The group of words to which **wemm** belongs is better-evidenced as referring to moral than to physical pollution, but the use of the noun as a simplex place-name can only be explained by postulating a sense appropriate to soil conditions. Much of the large parish of Wem is marshy.

The Wems occurs as a farm-name in Adderley, about 12 miles N.E. of Wem, also in wet ground. This has not been traced back further than the 19th-cent. OS map and the *TA*, but it is likely to be an ancient name. There is a single instance of Wem in Cheshire, as a 19th-cent. field-name in Great Warford, another marshy area.

MUCH WENLOCK SO 623000 Ancient Parish

Wininicas 675-90 (13th) S 1798, 901 S 221
Wenlocan, Wynlocan 9th Saints
Wenloch 1086 DB, *-loc* 1200 P *et passim* with variant spellings *-lok, -lock(e), -lok(k)e*; *Wenlac* 1200 P *et passim* with variant spellings *-lak(e)* to 1261-2 *ForProc*
Wuneloch 1138 SAS 66
Winloc' c.1147 SAS 66, *Wynnlok'* 1291-2 *Ass*
Weneloc 1167 P *et passim* with variant spellings *-loch', -lok'* to 1290 Ch, *Wenelach* 1196 P *et freq* with variant spelling *-lac* to 1237 Cl
Gueneloch 1191 Gir
Wanelak' 1212 Fees
Wentlok 1236 Cl, *Wendlok* 1281 (1348) Pat, *Wendlocke* 1607 PR(H) 3, 1670 PR(H) 1

Wonloc, -lok 1247 SAS 66
Wanlok 1255 RH, 1318 Cl
Wellok' 1271-2 *Ass* (p), *Welloke* 1319 Ipm

ME *muche* is a shortened form of *muchel* 'great'. An affix is first noted 1291-2 *Ass* (*Magna Wenlak'*), and the Latin form is fairly common, sometimes after the name, till 1535 VE (*Wenloke Magna*). Printed calendars of Charter Rolls and Inquisitions for the 14th cent. give *Much Wenlok*(*e*), but this may be the editors' translation of *Magna* -, so it is not clear how early the vernacular form occurs. It is certainly found in 1550-1 *RentSur* (*Moche - Much Wenlok'*) and is common after that. PR(L) 2 and PR(H) 8 have *Great Wenlock* from 1749 to 1756.

The form *Wininicas* in S 1789 (the document known as St Mildburg's Testament) and S 221 is said by H.P.R. Finberg (*Lucerna* p. 74, n.1) to be the correct reading of the MSS. The name has more frequently been transcribed as *Wimnicas*, but even if this were the likelier reading, emendation to *Wininicas* would be reasonable. The compilers of both documents are likely to have been using the monastery's foundation charter of c.685. *Wininicas* defies complete explanation, but *Win-* must surely be Welsh *gwyn* 'white'.

The monastery is called *Wenlocan, Wynlocan* in a 9th-cent. text giving the burial-places of saints, and this is most likely to be the first element of *Wininicas* with the addition of an element *loc*(*a*).

Wenlock has hitherto been explained as a Welsh name meaning 'white monastery', but this interpretation presents formidable problems. It is difficult to imagine such a name being coined in the late-7th cent. in an area where other place-name evidence does not suggest the late survival of Welsh speech. If the name had been coined at that date, the adjective would have been likely to come after the noun. The etymology assumes that Welsh *loc* could mean 'monastery', but this word does not seem likely to have been an active Welsh place-name-forming term c.685. Latin *locus*, from which Old Welsh *loc*, Modern Welsh *llog* were derived, did acquire a religious significance, and was adopted into Welsh with the meaning 'monastery'; but although well-represented in place-names in Brittany it is exceedingly rare in Welsh names, and a recent study of the corresponding Cornish word (EPNS

LVI/LVII, pp. 151-2) concludes that there is only one instance in Cornish names and points out that the Lok- names in Brittany date from the 11th cent. or later.

It is possible that what we have in Wenlock is rather the English word **loca** 'enclosed place', which would be a suitable term for a monastery. If this were combined with the first syllable of *Wininicas*, the whiteness referred to could be that of the limestone of Wenlock Edge, rather than the monastery buildings. Behind the name Wenlock there may be a pre-English district-name meaning something like 'white area'. Rumours in 1986 that a late-Roman Christian church had been found beneath the medieval buildings of the Priory suggested the exciting possibility that the name went back to Roman times. If so, Wenlock would have had the structure usual in Romano-British names, and it would have seemed reasonable to postulate a transient use of Latin *locus* in the sense 'religious place' at the end of the Roman period. But subsequent information stated that the 'Roman' building did not have features specifically indicating a church, and a recent discussion by Martin and Birthe Biddle in *Journ. Brit. Arch. Ass.* CXLI contests the claim that it is Roman rather than Anglo-Saxon.

LITTLE WENLOCK SJ 647068 Ancient Parish

Wenloch 1086 DB, *Parva Wenlok'* 1190 (15th) SAC, - *Wenlac* 1232 Cl, *Wenloke Parua* l.13th *ForProc*, *Parva Wenloc'* 1334 SR, *Wenlok Parva* 1535 VE, 1577 Saxton, *Littell Wenloke* 1609 PR(L) 20, *Little Wenlock* 1679 PR(L) 8 *et seq*
Parua Weneloc c.1200 *ForProc*
Parua Wellok' 1271-2 *Ass*
Little Wendlock 1692 PR(L) 14, *Wendlock Parva* 1706 *PRShifnal*

This can only be the name of Much Wenlock transferred to what was presumably a new settlement on the north-west border of its territory established by the religious house. DB notes that Little Wenlock had belonged to St Mildburg's church before the Norman Conquest. In some instances of name-sharing by settlements it can be shown that they are both (or all) using a district-name, but that explanation does not suit here as Little Wenlock is five miles away and in different terrain, on the other side of the R. Severn.

The forms mirror those for the parent settlement, exhibiting the variation of *-loc-* with *-lac-*, the occasional parasitic *-d-*, and *Wellok'*, in which *-n-* has been assimilated to *-l-*.

WENTNOR SO 385928 Ancient Parish

Wantenoure 1086 DB, *-ouura* 1121 SAC, *-overa* 1155 SAC
Wantenore 1138 SAC
Wontenoure c.1200 (1292) Ch *et freq* with variant spellings *-our, -owr* to 1305 Pat
Wentenour' 1251 Fees *et freq* with variant spellings *-overe, -ouere, -oure* to 1333 Cl
Wyntenouer 1291-2 *Ass*
Wentenore 1315 Cl *et passim* to 1397 Pat
Wontenore 1334 SR
Wentnore 1385 Cl, *-or* 1535 VE *et seq*
Wintnor 1672 HTR

'Wonta's/Wenta's flat-topped ridge'.

The first element appears to have had alternative forms, *Wonta* and *Wenta.* DEPN compares the interchange of ē and ō in names which refer to the god Woden. The *Want-* forms of DB and SAC probably exhibit Norman French *-a-* for *-e-*. A personal name *Wont* is on record.

The second element is **ofer**, a word consistently used in place-names for settlements in situations of which Wentnor affords a perfect specimen. The village covers the end-section of a flat-topped ridge, with the church standing on the tip and land falling away sharply on three sides.

WESTBURY SJ 355095 Ancient Parish

Wesberie 1086 DB, *Wesbury* 1346 FA, 1625 PR(H) 1, 1658 PR(StA) 4, 1811 PR(StA) 13
Westbir' 1203-4 *Ass et passim* with variant spellings *-bur', -biry, -buri(e), -bury(e)*
Wesbrey 1711 PR(StA) 2

v. **west, byrig**. The road system makes a small D-shaped enclosure in the centre of the village, and this may preserve the outline of a fortification. VCH VIII p. 300 points out that Westbury is at a junction of routes to Wales. Cf. Pontesbury, where the morphology of the village also suggests a fortified area. Westbury may be named from its position W. of Pontesbury.

VCH suggests that this, rather than Westbury on Severn Gl, is the *Wæstbyrig* of ASC C s.a. 1053. In this entry it is stated that Welshmen killed many English guards (*weardmenn*), but no context is given, and the Shropshire place is only a possibility.

WEST FELTON SJ 343252 Ancient Parish

Feltone 1086 DB, *Felton by le Knokyn* 1303 Pat, *Felton* 1344 *SBL 3621 et seq, West Felton* 1397 Pat *et seq, Westfeltoune* 1553 Pat, *Welch Felton* 1654 PR(L) 20, 1668 PR(L) 9, *Welsh* - 1670 PR(StA) 2, 1709-10 PR(H) 6

'Settlement in open ground'. 'West' for distinction from Felton Butler. The stretch of land between the two places may have been called *Feld* by contrast with the surrounding marshes. 'West' was sometimes mininterpreted as 'Welsh' in the 17th-18th cents.

WESTHOPE SO 471864 DB Manor

Weshope 1086 DB
Westhop' c.1200 *ForProc et passim* with variant spelling *-hope, Westhopp* 1549 Pat, *Westop* 1577 Saxton

This name is discussed under Easthope *supra.* Westhope is a township of Diddlebury.

WESTON

Shropshire contains at least ten examples of this name. The five which qualify for full treatment in this volume are set out below. The others are:

Weston in Nash, first noted 1255 RH, near the west boundary of the parish.

Weston in Monkhopton, also first recorded 1255 RH, also in the west of its parish. This is *Weston Monachorum* 1291 Ch, *Moncke Weston* 1569 AD, *Monk Weston* 1695 Morden.

Weston Lullingfields in Baschurch, again first recorded 1255 RH. This is not in the west of the parish. It is probably named in relation to the area called Lullingfield. It is *Weston' super Lullingfeld* 1291-2 *Ass, Westone in Lollyngfyld'* 1516 *SBL 3651.*

Weston in the parish of Stow, first recorded 1242 Fees. This is in the eastern part of Stow parish, and can only be named in relation to Bucknell. It is the next settlement to the west along the road from Bucknell.

Binweston in Worthen, which is *Binneweston* 1255 RH, and is only once - in 1271-2 *Ass* - recorded without the prefix. This is presumably 'Binna's west settlement'. It is in the western part of Worthen parish

Whitchurch (infra) was *Westune* in DB. No early spellings have been found for Weston in Clun.

WESTON SJ 297276 DB Manor

Westune 1086 DB, *Weston* 1271 Ipm *et passim*
Gweston 1582 PR(StA) 4
Westyn 1603 PR(StA) 4

Named in relation to Aston in Oswestry, *supra.* *Gweston* and *Westyn* are Welshified forms.

A hamlet called Coton, a mile N. of Weston, became Weston Coton in the 17th cent.

COLD WESTON SO 551830 Ancient Parish

Westona c.1090 SAC, *-tone* c.1155 SAC, *Coldeweston', Colde Weston'* 1255-6 *Ass et passim* with variant spelling *-ton* to 1562-3 *SBL 7146, Goldeweston* 1271-2 *Ass, Coldweston* 1393 *SBL 15760, Cold Weston* 1395 *ib*
Cold Wyston 1505 Ipm
Colwaston 1535 *SBL 7180*

This Weston is perhaps named from its position in relation to the Clee Hills. It may be a counterpart to Aston Botterell, *q.v.* The affix is 'cold', cf. Cold Hatton (under Hatton).

PRIESTWESTON SO 291974 DB Manor

Westune 1086 DB, *Weston* 1228 Lib *et freq* with variant spelling *-ton'*; *Presteweston', Prestes Weston', Weston' Prustes* 1291-2 *Ass, Preostes Weston* 1315 Ipm, *Presteswesten* 1317,39 Pat, 1346, 1421 Cl, *Weston Prestes* 1334 SR, *Prestweston* 1361, 1421 Cl, *Preste-* 1416 AD, 1421 Cl, *Pryst -, Prist Weston* 1535 VE, *Priest* - 1637 PR(H) 8, *Preece* - 1672 HTR

This place is in the eastern part of Chirbury parish, so the name presumably has the general sense of being west in the county. The affix refers to Chirbury Priory.

Little Weston (*Parua Weston'* 1291-2 *Ass*) is three-quarters of a mile N.

WESTON RHYN SJ 283357 Civil Parish

Westone 1086 DB, 1272 Ipm, *-ton'* 1272 Cl, *Weston Ryn* 1302 Ipm, - *Rhine* 1653 *RentSur,* - *Rynn* 1655 SAS 1/XLVII, - *Rhyn* 1670 *SBL 6158*

West of St Martin's, in which parish it lay. Rhyn is a settlement 1½ miles N.E., and the name is Welsh *rhyn* 'peak'. The affix was probably felt to be desirable for distinction from Weston in Oswestry.

WESTON-UNDER-REDCASTLE SJ 565288 Civil Parish

Westune 1086 DB, *-ton'* 1195 P *et passim* with variant spelling *-ton*, *Rede Castell Weston* 1514 *SBL 4537*
Wesson 1666,93 PR(L) 11

Together with Wixhill this formed the western part of the ancient parish of Hodnet. The castle, a 13th-cent. ruin in Hawkstone Park, is *Rubeum Castrum* 1255 RH *et freq* to 1353 Cl, *Rede Castel* 1306-7 *Ass, Le Chastiel Rous* c.1320 FFW, *Rougechastel* 1330 Pat, 1357 Cl, *Redecastell* 1401 Fine, *Redcastle* 1577 Saxton

WHEATHILL SO 623821 Ancient Parish

Waltham 1086 DB
Wethulla c.1188 SAC *et freq* with variant spellings *-hull', -hul(l)* to 1409 Pat
Hwethill' c.1200 *ForProc, Hwet-, Whethull* 1255 RH, *Whethull'* 1255-6 *Ass et freq* with variant spellings *-hull, -hill(e)* to 1690 *PRChetton, Wheathill* 1618 *SBL 6332 et seq*
Wathull 1231 Cur, Cl
Wetehull 1270 Pat
Whettill 1495 Ipm, *Whettle* 1577 Saxton, c.1612 *SBL 15691*, 1695 PR(H) 13, *Whetill* 1592 PR(H) 18, *Wheathill als Whettell* 1615 *SBL 6381, Whittoll* 1694 PR(H) 13, *Whettoll* 1697 ib, *Whettell* 1702 ib

'Wheat hill', *v.* **hwǣte, hyll**. The DB form is one of the rare instances in which that record is almost totally erroneous. OE **hyll** is used in this name because the eminence does not have the expanse of level summit which would make it a **dūn**.

WHITCHURCH SJ 542415 Ancient Parish

Westune 1086 DB
Album Monasterium 1199 P *et passim* to 1337 Pat
Blancmustier c.1200 MM, 1211 P, *Blancum Monasterium* 1207,9,14 P (p), *Blancmostiers* c.1320 FFW, *Blankmostier* 1327 Pat,

Blanmouster 1337 Cl, *-moster* 1339 Cl, *Blankmouster* 1343 Cl, *Blaunkmonst(i)er* 1346 Pat, *Blankmonster* 1349 Pat
Whytchyrche 1271-2 *Ass et freq* with variant spellings *Whit-* and *-chirch(e)*, *-church(e)*; *Wytcherche* 1304 Pat (p)
Whitechirche 1307 Pat *et freq* with variant spellings *Whyte-* and *-church(e)*, *-cherche* to 1750 PR(L) 8, *Wytechirche* 1324 Ipm
Blauminister (p), *Blammoster* (p), *Blaminister* 1281 Ipm, *Blammonster* 1345 Pat
Qwicherche, The - 1427 Cl

'West settlement', later 'white church'.

The precise significance of 'west' is obscure, and there is no record of the building of the church which brought about the change of name. Whit(e)church is the commonest -church compound in English place-names. Examples in Wales, He and Sa share the characteristic of translation into Latin, and sometimes French, in records. Oswestry (*supra*) was called *Album Monasterium* or *Blancmuster* before the modern name asserted its primacy. There is no record of the vernacular *Whit(e)church* in the Oswestry forms, however.

WHITTINGSLOW SO 432890 DB Manor

Witecheslawe 1086 DB, *Witikes-*, *Witekes-* 1201 Cur, *Wytekeslowe* 1208-9 *ForProc* (p), *Whitockeslowe* 1376 Pat
Wittingeslaw, *Withincckelawe* 1200 Cur, *Wyttingeslowe* l.13th *ForProc*, *Whittingeslowe* 1301 SAC *et freq* with variant spellings *Whytt-* and *-yng-* to 1502 Ipm, *Wyttyngesluwe* 1334 SR, *Wittingeslowe* 1346 FA, *Wyttynges-* 1428 FA
Witingeslaw 1203-4 *Ass*, *Whytynggeslawe* 1291-2 *Ass*, *Whityngeslowe* 1431 FA, 1453 Cl
Wittokeslawe 1242 Fees *et freq* with variant spellings *Wyttokes-* and *-lowe* to 1276 Cl
Whytyngslowe 1449 Fine
Whutinslow 1577 Saxton, *Whittenslow* 1702 PR(H) 17, *Wittens-* 1703 ib, *Whitinslow* 1722 PR(H) 11
Whittingslowe 1601 *SBL 6485*, *-loe* 1661 PR(H) 17, *-low* 1811 ib

'Hwittuc's burial-mound'. The problems associated with

names of this type are discussed under Beslow *supra.* The hill above the hamlet of Whittingslow would be a magnificent site for a tumulus, but there is a small quarry there and little chance of anything remaining, even below the surface.

WHITTINGTON SJ 327313 Ancient Parish

Wititone 1086 DB
Quitentona c.1127 Ordericus Vitalis
Witinton' 1160 P *et freq* with variant spellings *Wyt-*, *-yn-* and *-ton* to 1380 Fine
Witenton' 1163 P
Whitinton' 1198 P *et freq* with variant spellings *Whyt-*, *-yn-* and *-ton* to 1427 *SBL 4028*
Wytigton' 1230 P, *Whytygton* 1378 Fine, *Whitigton* c.1540 Leland
Trefwen 1254 Norwich
Whytenton 1264,97 Pat, *Whit-* 1295 InqMisc, *Whittenton* 1577 Saxton
Chwytunton c.1291 TN
Whitington 1304 Pat *et passim* with variant spellings *Whyt-* and *-yng-* to 1730 *SBL 4015, Whyttyngton* 1544 *SBL 6176, Whittington* 1711 PR(L) 9 *et seq*
Blauncheville, e englois Whytyntone c.1320 FFW
Wyttington 1544 *SBL 6176, Witt-* 1707-8 PR(StA) 3

Probably 'estate associated with Hwīta'. The persistent *-in-* of the early forms suggests an **-ingtūn** formation. If the name had been OE *Hwītantūne,* 'at the white settlement', early contraction to Whitton would be expected. The etymology 'white settlement' was the accepted one in the 13th and 14th cents., however, as Welsh *Trefwen* and French *Blauncheville* demonstrate. The modern Welsh name is Y Dref-wen or Y Drewen.

Whittington occurs also in Db, Gl, La, Nb, Wa and Wo. There is an OE form *Hwitingtun* for the Wo example. Groups of names of this type are discussed under Detton *supra.*

Whittington Sa has frequently been identified with the place called *Drefwen* which is the subject of a poem in the Welsh poetic cycle known as Canu Heledd, but there is no firm basis for this identification.

WHITTON SO 575729 Civil Parish

Witet' c.1174 Eyton (p)
Witinton c.1180 Eyton (p), *-tone* 1210-12 RBE (p), *W(h)ytinton* 1255-6 *Ass*
Whittington 1233 Eyton (p)
Witton 1236 Eyton (p), *Wyttone* 1255 RH, *-ton* 1271-2 *Ass, -ton'* 1291-2 *Ass,* 1334 SR
Whitenton 1237 Eyton
Whytton 1255-6 *Ass et passim* with variant spelling *Whit-*

The spellings can be divided into two groups, one suggesting OE *Hwītingtūn*, the source of the names discussed under Whittington *supra*, the other suggesting *Hwītantūne*, 'at the white settlement', which is the probable source of Whitton in Du, Mx, Nb and Sf.

Most of the spellings which suggest *Hwītingtūn* are surnames, belonging to members of a local family identified by Eyton (IV, pp. 341-2), and it is possible that a more authentic local form was distorted in the surname. Judging from the entries in DEPN under Whittington and Whitton, there is a fairly consistent distinction. The contracted form is more likely to contain the adjective, which would give forms with early ME *-en-*, than the connective **-ing-** used with a personal name. Whittington near Lichfield St is an exception, however, being *Hwituntune* in a charter of A.D. 915, so presumably (though the spelling is irregular) containing the adjective. The two groups of names may have influenced each other to some extent.

WHITTON SJ 347091 DB Manor

Wibetune 1086 DB
Witton' 1242 Fees *et freq* with variant spellings *Wyt-* and *-ton* to 1656
PR(H) 6
Wytone 1291-2 *Ass, Witon* 1347 Cl
Whitton 1316, 1431 FA, *Witton alias Whitton* 1618 *SBL 9943*

The late and sparse appearance of *Wh-* is against the interpretation of this name as 'white settlement'. It may be 'wood settlement', OE **widu-tūn*, which is the source of a number of names with the modern form Witton. If so, *Wibetune* in DB is an error for **Widetune*.

Whitton is in Westbury parish.

WHIXALL SJ 515345 Civil Parish

Witehala 1086 DB
Withekisall, Witcheshill 1203-4 *Ass* (p), *Whitekeshal* 1240 SAS 4/VI (FF)
Wykeshull 1221-2 *Ass*
Wickeshall, Wickis- 1255 RH, *Wickeshal'* 1255-6 *Ass et freq* with variant spellings *Wy(c)kes-*, *Wyches-* and *-hale* to 1316 FA
Quickeshale 1255-6 *Ass, Quekeshale* 1317 Cl, Ipm, *Quyxhale* 1334 SR, 1411 Fine, *Quiksale* 1341 HAC (p), 1346 Pat, *Quikeshale* 1362 Ipm, *Quixsale* 1369 Ipm, *Quykesale* 1392 Cl, Fine, *Quyckesall alias Whyckesall* 1569 *SBL 5458, Wixhall otherwise Quixhall* 1665 *SBL 8383*
Wykedeshal 1255-6 *Ass*
Wixhale 1290 Ipm, *Wixall* 1615 *et seq* to 1742 PR(L) 9
Whyckeshale 1291-2 *Ass, Whickesall* 1601 PR(L) 9
Whicsale 1363 Ipm, *Whicksall* 1590, 1604 PR(L) 9, 1677 PR(L) 12, *Whixall* 1645 PR(L) 9
Whicksoe 1577 Saxton

'Hwittuc's nook', with the same personal name as in Whittingslow, but shortened by dropping the *-tt-*. This name seems to be a clear instance of *halh* used of firm ground in a wet area.

WIGMORE SJ 346114, 355114 DB Manor

Wigemore 1086 DB, 1255-6 *Ass, Wygemor'* 1221-2 *Ass* (p)
Wyggemor' 1255-6 *Ass*
Wigmore 1625 PR(H) 6, *-mor* 1650 ib, *-moore* 1673 ib, *Lower Wigmore* 1722 *SBL 6195*

This is the same name as Wigmore He. Other examples occur as field-names in Berks and Ch (PN Berks 916, PN Ch 4,

55). The second element is *mōr* 'marsh'. The first is *wicga*, recorded as a term for an insect and surviving in modern *earwig*. It would be reasonable to postulate a meaning 'something which wiggles'.

At Wigmore He the castle overlooks an unstable marsh in which wet mounds erupt and disappear, and it is possible that OE **wicga-mōr* was a term for such a marsh. The Sa places (Upper and Lower) are in a low-lying, marshy area. Marsh (modern Marche) and Wigmore was a township of Westbury in the 19th cent, and the two farms are named on the 1st ed. OS map in the positions given above. They are not named on modern maps, however.

WIGWIG SJ 608015 DB Manor

Wigewic 1086 DB, 1255 RH *et freq* with variant spellings *Wyge-* and *-wyk(e), -wike* to l.13th *ForProc*
Wicewica 1121 SAC, *Wychewyca* 1138 SAC, *Wichewica* 1155 SAC
Wiggewich 1177 P (p) *et freq* with variant spellings *Wygge-* and *-wyk, -wyk', -wik, -wich'* to 1428 Fine
Wigewig 1255 RH (p), *Wiggewig'* 1274 RH (p), *-wyg'* 1271-2 *Ass*, *Wygewygg* 1625 PR(L) 2
Wiggeswych' 1261-2 *ForProc* (p)
Wygwyke 1264-79 APW (p), 1271-2 *Ass* (p), 1535 VE, *-wyk* 1301 SAC, 1446 Fine, *Wigwike* 1617 PR(L) 6, *-wicke* 1653 PR(L) 2
Wygenewyk c.1291 TN, *Wygelwyk* 1316 FA
Wykwyk 1368 Ipm (p)
Wigwig 1622 PR(L) 2, *Wygwygg* 1623 ib, *Wigwigh* 1656 ib, *Wiggwigg* 1672 HTR, *Whig Whig* 1808 PR(L) 20

Probably 'Wicga's dairy-farm'. The well-recorded personal name *Wicga* is indistinguishable from **wicga** 'insect, ?quaking object' considered to occur in Wigmore *supra*, but a personal name seems more appropriate with **wīc**. On the other hand, if the forms *Wygenewyk* and *Wygelwyk* were taken seriously, the meaning could be 'dairy-farm of the insects' with the gen.pl. of **wicga**.

The tendency for the *-g-* and *-c-* of the first and second elements to influence each other can be seen to have been operating in the 12th and 13th cents.

Wigwig is in Much Wenlock parish.

WILDERLEY SJ 434018 DB Manor

Wildredelega 1086 DB, *Wildredel'* 1201 Cur (p), 1261-2 *ForProc, -leg* 1203-4 *Ass* (p), *-lega* 1204 HAC, *-leye* l.13th *ForProc*, 1306-7 *Ass* (p), *Wyldredelegh'* 1271-2 *ForProc* (p), *-lye* 1271-2 *Ass*
Widerleg' 1195 *et seq* to 1204 P (p)
Wiudredelee 1201 Cur (p)
Wildrideleg' 1203-4 *Ass* (p), *Wildridleg* 1255 RH, *Wyldridelee* 1261-2 *ForProc, Wyldrideley* 1271-2 *Ass, -legh* 1301 SAC
Wildricheleg' 1203-4 *Ass* (p), *Wildritheleg* c.1250-80 HAC, *Wyldrichleye* c.1291 TN
Wildridesle 1203-4 *Ass* (p), *Wyldredeslegh'* 1271-2 *ForProc*
Wardredelegh' 1208-9 *ForProc* (p)
Wilderdeleg' 1242 Fees, *Wylderdeleye* 1320 Ch, *Wilderdeleye* 1334 SR, 1346, 1428 FA
Wydridel' 1255-6 *Ass*
Wildreley a.1244 HAC, *Wyldrelye* 1271-2 *Ass*
Wuldredeleg', Woldrede- 1261-2 *ForProc* (p)
Wilderleye 1291-2 *Ass, -ley* 1445 Fine *et seq*
Welderdeleye 1316 FA
Wilderley alias Wynderley 1551 Pat, *- alias Wynderleye* 1596 *SBL 3463, Wynderley alias Wilderley, Wilderley alias Wynderley* 1615 *SBL 3465, Wilderley, Winderley* 1674 *SBL 3467*

'Wilþrȳð's clearing', *v.* **lēah**. The personal name is feminine. Wilderley is in Church Pulverbatch parish.

WILLEY SO 673992 Ancient Parish

Wilit 1086 DB
Welileia 1120 (copy) Eyton (p), *Welyleye* 1357 Pat
Wililega c.1180 SAC *et passim* with variant spellings *Wyli-, Wyly-* and *-leia, -leg(h)', -lee, -ley(e)* to 1406 Pat, *Wilelee* 1205 Cur *et freq* with variant spellings *Wyle-* and *-leg(h), -ley* to 1408 Pat
Willileg', Willeleia 1203-4 *Ass, Willelee* 1204 Cur, *Willel'* 1261-2 *ForProc, Williley, Willy-* 1375 Pat, *Willeley* 1392 Pat, *Wyllyley*

1431 FA

Wilegh' 1209 For (p), *Wyleye* 1416 AD, *Willey* 1453 Fine *et seq,* *Wylley* 1535 VE, *Wyley* c.1540 Leland

Wilgelegh' 1231 Cur (p)

'Willow wood', OE **wilig-lēah.* The same name occurs in Ch, He and Wa.

WINSLEY SJ 356077 DB Manor

Wineslei 1086 DB *et passim* with variant spellings *Wynes-* and *-leg(a), -leg'* to 1291-2 *Ass*

Wynelega, Wene- 1138 SAC

Wynnesl' 1255-6 *Ass, -legh'* 1291-2 *Ass* (p), *Winnesleg'* l.14th SAC, *Wynnesley* 1535 VE

Winsley 1672 HTR, *Wynsley* 1705 *SBL 6042*

'Wine's clearing', *v.* **lēah**. The same name occurs in Db and Wa.

Winsley is in Westbury parish.

WISTANSTOW SO 431855 Ancient Parish

Wistanestou 1086 DB, *-stowa* 1177 P *et passim* with variant spellings *Wystane-* and *-stowe* to 1443 *SBL 15752, Wystonestowe* 1208-9 (p), 1271-2 *ForProc, Wystannestowe* 1291-2 *Ass, Wistanesstowe* 1301 SAC, *Wistannestowe* 1329 Ipm

Wystanstowe 1255 RH *et freq* with variant spellings *Wistan-* and *-stoue, -stow*; *Wystonstow* 1553 PR(H) 17, *Wiston-* 1664 ib, 1704 PR(H) 18, *Wisten-* 1699 PR(H) 8, 1720 PR(H) 14

Wnstanestowe, Wynstaneston' 1255-6 *Ass, Wynstanesstowe* c.1291 TN, *Wynstanestouwe* l.13th *ForProc,* 1306-7 *Ass* (p), *Winstanstow* 1726 PR(H) 18

Witstaneston' 1255-6 *Ass, Wytstanstowe* 1271-2 *Ass* (p), *Wit-* 1272 Cl, *Witstonstowe* 1272 Ipm

Wynstan(t)stowe 1291-2 *Ass, Winstonstone* 1695 Morden, 1731 PR(L) 4, *Winstenstow* 1708-9 PR(H) 2

Wonstanestowe c.1291 TN, *Wolstanstowe* 1340 Fine, *Wostanstow* 1752

PR(H) 8
Whitstanstowe 1306 Ch, *Whistonstowe, Whynstonstow* 1672 HTR, *Whistanstow* 1736 PR(H) 8, 1770 *SBL 10308*, 1796 *PRLudford*, *Whistenstow* 1752 PR(H) 1
Wystamstowe or Wistehamstowe 1492 Ipm
Wistingstow 1746 *PRLudford*, *Wistinstow* 1781 PR(H) 9
Wustenstow 1695 PR(H) 18, *Woostenstoe* 1699 ib

Probably 'holy place of St Wigstan'. **stōw**, literally 'place', can usually be shown to have a special significance in place-names. 'Meeting-place' and 'place associated with a saint' are early senses; in the 10th century it developed a more general meaning 'church or monastery'. When the first element is the name of a 9th-cent. saint a close association between that saint and the place is a reasonable hypothesis. Wistow Lei is the same name.

St Wigstan was a member of the Mercian royal family who was murdered in 849 or 850. His body was taken to Repton Db, where the crypt was adapted to accommodate pilgrims. The medieval account of the murder gives *Wistanstow* as the site. Wistow Lei suits better than the Sa place, since it is nearer to Repton. The Sa place may, however, have been the site of a hermitage associated with the saint in his lifetime.

WITHINGTON SJ 577130 Ancient Parish

Wientone 1086 DB
Widintona c.1155 SAC, *-ton'* 1193 P
Withentunie c.1160-72 HAC, *Withneton* 1203-4 *Ass* (p), *Wythinton'* 1242 Fees *et passim* with variant spellings *With-*, *-yn-* and *-ton* to 1743 PR(L) 8, *Wythyntoun* 1397 Cl
Widiton' 1194 P
Wythington 1271-2 *Ass* (p), 1535 VE, 1768 PR(L) 2, *Withyngden* 1576 *SBL 5865*, *Withington* 1646 *SBL 5827 et seq*
Whitinton 1316 FA, *Whityndon* 1375 Pat
Wythmerton' 1334 SR
Wethiton 1577 Saxton

'Willow settlement', OE **wīthign-tūn*. The name occurs also in Ch, He and La.

The entry in 1284-5 FA refers to *Wythinton* and *Parva Wythinton*, but 19th-cent. maps show the single nucleated settlement of the present day.

WOLLASTON SJ 330124 Civil Parish

Willavestune 1086 DB, *Willaueston'* c.1200 *ForProc* (p), 1203-4 *Ass*, 1255 RH, *Wylaveston* 1242 Fees, 1255-6 *Ass, Willaveston* c.1260 InqMisc
Wallaueston', Wullaueston 1203-4 *Ass*
Wilageston' 1221-2 *Ass*
Wilaston' 1242 Fees, *Magna Wylaston'* 1291-2 *Ass, Wylaston* 1316 FA, 1415 Fine, 1577 Saxton, *-ton'* 1334 SR, *Wyllaston* 1431 FA, *Willaston* 1608-9 PR(H) 6 *et freq* to 1655 SAS 1/XLVII, *Gr. Willaston* 1695 Morden
Wilauston, Willaustun m.13th (1322) Ch, *Wylaweston* c.1291 TN
Petite Wollaston' 1305-6 *Ass, Woolleston* 1660 PR(H) 6, *Wollaston* 1667 ib, *Woollaston* 1673,7 ib, *Great* and *Little Woolaston* 1707 *SBL 6042*
Wallaston 1610 *SBL 15757*
Wollesson, Wrolleson 1658 PR(L) 20
Woolleseston 1672 HTR
Woolston 1681 PR(H) 6

'Wīglāf's estate', identical with Wollaston Nth.

The earliest indication that there were two settlements is in 1255 RH, where *Willaueston* and *Willaueston Parva* are both listed. *Little Woolaston* is marked on the 19th-cent. OS map at G.R. 366117, where later maps show Orchard Fm. It is over two miles E. of Wollaston, and in Alberbury Parish (as the whole of Wollaston was). It is Wollaston Fm in the Alberbury *TA*.

WOLLERTON SJ 620301 DB Manor

Uluretone 1086 DB, *Wluretona* 1121 SAC, *Wlurut'* c.1138 SAC, *Wlureton'* e.13th, 1242 SAC, *Wlfreton'* 1241 SAC, *-ton* 1256 (1332) Ch, *Wluretone* c.1275 SAC, *Ulv'ton* 1535 VE
Wluruntona c.1135 SAC, *-ton'* c.1144 SAC

Wlueruntona 1138 SAC
Wulfrinton' 1200 P, *Wlurinton'* 1201 P, *Wulfrinton* 1240 SAS 3/VII (FF) (p)
Magna Wlrinton' 1271-2 Ass, *Wolrinton'* 1291-2 *Ass*
Wolverton c.1291 TN *et freq* with variant spelling *-ton'* to l.14th SAC
Wluirton' 1292-5 *Ass*
Wollerton 1535 VE *et seq, Wollerton' al' Ollerton'* Hy 8 *RentSur, Wullerton* 1540 PR(L) 1, *Wolarton* 1559 ib, *Wollarton* 1646 PR(L) 9, *Woollerton* 1685 ib, 1765 *SBL 4264, Woolerton* 1692 PR(L) 11 *et freq* to 1715 PR(L) 4

'Wulfrūn's estate'; the personal name is feminine. Wollerton is a township of Hodnet.

WOLVERLEY SJ 469312 DB Manor

Ulwardelege 1086 DB, *Wluardele* 1271-2 *Ass*
Wolewardelegh 1199 (1265) Ch, 1217 (1285) Ch
Woluardesl' 1255-6 *Ass*
Wolfardeleye 1380 *SBL 4213*
Wulverley 1446 Cl, *Wolverley* 1586-7 *RentSur et seq, Woolverley* 1619 PR(L) 9 *et freq* to 1782 PR(L) 10, *Woulverley* 1678,84,87 PR(L) 9
Overley 1577 Saxton

'Wulfward's clearing', *v.* **lēah**. The OE form may have been **Wulfwardinglēah*, which would explain the lack of *-s-* in all forms but one. Wolverley Wo is *Wulweardiglea* 866, *Ulwardelei* DB.

Wolverley is a township of Wem.

WOMERTON SO 456972 DB Manor

Umbruntune 1086 DB
Wimbriton' 1228 Cl
Wimbriston' 1255 RH
Womertons Wood c.1613 *SBL 6162*
Wombertons Chapple 1626,36 *SBL 6573*

Omertons Wood 1667 *et seq* PR(H) 8
Woom(b)ertons Wood c.1700 *SBL 4098*
Wymbertons Wood 1700,2 PR(H) 8

Possibly 'Wynbeorht's estate', with loss of genitival *s* for reasons discussed under Albrighton

The settlement is in All Stretton parish, where there is a single house called Womerton on OS maps. All the post-medieval references are to a wood or a chapel. The 1255 reference, also, is to *boscus de Wimbriston'*. The chapel is given the alternative name of *St Peters* in *SBL 6573*, where it is described as ruinous.

In DB, Womerton is described as an estate of 2½ hides which had been held as four manors TRE.

WOODCOTE SJ 767154 Civil Parish

Udecote 1086 DB
Wudecota 1177 (p) *et freq* with variant spelling *-cote* to 1204 P, *Wudicote* 1205 P (p)
Wodecot' 1200 Cur (p) *et passim* with variant spellings *-cote, -kote* to 1466 Fine
Wodcote 1316 FA
Woodcote 1577 Saxton, 1665 PR(L) 7, *-coat* 1691 ib, *-cott(e)* 1702 ib

'Cottages in or near a wood'. This compound, while much less common than Wootton, has given major names in Ha, O, Sr, Wa and Ch in addition to the two Sa examples. There are grounds for considering **cot(e)** to be an element characteristically of the middle Anglo-Saxon period. A relatively early origin is likely since both the Sa places became DB manors.

WOODCOTE SJ 452117 DB Manor

Udecote 1086 DB
Wodecote 1255 RH, 1255-6 *Ass*, 1361,2 *SBL 3610, 3792*
Woddecote 1255 RH (p), *Woddcote* 1610 PR(H) 1
Wudcot c.1291 TN

Wodcote 1478 *SBL 4446*, 1607 PR(H) 1, *-cott'* 1524 *SBL 3809*, *-cot* 1566 PR(H) 1
Woodcote 1552 Pat, 1606,90 PR(H) 1, *-cott* 1730 *SBL 40115*, *-cutt* 1806 PR(H) 7

See preceding name. This Woodcote is in Bicton parish.

WOODHOUSE

Shropshire has at least eight examples of this name which date from the ME period. Forms for the one which has become an administrative district are set out below. The others are:

1. Woodhouses in Boningale parish: *Bonycall Wodhous* 1437 Fine, *Woodhouse* 1672 HTR.
2. The Woodhouse in Shifnal parish. This place is well-documented, the earliest form being *La Wodehus'* 1250 Cl (p). There are late plural forms, e.g. *Woodhouses* 1736 *PRShifnal*. The Woodhouse in Lilleshall parish, only a mile north, is *Woodhouse* in the *TA*, but no early forms have been noted which certainly belong to it.
3. Woodhouse Fm in Stoke upon Tern parish: well-documented from 1221-2 *Ass* to 1284-5 FA.
4. Woodhouse in West Felton parish: *Wodehus'* 1255-6 *Ass* (p), *Wodehouses* 1279-80 *RentSur*.
5. Woodhouse in Wem parish: *Woodhowsen'* Eliz. *RentSur*, *The Wodehouse* 1601 PR(L) 9, *The Woodhousen* 1616 ib, some forms showing the dialectal plural *housen*.
6. New and Old Woodhouse in Whitchurch parish: *Wodehous* 1271-2 *Ass*, *Blakemere Wodehous* 1388 Pat.
7. *Woodhouse* (later Woodhall) in Pontesbury parish: well-documented from 1221-2 *Ass* onwards, occasionally with the def. art. in the 13th cent.

There are further examples on modern maps, and documentation for some of these will probably be discovered when all the minor-name and field-name material is examined. This recurring name appears to be the equivalent of Wood Hall, which recurs in more eastern counties, sometimes as a major, but more frequently as a minor name. The reference is not likely to be to building material, as timber was probably usual for all houses in the areas where these names are found. Woodhouse(s) and Wood Hall may have been technical terms for buildings housing people who had specialised woodland functions.

WOODHOUSE SO 647772 Civil Parish

La Wodehus 1255-6 *Ass* (p), *La Wodehouse* 1291-2 *Ass, La Wodehous* 1346 FA (p), *The Woodhouse* 1651 PR(H) 9, *Ye-* 1717 ib
Wodehous by Cleobury Mortymer 1352 Pat

A cell of Augustine Friars was founded here in 1250, and the place was an extra-parochial liberty until 1857, when it became a civil parish. It ceased to have this status in 1966, when it was transferred to Hopton Wafers.

WOOLSTASTON SO 451985 Ancient Parish

Ulestanestune 1086 DB
Wolstaneston' 1204-10 HAC *et freq* with variant spelling *-ton* to 1301 SAC, *Wlstaneston'* 1242 Fees
Wolstanston' 1204-10 HAC *et freq* with variant spellings *-ton*(*e*) to 1721 PR(H) 18, *Wlstanston* 1271-2 *Ass,* 1279 Cl
Wolfstaneston' 1255-6 *Ass, -ton* 1294 InqMisc, 1295 Ipm
Wulstoneston (p), *-stan-* 1261-2 *ForProc*
Wlstanton' 1271-2 *Ass, Wolstanton* 1286 Pat *et freq* to 1431 FA
Wlstatson 1271-2 *Ass*
Wolfstanston' l.15th HAC
Wusaston 1577 Saxton, *Wosseston* 1672 HTR, *Wosaston* 1695-6 PR(H) 17, *Woceston* 1787 PR(H) 14
Wolstaston 1601 PR(H) 1, 1695 Morden, 1780 PR(L) 6, *Woolstaston* 1749 PR(L) 1 *et seq*
Woolzaston 1608 PR(L) 14
Wostaston 1655 SAS 1/XLVII, 1763 PR(H) 8, 1796 PR(H) 11
Wolsaston 1671 PR(H) 18 *et freq* to 1774 PR(L) 6

'Wulfstān's estate'. *v.* **tūn**. The late continuance of varying forms was recognised by Plymley in 1803 "Wolstaston alias Wollaston, usually written Woolstaston and pronounced Woosasun". Plymley's *Wollaston* has not, however, appeared in the spellings.

WOOLSTON SJ 323244 DB Manor

Osulvestune 1086 DB, *-ton* c.1230 HAC
Offleston 1272 Cl
Osselton 1272 Ipm, *Osel-* 1416 Fine
Oseleston 1397 InqMisc, *Osleston* 1549 Pat, *Osselston* c.17th SAS 4/III
Wolston 1577 Saxton, 1693 PR(StA) 3, *Woolston* 1708 PR(StA) 3, *-tone* 1730 ib
Wooston 1672 HTR, 1808 PR(StA) 3

'Oswulf's estate'. It is not clear why *Osselston* was transformed into Woolston. The place is a township of West Felton.

WOOLSTON SO 424873 DB Manor

Wistanestune 1086 DB
Wlureston' 1208-9 *ForProc* (p), *Wolureston* 1255 RH, 1343 InqMisc (p), *Wolfreston', Wylfriston'* 1255-6 *Ass, Wlfereston'* (p), *Wolueerestone* 1271-2 *ForProc, Wolureston', Wolf-* 1271-2 *Ass, Wlfriston'* 1272 Cl
Wulfreston' 1261-2 *ForProc* (p), 1271-2 *Ass*
Woluerston' 1271-2 *Ass, Wolferston'* 1291-2 *Ass*
Wolfreton' 1272 Cl, *Wlfreton* 1272 Ipm
Wolverton 1329 Pat
Wolston 1431 FA *et freq* to 1745 PR(H) 17, *- or Wolleston* 1492 Ipm, *Wulston* 1577 Saxton, *Woolston* 1705 PR(H) 17, *Wolstone* 1720-1 ib, *Wool-* 1754 ib
Woson Eliz. *SBL Ms292, Wooson* 1717 PR(H) 17
Wooston 1703 PR(H) 17

'Wulfhere's estate', *v.* **tūn**. The DB form is probably due to confusion with Wistanstow. Woolston is in Wistanstow parish, and both had belonged to Spirtes the priest in 1066.

WOORE SJ 730423 Civil Parish

Wavre 1086 DB, *Waure* 1255-6 *Ass*, 1284-5 FA, *Wafre* 1255 RH
Wauere 1255-6 *Ass, Wavere* 1323 AD
Wourre 1291-2 *Ass*, (p), *Woure* 1294-9 *Ass* (p), 1334 SR
Wouere 1292-5 *Ass* (p), 1316 FA, *Wovere* 1323 AD, 1431 Fine
Wore 1429 Cl
Owre 1550 Pat, 1577 Saxton, *Oare* 1672 HTR
Woer 1655 SAS 1/XLVII, 1744 PR(L) 20, *Woor alias Wooer* 1701 *SBL 4244, Woore* 1703 PR(L) 4 *et seq, Wooer* 1706 PR(L) 12, *Woor otherwise Wore* 1758 *SBL 4748*

Woore derives from an OE place-name element *wæfre*, which occurs as a river-name in the form Waver in Cumberland. Another name in which the word is unqualified is Over Wa (*Wavre, Wavra, Gavra* DB), and here it is assumed to be an earlier name of the R. Swift. As a first element in compound names *wæfre* occurs in Waverley Sr, Wavertree La and in four instances with *-tūn*, these being Warton Wa, Wharton He, and Waverton and Wharton, Ch. It is agreed that the term means 'something wavering'. This is easily comprehensible as applied to rivers, trees and woods, but less easy in the compound with **tūn**, and very puzzling in Woore.

Woore stands on a ridge which forms part of the watershed dividing streams which flow to the Irish Sea from those which flow to the south. The name is certainly not that of a river, and the district is not exceptionally marshy. Nearby names (such as Gravenhunger, Syllenhurst, Bulkeley) indicate the presence of wood, and the name possibly refers to the appearance of trees on the ridge.

WOOTTON

Shropshire has four names derived from OE **wudu-tūn*. This is a recurring compound which is fairly widely distributed in counties as far north as Shropshire and Staffordshire. The corpus has not been studied, but a tentative translation 'settlement which performs some function in relation to a wood' seems worth offering as a hypothesis. The habitative term **tūn** is characteristic of non-forested areas, so it seems likely that a *wudu-tūn* was near a wood, rather than in it. Forms for the Shropshire example which appears in DB are set out below. The others are:

1. Wootton, also spelt Wooton, in Quatt parish (*Wodeton in foresta de Morf* 1255 RH);
2. Wootton in Onibury parish (*Wodeton* 1203-4 *Ass* (p));
3. Wooton in Whitton parish (*Wodeton;* 1255-6 *Ass*).

WOOTTON SJ 336278 DB Manor

Udetone 1086 DB
Wodetona, Parva - 1201 HAC, *Wodeton* c.1217 HAC, 1272 Ipm, *Magna* - 1307,40 HAC
Woditon' 1272 Cl
Wodton' 1331 HAC
Wotton 1346, 1428 FA *et freq* to 1634 PR(StA) 2, *Woton* 1607 PR(StA) 4
Utton 1579 PR(StA) 4, *Uttin, Uttyn* 1602-3 ib, *Utyn* 1604 ib, *Utten* 1624-5 ib
Wootten 1590 PR(StA) 4, *Wooton* 1655 PR(StA) 2, 1692 PR(StA) 5, *Wootton* 1669 PR(StA) 5, - *als Wooton* 1698 *SBL 3544*

Only one settlement is called Wootton on modern maps, but there were evidently two in the 13th and 14th cents. A large house three quarters of a mile W., which is White Hall on modern maps, is *Wootton Hall* in the *TA*.

-tyn in some of the forms from PR(StA) 4 is due to Welsh influence. This Wootton is a township of Oswestry.

WORFIELD SO 758958 Ancient Parish

Wrfeld 1086 DB, 1265 Pat, *Wrfeud* 1255 RH
Woresfeld 1167 P
Wurefeld' 1177 P, *-feld* 1214 P, 1229 Pat, *Wurrefeld'* 1230 P

Wordfeld' 1189,90,91 P, *Wurdefeud* 1240 SAS 4/VI (FF)
Werefeld' 1196 P, *-feld* 1199 *et freq* to 1214 P
Werfeld 1199 P
Wurfeld 1203 P *et freq* with variant spellings *-felt'*, *-feld'*, *-feud*, *-feud'* to 1449 Cl
Wirfeld 1205 P, 1265 Pat
Urfeld 1209 For
Weresfeld 1209 P
Wirefeld 1209 P, *Wiri-* 1212 P
Wyrfet 1221 Fees, 1221-2 *Ass*
Worfeld' 1230-1 MemR *et passim* with variant spellings *-feld(e)*, *-feud*, *-fyld*, *-feilde*, *-fyeld*, *-field*
Worefeud' 1250 Cl *et freq* with variant spellings *-feud*, *-feld'*, *-feld* to 1394 Pat
Worisfeld 1262 Pat
Wrefeld 1267 Pat
Wornfeld 1283 InqMisc
Worvelde 1334 SR, *-veld* 1570 *SBL Ms292*, *-vill* 1577 Saxton, 1765 PR(H) 16, *-veilde* 1639 PR(L) 3, *-vild* 1685 PR(H) 16, *-vel* 1703 PR(L) 3, *-ville* 1814 PR(H) 7
Worril 1695 Morden

'Open land on the R. Worfe'. For the river-name, Ekwall (RN and DEPN) proposed an OE **wōrig* 'wandering', a derivative of the verb *wōrian.* He explained the variation of *o* and *e* in the early forms as either analogous to that in *Wōden*, *Wēden*, or as indicating that the base was partly OE *wērig* 'weary'. A full collection of spellings suggests, however, that a base such as **wyrig* would suit better. The *-u-*, *-e-* and *-i-* spellings are appropriate to an OE *ȳ* or *y̆*, and the *-o-* forms could be due to the common scribal use of *o* instead of *u* in the vicinity of *w*. A derivative of OE *wyrgan* 'to strangle', modern *worry*, might be considered. The river is exceptionally convoluted.

Warminster W, which does appear to have a river-name *Worge* as first element, has no *-u-* spellings.

A form of Worfield which was similar to the later development of Morville had some currency, but did not prevail.

From the ridge called Grosvenor in the parish of Claverley the expanse of relatively level ground surrounding Worfield shows as a marked landscape feature.

WORTHEN SJ 329047 Ancient Parish

Wrdine 1086 DB
Worthyn 1246 Ch *et passim* with variant spelling *Worthin* to 1787 PR(StA) 2
Worthy 1271-2 *Ass*, 1294 Pat, *Worthi* 1306-7 *Ass*
Wortham 1334 SR
Wurthyn 1354 Ipm
Wrothyn 1403 Cl
Worthen 1501 *SBL 16170 et seq*
Worthinge c.1540 Leland, *-ing* 1682 PR(L) 3, 1697 PR(H) 2, 1733 PR(H) 14, 1810 PR(StA) 2, *Worting alias Worthen* 1803 Plymley
Woorthin 1563,8 PR(H) 12

'Enclosed settlement', OE *worðign.*

WOTHERTON SJ 284006 DB Manor

Udevertune 1086 DB
Wdeverton' 1206 Cur (p), 1226-8 Fees (p)
Wudeveston 1227 Ch (p), *Wudeverton* 1228 Lib (p)
Wodforton' 1242 Fees, *Wodeforton'* 1255-6 *Ass*
Wodeverton' 1242 Fees *et freq* with variant spelling *-ton* to 1326 Ipm, *Wadeverton* 1255 RH
Wodewerton' 1255-6 *Ass* (p), *-warton'* 1291-2 *Ass* (p)
Woderton, Wodurton, Wodeton 1274 RH, *Woderton'* 1291-2 *Ass* (p) *et freq* with variant spelling *-ton* to 1623 PR(H) 11
Wooderton 1629 *et seq* PR(H) 8
Wotherton, Wartherton 1649 SAS 4/VII, *Watherton* 1672 HTR

'Settlement at a woodland ford', OE **Wudufordtūn.* The E./W. road through the village crosses a small stream. Wotherton is in Chirbury parish.

WRENTNALL SJ 426037 DB Manor

Werentenehale 1086 DB

Wrontenhale 1271-2,91-2 *Ass, -hall* 1346 FA
Wrentehale 1364-6 *ForProc, Wrentall* 1577 Saxton
Wrentenhale 1365-6 *ForProc*
Wrentnall 1528 *SBL 4001 et seq*
Wrentnor c.1597 *SBL Plan 47, -nole* 1601 *SBL 7076*

'Wrenta's nook'. The personal name is not on record, but is conjectured in DEPN to explain this name and Wrentham Sf. It could be a nickname meaning 'sulky person'.

The settlement is not in a hollow; it is on a hillside between two valleys of the type for which **bæce** is used in Shropshire names. The administrative sense of **halh** may be the relevant one. Wrentnall is a township of Church Pulverbatch, and the north boundary of the parish makes a curve in order to accommodate the township area.

WROCKWARDINE SJ 625120 Ancient Parish

Recordine 1086 DB, *Recordina* 1121 SAC, *Roc-* 1138 SAC, *Rockardyne* 1316 Strange, *Recordyne, Rocordyn* 1535 VE, *Rokerden* 1547 Pat, *Rockerdyne* 1597 PR(L) 9, *-dine* 1628 PR(L) 6, *Rokerdyne* 1581 PR(L) 3, *Rockardine* 1655 SAS 1/XLVII, 1682 PR(L) 4, 1737 PR(L) 8, *Rockerdine* 1698 PR(H) 14, 1732 PR(L) 18
Werocordina c.1090 SAC, *Wor-* 1155 SAC
Wrocword c.1138 SAC, *Wrocwordina* c.1155 SAC *et passim* with variant spellings *Wroch-, Wrok-, Wrock-* and *-wurthin, -wurthin', -wurdin, -wurdin', -wardin(e), -wardyn, -warthyn, -worthin, -worthyn'; Wrocwrði* 1202,3 P, *-wardy* 1291-2 *Ass*
Wrokewurdin 1175 P, *Wrockewurthin* c.1176 CartAntiq, *Wro(c)kewrthyn* 1255-6 *Ass, Wrockewardyn* 1336 Ipm, *Wroke-* 1362 Pat, *Wroke Warden* 1553 Pat
Wrowurdin 1195, 1200 P, *Wrowrðin* 1204 P
Wrogwardyn 1443 Cl
Rock(e)wardyne 1549 Pat, *Rokewarden* 1553 Pat, 1554 *SBL 4528, Rockwardyne* 1672 HTR *et freq* with variant spelling *-dine* to 1796 PR(L) 14
Rocadyne 1577 Saxton, *-dine* 1690 PR(L) 9, *Rockadine* 1661 PR(H) 9, 1679 *PRShifnal*

Wrockerdyne 1602 PR(L) 8 *et freq* with variant spellings *-din(e)* to 1658 *SBL 5658, Wrockardine* 1651 *SBL 6315*, 1687 *PRShifnal*
Wrockadine 1666 PR(L) 11, 1689 *PRShifnal*

'Enclosed settlement by The Wrekin', second element **worðign**. The name Wrekin is discussed under Wroxeter *infra.* As frequently in Shropshire, a long form of the name has prevailed, though simplified forms are evidenced from 1086 to the 18th cent. The modern form appears early, in *Wrockwardyn* 1284-5 FA. The precise spelling *Wrockwardine* is first noted 1616 PR(L) 8.

WROXETER SJ 573083 Ancient Parish

Rochecestre 1086 DB
Wrochecestria 1155 SAC (p), *Wroccecest'* 1255 RH, *Wrokecestr'* 1255-6 *Ass*
Wroxcestr' 1155 HAC *et freq* with variant spellings *-cestre, -cester* to 1737 PR(L) 4
Wroccestr' c.1176-82 HAC *et freq* with variant spelling *-cestre* to 1331 Pat, *Wrokcestr'* 1271-2 *Ass,* c.1291 TN, *-cester* 1736 PR(L) 8
Wrogcestr' 1271-2 *Ass*
Wrocestr' 1272 Cl
Wroxestre 1327 Pat, *-ester* 1738,9 PR(L) 4
Wroxcetr' 1408 *SBL 3054, Wroksetur* 1497 Ipm, *Wroxceter* 1535 *SBL 7180,* 1742 PR(H) 18, *-cetour'* 1535 VE, *Wroxiter* 1614 PR(L) 20, 1655 SAS I/XLVII, 1670, 1725 PR(L) 14, *Wroxeter* 1636 PR(L) 11 *et seq*
Rockcetor 1535 VE, *-ceter* 1613 PR(H) 6, *-siter* 1760 PR(L) 2
Wroxtor 1535 VE
Roxcester c.1540 Leland
Roxater 1577 Saxton, *Roxiter* 1588 PR(L) 20, 1654-5 PR(StA) 4, 1669 *SBL 15748, Roxeter* 1619 PR(L) 20, 1668 *SBL 6021*, 1773 PR(H) 8
Roxalter, Rocksolter 1684 *PRShifnal*

'Roman town called *Uricon*', second element **ceaster**.

The recorded forms of the RB name are *Ouirokónion* c.150 Ptolemy, *Uiroconium, Uiriconium* 4th cent. Antonine Itinerary. The form in the Ravenna Cosmography (*Utriconion*) is corrupt. This was the capital of the Cornovii, and the name probably belonged to the hill-fort on The Wrekin (which may have been their pre-Roman capital) before it was transferred to the new town. The meaning may be 'place associated with Virico'.

Jackson (LHEB, pp. 601-2) postulates a British bye-form **uricono-*. This would be the proximate source of early OE **Wricun*, which became *Wreocen*, modern Wrekin. The best OE forms for the name are found in the province-name *Wreocensœte*, which is recorded as *Wreocensetun* 855 S 206. The OE form of Wroxeter was probably **Wreocenceaster*, but *Wreocen-* was shortened to *Wroc-* in this name and in Wrockwardine *supra*. The conjunction of the final [k] of *Wroc-* with the initial [s] of the Norman French pronunciation of *ceaster* produced the *-x-* of Wroxeter.

A full collection of spellings makes it clear that *Wroxcester* or *Wroxester* were the commonest forms down to the 18th cent. Leland's *Roxcester* shows that he heard the *-s-* of the second element. This tells against the conventional view that the reduction of *-cester* to *-ceter* is due to Norman French simplification of consonant clusters. It appears, at least in this name, to be a late ME development, probably due to dissimilation, since *-cester* contains two [s] sounds. The spellings for Exeter (PN D 20-21) are comparable; there also forms such as *Excetur, Exceter* first appear in the 15th cent.

There is only a single spelling (*Wroxtor* 1535) which suggests a disyllabic pronunciation, and it is doubtful whether the name was ever shortened in this way.

WYKEY SJ 391249 DB Manor

Wiche 1086 DB
Wikes, Wykes 1254 Pat
Wikey 1577 Saxton *et freq* to 1810 PR(StA) 3, *Wykie* 1615 *SBL 15755, PR(StA) 4, Wykey* 1672 *SBL 8545 et seq*
Wicke e.17th SAS 4/III
Wickie 1604-5 PR(StA) 4
Weykie 1656 PR(StA) 4, *Weykey* 1672 HTR, *Weikie* 1697 *SBL 7178,* *- Town* 1685 *SBL 10258*

v. **wīc**, probably used here in its late OE sense of 'dairy-farm'. The DB spelling *Wiche* probably represents the dat.pl., OE *wīcum*. This sometimes becomes Wyke, Week or Wyken, but the development to Wykey appears to be unique to this name.

There are three other simplex names from *wīcum* in Shropshire: these are The Wyke in Shifnal, Wyke in Much Wenlock, and Wyken in Worfield.

Wykey is a township of Ruyton of the Eleven Towns parish.

WYTHEFORD, Great and Little SJ 572192, 552195 DB Manors

Wicford (bis) 1086 DB
Wideford (bis) 1086 DB, *-forde* 1257 HAC
Withiforde 1155-62 HAC *et passim* with variant spellings *Wythy-*, *Withy-*, *Wythi-* and *-ford* to m.19th OS
Wiford 1199 P
Witford, *Wis-* 1201 P, *Wytford'* 1223 Cur
Wytheford' 1242 Fees, *Witheforde* 1255-63 HAC
Wydiford 1255-6 *Ass*, *Widiforde* 1255-63, 1260-70 HAC
Wediforde 1255-63 HAC
Wytesford 1379 Cl
Wethiford 1577 Saxton
Withford e.17th SAS 4/III

'Willow ford', first element OE **wīðig**. The expected DB spelling for *wīðig-* is *Wide-*, which in this instance is used for the two manors in Little Wytheford. The two in Great Wytheford are referred to as *Wicford*. There is no systematic differentiation in later sources. The affix *Magna* is first noted 1255-6 *Ass*. *Parva* (rendered Little in the printed Calendar) appears 1293 Ipm.

Both places are in Shawbury parish. They are half a mile apart, on either side of the R. Roden, neither being immediately adjacent to the river. Wytheford may have been the name of the southern portion of the parish.

YAGDON'S LANE SJ 457193 DB Manor

Iagedone 1086 DB, *-don* 1185 Templars (p), *-dune* c.1200 *SBL*

5392, -don' 1271-2 *Ass*
Jagedun 1197-1203 (p), c.1230-5 HAC, *-don* c.1220-30 HAC, 1255 RH, 1272 Ipm, 1335 HAC, *-don'* 1272 Cl
Hiaged' c.1205 *SBL 5393, Haggedene* 1271-2 *Ass* (p)
Yagindon' 1255-6 *Ass* (p)
Yaggedon,| Yagedon' 1271-2 *Ass* (p)
Yakedon 1310 Ipm, 1344,50 *SBL 3903,4* (p), 1404 Pat, *-doun* 1404 Cl
Jagdon e.17th SAS 4/III
Yagdon 1629,43 PR(L) 4, *The -* 1630 ib, *Yagdon Lane* 1648 ib, *Yagden* 1656 ib, *Yagdone* 1722 ib, *Yagdon's Lane* 1798 ib
Agdons Lane m.19th OS
Yaggon's Lane 1888 OS 6"

'Cuckoos' hill', *v.* **gēac** (here in gen.pl.), **dūn**

The G.R. is for Yagdon's Lane, a scatter of houses on either side of a road, which may have been an outlying hamlet from a settlement named *Yagdon* which has disappeared. The Baschurch *TA* map shows a number of fields called *Yagdens* which surround a noated site, and the moat is shown on the 1961 1" map at 448191. This is likely to have been the site of the manor house, but there may have been a small settlement elsewhere in the vicinity.

YEATON SJ 433194 DB Manor

Aitone 1086 DB
Eton 1271-2 *Ass,* 1310 Ipm, 1335 HAC
Eaton 1687 PR(L) 4
Yeaton 1702 PR(L) 15 *et seq*

See Eaton *supra.* This 'river-settlement' is by the R. Perry in Baschurch parish. The modern pronunciation is [jeton].

YOCKLETON SJ 400101 DB Manor

Ioclehuile 1086 DB, *-hulle* 1121 SAC
Iochehulle 1138 SAC
Thokethul c.1143 SAC

Iocheshulla 1155 SAC, *Yokeshull'* 1255-6 *Ass*
Lokethull' c.1155 SAC
Yokethil 1246 Ch *et freq* with variant spellings *-hull(e)* to 1333 Cl
Yokelcul 1255 RH
Yukehull' 1268 Cl (p)
Yokelthul 1274 Ipm, *Yocultul*, *Yokeltul* 1291-2 *Ass*, *Yokelthull* 1301 Ipm
Yekelton 1316 FA, 1357 Pat
Jokelhull 1322 Cl
Jokethull 1322 Cl
Yokenhulle 1334 SR
Yokton 1347 Ipm
Yokelton 1349 Ipm *et freq* to 1430 Fine, *Yoculton* 1381 Pat, *Yokilton* 1474 Cl, *Yockylton* 1535 VE, *Yockleton* 1577 Saxton
Yokelynton 1390,1 Cl

Second element **hyll** 'hill', with 14th-cent. substitution of *-ton*. For the first, DEPN (followed by EPN) suggests *geocled*, *geoclet*, a Kentish term for a small manor. This word would suit the spellings, but it is unlikely to have been in use so far from Kent, and it does not give a satisfactory compound with **hyll**. The word **geoc** 'yoke', which is the basis of the Kentish term, is more widespread in place-names; it is the only suggestion available, e.g. for the first part of Yoxall St. The first element of Yockleton is not certain to have contained *-l-*. In forms such as *Ioclehuile* DB, and later *Yokelthul*, it could be an inorganic letter introduced by influence of the *-ll-* of **hyll**. If the OE form were **geocedhyll*, the first element could be the past participle of the verb *geocian*, 'to yoke'; but it is not clear what a 'yoked hill' would be, any more than it is clear what 'yoke nook' means in Yoxall.

Yockleton is a township of Westbury parish.

YORTON SJ 504237 DB Manor

Iartune 1086 DB, *Iorthon'* 1255-6 *Ass* (p), *Iyarton* 1255 RH
Yorton c.1250-63 HAC (p) *et passim* with variant spelling *-ton'*
Yoreton 1542 *SBL 5977*, 1824 *PRHadnall*, *Yoarton* 1655 SAS 1/XLVII, *Yourghton* 1804 PR(L) 11

A compound of **geard** 'yard, enclosure' and **tūn**. Yorton is in Broughton parish.

ENGLISH PLACE-NAME SOCIETY

The English Place-Name Society was founded in 1923 to carry out the survey of English place-names and to issue annual volumes to members who subscribe to the work of the Society. The Society has issued the following volumes:

I. (Part 1) *Introduction to the Survey of English Place-Names.*
(Part 2) *The Chief Elements used in English Place-Names.*
(Reprinted as one volume).
II. *The Place-Names of Buckinghamshire.*
III. *The Place-Names of Bedfordshire and Huntingdonshire.*
IV. *The Place-Names of Worcestershire.*
V. *The Place-Names of the North Riding of Yorkshire.*
VI, VII. *The Place-Names of Sussex,* Parts 1 and 2
VIII, IX. *The Place-Names of Devon,* Parts 1 and 2.
X. *The Place-Names of Northamptonshire.*
XI. *The Place-Names of Surrey.*
XII. *The Place-Names of Essex.*
XIII. *The Place-Names of Warwickshire.*
XIV. *The Place-Names of the East Riding of Yorkshire and York.*
XV. *The Place-Names of Hertfordshire.*
XVI. *The Place-Names of Wiltshire.*
XVII. *The Place-Names of Nottinghamshire.*
XVIII. *The Place-Names of Middlesex* (apart from the *City of London*).
XIX. *The Place-Names of Cambridgeshire and the Isle of Ely.*
XX, XXI, XXII. *The Place-Names of Cumberland,* Parts 1, 2 and 3.
XXIII, XXIV. *The Place-Names of Oxfordshire,* Parts 1 and 2.
XXV, XXVI. *English Place-Name Elements,* Parts 1 and 2.
XXVII, XXVIII, XXIX. *The Place-Names of Derbyshire,* Parts 1, 2 and 3.
XXX, XXXI, XXXII. XXXIII, XXXIV, XXXV, XXXVI, XXXVII. *The Place-Names of the West Riding of Yorkshire,* Parts 1-8.
XXXVIII, XXXIX, XL, XLI *The- Place-Names of Gloucestershire,* Parts 1-4.
XLII, XLIII *The Place-Names of Westmorland,* Parts 1 and 2.
XLIV, XLV, XLVI, XLVII, XLVIII *The Place-Names of Cheshire,* Parts 1, 2, 3, 4, 5 I:i
XLIX, L, LI. *The Place-Names of Berkshire,* Parts 1, 2 and 3
LII, LIII. *The Place-Names of Dorset,* Parts 1 and 2.
LIV. *The Place-Names of Cheshire,* Part 5 I:ii.
LV. *The Place-Names of Staffordshire,* Part 1.
LVI, LVII. *Cornish Place-Name Elements.*
LVIII. *The Place-Names of Lincolnshire,* Part 1.
LIX, LX. *The Place-Names of Dorset,* Part 3.
LXI *The Place-Names of Norfolk,* Part 1.
LXII. LXIII *The Place-Names of Shropshire,* Part 1.

All communications concerning the Society and membership should be addressed to:

THE HON. DIRECTOR, English Place-Name Society,
The University, Nottingham, NG7 2RD.